Glossary of educational technology terms

Glossaire des termes de technologie éducative

Prepared by the Division of Educational Sciences, Contents and Methods of Education, Unesco,
for the International Bureau of Education

Préparé par la Division des sciences de l'éducation, contenus et méthodes de l'Unesco
pour le Bureau international d'éducation

**Second edition,
revised and enlarged**

**Deuxième édition,
revue et augmentée**

Ministry of Education, Ontario
Information Centre, 13th Floor,
Mowat Block, Queen's Park,
Toronto, Ont.   M7A 1L2

Second edition: revised and enlarged, 1987.

First published in 1984 by the
United Nations Educational,
Scientific and Cultural Organization,
7 Place de Fontenoy, 75700 Paris (France)

Deuxième édition: revue et augmentée, 1987.

Publié pour la première fois en 1984 par
l'Organisation des Nations Unies pour
l'éducation, la science et la culture,
7, place de Fontenoy, 75700 Paris (France)

ISBN 92-3-002517-8

Printed in Switzerland by Presses Centrales, Lausanne

© Unesco 1984, 1987

Preface

Within the framework of Unesco's activities for the promotion of new educational methods and techniques, foreseen in its Approved Programme and Budget for 1981-83, the Secretariat has undertaken the publication of a multilingual glossary of educational technology terms.

Educational technology has developed considerably over the last two decades, covering not only audio-visual media, but also fields such as informatics, telecommunications, evaluation, systems analysis and educational sciences in general. The new meaning given to the term 'educational technology' in its widest sense is that of 'a systematic method of devising, applying and assessing the whole process of teaching and learning by taking into account both technical and human resources, and the interactions between these, so as to obtain a more effective form of education.'

This glossary groups in one volume the terms related to educational technology which exist, in part, in various specialized vocabularies, lexicons or dictionaries. It should assist in facilitating understanding of these terms and thus promote and encourage communication at the international level.

Therefore, it should be of interest to all those specialists or laymen involved to a greater or lesser extent in educational technology: specialists, researchers, documentalists, interpreters and translators, technicians, administrators and, of course, adult educators and teachers. However, the glossary is in no way intended as an encyclopaedia or a textbook, but rather as an up-to-date, easily useable, reference book.

Unesco requested the International Council of Educational Media (ICEM) to prepare the glossary. After an in-depth analysis of terms pertaining to the fields of audio-visual teaching, programmed learning, educational television and documentation, ICEM drew up a preliminary inventory of some 3,000 words and constituted a working group under the chairmanship of Dr. Anna L. Hyer and Dr. Howard Hitchens, whose first task was to decide which were the most important terms, according to criteria of relevance and frequency of use.

This list, which included about a hundred words relating to computer technology provided by the International Federation of Information Processing, was submitted for examination and comment to experts from ten different ICEM member countries. It was then reduced to about 1,650 terms, before being once more revised during a meeting of international specialists organized in Paris by ICEM in December 1981. (The participants at both of these meetings are listed in the appendix.)

At the conclusion of this meeting a basic inventory of terms had been established. Teams were then set up for each of the three languages chosen – English, French and Spanish – co-ordinated respectively by Dr. Anna L. Hyer (United States), Dr. Paul

Chaix (France) and Dr. Ernesto Zierer (Peru). Apart from the co-ordinator, the English-language team was composed of Professor Howard Hitchins, Dr. Raymond Wyman; the French-language team included Messrs. Paul Chaix, Robert Lefranc, Guy Berger, Jean Valérien and Jacques Rubenach.

This volume is the English-French, French-English version; other volumes in English-Spanish, Spanish-English, and English-Russian, Russian-English have been prepared.

In order to work out the definitions, these groups consulted existing specialized literature in the different languages. A concise bibliography is given in the appendix. When appropriate, the definitions proposed in terminologies prepared by the International Electrotechnical Commission and the International Organization for Standardization were retained. Entries are classified in alphabetical order. However, as in French the determiner is put before the element that it determines, entries in the French version are more homogenous than in the English version and, therefore, more numerous cross-references have been introduced in this latter. When an item has several meanings, these have been numbered and the semantic field is mentioned. Correlates in italics, which sometimes follow the definitions, enable the reader, by synonymy or antonymy, to better understand the different significations of the word. Some entries have not been translated and appear in brackets in the original language.

It will be seen that each version has kept its own specificity. Unesco undertook responsibility for the final text in order to harmonize, as far as possible, the different versions.

As a useful working tool — but deemed open to improvement — this glossary makes no pretence at being perfect, inspite of the precautions taken. The Secretariat of Unesco intends to revise it at regular intervals, not only to take account of rapid new developments in the field of educational technology, but also to fill the gaps or strengthen the all but inevitable weaknesses which might be found therein. To this end, readers and users of the glossary, who are the best placed to discover any such lacuna, are invited to send their comments and suggestions to the Division of Educational Sciences, Contents and Methods of Education at Unesco, 7 Place de Fontenoy, 75700 Paris, France.

As it stands, the glossary offers prospective users a common and up-to-date vocabulary which it is hoped will lead them to mutual understanding and encourage closer co-operation. The valuable assistance given by the International Electrotechnical Commission and the International Organization for Standardization should be noted here. The help and assistance given by the co-ordinators of the editing teams and all members of the committees and working groups in the production of this work has been invaluable. The Unesco Secretariat wishes to thank them once more, and especially Dr. Anna L. Hyer, Mr. Paul Chaix, Dr. Howard Hitchins, Mr. Robert Lefranc, Mr. John Mercer, Dr. Raymond Wyman and Professor E. Zierer.

The overall co-ordination and joint responsibility for this version rests with Mr Robert Lefranc (ICEM) and the Division of Educational Sciences, Contents and Methods of Education of Unesco.

The Secretariat has revised and updated this *Glossary* so that it now contains nearly 2000 entries.

Préface

Dans le cadre des activités visant à promouvoir l'utilisation des méthodes et techniques nouvelles d'éducation prévues par son programme pour 1981-1983 approuvé par sa Conférence générale à sa vingt et unième session, l'Unesco a entrepris de publier un glossaire multilingue des termes de technologie de l'éducation.

Le concept de technologie de l'éducation s'est considérablement enrichi au cours des deux dernières décennies, débordant largement les moyens audio-visuels pour s'élargir à d'autres domaines tels que l'informatique, les télécommunications, l'évaluation et l'analyse systémique, ainsi qu'aux sciences de l'éducation en général. Dans son acception nouvelle et dans son sens large, on entend par technologie de l'éducation la «façon systématique de concevoir, de mettre en œuvre et d'évaluer l'ensemble du processus d'enseignement/et d'apprentissage en tenant compte à la fois des moyens techniques, des moyens humains et des interactions entre les uns et les autres, de manière à aboutir à une éducation plus efficace».

Le présent glossaire regroupe en un seul volume l'ensemble des termes utilisés en technologie de l'éducation que l'on peut trouver pour partie dans les divers vocabulaires, lexiques ou dictionnaires spécialisés. Il se propose de faciliter la compréhension de ces termes et de favoriser ainsi la communication au plan international.

Il s'adresse donc à tous ceux, qu'ils soient ou non spécialistes, qui s'intéressent de près ou de loin à la technologie de l'éducation : les professionnels, les chercheurs, les documentalistes, les interprètes et les traducteurs, les techniciens, les administrateurs, et, naturellement, les formateurs et les enseignants. Cependant, ce glossaire ne se veut ni encyclopédie, ni instrument de formation, mais, plutôt, il se présente comme un ouvrage de référence actualisé et aisément utilisable.

L'Unesco en a confié la réalisation au Conseil international des moyens d'enseignement. Après une analyse approfondie des termes appartenant aux domaines de l'enseignement audio-visuel, de l'enseignement programmé, de la télévision éducative et de la documentation, le CIME a dressé un premier inventaire de quelque 3000 mots et a constitué un groupe de travail sous la direction du Dr Anna L. Hyer et du Dr Howard Hitchens, pour arrêter la liste des termes les plus importants en fonction des critères de pertinence et de fréquence d'emploi.

Cette liste, qui a inclus une centaine de mots relatifs à l'informatique fournis par la Fédération internationale du traitement de l'information, a été soumise à l'examen critique d'experts de 10 pays différents membres du CIME (voir annexe). Elle a été ramenée à environ 1 650 termes avant d'être une nouvelle fois révisée au cours d'une réunion de spécialistes internationaux organisée à Paris par le CIME en décembre 1981 (voir annexe).

A l'issue de cette réunion, un répertoire de base a été arrêté. Des équipes ont été constituées pour chacune des trois langues prévues : anglais, français et espagnol, et respectivement coordonnées par Anna L. Hyer (Etats-Unis d'Amérique), Paul Chaix (France), et Ernesto Zierer (Pérou), afin d'élaborer les différentes versions linguistiques. L'équipe anglophone était composée, à part le coordinateur, de Howard Hitchens et de Raymond Wymans ; l'équipe francophone comprenait, en plus de Paul Chaix, Robert Lefranc, Guy Berger, Jean Valérien et Jacques Rubenach. Le présent volume présente les versions anglaise et française ; d'autres volumes présentent les versions anglais-espagnol et anglais-russe.

Pour mettre au point les définitions, les groupes ont consulté les ouvrages spécialisés existant dans les différentes langues (voir bibliographie en annexe). Chaque fois que possible, les définitions proposées dans les terminologies préparées par la Commission électronique internationale et l'Organisation internationale de normalisation ont été retenues. Les entrées ont été classées par ordre alphabétique. Mais, comme en français le déterminé précède le déterminant, la version française compte des entrées plus synthétiques que la version anglaise. De ce fait, des renvois plus nombreux ont été introduits dans la version anglaise. Lorsqu'un item fait l'objet de plusieurs acceptions, celles-ci sont numérotées. Des corrélats présentés en italique font parfois suite aux définitions et permettent au lecteur, par synonymie ou antonymie, de mieux comprendre les différentes significations des termes. Certaines entrées n'ont pas fait l'objet de traductions et sont présentées entre parenthèses.

On remarquera que chacune des versions conserve une spécificité propre. En vue d'harmoniser autant que faire se peut les différentes versions, le Secrétariat de l'Unesco s'est chargé de la révision finale.

Outil de travail utile et perfectible, le présent ouvrage ne prétend nullement être parfait en dépit des précautions prises. Aussi, le Secrétariat de l'Unesco souhaite-t-il pouvoir le réviser à intervalles réguliers, non seulement pour tenir compte des nouveaux développements particulièrement rapides dans le domaine de la technologie de l'éducation, mais encore pour combler les lacunes ou les faiblesses inévitables qu'il pourrait éventuellement comporter. Dans cette perspective, les lecteurs et les utilisateurs du glossaire, qui sont les mieux placés pour les découvrir, sont invités à communiquer leurs remarques et leurs suggestions au Secrétariat de l'Unesco, Division des sciences de l'éducation, contenus et méthodes 7, place de Fontenoy, 75700 Paris, France.

Tel qu'il est, le glossaire offre néanmoins à ceux qui l'emploieront la possibilité d'utiliser un vocabulaire commun et actualisé, donc de pouvoir mieux se comprendre et de coopérer plus étroitement. L'aide qu'ont apportée à la réalisation de l'ouvrage les coordinateurs des équipes rédactionnelles et tous les membres des commissions et groupes de travail constitués à cet effet a été très précieuse. Le Secrétariat de l'Unesco tient à les en remercier vivement, et plus particulièrement Mme Anna L. Hyer, MM. Raymond Wyman, John Mercer, Howard Hitchens, Robert Lefranc, Paul Chaix et E. Zierer.

Le Secrétariat est également très reconnaissant à la Commission électronique internationale et à l'Organisation internationale de normalisation pour leur précieux concours. Robert Lefranc (CIME) et la Division des sciences de l'éducation, contenus et méthodes de l'Unesco ont assuré conjointement la coordination de cette version et en assument la responsabilité générale.

Le Secrétariat, à l'occasion de cette seconde édition, a revu et actualisé ce glossaire qui propose maintenant près de 2 000 entrées.

Contents

Table des matières

English glossary p. 9

Bibliography p. 129

French glossary p. 133

Appendix p. 267

Glossaire anglais p. 9

Glossaire français p. 133

Bibliographie p. 265

Annexe p. 267

Abbreviations and conventions

C = a correlate included for purposes of comparison.
F = French translation.
() = Terms within parentheses are considered to have no acceptable equivalent in the other language.
* = A translation as near as possible to the original.

AA: see **audio-active laboratory/system**

AAC: see **audio-active comparative laboratory/system**

AAC: amplitude automatic control

F commande automatique d'amplitude

ability: aptitude to carry out a particular task.

F capacité

ability grouping: grouping of pupils for learning or teaching purposes according to some measured ability.

C *setting, grouping, streaming*

F groupement selon les aptitudes; groupement par niveau.

abstract: 1. a summary giving the significant content of an article or a publication; **2.** a film which shows only the essential elements of the original film.

F 1. résumé analytique (abstract); 2. film de présentation

AC: alternating current

F courant alternatif

accessory materials: another word for accompanying documents

access point: 1. in indexing, any unique heading or qualified heading in an index; it may have subdivisions, modifiers, and/or other references; **2.** in a network, a location or point in the network where a user may gain access to the network to enter or retrieve data; **3.** in a computer system, the terminal or input/output device or physical means and location from which a user can interact with the computer; also used to describe the point of access or entry for a data file.

C *remote access; direct access, dial access, sequential access.*

F 1. point d'entrée; 2. point d'accès; 3. poste d'accès

access term: in indexing, the initial or first word of a multi-word entry; the word which will determine the complete entry.

F mot d'entrée

access time: in data processing, the time interval between the time a computer is requested to locate some specific data and the time that data is delivered to a designated point.

F temps d'accès à l'information; temps de réponse

accession: 1. the process of recording items and materials added to a library or learning resource centre; usually in the order of acquisition; **2.** item(s) and material(s) acquired by a library or learning resource centre for its collection.

F 1. entrée d'une acquisition; 2. acquisition

accompaniments: see **accompanying documents**

accompanying documents: audio-visual or printed material (notes, guides, etc.) accompanying a work (book, film, radio or television programme) to further explain it or enhance its use.

F documents d'accompagnement

accountability: see **educational accountability**

accumulator: 1. a temporary, manipulative register, located in the arithmetic unit of a computer, where data may be held, be operated on so as to perform various mathematical operations, and be otherwise manipulated; **2.** a storage or rechargeable battery.

F 1. accumulateur; 2. batterie

9

acetate: a transparent plastic film, sheet or roll used for photographic stock, and for overhead transparencies and animation cells.

F (film/feuille/rouleau) d'acétate

achievement: 1. proficiency of performance in a given area; **2.** progress in school.

F 1. acquis; accomplissement; performance; 2. rendement; résultats scolaires

achievement objective: see **performance objective**

achievement test: a test designed to measure a person's knowledge, skills, understanding, etc., in a given area.

F test de rendement; test de connaissances

achromatic: a term applied to a lens which is specially designed in a way that minimizes chromatic aberration.

F achromatique

acoustic coupler: a form of modem which, when attached to an ordinary telephone handset, permits communication between computers.

F coupleur acoustique

action frame: another word for response frame

action research: an on-the-job type of research used to develop new skills or new approaches and used to solve problems with direct application to the classroom or other educational situations.

C *operations research*

F recherche action

(activités d'éveil): French term grouping together the following subjects as taught in elementary school: history; geography; natural science; moral studies; drawing; handicrafts and music. Whilst not precluding the acquisition of knowledge, these 'activités d'éveil' aim to foster skills constituting a psychological and intellectual preparation for subsequent activities.

F activités d'éveil

activity learning/method: learning approach that requires the learner to do something more than look at and listen to a teacher and involving his/her active participation in the learning process – also called active learning.

F méthodes actives

ADA: a high-level programming language, based on PASCAL with important additions

F ADA

adaptation: 1. a new version of a work which has been modified for a purpose or use other than that for which the work was originally intended or designed; **2.** in cinematography, a procedure which consists of rewriting a literary work by finding audio-visual equivalents; **3.** a modification of equipment for a specific purpose; **4.** in psychology, the process whereby a person meets the demands of his environment.

F 1. 2. 3. 4. adaptation

adapter: a device which permits the interconnection of two or more machines using different sizes or shapes of ring, plug, cable or jack. The adapter is usually a single unit which is fitted on one end of a pre-existing connecting cable.

F adapteur; d'adaptation (bague, cordon, fiche, jack)

adaptive teaching: educational approach which adjusts to inter-individual differences of a group of students and to the intra-individual changes in knowledge, cognitive skills and motivation of each student in order to assist students in reaching common goals.

C *mastery learning*

F pédagogie différenciée

address: in computer terminology, a character or group of characters that identifies a register, a particular part of a storage or some other data source or destination.

F adresse

adjustment: the bringing into proper, exact or conforming position or condition.

F réglage.

ADP: see **automatic data processing**

advance organizer: a short piece of text placed before a major section of information to be learned. It acts as a guide to the main points of the section without supplanting this as the real source of learning.

F organisateur avancé

adviser: see **educational adviser; technical adviser**

aerial: see **antenna**

AFC: see **automatic frequency control**

affective domain: part of Bloom's taxonomy of educational objectives, including those objectives which describe changes in interest, attitudes and values and the development of appreciations and adequate adjustment.

C *cognitive domain; psychomotor domain*

F domaine affectif

afterimage: visual sensation occurring after the external stimulus causing it has ceased to operate. Also called persistence of vision.

F persistance rétinienne

AGC: see **automatic gain control**

(agents pédagogiques): generic term, in French, for people directly or indirectly involved in the pedagogic process: teachers, documentalists, producers and technicians of educational media, careers advisers, organizers of out-of-school activities, etc.

F agents pédagogiques

AI: see **artificial intelligence**

aids: see **visual aids, instructional aids**

aide: in the United States, a person with few or no special skills who performs simple tasks usually under the supervision of a technician or a specialist; (assistant in the United Kingdom).

F aide; assistant

aim: a general statement which gives shape and direction to a set of intentions for the future. In practice, aims are less clearly defined than behavioural objectives.

F fins

airbrush: a precision spraying device used to give soft and even areas of tone or shading in artwork.

F aérographe

ALGOL: an algebraic and logic language used by many computer groups as a common international language for the precise presentation of numerical procedures in a standard form to a computer.

F ALGOL

algorithm: a finite set of well-defined rules for the solution of a problem in a finite number of steps.

F algorithme

algorithmic language: see **ALGOL**

algorithmic oriented language: see **ALGOL**

alkaline battery: see **battery**

all-purpose computer: see **general-purpose computer**

alphanumeric: a contraction of alphabetic-numeric, a set of characters including letters, numerals, and usually a set of additional special symbols used as punctuation marks, special meaning marks, etc.

F alphanumérique

alternative strategy: a different approach to a problem or a task.

F stratégie alternative

aluminium screen: a projection screen which uses an aluminium coating as the reflective medium.

F écran aluminium

11

AM: amplitude modulation; see **modulation**.

F MA – modulation d'amplitude.

ambience: natural reverberation, particularly of recording venue.

F ambiance

amplifier: an electronic device for increasing the strength of an electric signal while minimizing any distortion.

C *loudspeaker*

F amplificateur

amplitude automatic control: see **AAC**

analog computer: a computer designed to handle information supplied in analog form, i.e. which varies in a continuous manner and has not been converted into digital form; such computers are mainly used in scientific research.

C *digital computer*

F calculateur analogique

analog image: visual representation of information by means of a physical phenomenon varying in a continuum which corresponds to human perception.

C *digital image*

F image analogique

analogy: **1.** a form of logic based on the inference from known resemblances to other resemblances not directly known; **2.** in semiotics, perceptual resemblance between a notion and its acoustic or visual representation, for instance between an object and its photograph.

C *iconic sign*

F 1. 2. analogie

analysis: the breakdown of the material into its constituent parts and detection of the relationships of the parts and of the way they are organized.

C *item analysis; task analysis; content analysis; comparative analysis; behavioural analysis*

F analyse

anamorphic lens: a lens composed of elements which, used as a 'taking' lens, compresses a wide image onto a standard frame of film; when used as a projection lens, it spreads the 'squeezed' image out to its proper width.

F objectif anamorphoseur; anamorphoseur

anastigmatic lens: a lens optically corrected, in manufacture, for astigmatism.

F objectif anastigmatique

andragogy: the science and art of teaching adults. The term was introduced to distinguish this subject from the teaching of children (pedagogy).

F andragogie

angle of view: see **view angle**

(animateur): a French term which denotes a person in the field of education, social work or community development who works to stimulate people to awareness of their own needs as a group, so that they define the nature of the needs, determine the means to satisfy them and act to do so. Equivalents in English are: extension worker; change agent; community development agent; resource person.

C *facilitator*

F animateur

animation: **1.** a film production technique that brings to apparent life and movement inanimate objects or drawings, cartoons, diagrams and captions; **2.** in education, social work and community development, a concept of French origin denoting the process of the stimulation of people to awareness of their own needs as a group, so that they define the nature of the needs, determine the means to satisfy these needs and act to do so. The term is currently used of functions which have a large element of direction, organization and instruction.

F 1. 2. animation

animation stand: an adjustable stand which holds a motion picture camera in vertical relationship to flat artwork on a moveable bench with registration points. It is used to produce animated motion pictures and sometimes used to produce filmstrips and slides. Also called 'caption stand'.

F banc titre

animator: 1. the person who prepares objects or drawings used for animation; 2. see **animateur**

F animateur

ANTIOPE: see **information network system**

answer print: the first composite print from a negative used as a guide for corrections in colour, density, etc. The first acceptable answer print becomes the first release print.

F copie d'étalonnage; copie de contrôle

antenna: a device that picks up or transmits a radio or television signal; UK: aerial.

C *dish antenna; parabolic antenna*

F antenne

anti-flare: see **flare**

F antireflet

aperture: 1. the opening or diameter of a lens, each lens opening being known as a 'stop'; 2. the opening on an overhead projector where the transparency is placed; 3. the open end of a horn, reflector or similar item.

F 1. ouverture; 2. fenêtre; 3. ouverture

aperture card: a punched or coded data card with microfilm images.

F carte à fenêtre

aperture preferred: a camera in which the aperture is manually set and the exposure is automatically adjusted.

F priorité au diaphragme

apparatus: equipment, appliances and materials other than books used in teaching.

F appareils

application(s) program: computer program or set of programs designed to carry out specific tasks and for which the user has to provide his/her own data and parameters, as distinct from systems software which controls the operation of the computer itself. Also called 'package'.

C *service program; software*

F logiciel ou programme d'application; progiciel

apprehension span: see **span of apprehension**

appraisal: the critical assessment of the relevance, feasibility and potential effectiveness of an activity before a decision is made to undertake that activity or to approve assistance for it.

C *assessment; evaluation*

F examen préalable

appropriate technology: this term, which tends today to be somewhat more popular than 'low cost' or 'intermediate technology', indicates that the value of a technology lies not only in its economic viability and its technical soundness, but in its adaptation to the local, social and cultural environment.

F technologie appropriée

approach: see **systems approach**

aptitude: group of attributes deemed to be characteristic of an individual's ability to acquire proficiency in a given area.

F aptitude

aptitude test: a test designed to measure the capacity of a person in a given area.

F test d'aptitude

architecture: a set of design principles specifying the way hardware and software interact so as to provide the type of facilities and services required in computing systems, a data base, a communications network.

C *configuration*

F architecture

arc lamp: a lamp with a very bright light made by electricity arcing between two electrodes.

F lampe à arc

archives: an organized body of records, usually of historical nature, e.g. papers, films, video, etc.

F archives

arithmetic unit: that portion of the hardware of an automatic computer in which arithmetical and logical operations are performed.

F unité (organe) arithmétique

array: in computer terminology, a list of numbers or strings, the elements of which can be referenced by their position in the list.

F tableau

art director: professional responsible for designing sets used in filming and providing every property required by the script.

F décorateur

artificial intelligence—AI: the logical operations performed by a computer and which are analogous to the human abilities of learning, adapting, reasoning, self-correction, decision-making.

F intelligence artificielle

ASA: American Standards Association (now American National Standards Institute). A system of rating film emulsion speeds. Speeds are usually quoted using an arithmetical scale, e.g. double the speed, double the number.

F ASA.

ASCII - American Standard Code for Information Interchanges: a standard system used to code alphanumerical and other symbols into binary form for computing and communication purposes.

F ASCII; code ASCII

aspect ratio: the ratio of the width to the height of the picture.

F format de l'image; rapport des dimensions

assemble: 1. to translate a symbolic language program into a machine language program by substituting absolute operation codes and addresses for symbolic operation codes and addresses; **2.** to set up and interconnect equipment components.

F 1. 2. assembler

assembler: a computer program written in assembly language which directs the computer to translate a program written in symbolic language (which humans read and understand) into machine (binary) language (which computers can read and understand) and the computer can execute.

C *assembly language*

F assembleur

assembly: in cinematography, the juxtaposition of shots in order to present contrast, comparisons, similarities or ideas.

F assemblage, bout à bout

assembly language: a computer programming language very near to the machine language, but using symbolic operation codes and addresses.

C *assembler*

F langage d'assemblage

assess: to analyse critically and judge definitively the nature, significance, size or value.

F examiner; évaluer

assessment: the process of quantifying or qualifying the performance of an individual, group, device or material.

C *appraisal; evaluation*

F examen critique

assignment: in education, a term to describe the project or work to be completed by a pupil during a given period.

C *project method*

F devoirs

assistant: see **aide**

assistant director: the person to whom the film director assigns certain tasks which must be performed in connection with a production, but which can be done without the director's supervision.

F assistant réalisateur

astigmatism: structural defect in a lens preventing rays of light being brought to a common focus.

F astigmatisme

asynchronous: in computer terminology, a mode of operation such that the execution of the next instruction or the next event is initiated by a signal that is generated upon completion of the previous command.

C *synchronous*

F asynchrone

attainment test: a test designed to measure the level of learning reached by a person in a given area.

F test d'acquisition.

attitude scale: a procedure designed to measure the likes and dislikes of a person.

F échelle d'attitudes

audience analysis: systematic study of the actual or potential learners or viewers of a programme in order to obtain salient facts about them including such aspects as educational needs, socio-economic background, geographical location, leisure and study preferences.

F analyse de public

audience measurement: measurement through sampling of the number of persons or households who watch or listen to a broadcast programme at a given moment in time. Principal measurement methods are: diary, door-to-door, telephone interviews, audimeter.

F sondage d'écoute

audience rating: rate of points/percentage given to a broadcast programme based on estimated audience viewing or listening figures compared with total number of households with TV or radio.

F mesure d'audience

audience share: percentage of all TV or radio sets in use tuned to any one of several channels available.

F indice d'écoute

audio: 1. a term designating devices or communications systems used in origination, transmission or reception of aural information (sound); **2.** more specifically, the electrical currents representing sound or the sound portion of a transmitted, recorded or received programme.

C *video*

F 1. 2. audio

audio-active comparative laboratory – AAC: a language teaching system where the listener (student) can reproduce the pre-recorded information (teacher), respond to it, during the interposed gaps, if any, and simultaneously hear his response by means of a microphone/headphone device (headset). The response is recorded so that the pre-recorded information · (teacher) and the · response (student) can both be reproduced.

F laboratoire/système audio-actif-comparatif

audio-active comparative system: see **audio-active comparative laboratory**

audio-active laboratory – AA: a language teaching system where the listener (student) can reproduce the pre-recorded information (teacher), respond to it during the interposed gaps, if any, and simultaneously hear his response by means of a microphone/headphone device (headset), his response not being recorded.

F laboratoire/système audio-actif.

audio-active system: see **audio-active laboratory**

audiocard: a thin card with a strip of audiotape across the bottom of its width. Sounds recorded on tape are usually thirty seconds or less in length. Space is provided above the audiotape for pictures or words. It must be recorded and played on a special device.

C *sound page*

F audio-carte

audiocassette: see **audiotape**

audiochannel

F voie son

audiodisc: a piece of plastic material in the form of a disc on which audio information

15

is mechanically recorded. Also called phonodisc, phonograph record, phonorecord and variants of these terms.

F disque audio

audiodisc player: see **record player**

audio frequency: that range of sound frequencies lying within the range of human hearing; approximately 20 to 20,000 hertz.

F fréquence acoustique; basse fréquence

audiolingual method: an approach to foreign language teaching that considers languages as a set of habits that are mastered by repetition drills and over-learning; listening and speaking are considered the central skills that are followed by reading and writing.

C *audio-visual method*

F méthode audiolinguale

audio mix: electronic combination of two or more sound elements into a single or stereo track.

F mixage son

audio-oral: refers to teaching aids or materials without visual elements and which emphasize oral activities.

F audio-oral

audiopage: see **sound page**.

audio-passive laboratory – AP: a language teaching system where the listener (student) can reproduce only the pre-recorded information (teacher).

C *audio-active*

F laboratoire/système audio-passif

audio-passive system: see **audio-passive laboratory**

audioslide: a 2″ × 2″ slide with a brief audio-recording on a magnetic coating on the slide mount or a specific holder for the slide. An audioslide requires a special projector.

C *tape slide*

F diapositive sonorisée

16

audiotape: a magnetic tape for the recording of sound. Audiotape comes in reels, cassettes and cartridges.

F bande magnétique audio

audiotape recorder: apparatus for recording on and playing magnetic tape on reels. One or more tracks can be used on this tape according to the type of recorder.

F magnétophone à bande

audiotutorial method: a self-pacing multi-media method of instruction that features tape recorded lessons with kits of learning materials and instruction sheets for individual learning in study carrels.

C *auto-instructional device; self-study materials; teaching machine, personalized system of instruction*

F méthode d'audio-instruction

audio-visual: descriptive of the transmission of information by visual and/or audio displays.

F audiovisuel

audio-visual aids: see **audio-visual materials**

audio-visual cartridge: see **videotape**

audio-visual centre: see **educational media centre**

audio-visual materials: a collection of materials and devices used for communication in instruction and which are displayed by visual projection and/or sound reproduction.

C *educational media; instructional aids; instructional materials*

F moyens audiovisuels; aides audiovisuelles

audio-visual method: an approach to foreign language teaching using an audio-visual context (taped dialogues in situations illustrated by corresponding pictures usually on filmstrips) to make the language forms meaningful. Use of the mother tongue is avoided and the presentation and practice of the language are primarily oral.

C *audiolingual method*

F méthode audiovisuelle

(audiovisuel léger): French term for audiovisual media which are always readily available to the teacher, such as slides, sound recordings and records, as opposed to mass media such as radio or television which require a complex infrastructure.

F audiovisuel léger

audit: examination or review which establishes to what extent a condition, process or output (performance) conforms to predetermined standards or criteria.

F vérification*

auditing: 1. taking a course not leading to an academic credit; 2. independent examination of financial accounts.

F 1. statut d'auditeur libre; 2. vérification comptable

auditorium: a space with a built-in stage and sloping floor or fixed seating, for use as an assembly centre.

F auditorium

aural-oral method: see **audiolingual method**

author: 1. in computer technology, someone who designs instructional material for presentation by the computer; 2. someone who is the source of some form of intellectual or creative work.

F 1. 2. auteur

authoring language: a computer language more or less closely related to a natural language with which an author can develop software.

F langage auteur

authoring system: a program designed to assist with the production of software packages through special commands and editors for the creation of text, graphics and animated images, for handling dialogue and analysing user response.

C *courseware editor; expert system*

F système auteur

author's rights: the rights granted to an author under national law on copyright in respect of works created by him (usually of an economic and moral nature).

C *copyright*

F droits de l'auteur

autodidaxy: refers to a range of situations where learners study outside a formal educational framework. Autodidaxy can be 'pure' or assisted, can involve a single person or a group, can be adopted out of preference or through force of circumstances. (Not to be confused with self-directed learning.)

C *autonomy; independent study; individualized instruction; self-directed learning; self-instruction*

F autodidaxie

autofocus: a term applied to a camera that provides automatic self-induced focusing.

F mise au point automatique

auto-instructional device: a device for individual instruction. Includes individual reading pacers, individual viewing and listening equipment, language laboratories, and other teaching machines which present verbal and pictorial programmes in various ways — electronic and mechanical — so that the individual responds and is informed of errors and progress.

C *audiotutorial method; self-study materials; teaching machine*

F dispositif d'auto-instruction

automatic changeover: a device which, when hooked up to two projectors, will automatically switch one projector off and the other one on to provide continuous projection, especially with multiple-reel films.

F changeur automatique

automatic data processing – ADP: 1. data processing largely performed by automatic means whether mechanical, electro-mechanical or electronic; 2. the branch of science and technology that is concerned with methods and techniques relating to data processing largely performed by automatic means.

C *informatics, computer science*

F 1. traitement automatique de données; 2. informatique

automatic frequency control - AFC: a self-actuating device incorporated in a receiver to compensate for small variations in the frequencies of incoming signals and/or local oscillations.

F régulateur automatique d'accord; de fréquence; RAF

automatic gain control - AGC: a self-actuating device incorporated in a receiver to maintain the output level of a sound transmission constant.

F commande automatique de gain; CAG

autonomous learning: see **autonomy**

autonomy: either the ability to take responsibility for one's own learning, or the option to conduct one's learning process in the way one wishes, or the degree of freedom of the learner within the constraints of a given situation or environment.

C *autodidaxy; independent study; individualized instruction; self-directed learning; self-instruction*

F autonomie (dans l'apprentissage)

(autoscopie): French term for the use, mainly but not exclusively in teacher training, of recordings, generally video, to analyse one's own behaviour in a given situation.

F autoscopie

auxiliary storage: see **auxiliary store**

auxiliary store: a storage device in addition to the main storage of a computer, such as a disk, magnetic tape, or other types of storage.

C *store*

F mémoire auxiliaire

A-V: audio-visual

B

BAW: black and white
F noir et blanc

back projection: a term used in the United Kingdom for the optical projection of a visual image onto a translucent screen from a point located on the opposite side to the viewer. In the United States the term used is:
C *rear projection (United States)*
F projection par transparence

background noise: 1. noises which exist in any situation that may encroach on desired sounds such as those being recorded. Sound-proofing is used to exclude ambient noise from recording studios; **2.** unwanted signals present at the output of a transmission channel in the absence of the wanted signal, when the channel is in normal operation.

F 1. 2. bruit de fond

background projection: an effect consisting of putting actors in front of a translucent screen and projecting a filmed background on it.

F projection par transparence

backup: descriptive of additional people, equipment or materials (for emergency use). It can be used as a noun with the meaning of 'support'.

F de secours; de réserve

baffle: container for a loudspeaker to improve sound.

F enceinte (acoustique)

balance: 1. in photography, equality of level in the red, green and blue images which produce neutral blacks and clean whites; **2.** in audio systems, balance has been achieved when the output of loudspeakers approximates the original ambience of the environment in which the material was recorded.

F 1. équilibre; 2. équilibrage; balance

balance control: device for adjusting relative levels of right and left signals in a stereo sound system.

F balance

balun transformer: (BALanced/UNbalanced); a device for connecting some TV receivers to some antennas or cables.

F transformateur symétrique-dissymétrique; symétriseur; balun

banana plug: a single conductor electrical plug with a banana-shaped metallic spring.

F fiche banane

bandwidth: the carrying capacity of a communication channel.

C *frequency range*

F bande passante

bank: see **data bank**

barney: another world for blimp.

base: 1. a number base – a quantity used implicitly to define some system of representing numbers by position; **2.** the flexible material, usually cellulose triacetate, which supports film emulsions and other coatings; **3.** the place where a team works.

C *data base*

F 1. base de numération; 2. support; 3. base

BASIC: Beginners All-purpose Symbolic Instruction Code; see **computer language**

F BASIC

basket method: see **case study method**

bass: the lower range of frequencies in the audio spectrum.

F basses

batch processing: data processing in which, for operating convenience and efficiency, a number of similar input data items are grouped together before the run and then processed during a single machine run with the same programme.

F traitement par lots

battery: 1. a number of similar articles, devices or machines arranged, connected or used together; **2.** a group of voltaïc cells used to provide electricity by chemical means. Common types include carbon-zinc, alkaline, lead-acid and silver; **3.** a group of tests specially selected for a given purpose.

F 1. batterie; 2. pile; batterie; 3. batterie (de tests)

bayonet mount: a type of mount for a camera lens or projection lamp in which the lens or lamp is held by two small spurs. The spurs on the lens or lamp fit into slots or under projections on the mount.

F monture à baïonnette

beaded screen: a front-projection screen coated with many tiny glass or plastic beads giving a highly reflecting surface and a narrow angle of dispersion.

F écran perlé

beam: 1. the concentration of the radiation energy of a signalling system towards a given direction; **2.** the region of space illuminated by this radiation.

F 1. 2. faisceau (électro-magnétique).

beep: a brief audio signal placed on the cue track portion of audio or video tape for editing purposes.

F top

behaviour: anything that an organism does that involves action and response to stimulation.

F comportement

behavioural analysis: an approach to curriculum development that initially renders educational aims into a description of terminal behaviours and then describes the sequence of behaviours and enabling tasks that students must be capable of performing en route to the desired curricular outcome.

F analyse comportementale

19

behavioural instruction: a term usually applied to a learning approach where the desired outcomes are specified as performance objectives.

C *mastery learning*

F pédagogie par objectifs

behavioural objective: see **performance objective**

Beta: see **video format**

Betamax: see **video format**

bias: 1. any irrelevant characteristic of the experimental design or procedure other than deliberate variations in the experimental variable, that will systematically affect the differences (in the criterion measure) between treatments; **2.** intentional or unintentional point of view included in a film or programme; **3.** adjustment to an electronic or magnetic signal to improve fidelity.

F 1. erreur systématique; 2. orientation tendancieuse; 3. polarisation; prémagnétisation

binary: having just two possible states or conditions, such as 'on' or 'off', or '1' and '2'.

F binaire

binary number system: a numbering system used internally by computers that use number 2 as a base (as opposed to the decimal system that uses the number 10).

F numération binaire

binaural: see **stereophonic**

bit: contraction of 'binary digit'; a unit of information; it is the smallest unit of information in a binary system of notation.

C *byte; octet*

F bit; élément binaire

blackboard: a smooth surface of slate, glass, or other material used for presentation by writing or drawing with chalk, crayon, pen, or other easily erased materials.

C *chalkboard; markerboard*

F tableau (noir)

black box: electronic device whose internal mechanism is hidden from (or irrelevant to) the user. Also a term widely used in curriculum evaluation and classroom research referring to a situation where only the inputs and the outputs are considered.

F boîte noire

blimp: a sound-proof camera box that allows full control of all the functions of the camera.

F blimp; caisson insonore

blinking: a method of signalling important messages by flashing characters on a VDU.

F clignotement

block: a quantity of transmitted information regarded as a discrete entity by size or more commonly by its own starting and ending delineators, usually with its own self-contained control routines and coordinating information.

F bloc

block diagram: a diagram of a system, instrument or computer in which the principal parts are represented by suitably annotated geometrical figures to show both basic functions and relationships amongst the parts.

C *flowchart*

F schéma fonctionnel; schéma de principe

bloop: noise made by the passage of a splice through an optical film reproducer.

F raccord sonore défectueux

blow up: 1. a process used in making larger prints of smaller gauged film, such as 'blowing up' 16 mm prints to 35 mm for theatrical showings; **2.** to enlarge a photographic or other image; **3.** the resulting enlarged image.

C *enlargement*

F 1. gonflage; 2. agrandir; 3. agrandissement

blueprint: originally, copies of drawings or plans produced by a ferroprussiate process that gives an image on a blue background. The term is now used for all large copies of

plans or engineering drawings reproduced by various processes.
F bleu; calque

blurred: characterized by dimness, lack of sharpness or obscurity.
F flou

book: see **handbook; textbook; reference book**

bookmobile: a library travelling in a truck, lorry or van
F bibliobus

boom: 1. a generic term for a crane-like apparatus to suspend a microphone, a motion picture camera, and sometimes lighting equipment; **2.** a loud momentary bass sound.
F 1. grue; perche; 2. son creux

boomer: see **woofer**

boom man: sound technician operating a microphone boom.
F perchiste

boom operator (United Kingdom): see **boom man**

boost: an increase or the act of increasing.
F amplification

booth: 1. a small soundproof enclosure from which a message can be delivered live to an audience; **2.** a small soundproof enclosure which is used for voice recording in film or video tape; **3.** small space designed for individual learning activities, as in a language laboratory.
C carrel
F 1. 2. 3. cabine

bootlegging: see **piracy**.
F piraterie; (piratage)

bootstrap: a procedure for initiating the reading of a programme by a computer.
F amorce

brainstorming: a technique used to solve a problem demanding an original solution. It consists of presenting the problem to a group of people and asking them to think up as many possible solutions as they can in a set period of time. The emphasis is on the generation of many ideas, and not on criticizing the ideas generated.
F (brainstorming); remue-méninges

branch: 1. a point of choice at which students are sent to alternative items depending on their responses to the particular item. A common use of branching is in intrinsic programmes, where the branch (or loop) consists of a single item explaining why a particular answer is incorrect and returning the student to the original item for another try; **2.** a computer instruction that requires that the selection of the next instruction be based on the result or outcome of some arithmetical or logical operation, or on the state of some indicator.
F 1. 2. branchement; ramification

branch of knowledge: see **discipline**

branching: altering the course of a set of instructions by switching where some pre-designated event occurs.
C intrinsic programming; branch; jump
F branchement

breakdown: 1. in film production, directional analysis, in terms of shots, of action to be photographed; **2.** as a preliminary to cutting, the planning of the use of shots, or the process of reorganizing scenes from random shooting sequences to the desired presentation sequence.
F 1. calendrier de travail; 2. dépouillement

breakout lug: a small ear or projection on a cassette that can be broken out to prevent recording.
F ergot de sécurité

brightness: 1. (UK) the brightness of colour (i.e. the opposite of dullness, as used in the dyeing industry); **2.** (USA) attribute of visual sensation according to which an area appears to emit more or less light.
C luminosity
F 1. éclat de la couleur; 2. luminosité

broadband: a general term used to describe equipment or systems which can carry a wide range of frequencies or channels.
F à large bande (de fréquences)

broadcast: 1. (noun) any transmitted radio or television programme; **2.** (verb) to transmit electronic signals by means of a radio frequency (RF) carrier over the waves; **3.** (material) standard professional radio or television equipment classification.
F 1. programme; émission (de radio ou de télévision); 2. radiodiffuser; émettre; 3. matériel professionnel

broadcasting: distributing a programme or a signal on the airwaves which can be received by all radio and television sets in the coverage of the station.
C *narrowcasting*
F radiodiffusion

bubble screen: screen using magnetic bubbles for the display of video images.
F écran à bulles

buffer: a temporary storage device used to compensate for the difference in rate of data flow or events when transmitting between two devices, often the memory of the computer and an input/output device or other storage device. It collects and holds the incoming data and delivers them to the processing unit when needed.
F mémoire tampon

bug: a mechanical, electrical, electronic or logical defect in a piece of equipment or in its operation, or a defect or error in a coded programme; thus, a malfunction or a mistake.
C *debug*
F erreur; élément parasite; bogue

builder: computer program for manipulating shapes and exploring geometric concepts that relate to drawing figures.
F imagiciel

bulb: a dilated glass tube containing a filament for electric lighting. Also called a lamp.
F ampoule; lampe

bulk eraser: a device for the erasure of the whole recording at the same time.
F démagnétiseur; effaceur total

burn-in: image impregnated onto camera pick-up tube, caused by extremely bright light, or camera focused on high-contrast image for too long a period of time.
F marquage

bus: in computer terminology, a circuit over which data are carried from any of several sources to any of several directions.
F bus

buzz board: a generic term applied to numerous devices generated to test, drill or demonstrate. It usually features an electric circuit which activates a buzzer, a bell or light when appropriate contacts or switches are manipulated in response to a question or pictorial materials displayed on the board.
F panneau électrique

buzz group session: a group discussion technique used to involve all members of a large group in the procedures pursued by forming small groups to carry on during a short period informal discussion of a topic previously selected.
F discussion en petits groupes

by-passing: see **skip branching**

byte: 1. a sequence of adjacent binary digits operated on as a unit, e.g. a 6-bit or a 8-bit byte, shorter than a computer word and representing usually one alphabetic or numeric symbol; **2.** the 8-bit byte (octet) which constitutes the smallest addressable unit in certain systems.
C *bit; octet*
F 1. multiplet; 2. octet

B & W: see **BAW**

C

cablecasting: see **cable television**

cable release: a flexible sheath with inner shaft, used to activate the single-frame mechanism or the running mechanism on some motion picture cameras and the shutter of still cameras.

F déclencheur souple

cable television: a television system in which the signal is distributed via cable links rather than by broadcasting.

F télédistribution; câblodiffusion; câblodistribution; distribution par câble; télévision par câble

CAI: see **computer-assisted instruction**

CAL: see **computer-assisted learning**

calc: see **spreadsheet**

calculator: a device capable of performing arithmetical operations that requires frequent interventions by a human operator.

F calculatrice

camera: a device used for making a record of the image formed when light rays pass through a lens or opening and fall upon light-sensitive material. 1. a film camera is a camera which can make motion pictures and is available for making sound or silent motion pictures; 2. a television camera is a device which converts visual images into electrical signals which can be recorded and/or viewed on a television monitor; 3. a still camera is used for making photographs or negatives intended to be shown as single, still photographs.

F 1. caméra (cinématographique); 2. caméra (de télévision); 3. appareil photographique

camera control unit - CCU: the equipment in a television camera channel which contains the major part of the electronic circuitry. It provides the camera with operating signals and processes the signals from the camera. It enables the amount of electronics housed in the actual camera to be kept to a minimum.

F ensemble de commande de caméra; système de contrôle de caméra

camera man: a technician in charge of operating a film or television camera and responsible for manipulating it as the director requires.

F cadreur; opérateur de prise de vues

can: any metal or plastic container used for the safekeeping of film or videotape.

F boîte

capacitor: see **condenser**

capstan: a motor-driven roller which controls the speed at which magnetic tape passes the heads in a tape machine.

F cabestan

CAPTAIN: see **information network system**

caption: the printed information to accompany the visuals of an audio-visual material.

C title caption

F légende

caption stand: see **animation stand**

captive audience: groups of learners attending a broadcast programme under supervision.

F auditoire encadré

card: a small board containing electronic components (chips) which can be plugged into a micro-computer to give extra facilities.

F carte

cardioid: heart-shaped, as the pick-up pattern of a microphone.

F cardioïde

carousel: a horizontally rotating slide tray.

F carrousel

carrel: 1. a small cubicle or study desk set aside for individual study; **2.** a student study station with a desk, table or booth unit designed to facilitate effective study by the student; described as 'wet' when it includes electronic devices and 'dry' when it lacks such devices.

F 1. 2. carrel; cabine d'audition; alvéole d'étude

carriage: in computer technology, a control mechanism for a typewriter or other listing device that can automatically control the feeding, spacing, skipping and ejection of paper or preprinted forms.

F chariot automatique

carrier: 1. the transmitted electromagnetic wave upon which video or audio signals or impulses are impressed, and thereby transmitted, through a process called modulation; **2.** an entity capable of carrying an electric charge through a solid; **3.** a wave of constant amplitude, frequency and phase which can be modulated by changing amplitude, frequency or phase; **4.** the physical material on which an audio-visual message is recorded: film, record, magnetic tape, etc.

F 1. onde porteuse; 2. porteur (de charge); 3. porteuse; 4. support

cartoon: 1. an interpretative drawing which satirizes or exaggerates in order to stress a point; **2.** (animated cartoon); (cartoon film); film made by photographing a succession of drawings.

F 1. caricature; dessin humoristique; 2. dessin animé

cartridge: 1. a type of container carrying a closed loop of audiotape, videotape or film that does not require rewinding. **2.** a memory chip container containing software that can be plugged into a microcomputer: 'language cartridge', 'game cartridge'.

F 1. 2. cartouche

cartridge film: a motion picture spliced in a continuous loop for continuous playing without rewinding, and encased in a cartridge.

F film en cartouche

case study method: the use by learners of a written description of an event, incident or situation as resource material to aid the process of analysing and discussing theories, concepts and real life phenomena. Also called 'basket method'.

F méthode des cas

cassette: a self-contained unit consisting of an empty take-up reel and a full reel of either audio-tape, video-tape or film.

F cassette

cassette deck: an incomplete device for playing or recording tapes when mounted in a carrel or desk and connected to auxiliary equipment.

F platine cassette

cassette recorder: a recorder which only records and plays cassettes.

F magnétophone à cassette; magnétocassette

cassette storage: the storage of information on ordinary cassette tape.

F mémoire à cassette

cast: the title list of actors and their parts appearing among the titles at the head (or the end) of a film.

F distribution artistique

casting: selecting people to play the various roles in a play or a film.

F casting

cast list: see **casting**

catalog: a list of materials or items arranged in some definite order. It records, describes and indexes (usually completely) the resources.

F catalogue

cataloging: 1. the process of preparing a description of and bibliographic record for an item to be housed in a particular collection; **2.** the process of preparing entries for a catalogue. In a broad sense, all the processes connected with the preparation and maintenance of a catalogue, including classification and assignment of subject headings.

F 1. 2. catalogage

catalogue: see **catalog**

cathode-ray tube – CRT: an output device that displays characters or graphics via electrically stimulated phosphorescence on a glass surface. The screen of an ordinary television set is an example of a CRT.

F tube à rayons cathodiques; écran cathodique

CATV: see **community antenna television**

CB: see **citizens' band**

CBI: computer-based instruction

CBL: computer-based learning: see **computer-based instruction**

CBT: computer-based training: see **computer-based instruction**

CCIR: International Radio Consultative Committee

F CCIR

CCTV: see **closed-circuit television**

CD: see **compact disc**

CEEFAX: see **information network system**

cell: 1. a location in a memory unit of a computer, usually with an assigned address; **2.** a unit of an electric battery; **3.** a piece of plastic (cellophane) used for making animated films or overlays.

C *photoelectric cell*

F 1. cellule de mémoire; 2. élément de pile; 3. cellulo

centre: see **educational media centre; listening centre; production centre**

central antenna system: a device or devices to intercept radio or television broadcast signals and distribute them efficiently to radios or television receivers. Includes antenna, antenna distribution systems and amplifiers related to the antenna system.

C *community antenna system*

F système d'antenne centrale

central processing unit – CPU: the group of components of a data-processing system that contains the logical, arithmetic and control circuits for the basic system.

F unité centrale

(centre d'intérêt): French term for a topic providing the basis for relatively lengthy educational activities which may extend over several weeks.

F centre d'intérêt

chaining: the linking together of a series of separate responses in a particular order in which the completion of the first response provides the stimulus for the second response; in typical laboratory examples reinforcement is given at the end of the chain of response.

F enchaînement

chalkboard: see **blackboard**

changeover: small spot or other mark in the top right-hand corner of a certain frame near the end of a reel of film to give the projectionist a signal for the changeover to the next reel.

C *cue*

F marque de fin de bobine

channel: 1. (communication theory) the connection between sender and receiver; **2.** (broadcasting) a specific band of frequencies assigned to each radio or television station or to which a closed-circuit television camera is tuned when transmitting via radio frequencies; **3.** (computer) a path in the computer system along which signals can be sent, such as data channel, output channel.

F 1. canal; 2. voie; canal; chaîne; 3. canal

channel capacity: the amount of information that a space channel can transmit per time unit or that a time channel can retain.

F capacité en voies (d'un canal radioélectrique)

character: 1. a letter, digit, punctuation mark, or other symbol used in the representation of information; **2.** a personage in a film.

F 1. caractère; 2. personnage

character generator: electronic device used to display alphanumeric characters on a TV screen.

F générateur de caractères

chart: an opaque sheet exhibiting information in graphic or tabular form, or by use of contours, shapes or figures.

C *flip chart; flow chart; test chart*

F tableau; graphique

check print: see **answer print**

chest microphone: see **Lavalier microphone**

chip: a single, solid state device, containing integrated electronic circuit components.

F puce

chrominance: the chromatic or colour content of the video display.

F chrominance

cinch marks: scratches on film caused by pulling on the free end of a roll of film.

F rayures d'enroulement

cine: see **cinema**

cineclub: an association to show films outside the commercial circuits and generally using the projection of a film to lead up to discussions on topics directly or indirectly related to the projected film. Also called 'film club'.

F ciné-club

cinema: 1. a motion picture show or theatre; **2.** the art or technique of making motion pictures.

F 1. salle (de cinéma); 2. cinéma

cinemascope: trade name of one method of wide-screen presentation. An anamorphic lens is used to obtain the effect.

F cinémascope

cinemicrography: motion picture production in which the action is photographed by a motion picture camera attached to a microscope.

F microcinématographie

cinemicroscopy: see **cinemicrography**

cineradiography: X-ray cinematography done by means of any of several techniques available, especially image intensifiers.

F radiocinématographie

cinerama: projection technique using three different films projected on a wide screen.

F cinérama

circuit: see **closed circuit**; **integrated circuit**

circuit board: 1. a flat piece of material drilled or otherwise modified to facilitate the mounting and connection of various electrical components such as resistors, coils, batteries, transistors, etc. Used to assemble experimental electronic devices; **2.** a flat piece of material with several points for making electrical contact and a hidden network of wires connecting certain pairs of the contact points, used especially in teaching inference to younger learners.

F 1. 2. panneau de montage

circulation: the average number of copies of a periodical publication sold or otherwise distributed over a given period.

F diffusion

citizens' band—CB: assigned frequencies for radio transmission using low-power transmitters over short distance for private use.

F bande de fréquences banalisée; bande CB

clapper board: two hinged pieces of wood which are 'slapped' together to serve as a synchronization mark on the soundtrack of each shot of a motion picture production.

F claquette; clap

classical conditioning: see **respondent conditioning**

classification system: a systematic scheme for the arrangement of materials according to subject or form.

F système de classification

class management: organizing class member activities, student/student interaction, student/teacher interaction, taking into consideration teaching aims, inherent class variables and external interference.

F organisation de la classe; conduite de la classe

claw: the pull-down mechanism on a movie camera or projector which pulls down one frame of film at a time while a shutter covers the movement. The result provides an illusion of movement.

F griffe (d'entraînement)

client centred: educational or therapeutic attitude focusing not on the content to be transmitted or on the transformation to be performed, but on the person as such. It is based on being receptive to others and accepting them as they are. Not to be confused with 'laissez faire' which is one possible mode of exercising authority (C. Rogers).

C *teacher centred; subject centred*

F non directif

clientèle analysis: see **audience analysis**

clip: 1. a short film insert used in live TV programming; **2.** plastic or metal fasteners used to join the ends of rolls of film without splicing.

F 1. insert filmé; 2. attache

closed/open-ended: 1. a 'closed' film provides the ending whereas an open-ended film does not provide closure but leaves the ending to the imagination or reasoning of the viewer; **2.** a 'closed' set, question, etc., contains all its limit points or required elements. An open-ended item does not.

C *open-ended question; constructed response; multiple-choice question*

F 1. 2. fermé/ouvert

closed/open system: a 'closed system' is one which is cut off from its environment. Here, equilibrium therefore also means the death of the system, i.e. the end of any exchange or interaction. An 'open system' is one which is continually in communication with its environment, from which it receives a flow of energy, information and people. This openness enables the system to tend towards a dynamic equilibrium and ever-increasing complexity.

F système fermé/système ouvert

closed-circuit television – CCTV: a transmission system that distributes television programmes, live or on tape, both audio and video, to a limited network connected by cable or special microwave relay. CCTV is usually limited to a single area, building, site or campus.

F télévision en circuit fermé.

cloze test: a test of reading and comprehension skill which involves the insertion or deletion of appropriate words in a test.

C *legibility, readability*

F test de closure

clue: a stimulus that gives unintended assistance in answering objective-type test items.

C *prompt; cue*

F indice

CMI: see **computer-managed instruction**

coated lens: a lens whose surfaces are coated to reduce reflection and thus increase transmission of light through the lens.

F objectif traité

coaxial cable: a transmission line formed by a number of conductors, each insulated from the other and used for the transmission of a signal or many signals simultaneously.

F câble coaxial

COBOL: Common Business Oriented Language; a business data-processing language designed to express data manipulation and processing problems in a precise and standard manner.

F COBOL

code: an agreed transformation, or set of unambiguous rules, whereby messages are converted from one representation to another.

F code

cognitive domain: part of Bloom's taxonomy of educational objectives which includes those objectives which deal with the recall or recognition of knowledge and the development of intellectual abilities and skills.

C *affective domain; psychomotor domain*

F domaine cognitif

collator: a device used in reprography, book binding or data processing to sort or order sheets, cards, etc., automatically.

C *sorter*

F trieuse

collection: 1. the holdings of a library or learning resource centre; 2. a number of separate individual works brought together and issued as a single work.

F 1. fonds; 2. collection

colour film: 1. stock with one or more layers of colour sensitive emulsion; 2. cinematographic film produced with this material.

F 1. pellicule couleur; film couleur; 2. film en couleurs

colour saturation: the amount of colour present in a direction away from white.

F saturation

colour temperature: the absolute temperature at which a black-body radiator must be operated to have a chromaticity equal to that of the light source (a rating in Kelvin degrees which is generally used as an indicator of a lamp's apparent colour).

F température de couleur

(combinatoire): French term, used in educational technology, taken from logic, mathematics and linguistics, which refers to a strategy using a combination of several media so that they mutually complement and reinforce their educational effect in given circumstances.

C *multimedia approach*

F combinatoire

combined negative: see **composite negative**

combined magnetic sound – COMMAG: magnetic soundtrack on a film which also carries pictures.

F piste magnétique couchée

combined optical sound – COMOPT: optical soundtrack printed on to a film which also carries pictures.

F piste optique

comic book: see **comic strip.**

F album de bandes dessinées

comic strip: combination of a cartoon with a storyline laid out in a series of pictorial panels across a page and concerning a continuous character or set of characters whose thoughts and dialogues are indicated by means of 'balloons' containing written script.

C *cartoon*

F bande dessinée; BD

COMMAG: see **combined magnetic sound**

command: any instruction given to a computer.

F commande

command-driven program: a computer program where events are controlled by commands entered by the user.

C *menu-driven program*

F programme manœuvré en mode commande

commentary: 1. the narration for a film spoken by an off-screen person; 2. a spoken description or series of comments accompanying a motion picture or other exhibition.

F 1. 2. commentaire

commentator: one who comments or makes or writes a commentary.

F commentateur

common business oriented language: see **COBOL**

communication: the process of transferring information in the various media from one point, person, or device to another.

F communication

communication skills: skills associated with the transfer of information in oral, written, pictorial or audio-visual form.

F compétences en matière de communication; techniques de communication

communications satellite: satellite used for the transmission of all types of information-telephone, telegraph, telex, facsimile, radio, television and data transfer between computers. The satellite may have an eliptical orbit (low orbit) or a synchronous orbit (geostationary above the equator).

C *direct broadcast satellite; distribution satellite*

F satellite de télécommunication

communicative approach: an approach to foreign language teaching relating the teaching techniques, language content and materials to the acquisition of a communicative competence by the learners.

C *communicative competence*

F approche communicative

communicative competence: knowledge and ability to apply linguistic and paralinguistic code rules necessary to master successfully a given communicative situation.

F compétence de communication

community antenna television − CATV: a distribution system that receives television programmes from regular broadcasting stations by means of an antenna and then relays them via a closed-circuit system to subscribers in a particular area.

C *central antenna system, cable television*

F télévision par antenne communautaire; câblodistribution

community-based learning: a learning situation in which the student learns not in a classroom, but rather by using the cultural, governmental, business, industrial and physical resources of the community and the people, materials, events, institutions and services present in it as the motivation for, site of, and learning tools for learning (as opposed to school-based learning).

F apprentissage fondé sur les ressources de la collectivité*

community development: 1. activities directed to the improvement of the material and social welfare of the inhabitants of a limited urban or rural locality, sharing a sense of group identity and a body of common interests. The inhabitants should in principle play a major role in decision-making and participate in the activities; **2.** body of principles and methods evolved to stimulate the people of a community to take an interest in, and responsibility for, its material and social improvement.

F 1. animation globale; 2. développement communautaire

community education: enabling process through which children and adults receive a sense of identification with their community, become sensitive to its shortcomings and develop methods of participation in those activities directed to improving its quality of life.

F éducation communautaire

community listening: see **community viewing**

community viewing: viewing or listening done by residents of a limited geographical location frequently in a community social or cultural centre serving the neighbourhood.

F réception collective

COMOPT: see **combined optical sound**

compact cassette: see **tape cassette**

compact disc−CD: 1. a. small metallic disc on which audio information is stored in the form of digital signals which are read optically with a laser beam; **2.** the reading equipment for such a disc.

F 1. disque compact; disque audio-numérique; 2. lecteur de disque compact

comparative analysis: the description, classification and analysis of more than one system, group or the like so as to ascertain and evaluate similarities and differences.

F analyse comparée

compatibility: 1. the suitability of one learning resource as it relates to other learning resources in content, format, etc.; 2. the ability of one manufacturer's equipment to work with that of another manufacturer.

F 1. 2. compatibilité

compensatory education: education intended to compensate those who, for whatever reason, were deprived of part or all of the education they would normally have received during the period of compulsory schooling.

F éducation compensatoire

competency-based education: education deriving from the specification, learning and demonstration of the knowledge, skills, behaviour and attitudes required for a given role, profession or career.

C *mastery learning; performance-based instruction*

F éducation axée sur la compétence; méthode compétencialiste

compiler: 1. a collector or editor of materials gleaned from various sources who arranges them for publication; 2. a computer program that converts a high-level programming language (source language) into machine language before the program is executed.

F 1. 2. compilateur

completion test: an intelligence test requiring that the person to be tested complete a whole (such as a sentence or picture) from which certain parts have been omitted.

C *cloze test*

F test de complètement

components: elements that compose a system.

F composants; éléments

composite negative: a negative bearing the edited picture and matching sound in their correct relationship.

F négatif combiné (image et son)

composite video waveform: the signal produced by a television camera or tape before or without the carrier wave necessary for broadcast or use by a television receiver. A TV monitor without a channel tuner can use composite video.

F signal vidéo composite

compressed speech: speech which has been speeded up by means of an electronic device (audiocompressor) without distorting it.

F parole comprimée

computer: a data processor that can perform substantial computation, including numerous arithmetical operations or logical operations without intervention of a human operator during the run. Computers are differentiated by internal memory capacity among mainframe, mini- and micro-computers.

C *analog computer; digital computer; microcomputer; mini-computer; calculator.*

F ordinateur

computeracy: colloquial for computer literacy.

computer-aided instruction: see **computer-assisted instruction**

computer-aided learning: see **computer-assisted learning**

computer-assisted instruction – CAI: an instructional technique based on the two-way interaction of a learner and a computer with the objective of human learning and retention.

C *computer-managed instruction; computer-developed instruction*

F enseignement assisté par ordinateur; EAO

computer-assisted learning – CAL: a method of using a computer system as a means of presenting individualized instructional material.

F enseignement assisté par ordinateur*

computer-based instruction—CBI: any instructional or training technique which utilizes a computer, sometimes referred to as 'computer-mediated instruction'; 'computer-based learning – CBL'; 'computer-based training – CBT'.

C *media-based instruction*

F enseignement (formation) par l'informatique; enseignement informatisé

computer-developed instruction – CDI: an instructional technique which uses a computer as an integral part of the arrangement, selection and/or production of material designed to facilitate learning. Does not include procedures in which the learner directly interacts with the computer.

F enseignement généré par ordinateur

computer education: general term applied to the various uses of computers in education, computer literacy, computer-based instruction, computer studies, sometimes referred to as educational computing.

F informatique éducative

computer graphics: the use of computers to generate and display graphic materials such as diagrams, etc.

F infographie

computer language: a computer-oriented language whose instructions consist only of computer instructions.

C *programming language*
F langage machine

computer literacy: basic familiarity with computers and their applications.

F *initiation informatique; *alphabétisation informatique

computer-managed instruction – CMI: the use of a computer in education, not for instruction, but for recording the progress of a student through a learning sequence, prescribing lessons for the student, grading tests, scheduling non-computer learning experiences, etc., and making all this data available to both the student and the teacher.

F enseignement géré par ordinateur

computer-managed learning: see **computer-managed instruction**

computer-mediated instruction: see **computer-based instruction**

computer science: the science of rationally processing information, especially by means of automatic machines. Also referred to as 'informatics'.

F informatique

computer simulation: a technique in which a learner using direct access to a computer interacts with a mathematical model or simulation of a real situation in order to learn the process.

F simulation sur ordinateur

computer studies: study of computer science.

F informatique (comme matière d'enseignement)

computer system: a system consisting of one or more central processing units, input/output devices and other peripheral hardware that is related, interconnected and capable of simultaneous operation.

F système informatique

computer terminal: see **terminal**

concept film: see **single concept film**

condenser: a device which stores or partially blocks the flow of electric current.

F condensateur

condenser microphone: a type of microphone where sound waves cause varying changes in the capacity of a condenser. With the condenser forming part of an electrical circuit, sound energy is thus transformed into an electric voltage.

F microphone électrostatique

condensing lens: lenses used to concentrate or collect light rays from a source such as a projection lamp.

F lentille condensatrice; condensateur

conditional branch: see **conditional jump**

conditional jump: a jump (out of the normal execution sequence in a programme) which is only executed if certain conditions are met.

F saut conditionnel

conditioning: see **operant conditioning; respondent conditioning**

configuration: the layout of the hardware in a particular computer system.

C *architecture*

F configuration

connecting cable: see **patch cord**

connotation: 1. the sum of qualities implied by a term; 2. any meaning to which a given message refers by way of generally accepted terms.

C *denotation*

F 1. 2. connotation

conscientization: term created by Paolo Freire, denoting an educational process to enable an illiterate public living in conditions of extreme deprivation to achieve freedom and mastery over its own destiny. It attempts to develop consciousness and a critical appreciation of one's situation in order that one may act to transform it. The method of dialogue is used to prepare for action.

F conscientisation

consistency: see **reliability**

console: 1. a generic term for a large piece of equipment (often desk-like and non-movable) with control board(s) and related electronic equipment used for: *(i)* mixing and/or recording of sound; and/or *(ii)* direction and/or production of television programmes; and/or *(iii)* videorecordings; 2. peripheral unit of a computer used for communication between the operators or service personnel and the system. The console usually contains a panel for lights, keys, switches and related circuits for man-machine communication.

F 1. console; 2. pupitre de commande

console operator: in computer technology, an employee who sets up and operates the console and other peripheral units of an electronic data-processing system.

F pupitreur

constraints: the set of institutional, human, physical and technical determinants which, in a given situation, condition the application of a strategy and the reaching of an objective.

F contraintes

constructed response: a response to a question or frame in a programme or test which has to be elicited from the student, i.e. he does not select from a list of alternatives as with multiple-choice responding.

C *closed/open ended; open-ended question*

F réponse libre

contact print: a photographic print the same size as the negative, prepared by exposing to light the negative and positive films (or paper) placed together.

F planche de contact; copie contact

content analysis: 1. a procedure for identifying intellectual tasks including *(a)* the concepts involved in competence; *(b)* the relationships among concepts; *(c)* behaviours, performances using the concepts and relationships; 2. a systematic attempt to establish the characteristics of a message in order to analyse overt (explicit) and covert (latent) meanings, conceptual trends, biases, etc.

F 1. 2. analyse de contenu

contents of education: totality of knowledge, know-how, values, attitudes and behavioural patterns conveyed and transmitted by the educational institution or during out-of-school activities. It should be borne in mind that the concept of educational contents covers both taught content, i.e. that forming part of an explicit programme; and latent content offered by school life, teacher-pupil relations, work experience and the totality of the oral, written and audio-visual 'messages' encountered by pupils.

C *hidden curriculum; curriculum*

F contenu de l'éducation

context analysis: analysis of meaning as related to the environment or particular circumstances in which anything occurs or is found.

F analyse contextuelle

context-free answer: an answer not influenced by words or data directly before or after the required answer. Opposed to context sensitive response.

F réponse indépendante du contexte

context-free response: see **context-free answer**

contingency management: the advance preparation of a set of programmes, plans or alternatives to deal with unexpected or uncertain events that may occur within an organization.

F gestion des imprévus

contingency planning: see **contingency management**

continuity: of a sequence of programmes or of the parts of a single programme. The orderly progression from one part to the next according to a prearranged plan in order to produce a desired effect.

F continuité; enchaînement

continuity girl: see **script girl**

continuous assessment: assessment of an individual throughout a course of instruction, as opposed to terminal assessment which takes place only at the conclusion. Intended to provide frequent feedback to the learner.

C *assessment; feedback*

F contrôle continu

continuous loop: two open ends of a short length of film – 1½ to 2 metres – spliced and threaded into a projector and presented over and over again.

F boucle sans fin

continuous tone: an image made up of many shades of grey as well as black and white.

F dégradé

contract: see **learning contract**; **student contract**

contrast: relationship between light and dark elements of a picture. High contrast has extremes of light and dark; low contrast has middle tones.

F contraste

control board: see **control console**; **console**

control console: a console for processing audio and/or video signals.

C *console*

F pupitre de régie

control group: a collection of subjects in a sample which resembles the experimental group in all important respects except for the presence of a characteristic of interest. In true experimental studies, the control and experimental groups are presumed, for practical purposes, to be identical.

F groupe témoin

control panel: see **control console**; **console**

control room: a special area where the production output of a single studio is controlled. A small control room is often called a control booth or control cubicle.

F (salle de) régie

control unit: the part of a computer which directs the operations of all the other parts of the computer.

F unité de commande

convergent thinking: a rational, systematic approach to problem solving normally leading to the single correct, most conventional or most logical solution.

C *divergent thinking*

F production convergente; convergence

conversational chaining: in programmed instruction, a technique in which the correct answer to an item is not presented by itself but is rather embedded in the text of the following item. Consecutive items are those closely linked by the necessity of repeating in the new item the word or words that were elicited in the previous item. The response to one item becomes part of the stimulus in the next.

F programmation en chaîne

conversational mode: a method of operation in which the user is in direct communication with the computer and is able to obtain immediate response to his input message.

C *on-line; tutorial mode*

F mode dialogué

copy: 1. typescript or graphic material prior to being typeset or photographed; **2.** material prepared for photographic or more especially photo-mechanical processes; **3.** to reproduce information in a new location replacing whatever was previously stored there and leaving the source of the information unchanged.

F 1. 2. document à copier; copie; 3. copier

copyright: 1. institution or branch of law; **2.** set of rights granted to an author under national law on copyright (may be considered as synonymous to the term 'author's rights').

C *author's rights*

F droit d'auteur

copystand: a vertical or horizontal stand with an adjustable bracket to hold a camera for photographing flat materials at close range.

F statif de reproduction

core: 1. a small piece of magnetic material used as a storage medium in computers; **2.** a plastic centre on which a film is wound.

F 1. tore; 2. noyau

core curriculum: a term usually employed in secondary education, although it may be applied in some higher education programmes, referring to the organized curriculum which is considered essential and obligatory for all students in a particular educational programme regardless of their fields of specialization or their interests.

F tronc commun

correlation: the degree to which two variables vary together, that is, the degree to which changes in one are accompanied by changes in the other.

F corrélation

correspondence education: a form of distance education that emphasizes individual study making almost exclusive use of print material and exchange by post of written communication between tutors and students. Also called 'correspondence instruction'.

C *distance education*

F enseignement par correspondance

correspondence instruction: see **correspondence education**

cost/benefit analysis: a specialized form of cost-effectiveness analysis which allows the comparison of widely differing activities through the expression of all costs and benefits in common monetary terms.

F analyse coût-bénéfices; analyse coût-avantages

cost/effectiveness analysis: seeks to determine the costs and the effectiveness of an activity, or to compare similar alternative activities to determine the relative degree to which they will achieve the desired objective.

F analyse coût-efficacité

course: 1. an organization of subject matter and related learning experiences provided for the instruction of pupils on a regular or systematic basis, usually for a predetermined period of time (e.g. a semester, a regular school term, or a 2-week workshop); **2.** published materials designated to assist learning of some subject.

C *crash course; refresher course*

F 1. 2. cours

course design: 1. the designing of a course: developing the structure of a set of teaching units in accordance with given learning objectives; **2.** the structure of a set of teaching units, produced in accordance with given learning objectives.

F 1. organisation et conception d'un cours*; 2. structure d'un cours*

courseware: 1. the actual instructional material – including both content and technique – installed in a CAI system. Courseware is different from software in that the software is the actual program which directs the computer operation; **2.** as a generic term, any instructional materials, particularly items which must be used with equipment.

F 1. logiciel d'enseignement didacticiel; 2. programme

courseware editor: see **editor 2**

coverage: the size of, or the total number of inhabitants within the service area of a broadcasting station.

F couverture (d'un émetteur)

covert/overt: 1. 'covert' refers to performance that cannot be observed directly, performance that is mental, cognitive, internal or subliminal; 'overt' refers to any kind of performance which can be observed directly, whether the performance is visible or audible; **2.** distinction introduced by psychoanalysis which is of importance in content analysis and semiotics. The 'covert' content is the set of specifications which are gradually revealed by the work of analysis and which in certain cases contradict the apparent specifications. The 'overt' content is the set of specifications which are explicitly present.

F 1. invisible/observable; 2. latent/manifeste

covert response: behaviour or a response that cannot be detected by an observer. Such behaviour can only be established from observation of further behaviour or by introspection on the part of the subject.

C *overt response; free response*

F réponse invisible; réponse implicite

CPM: see **critical path method**

CPU: see **central processing unit**

crash course: an intensive course designed to meet emergency conditions in the shortest possible time by maximum utilization of resources.

F cours accéléré

credit: 1. the unit of value awarded for the successful completion of certain courses. The credit is intended to indicate the quantity (but not necessarily the quality) of course instruction in relation to the total requirements for a diploma, certificate or degree; **2.** to give credit, mention the source and the name of the author of the work used.

F 1. unité de valeur (universitaire); 2. faire mention de réserve

credits: the names of people that participated in the creation of a programme.

F générique

crew: any group of persons who collaborate on some aspect of a film production, such as a camera crew or sound crew.

F équipe de prise de vues, ou de son

criterion: 1. a characteristic or measurement with which other characteristics are measured; **2.** a standard or established level of performance against which individual scores may be compared; **3.** set of scores or rating that a test is supposed to produce.

F 1. 2. 3. critère; critérium

criterion-referenced test: a testing procedure in which a student is evaluated on how well he performs a given standard rather than in relation to the performance of a reference group.

C *norm-referenced test*

F test critériel; test à étalonnage critériel

critical-incident technique: method for determining what abilities are needed to do a particular job in order to establish standards of success through actual incidents occurring on the job. Critical incident films and tapes are sometimes used in teacher-training to study behaviour of teachers or students in given situations.

F technique des incidents critiques

critical mass: refers to the required size or extent of a project, programme, etc., to ensure an opportunity for it to have the desired, observable effect.

F masse critique

critical path method – CPM: the determination of the critical path, i.e. a sequence of interconnected events and activities between the start of a project and its completion that requires the longest time to accomplish. This gives the shortest time in which the project can be completed and is used as a planning aid.

F méthode du chemin critique

cross-age teaching: a technique in which learners are taught not by a teacher but

35

rather by other learners, usually older, who have already learned the content or gained the skills being taught.

C *peer instruction*

F enseignement mutuel inter-niveaux

cross dissolve: see **cross fade**

cross fade: in sound and television mixing, fading out one source while simultaneously fading in another source. Also sometimes called a segue.

F fondu enchaîné

cross modulation: in a receiver, the modulation of a wanted signal by the modulation of an unwanted signal on a different carrier frequency arising from the interaction of the radio frequency signals in non-linear circuits of the receiver preceding the detector.

F transmodulation; modulation transversale

crosstalk: the undesired mixing of two separate audio or video signals.

F diaphonie; interférence

Crowderian programme: see **intrinsic programming**

CRT: see **cathode ray tube**

crystal microphone: a low-fidelity microphone that uses a piezoelectric crystal to convert a sound into an electric signal.

F microphone piézoélectrique

cue: 1. to prepare a film, tape or audiodisc for playback so that when the material starts it will be in synchronization with other portions of the presentation or broadcast; **2.** a pre-arranged signal, for production purposes, to a studio or other programme source; **3.** see **clue**.

C *changeover; prompt*

F 1. (film, bande, disque audio) repérer; 2. signal d'avertissement; 3. indice

cue tone: an audio frequency of specified duration recorded on the cue track so as to provide a signalling system for functions as may be required.

F signal de commande

cueing: 1. adding a prompt or stimulus to make the correct response more likely while the student is learning; **2.** any system used by a second person to signal a narrator during narration recording.

F 1. présentation d'indices; 2. signalisation; soufflage

cultural centre: a centre equipped with rooms for meetings and exhibitions, libraries and records and workshops.

C *community viewing*

F centre culturel

cumulative record: a record (file, folder, report, etc.) designed to receive additional new material of the same kind as that already collected. Provides a running account over time.

F registre cumulatif

curriculum: the planned interaction of students with instructional content, instructional resources and instructional processes for the attainment of educational objectives.

C *core curriculum; hidden curriculum; contents of education; instructional programme; syllabus; programme*

F programme (d'enseignement); (curriculum)

curriculum development: the process of organizing, combining and co-ordinating the various courses which form the curricula so that they lead to different levels of knowledge and qualification. Such process also includes experimentation, evaluation of content and effectiveness, as well as selection of appropriate teaching and learning methods and materials.

F élaboration des programmes d'enseignement

curriculum guide: a written guide to a particular curriculum specifying what is to be covered and how it is to be taught. Such a guide may be as narrow in scope as a unit or topic of instruction, or as broad as the entire curriculum of a school system or level of instruction within a country.

F plan d'études; *guide (d'enseignement) du programme

cursor: a symbol placed on the screen to let the user know where the next typed character will appear.

F curseur

custom network: dedicated, non-standard liaison between computers.

C *local area network; network*

F réseau local

cut: 1. a cut is defined as 'each time the camera changes position or a new shot appears on the screen'; **2.** when a film director calls 'cut' he is indicating that the camera should be stopped and the 'take' is over; **3.** to delete part of a programme; **4.** to terminate abruptly the output of a channel.

F 1. coupe; 2. coupez!; 3. couper; 4. interrompre

cutting: the process of editing film.

F montage

cutting copy: film editor's rough combination of picture and soundtrack.

F copie de montage

cutting room: a room for cutting or editing of film.

C *cutting; editing*

F salle de montage

cybernetics: the study of information processing systems and control mechanisms in living beings and machines, in particular those that function on the basis of the principle of feedback.

F cybernétique

D

daisy wheel printer: a printer with interchangeable circular typeheads with the characters attached on the end of stalks.

C *matrix printer; laser printer*

F imprimante à marguerite

dark-room: an area specially equipped for the processing of photographic films and papers. It is lightproof and has special photographic safelights and ventilation.

F chambre noire

data: a representation of facts, concepts or instructions in a formalized manner suitable for processing by humans or by automatic means.

F données

data bank: a set of very large files of data held on mass storage devices for information-retrieval purposes.

F banque de données

data base: a collection of data fundamental to an operation organized in some predefined structure.

F base de données

data capture: a general term for techniques by which data are converted into machine readable format.

F saisie de données

data management program system: application software which permits the monitoring of a data base.

C *file management program*

F gestionnaire de données; système de gestion de données de base

data processing: any operation or combination of operations on data, usually in accordance with a specified or implied set of discrete steps including operations such as compute, assemble, compile, interpret, generate, translate, store, retrieve, transfer, select, extract, shift, search, sort, merge, transliterate, read, write, print, erase, punch, etc. The processing of data in an organization can be centralized when all data is processed at a single location, usually with a given configuration or equipment in one building; or decentralized.

F traitement de l'information

37

daylight projection: a projection system that in one way or another provides a screen image bright enough to be used in high levels of ambient light. Generally a rear projection set-up is used, but some front projection systems using special screens and/or special light sources can be used.

F projection plein jour

dB: decibel.

F décibel

DC: direct current.

F courant continu

debug: 1. to search for and correct errors in a computer programme; **2.** to correct a technical malfunction.

F 1. mettre au point; 2. déparasiter; dépanner

decision tree: a technique for portraying a number of decision alternatives or possible outcomes, assigning a value to each, and determining which one will best achieve some predetermined objective.

F arbre de décision; arbre de pertinence

deck: see **cassette deck**

decoder: an electronic device that is capable of accepting encoded data at its input and generating decoded data at its output, e.g. pay TV.

F décodeur

decoding: the process of converting code symbols to the original value or information for which the code stands.

C *encoding*

F décodage; déchiffrement

decoy: see **distractor**

dedicated: (of a program, machine, network, channel or system) set apart for special use.

F dédié; spécialisé

deductive method: a method of teaching, study or argument which proceeds from general or universally applicable principles to particular applications of these principles and shows the validity of the conclusions.

F méthode déductive

definition: 1. the fidelity with which the detail of an image is reproduced; **2.** the degree with which a communication system reproduces sound images or messages; **3.** the fidelity with which the pattern edges in a printed circuit (conductors, inductors, etc.) are reproduced relative to the original master pattern.

F 1. 2. 3. définition

degauss: remove stray magnetism from any recording, editing or playback equipment.

F démagnétiser

degree of freedom: any way an element (component) may move or change in a system, without changing the system.

F degré de liberté

delayed feedback: the return of the student's performance in an audio-active comparative language laboratory that occurs only at the end of a set of drills, as opposed to immediate feedback in an audio-active-comparative-corrective language laboratory where the student can compare his utterance with the correct (master) solution immediately after having produced it.

F retour d'écoute différé

delivery reel: see **delivery spool**

delivery spool: the spool (reel) from which the tape or film issues during the recording or reproducing process.

C *feed reel; reel-to-reel; take-up spool*

F bobine débitrice

delivery system: 1. the organization of the distribution of printed and audio-visual material by mail or other systems; **2.** the use of radio/television information networks and relay systems for the distribution of instruction and educational information to users.

F 1. routage; 2. système de distribution

Delphi technique: a method for the systematic solicitation and collation of judgements on a particular topic through a set of carefully designed sequential questionnaires interspersed with summarized information and feedback of opinions derived from earlier responses.

F technique delphi

democratic: liberal attitude in dealing with a class, as opposed to an authoritarian attitude.

F non directif

demodulation: the extraction of information from a modulated carrier signal.

C *modulation*

F démodulation

demonstration: an activity in which the teacher or another person uses examples, experiments, and/or other actual performance in order to illustrate a principle or show others how to do something.

F démonstration

demonstration lesson: the learning and instruction activities that are used in a demonstration class for observation by a group of prospective or experienced teachers.

C *practice lesson; microteaching*

F leçon modèle

denotation: the aggregate or class of individuals or instances falling under a conception or named by a term.

C *connotation*

F dénotation

density: 1. in general, the compactness of space distribution on a storage medium such as magnetic disk, magnetic tape or cathode-ray tube; **2.** packing density – the number of storage cells per unit length, unit area or unit volume, e.g. the number of bits per millimetre stored on a track; **3.** in film, the degree of opaqueness or transparency to light.

F 1. densité; 2. densité d'enregistrement; 3. densité

deposited negative: a film negative placed in a deposit library or storage area available on request to co-operating groups.

F négatif déposé

depth of field: the distance within a scene from the point closest to the camera in focus to the farthest in focus.

C *depth of focus*

F profondeur de champ

depth of focus: the distance between the lens and the film in a camera during exposure in which the subject matter being photographed will be sharply defined.

C *depth of field*

F profondeur de foyer

descriptor: a term or terms attached to a document to permit its subsequent location and retrieval. Also known as 'keyword'.

C *information retrieval system*

F descripteur

desk-top computer: see **microcomputer**

developer: a solution in which the chemicals set the photographic image by acting upon silver salts on exposed film that has been affected by light during picture-taking.

C *instructional developer*

F révélateur

developing tank: a large container in which film is developed

F cuve à développer

development bath: any liquid, chemical solution or water rinse used in film processing.

F bain de développement

developmental testing: empirical testing of learning materials so that the author can ascertain the ineffective and/or inefficient parts that need to be modified; often referred to as 'de-bugging'.

C *formative evaluation; validation; field testing*

F expérimentation de mise au point

device: see **apparatus; hardware; equipment; instructional aids**

diagnosis: the process of determining the existing capabilities of a student by analysing his/her performance of a hierarchy of essential tasks in a specific subject, such as mathematics or music, with the intent of facilitating

39

his/her learning by assigning appropriate remedial or advanced learning tasks.

F diagnostic

diagram: 1. a schematic representation of a sequence of sub-routines designed to solve a problem; **2.** a coarser and less symbolic representation than a flowchart, frequently including descriptions in words; **3.** a schematic or logical drawing showing the electrical circuit or logical arrangements within a component.

C *graph; flow chart*

F 1.2. diagramme; 2. schéma

dial: 1. a face upon which some measurement or other number is registered; **2.** a disk, usually with a knob or slot that may be turned to take electric connections or to regulate the operation of a machine; **3.** to manipulate a dial.

F 1. 2. cadran; 3. composer; appeler (par cadran)

dial access information retrieval: telephone-type dial access to a data bank of films, slides and/or tapes.

F accès automatisé à l'information

diaphragm: 1. the device that controls the opening through which light enters a camera; **2.** the disc in a microphone that responds to sound, or the cone in a loudspeaker that produces sound.

F 1. diaphragme; 2. membrane

(diaporama): combination of slides and sound recordings (on magnetic tape) used to present or illustrate. The operation is generally automatic, with the slide projectors controlled by a multi-track tape-recorder.

F diaporama

diazo process: duplicating procedure in which a translucent master with an opaque or light absorbing image is placed between an ultraviolet light source and a diazo paper or film which is developed in ammonia fumes. Diazo process is often used to make overhead transparencies.

F diazotypie

dichroic: a mirror or reflector for a projection lamp that transmits heat and reflects light.

Also called a cold mirror.

F dichroïque

didactic teaching: a method of instruction predominantly based on verbal presentations that emphasizes rules, principles, standards of conduct, and authoritative guidelines usually directly given to the student by someone else.

F méthode didactique

differential sensitivity: ability of a test or measuring instrument to express small variations in the object being measured.

C *reliability; validity*

F sensibilité (d'un test); finesse discriminatoire

diffuse lighting: light softened through the use of diffusers.

F éclairage diffus

diffusion-transfer process: a method for preparing overhead transparencies requiring the exposure to light of negative paper placed against the original material, then development of the negative in contact with a sheet of positive film in a photographic solution.

F diffusion-transfert

digital computer: a computer that processes information in the form of binary-coded signals. The five functional parts of all digital computers are the control unit, the memory, the arithmetic unit, the input unit and the output unit.

C *analog computer*

F ordinateur

digital image: visual representation of information in discrete units coded onto a grid of points.

C *analog image*

F image digitale; numérisée

digital optical disc—DOD: a disc designed for the recording, storage and retrieval of digital information using laser optics.

C *videodisc*

F disque optique numérique

40

digital transmission: the transmission of radio and television signals in a coded form, usually mathematical bits or binary codes providing easy signal regeneration without noise, drift or distortion.

F transmission numérisée

digitizing: converting an analog transmission into a digital transmission

F numérisation

dimmer: rheostat controlling illumination brightness.

F gradateur

DIN: abbreviation for Deutsche Industrie Normen (German industrial standards); DIN standards apply to a wide range of products including items of equipment such as plugs and sockets.

F DIN

diode: a solid-state electronic device that permits current to flow in only one direction.

F diode

diorama: a three-dimensional representation of a scene.

F diorama

direct access: a type of storage device which allows the particular address to be accessed in a manner independent of the location of that address. Thus, access by a programme is not dependent upon the previously accessed position. Sometimes called 'random access'.

C *sequential access*

F accès direct

direct-access store: a device that is used for temporary storage of information placed into the computer by the user, often termed RAM – random access memory. It is volatile storage, in that the information in RAM is often lost when power to the computer is shut off.

F mémoire vive

direct broadcast satellite: satellite used to broadcast direct to the audience via special receiving gear, rather than an intermediate receiving station and terrestrial transmitter.

C *distribution satellite; communications satellite*

F satellite de (radio) diffusion directe

direct experience: a term generally used to mean a learning process based upon actual experience with real things in a real (true-to-life) situation, e.g., learning to sell by working in a store.

F apprentissage en situation

direct method: a method of teaching a foreign language which stresses the actual use of the foreign language.

F méthode directe

direct oral method: see **direct method**

direct print: a print made in one step from original film.

F copie directe

direct learning: see **direct teaching**

direct teaching: instructions given in a face-to-face manner between teacher and students.

C *face-to-face*

F enseignement/apprentissage direct

directed observation: a guided observation provided for the purpose of improving the study, understanding and evaluation of that which is observed.

F observation dirigée

directed teaching: teaching in which there is a strong element of teacher direction and guidance.

C *discovery learning; independent study*

F pédagogie directive; méthode directive

director: the person mainly responsible for the final result of a film, a recording, or other production and who controls all phases of the work involved.

F réalisateur

disc: see **audio disc; video disc; optical disc; long-playing disc; compact disc; digital optical disc.**

discipline: 1. branch of knowledge or instruction, e.g. a general subject area, such as psychology, linguistics, etc.; **2.** order maintained amongst students.

F 1. 2. discipline

discovery learning method: the learning of principles or concepts which occurs as a generalization of experiences by the individual learner in the absence of direct telling by someone else.

C *heuristic approach*

F méthode d'apprentissage par la découverte

discrimination: a capability of making different responses to previously learned stimuli that differ from each other along one or more dimensions (one of the types of intellectual skills)

F discrimination

dish antenna: see **parabolic antenna**

dish-reflector antenna: see **parabolic antenna**

disk: alternative spelling for 'disc', used in relation to computers; see **floppy disk, hard disk, magnetic disk.**

disk drive: a peripheral of a computer system that operates disks used to store, file and retrieve information.

F unité de disques

diskette: a flexible magnetic disk enclosed in a protective container.

C *floppy disk; hard disk*

F disquette

disk pack: in data processing, a grouping of magnetic disks used to store data. Disk packs offer very large storage capacities and direct access to the stored data.

F pile de disques

display: any operation in which a message or selected data are presented for visual inspection.

C *visual display*

F affichage; visualisation; présentation sur écran

display board: a vertical surface used as a teaching device upon which are mounted displays of various kinds.

F tableau mural

display panel: see **display board**

dissolve: an optical effect in motion pictures involving two superimposed scenes in which the second one gradually appears as the first one gradually disappears.

F fondu enchaîné

distance education: an instructional system in which the learner is separated from the institution organizing the instruction by space and/or time. Communication in distance education uses various media (e.g. printed, audiovisual materials, radio, television, computer software) and includes usually tutors and group sessions.

C *correspondence education*

F enseignement à distance; téléenseignement

distortion: any change, whether caused by the recording transmission, or the reproducing equipment, from the original audio or visual programme.

F distorsion

distractor: any plausible but incorrect alternative in a multiple-choice or matching-test item; also known as 'decoy', 'foil'.

F distracteur

distribution: 1. delivery or conveyance of items, data, or goods; 2. delivery of media or video signals to designated places; 3. a statistical tabulation showing the frequencies or percentage of the values of a variable.

C *normal distribution curve*

F 1. 2. 3. distribution

distribution agency: the organization authorized to handle distribution of a commodity or item of equipment.

F agence de distribution

distribution frame: a structure providing for the termination of wires and cables and their interconnection in a desired order.

F répartiteur

distribution right: the right to offer copies of a work to the general public or any section thereof (mainly through appropriate commercial channels).

F droit de mise en circulation

distribution satellite: satellite used to circulate television and radio signals among broadcasting organizations or between transmitters, as opposed to a direct broadcast satellite.

C *communications satellite*

F satellite de distribution

distributor: 1. one who sells, rents or circulates a commodity; **2.** a commercial firm, agency or film library service which sells, rents or circulates films.

F 1. 2. distributeur

divergent thinking: a creative approach to solving a problem or tackling a task that is aimed at producing a range of original solutions.

C *convergent thinking; brainstorming*

F production divergente; créativité; divergence

(docimologie): French term for the science whose object is the systematic study of examinations, especially marking systems and the behaviour of examiners and examinees.

C *measurement*

F docimologie

documentalist: a person who carries out responsible work in the field of documentation.

F documentaliste

documentary film: factual film that records some historic event, the life of a person, the way of life of a group or society, a process or the like.

F film documentaire

document reproduction: see **reprography**

DOD: see **digital optical disc**

Dolby system: a method of sound recording and reproduction which reduces noise in tapes and disks.

F procédé Dolby

dolly: a wheeled carriage to support and transport equipment.

F chariot

dolly-in/dolly-out: moving camera towards object (dolly-in) or away (dolly-out).

F travelling avant/arrière

domestic satellite: satellite used to broadcast or relay signals within the country operating it.

F satellite national

dot printer: see **matrix printer**

double-band projector: see **double system projector**

double exposure: the photographic recording of two (or more) images on a single strip of film. The images may be either superimposed or side-by-side in any relationship, sometimes individually vignetted.

F surimpression

double frame: a filmstrip with images twice the size of single frame images.

F double image

double perforated stock: film having perforations along both edges.

F pellicule à double perforation

double system projector: a device designed to project 16 mm motion picture films with synchronized sound recorded on a separate 16 mm magnetic sound track.

F projecteur double bande

double system sound: see **double track**

double track: the storing of motion picture images and sounds in synchronization but recorded on separate materials and usually with separate machines or devices.

F double bande

43

down-link: transmission from satellite to earth.

C *feeder link; up-link*

F liaison espace-Terre; liaison descendante

down-loading: the use of data communication facilities to transfer data or programs from one computer to another, e.g. from a mainframe to a microcomputer.

C *teleprocessing; telesoftware; remote access*

F téléchargement

down time: the period of time a learning resource (usually a device) is out of service use awaiting repair/maintenance or being repaired/maintained.

F temps d'immobilisation; durée d'indisponibilité

dramatization: 1. an activity in which learners interpret, synthesize and express ideas, feelings, concepts or roles in the acted-out form of a verbal or non-verbal play; **2.** a technique to help the individual disclose indirectly feelings and attitudes he or she may not be able to express directly and to help group members to express, practice and facilitate interpersonal skills.

F 1. jeu de rôles; 2. psychodrame

drill: an orderly, repetitive, learning activity intended to help develop or fix a specific skill or aspect of knowledge.

F (drill); exercice d'automatisation

drill and practice program: a courseware that rehearses basic facts with a view to reinforcing skill acquisition.

C *tutorial program; simulation program; utility software*

F logiciel d'exercice(s); exerciseur

drop-out: 1. a serious momentary reduction of the reproduced signal level; **2.** person who abandons a course of study on which he has embarked before its completion.

F 1. perte de niveau; 2. élève ayant abandonné les études.

drop-out rate: percentage of pupils or students who leave school before completing a grade or a level.

F taux d'abandon

dry carrel: see **carrel**

dry cell: a battery whose contents are made non-spillable by the use of some absorbent.

F pile sèche

dry mounting: affixing art work to supporting mount boards by the use of a sheet of dry-mounting tissue and a heated press.

C *mounting*

F montage à sec

dry press: see **mounting press**

dry run: a practice tryout of equipment or programmes.

F essai général; répétition

dry transfer: method of preparing lettering or graphics from pressure-sensitive master sheets.

F transfert à sec; décalcomanie

dual cable: a method of doubling channel capacity by using two cables installed side by side to carry different signals.

F double câble

dual operation apparatus: apparatus controlled by two mechanisms under the command of the pupil and instructor respectively; used in training activities with an element of risk.

F appareil en double commande

dub: electronic copying of recorded information.

F repiquage

dubbing: 1. a process by which actors put new words on to the soundtrack of a motion picture made in a foreign language, such as 'dubbing' an Italian film into English; **2.** adding sound of any kind to a film which was not recorded at the time of the shooting; this is also known as 'post-dubbing';

3. the transfer of recorded sound from one unit to another; commonly record-to-tape, tape-to-tape, tape-to-film; **4.** the combination of two or more recordings into a composite recording by re-recording.

F 1. doublage; 2. post-sonorisation; 3. repiquage; 4. montage

dumb terminal: user terminal which only facilitates input and output without independent data processing capacity.

C *intelligent terminal; smart terminal*

F terminal passif

dupe: short for 'duplicate'. A dupe negative of a film is a negative produced from a master negative to protect the master or to enable it to be at different laboratories simultaneously. A dupe positive is produced from a reversal master for the same purposes.

F contretype; internégatif

duplex operation: the method of operation whereby radio transmission is made possible alternately in each direction, for example by means of manual control.

C *multiplex*

F exploitation en duplex

duplicating: 1. the making of one or more copies from an original tape, film document, etc.; **2.** the non-photographic reproduction of an original, two-dimensional material with the intermediate step of preparing a re-usable master from which multiple copies can be made.

F 1. duplication; 2. polycopie; multigraphie

dynamic microphone: a generic term for a microphone which works on electrodynamic principles, i.e. moving coil and ribbon.

F microphone électrodynamique

E

earphone: see **headset**

earth: 1. a conducting line between electrical equipment and the earth; **2.** the zero electrical point in a circuit or system. This is the term used in the United Kingdom; the term used in the United States is:

C *ground*

F 1. 2. terre

Earth station: transmitting or receiving station on Earth used as a link in receiving signals from a satellite or transmitting to it. This is the term used in the United Kingdom; the term used in the United States is:

C *ground station*

F station au sol

EBR: see **electron beam recording**

echo: the repetition of a sound or an image caused by reflection of radioelectrical waves.

F écho; écho sonore; image fantôme.

(école parallèle): term created by the French sociologist G. Friedman to characterize the information, knowledge, values, attitudes and behavioural patterns conveyed and transmitted outside the school by the mass media, press, comics, radio, films and television.

F école parallèle

edge number: a series of matching numbers printed at intervals along the edge of original motion-picture footage and also along the workprint edge so that after editing the workprint and original can be easily matched together.

F numéro de bord

editing: 1. the process of selecting and rearranging into an orderly continuity segments of either print, recorded sound, videorecordings or motion picture film; **2.** the process of editing a program on a computer, removing unwanted material from and/or inserting new material into a document.

C *cutting*

F 1. montage; préparation de copie; 2. édition

editing bench: see **editing table**

editing table: device for viewing motion picture film for editing purposes.

F table de montage

editor: 1. a person who performs editing as opposed to the author or director; **2.** utility program which aids the user of a computer to edit a file or to develop a special application, e.g. courseware editor.

F 1. monteur; monteuse (film); rédacteur; 2. éditeur

EDP: electronic data processing: see **data processing**

education system: the structural organization by which teaching and education at all levels is dispensed to the population.

C *instructional system*

F système éducatif

educational accountability: 1. the theory that teachers and school systems may be held responsible for actual improvement in pupil achievement and that such improvement is measurable through tests of teacher effectiveness conducted by outside agencies; **2.** educational technology term for the extent to which student performance is attributable to instruction rather than ageing, selective admission, etc.

F 1. *responsabilité éducative; 2. *efficacité pédagogique

educational advisor: a subject-matter or pedagogical expert for a programme.

F conseiller pédagogique

educational computing: see **computer education**

educational film: broadly speaking, any film used in an educational context for the teaching of skills, facts, concepts, attitudes and values. In a narrower sense, a classroom film or school film.

F film éducatif

educational media: the devices and materials used in the teaching-learning process. The term is often used as opposed to instructional aids to denote those means which present a complete body of information and are largely self-supporting rather than supplementary in the teaching-learning process.

C *learning resources; audio-visual aids; instructional aids; media; mass media*

F moyens d'enseignement

educational media centre: the area in a school used primarily for the storage, supply and utilization of learning resources which have been organized into an integrated collection of materials of all types (print, auditory, visual, kits, games) along with any devices and special settings (e.g. carrels) needed to use the materials. Also called 'learning resources centre – LRC'.

F médiathèque scolaire ou universitaire

educational objectives: the concrete results which one hopes to obtain within a planned period through strategic action and clearly established targets, in order to face up to some existing problems and the needs resulting from the expansion of the education system and to meet the social needs of the community.

F objectifs de l'éducation

educational programme: series of planned activities with administrative connotations relating to the development of institutions. What goes on in them and budget provision. To be distinguished from:

C *instructional programme*

F programme d'éducation; activité d'éducation

educational specification: detailed, precise expert presentation of a plan or proposal for educational facilities, including equipment, classrooms, laboratories, curriculum.

F programme pédagogique

educational strategy: preparation of plans, programmes and projects in order to meet general or specific objectives or to solve problems which the education system has to solve.

C *instructional strategy*

F *stratégie de l'éducation*

educational technology: 1. in its original sense, it concerns the use for educational purposes of the media born of the communications revolution, such as audiovisual media, television, computers, and other items of 'hardware' and 'software'; **2.** in new and broader terms, systematic method of devising, applying and assessing the whole process of teaching and learning by taking into account both technical and human resources, and the interactions between these, so as to obtain a more effective form of education. In this sense, educational technology uses systems analysis as a theoretical tool.

F 1.2. *technologie de l'éducation*

educational television — ETV: any television programming – broadcast or closed-circuit – designed to cover a broad range of educational and cultural subjects for information enrichment. Such programming may be used for instruction but is not specifically designed to be instructional.

C *school television; instructional television*

F *télévision éducative**

effect: see **placebo effect; Hawthorne effect**

effects – FX: depending on context, either sound effects, optical effects or special effects.

F *effets*

effects analysis: the special techniques to determine in objective and quantitative terms the effects of particular communication contents. The varied techniques include information and attitude tests and interviews.

F *analyse des effets*

effectiveness: a measure of the extent to which an activity achieves its objectives.

F *efficacité*

efficiency: the productivity of an activity's implementation process; how well inputs were converted into outputs.

F *efficience*

EGRUL: see **RULEG**

EIAJ: Electronic Industry Association of Japan.

electric board: see **buzz board**

electromagnetic: referring to the combined electric and magnetic fields caused by electron motion through conductors.

F *électromagnétique*

electron beam recording – EBR: high quality videotape-to-film transfer system.

F *enregistrement par faisceau cathodique*

electronic classroom: a classroom that can also be used as an audio-language laboratory, equipped with a simple master console and headsets for the students, or a loudspeaker.

F *classe équipée en laboratoire de langues**

electronic editing: a method wherein editing of videotapes is carried out by recording without physically cutting the tapes, whilst maintaining the continuity of all tracks.

F *montage électronique*

electronic flash: an electronic lighting device which gives off a brief but intense flash of light to illuminate the object to be photographed. Many are portable and may be attached to the camera.

F *flash électronique*

electronic mail: message service using teletext or videotèx facilities; messages are stored in an electronic mailbox at users' terminal.

C *delivery system*

F *courrier électronique; messagerie électronique; télémessagerie*

electrostatic copy: see **xerography**

47

embossed screen: a projection screen covered with raised dots of light-reflecting material. One type is called lenticular.

F écran gaufré

emulsion: the image-bearing layer of a film.

F émulsion

emulsion side: the side of a film on which the emulsion coating lies.

F côté émulsion

emulsion speed: the photosensitivity of a film emulsion, usually expressed as an index number based on the film manufacturer's recommendations for the use of the film under typical conditions of exposure and development.

C *exposure index*

F sensibilité

enabling objective: the component actions, knowledge and skills the student must learn if he/she is to attain the terminal objective. They represent the learning difference between where the learner is now and where one wants him/her to be.

F objectif intermédiaire; objectif médiateur

encoding: 1. process whereby a message is transformed into signals that can be carried by a communication channel; **2.** process whereby a person transforms his intention into such behaviour as can be a signal in a communicative system – usually oral or graphic language, but gestures, etc., may also serve. The entire encoding may involve several steps; e.g., a person writes out a telegram (first encoding) which in turn is tranformed by another into electric signals (second encoding).

C *decoding*

F 1. 2. codage

encryption: the conversion of data such as a computer program or a satellite transmission to a code format so that the data cannot be illegally or improperly read and copied.

C *scrambler*

F embrouillage; chiffrement

end title: the formal title which brings the audiovisual material to a conclusion.

F titre final

enhancement materials: see **enrichment programmes**

enlargement: a photograph made from a smaller negative through a projection process.

C *blow-up*

F agrandissement

enlarger: a projection device used for printing images of increased or reduced size on paper or film from a photographic negative.

F agrandisseur

enrichment programme: 1. supplementary instructional experience providing for special needs, abilities and interests; **2.** any educational broadcast programme which is not intended for direct instruction.

F 1. programme complémentaire d'appui*; 2. émission non didactique*

entropy: quantity specifying the amount of disorder or randomness in a system bearing energy or information. Originally defined in thermodynamics in terms of heat and temperature, entropy indicates the degree to which a given quantity of thermal energy is available for doing useful work; the greater the entropy, the less available the energy. In information theory, entropy represents the noise or random errors that occur in the transmission of signals or messages.

F entropie

entry behaviour: the skills which a student possesses at the time he or she enters or begins a sequence of instruction.

F comportement initial

entry point: part of a system, specially selected for introducing modifications, because it is particularly receptive and closely interconnected with the other parts, thereby making it possible to act upon the whole system. Example: modifying the structure of an examination so as to create a chain reaction leading to changes in curricula, in the attitudes of teachers, pupils, etc.

C *systems approach in education*

F point d'entrée

entry profile: abilities or attitudes which a student must possess before taking up training for a specific course.

C *outgoing profile; prerequisite; pre-test*

F profil d'entrée

environmental studies: organization of activities so as to provide pupils with an integrated approach to the study of their immediate environment; aims to give a common focus to the teaching of subjects such as geography, economics, history, biology and physics.

F étude du milieu

epidiascope: a device that will project both opaque and transparent pictures.

F épidiascope

episcope: a device designed to project images of opaque print materials and flat objects by using reflected light. This is the term used in the United Kingdom; the term used in the United States is:

C *opaque projector*

F épiscope

equalizer: an audio device designed to complement a regular audio system. It allows a finer control (often octave by octave) of the audible frequency range than ordinary tone controls can.

F égaliseur

equipment: usually covers everything, except personnel, needed for efficient operation or service.

C *apparatus; hardware; materials*

F équipement

erasing: 1. electronic degaussing (or wiping clean) of all pictures and sound from a tape; removing all previously recorded signals so that the tape can be used again; **2.** removing data from storage leaving the remaining space in a blank condition.

F 1. 2. effacer

erasing head: a device on a magnetic tape drive whose sole function is to erase previous information prior to writing new information.

F tête d'effacement

ergonomics: a scientific approach to the technology of work design based on the human biological sciences: anatomy, physiology and psychology. In education, it refers to the relationship of learner(s) and educator(s) to their occupations, equipment and aids used in the teaching-learning process, their working and learning environment, the temporal and social conditions of their work. Sometimes called 'human engineering'.

F ergonomie

error rate: the percentage of incorrect responses on an item, a set of items or a whole programme.

F taux d'erreur

estimate: 1. in evaluation, the value arrived at by a rough calculation; **2.** a value derived from a specific sample of statistics.

F 1. 2. estimation

ETV: see educational television

evaluation: the process of delineating, obtaining and providing useful information for judging decision alternatives.

C *formative evaluation; summative evaluation; assessment; appraisal*

F évaluation

exciter lamp: a bulb which illuminates the sound track of a film so that it can be translated into electrical energy which comes through the loudspeakers as music, sound effects and/or dialogue.

F lampe excitatrice

exclusive rights: a formal agreement giving sole rights to sell, rent or distribute a property during a specific period of time.

F droits d'exclusivité

executive producer: a studio administrator who does not directly produce films but supervises the work of producers.

F producteur exécutif

exhibit: a display of objects and/or materials arranged in a setting to convey a unified idea.

F exposition

expendable materials: things that are perforce used up in education such as candles, matches, filter paper, chemicals, workbooks, etc. Things that must be purchased prior to a teaching sequence. Sometimes called 'expendables' or 'consumables'.

F matériel fongible

experimental group: a collection of subjects in a sample presumed to be the only subjects possessing characteristics of the independent variable or the only subjects receiving the experimental treatment.

F groupe expérimental

experimental school: an elementary or secondary school connected with an educational research institution in which new teaching methods, new techniques, new structures and personnel practices are tested.

F école expérimentale

expert system: a particular development of artificial intelligence, highly specialized software applied to a specific domain and combining formal reasoning procedures with expert knowledge stored in the computer's memory.

C *intelligent tutoring system*

F système expert

exposed film: film which has been run through a camera or printer and is ready for development of its latent images.

C *over-exposed; under-exposed*

F film exposé; film impressionné

exposure: the amount of light allowed through the lens to register on the light-sensitive film.

C *double exposure*

F exposition

exposure index: a number assigned to a film by the manufacturer which indicates the relative emulsion speed of the film for determining camera settings, f number and shutter speed.

F indice de pose

exposure meter: a device used to measure light either falling on or reflected from the object to be photographed. Also called light meter.

F posemètre

extension cable: see **extension cord**

extension cord: a length of wire to connect electric power to a distant device.

F prolongateur; rallonge

extension education: instructional activities of educational institutions directed to clientele outside the immediate student body. They may include short courses, radio and television courses, correspondence study, conferences, workshops, counselling.

F enseignement périscolaire ou péri-universitaire

extension tube: a threaded tube or ring enabling a lens to be mounted at a greater distance from a camera than normal. This allows objects to be focused which are closer to the camera than normal.

F bague rallonge

external memory: see **external store**

external motivation: see **extrinsic motivation**

external storage: see **external store**

external store: a storage unit which is external to the computer (i.e. magnetic tapes, magnetic disks and punched cards) and accessible by a computer only through input-output channels.

F mémoire externe

extinction: the elimination or progressive reduction in magnitude or frequency of a conditioned response upon the withdrawal

50

of the reinforcement. The term is applied to both classical conditioning and operant conditioning.

F extinction

extra-curricular activities: activities associated with schools, but which take place outside of the usual schedule of classes, and which are optional for learners. Includes meetings of the science club, project work, science fairs, school societies, singing, dancing, acting, making music, etc.

F activités dirigées; activités hors programme

extra-mural: descriptive of: **1.** teaching given outside the university by correspondence and different media; **2.** students studying away from university through different forms of correspondence education.

F extra-muros

extrinsic meaning: see **connotation**

extrinsic motivation: the use of rewards or punishments external to intrinsic interest in the material itself in an attempt to control behaviour.

F motivation extrinsèque

F

face-to-face: sitting or standing opposite a speaker; or in a position facing an audience or person(s).

C *direct teaching*

F face à face

facilitator: a person whose task is to encourage the productive interaction of other people in a group situation.

C *animator; tutor*

F facilitateur; animateur

facsimile: **1.** exact copy of an original document; **2.** hard copy produced by facsimile transmission.

C *telewriter*

F 1. 2. facsimilé

facsimile transmission—fax: electronic system which scans graphic images, transmitting them by telephone lines and reproducing them.

C *telewriter*

F télécopie

factor analysis: method of describing correlations between tests with smallest number of factors, i.e. hypothetical entities such as skill, ability or personality traits which are assumed to underlie and influence tests.

F analyse factorielle

fade: **1.** in video, the gradual appearance of a picture from black (fade-in) or disappearance to black (fade-out); **2.** in audio, the gradual decrease of sound volume.

C *cross fade; sound fade*

F 1. 2. fondu

fading: **1.** in programmed learning, the gradual removal of the prompts in a sequence of items teaching a particular topic. Sequences typically begin with highly prompted items and end with unprompted terminal items. The word is sometimes used as a synonym of 'vanishing'; **2.** in audio/video, variation of strength of received signals due to variations with time in the conditions of propagation.

C *vanishing*

F 1. estompage; 2. évanouissement

failure rate: see **error rate**

fast motion: action which has been photographed at a filming rate less than normal, then projected at normal speed.

51

Sometimes called accelerated motion or speeded-up action.

C *slow motion; time lapse*

F accéléré

fax: see **facsimile transmission**

feasibility study: a study to determine the degree to which some strategy or project is possible or practical.

F étude de faisabilité

feature film: a film which runs over 48 minutes or which is on more than one reel. Sometimes loosely used to describe any fictional film.

F film de long métrage

feedback: 1. the return of part of a system's output that may influence its input. Incorrectly used to mean 'response to a stimulus'. In teaching, training and self-instruction, feedback signifies usable knowledge of results; **2.** the distressing howl or squeal produced by sound from a loudspeaker getting back into the microphone in a public address system; **3.** a circuit within an electric device to reduce distortion.

C *evaluation; delayed feedback*

F 1. (feedback), rétroaction*; information en retour; réaction; 2. effet Larsen; 3. circuit feedback

feedback classroom: see **student response system**

feed reel: the full reel (spool) of film or tape which is threaded into the machine for showing or playing.

C *delivery spool*

F bobine débitrice

feeder link: see **uplink**

feltboard: see **flannel board**

fiber optics: see **optical fibre**

field of study: subject of study in one department or field of learning.

F champ d'étude

52

field research: 1. the research whose purpose is to study intensively the background, current status and environmental interactions of a given social unit: an individual, a group, an institution, an organization or a community; **2.** research conducted in a remote or practical situation.

F 1. 2. recherche sur le terrain

field testing: large-scale testing of a near final model of an instructional material outside or away from the producing agency, to determine general weaknesses of materials and equipment and/or its ultimate viability and utility or to measure its effectiveness, cost, endurance and potential.

C *developmental testing*

F expérimentation sur le terrain

filament: a fine conductor that is rendered incandescent by the passage of an electric current.

F filament

file: in computer terminology, an orderly self-contained collection of data that is usually stored on a permanent storage device such as a disk. Although files are not part of programmes, they can be accessed for use in any programme.

F fichier

file management program: see **file manager**

file manager: utility program which assigns, or recognizes, labels identifying data files and enables them to be called from storage as required.

F gestionnaire de fichiers

filing system: an organization or set of procedures developed to identify records for efficient retrieval. Filing systems may be sequential, alphabetical, numeric or coded in various ways.

F classement

film: 1. the support of photographic emulsion; **2.** a term synonymous with a motion picture.

C *loop film; green film; sound film; colour film; safety film; silent film; feature film; striped film; magnetic film; reversal film;*

sound-on film; cartridge film; documentary film; educational film; single-concept film; teaching film

F 1. pellicule; 2. film

film archives: a depository of films and associated print materials, used for study and research.

C *film library*

F archives cinématographiques

film chain: a system of fixed television camera(s) and appropriate projectors utilized to transmit projected materials (usually slides, motion pictures, or filmstrips) into a television system. Also called telecine equipment.

F télécinéma; analyseur de vues fixes

film clip: see **film insert**

film club: see **cineclub**

film insert: filmed sequence played into a television programme.

F insert filmé

film laboratory: facility for developing and printing exposed film.

F laboratoire de développement et de tirage

film library: a depository of prints of films, usually to be circulated, but in some cases used for study only.

C *film archives*

F cinémathèque

film loop: an instructional device that contains a single event or related series of events on film of about three minutes running time. Often packaged in a self-rewinding cartridge which requires a special projector. Widely used in individualized science instruction. Frequently illustrates phenomena such as the opening of a flower or the impact of a moving car and a brick wall by the process of speeding up or slowing down the movements involved.

C *single concept film*

F film monovalent; film court

film rights: 1. the rights of a copyright owner in a cinematographic work (e.g. the right to sell and distribute copies of a work, to authorize its projection, broadcasting, etc.); **2.** the exclusive right of an author of pre-existing work to authorize its adaptation for cinematographic use.

F 1. droits sur une œuvre cinématographique; 2. droits d'adaptation cinématographique

film scanner: see **telecine**

filmograph: a motion picture made from still pictures, usually with special effects.

F film de banc titre

filmstrip: a length of film that presents a sequence of related still pictures for projection one at a time. Most filmstrips are on 35 mm film, but some are 16 mm or smaller. A filmstrip is double-frame if the horizontal axis of the picture is parallel to the sprocked holes and single frame if the images go across the film. It may or may not have provision for sound accompaniment; the advance signal may be audible or inaudible.

F film fixe

filmstrip projector: a device designed to project filmstrips (usually 35 mm) and which normally projects either a single-frame or a double-frame filmstrip. Sound filmstrip projectors have provision for playing accompanying audiorecordings. Some models have automatic advance mechanisms keyed to the audiorecordings.

F projecteur de films fixes

filter: 1. a piece of tinted or treated glass or other transparent material to change the amount, colour or patterns of light reaching the film; **2.** an electronic device for limiting or controlling frequency responses.

F 1. 2. filtre

final cut: the final step in editing a motion picture, on completion of which the scenes are of proper length and action between adjacent scences is matched.

F montage final

final print: see **release print**

final shooting script: the draft of a script which is approved for shooting.

F découpage technique final

final test: test given at the end of a course of instruction.

C *pre-test; post-test*

F test final

firmware: system software that is contained in the read only memory–ROM.

F microprogramme

first generation duplicate: a duplicate made directly from the original film.

F premier contretype

first print: the first print of a film which is projected and examined by the producer to determine whether the timing, colour corrections and sound are satisfactory.

F copie zéro

first release: the first distribution and exhibition of a film in a large market.

F première exclusivité

first trial print composite: see **first print**

fisheye: a lens with very short focal length for taking very wide angle photographs.

F (fisheye); très grand angulaire

flange: a disc with hub for holding or guiding tape or film.

F flasque

flannelboard: a display board made of cardboard or thin wood and covered with flannel, felt, flocking or similar cloth to which pictures and symbols backed with the same or similar materials will adhere.

C *feltboard; flannelograph*

F tableau de feutre; flanellographe

flare: areas in the film emulsion exposed to light in some way other than through the usual image-forming properties of lenses, such as internal reflections between the various surfaces of lens components, 'leaky' camera turrets, doors or magazines.

F taches lumineuses; reflets

flash: 1. an unwanted moulding material at the edge of a disk, formed during the compression moulding operation; **2.** supplementary light for taking still pictures; **3.** a momentary superposition of a sound or picture in a programme.

F 1. bavure; 2. (flash); 3. surimpression

flashbulb: a high intensity photographic bulb or lamp that is fired electrically or mechanically. It has a relatively short flashing duration and can be used only once.

F lampe éclair

flashcard: a card or other opaque material with words, numerals or pictures designed to be displayed briefly by hand or by mechanical device for the purpose of drill or recognition training.

F carte flash

flashlamp: see **flashbulb**

flexible schedule: an organization for instruction allowing for varying class size within and among courses, and providing for instructional groups which meet at varying frequencies and for varying lengths of time.

F emploi du temps souple*

flicker: an unwanted rhythmic variation in the reproduced image of the perceived picture due to the intermittent character of its luminosity.

F papillotement

flip chart: a set of large sheets of paper hinged together and mounted on an easel so that they can be flipped over the top into or out of view as required.

F tableau de papier

floating-point notation: a form of number representation in which quantities are represented by a number multiplied by the number base raised to a power. The decimal number 338 can be written as 3.38×10^2 or 0.338×10^3. A computer that has built-in circuitry for automatically controlling the location of the decimal or binary point is called a floating-point computer.

F virgule flottante

flocking: the process of projecting textile fibres or other particles on cardboard so as to make it adhesive.

F flocage

flood lamp: see **floodlight**

floodlight: a single light or bank of lights which are non-directional, yet light a specific area without glare or shadows.

F lumière d'ambiance

floor: studio performance area.

F plateau

floor manager: director's representative in charge of television floor activity. Also called stage manager.

F régisseur de plateau

floppy disk: a mass storage device that uses a flexible disk (diskette). Cheaper than hard disk. Also called 'floppy'.

F disquette; disque souple

flow chart: 1. a graphic representation for the definition, analysis or solution of a problem or a system in operation in which symbols are used to represent operations, data flow and equipment; **2.** graphic display of the logic for a computer programme.

C *block diagram*

F 1. 2. organigramme

flutter: an undesired form of frequency modulation introduced into the recorded signal by an irregular motion of the recording medium during the recording/reproducing process.

F scintillement

FM: frequency modulation; see **modulation**

F MF – modulation de fréquence

focal axis: a shutter mechanism used mainly in reflex cameras.

F obturateur à rideau

focal length: a lens parameter, being the distance from the optical centre of a lens to the film plane within the camera when the lens is focused at infinity.

F distance focale

focal plane: the plane at right angles to the axis of a lens at which rays of light are brought to a focus. To record a sharp image, the emulsion surface of the film in a camera must be positioned in the focal plane of the camera lens.

F plan focal

focal plane shutter: see **focal axis**

focus: 1. optical point at which light coming in through a lens forms a sharp colour image; **2.** sharpest image obtainable by adjusting the optical or electronic system.

F 1. foyer; 2. mise au point

foil: see **distractor**

follow-up activities: 1. the whole range of activities and exercises suggested and proposed to the teacher – and/or all the activities carried out by the teacher – with a view to integrating a relatively long and complex item (radio or TV programme, film, etc.) into an organized pedagogic sequence; **2.** additional and/or enrichment activities which follow a lesson.

F 1. exploitation pédagogique; 2. activités complémentaires

footage: the length of a film expressed in feet. Also sometimes used to refer to a strip of film.

F métrage

format: 1. a term used to denote the medium (physical material, container and arrangement) in which materials are produced, e.g. a film format or video-tape format. The term is also used to denote particular sub-divisions or sub-classifications within a particular medium, e.g. EIAJ-format, helical-scan format, quad format, eight-track format, cassette format. May also apply to the organization of the content, as well as the medium, e.g. programmed instruction format, audio-tutorial format; **2.** in computer terminology, the predetermined arrangement of characters, fields, lines, pages, numbers, punctuation marks. Refers to input, output and files; **3.** a term used to describe the appearance and make-up of a material, particularly a book; its size, shape, paper, type, binding, illustrations; 4. in videotex refers to one screen full of information.

F 1. format; 2. structure de données; disposition; 3. présentation; 4. écran; page

formatting: preparing a storage medium such as a disk into sectors so that it is ready to receive data.

F formatage

formative evaluation: 1. evaluation of instructional programmes whilst they are still in some stage of development; 2. evaluation which is intended to provide data for instruction product revision; 3. evaluation that occurs within and during the entire process of product, course, or programme design and production. Also referred to as 'on-going evaluation'.

C *summative evaluation; developmental testing*

F 1.2.3. évaluation formative

FORTRAN: FORmula TRANslation; a widely used programming language that translates statements expressed in a format similar to algebraic equations into computer language.

F FORTRAN

fotonovella: a narrative technique using a series of photographs with text superimposed as in strip cartoons. Also called 'photonovel'.

F photoroman

foundation courses: courses designed to provide a basis for advanced or specialized studies.

F enseignements généraux; enseignements fondamentaux

FPS: frames per second.

F images par seconde

frame: 1. each separate presentation of a small basic unit of material; 2. an individual picture in a filmstrip or motion picture; 3. one complete television picture.

F 1. élément de programme; 2. 3. image.

framer: a device on a filmstrip or movie projector that can be adjusted to obtain exactly one frame.

F dispositif de cadrage

framing: 1. moving the film gate aperture or claw so that the frame is correctly centered on the screen; 2. centering the film or video camera on the desired area.

F 1. 2. cadrage

free activities: in primary education, individual occupations of the pupils in which they themselves freely choose the subject and the ways in which they learn about it.

C *activity method; independent work*

F activités libres

freeze: to stop a motion picture or videotape on one still image during the projection or to simulate such suspended action.

F faire un arrêt sur image

frequency: oscillations of a wave or of a signal expressed in hertz, formerly 'cycles per second'. Frequency is also used to describe any flow that has regular periodicity such as an alternating current.

C *audio frequency; radio frequency*

F fréquence

frequency range: the portion of electromagnetic spectrum within an upper and lower frequency limit that a receiver is capable of accepting as an input.

C *bandwidth*

F largeur de bande

Fresnel lens: a condenser lens having a system of concentric prismatic ridges. This arrangement acts as an effective condenser for overhead projectors, spotlights and the like, but with considerable economy of bulk and weight.

F lentille de Fresnel

front projection: the optical projection of a visual image onto a screen from a point located on the same side as the viewer.

F projection frontale

full rights: a colloquial term for 'all rights composing copyright'.

F tous les droits

further training: additional training in a field or activity in which one has already a certain level of competence.

C *up-grading*

F perfectionnement

future studies on education: in contrast with forecasting, future studies are the methodological investigation of the future starting from an approach that favours change and newness while avoiding — unlike futurology — a break between the past and the future. In the field of education, future studies thus identify those facts that are portents of the future and that, while often imperceptible, are capable of having profound and extensive repercussions on present trends; such studies thereby serve to point out the already existing divergencies between educational content and the development of societies.

F prospective de l'éducation

FX: see **effects**

G

gage: see **gauge**

gain: for an amplifier or receiver, the ratio of two similar quantities, real or complex, measured respectively at the output and input of the networks. Examples: power gain, voltage gain, current gain.

F gain

gaming: practising responses to a real-life situation by means of an organized game with players, a set of allowable actions, a segment of time and a specific context.

C *simulation game*

F jeu de simulation

garbage: unwanted and meaningless information in the memory or output of a computer.

F informations parasites

gauge: 1. an instrument or means of testing; 2. the width of a film.

F 1. jauge; calibre; 2. largeur de film

general-purpose computer: a computer designed to solve a large variety of problems.

F ordinateur universel

general-purpose space: a space designed and/or adapted for a number of purposes, one of which is instructional.

C *multipurpose room*

F salle banalisée

general semantics: the study of the many ways in which the meaning of words and other symbols influences the response of human beings to their environment and to each other.

F sémantique générale

generalization: the process by which results obtained through the specific subjects involved in a study can be applied with confidence to a much larger group.

F généralisation

generation: 1. term used in describing the relationship of a film or tape to the original. The master tape is considered as the first generation and a copy from the master is the second generation. A copy of a first copy is the third generation, etc.; 2. the production of graphics by a computer on a cathode-ray tube.

F 1. génération; 2. génération d'images

57

generator: mobile electric power supply for lighting, etc.

C *special effects generator; synchronizing pulse generator*

F source d'énergie; génératrice

genlock: an electronic device to keep several TV images in synchronization.

F (genlock); verrouilleur de synchronisation

ghost: a defect, apparent in reproduction, in which an additional outline (ghost) or succession of outlines (multiple image) of prominent features of a picture may be observed displaced from the correct position of the outline by a noticeable amount.

F image fantôme; écho d'image

glitch: in television, a form of low frequency interference, appearing as a narrow horizontal bar moving vertically or horizontally through the picture.

F interférence basses fréquences

goal: 1. a general statement of intent; an expression of the desires and expectations of the developers and/or consumers of an educational programme; **2.** a substance, object or situation capable of satisfying a need or want and toward which motivated behaviour is directed.

C *aim; objective*

F 1. 2. but

grade: see **mark**

grading: 1. marking or rating of a student's work; **2.** in the United Kingdom, subjective alteration of printing light intensities and colour filters to achieve a balanced film positive from unbalanced negative material. (United States – timing).

F 1. classement; 2. étalonnage

grain: developed chemical particles comprising a film image. If the particles are very small, the image is described as fine grained. If the image under normal viewing conditions appears to be made up of distinguishable particles or grains, the condition is described as graininess.

F grain

gramophone: a record player with an amplifying system and one or more built-in or separate loudspeakers. This is the United Kingdom term; the United States term is phonograph. Also called 'record player', 'audiodisc player'.

F électrophone

graph: a diagram using dots, bars, lines or other symbols to represent and to visually display the interrelationship of two or more pieces of information.

F graphique; tracé; courbe

graphic materials: a generic term for two-dimensional, illustrative, representational materials (often incorporating words or well-known symbols) designed to communicate a brief message. The term is often used to include any printed materials which are not photographic and not textual in nature. Graphic materials are often referred to by the collective term 'graphics'.

F moyens graphiques

graphics tablet: an image input device that allows the user to enter pictorial information directly into the computer by sketching or tracing any shape or series of shapes on the tablet surface.

C *computer graphics*

F tablette graphique

graph plotter: an output device used to draw graphs on paper by plotting the course of co-ordinates. Also called 'x-y plotter'.

F traceur de courbes

green film: any film which is new and has not yet been treated with the proper coating.

F copie neuve

grip: set worker charged with lifting, carrying or pushing. Also called 'scene-shifter', 'stage hand'.

F machiniste

ground: see **earth**

ground station: see **Earth station**

group dynamics: the principles underlying the interaction of the behaviour of individuals as members of a group and of the behaviour of groups generally. The study of group dynamics provides theoretical support for group methods in education and training.

F dynamique des groupes.

group instruction: teaching a number of persons the same thing at the same time.

C *group learning; group teaching*

F enseignement collectif

group learning: learning that takes place through some form of interactive small group activity.

C *group instruction; group teaching*

F pédagogie de groupe

group teaching: teaching a class of pupils divided into groups according to some aspects of their ability.

C *group instruction; group learning; team teaching*

F enseignement par groupes de niveau

group work: a process in which members working co-operatively rather than individually, formulate and work toward common objectives under the guidance of one or more leaders.

F travail en groupe

grouping: 1. organizing study groups according to criteria such as age, learning capacity, motivation, achievement, course objectives, etc.; **2.** in computer technology the collation of data which come under classifiable headings.

F 1. organisation en groupes; 2. groupement

guided discovery: an inductive procedure for promoting learning in which learners are expected to learn a specific thing, although the latter is never explicitly stated by the teacher. Should be compared to 'discovery learning' in which that which is learned is not specified in advance.

C *discovery learning*

F observation dirigée

H

halation: 1. dark television picture tube area ringing an over-loaded bright area; also print flare caused by excessive light bouncing back through emulsion from film base; **2.** a parasitic image around a lens-formed image in film.

F 1. 2. halo

half-frame: a filmstrip picture area half of the full 24-36 mm frame size.

F demi-image

halo: see **halation**

handouts: inexpensive, supplementary materials given at no cost to participants in an educational activity, e.g. leaflets, printed notes, etc.

F documents distribués aux élèves

handbook: 1. a treatise on a special subject, often giving a simple, but all-embracing treatment; **2.** a book of science or technology written primarily for practitioners and serving as a book for constant revision or reference.

C *textbook; workbook*

F manuel

hard copy: a paper printout as opposed to the presentation on a visual display unit.

F tirage; copie papier

hard disk: a mass storage device that uses a disk with magnetic coating which is not flexible and provides much larger store capacity than a floppy disk (up to 600 million bytes).

F disque magnétique

hardware: 1. the technical facilities used to produce, distribute and present information as against the programme or content being recorded or reproduced; 2. a term used to describe the mechanical, electrical and electronic element of a data processing system.
C *apparatus; software*
F 1. équipement; appareillage; 2. matériel de (traitement de l'information)

Hawthorne effect: used to describe the situation in learning where improvement is due to the introduction of a new technique – and to the interest this attracts – as much as to the technique itself. Name derived from experiments on incentives in the Hawthorne works of the Western Electric Company, United States.
F effet Hawthorne

head: see **sound head; erasing head; magnetic head; playback head; recording head; pan-and-tilt head**

headphone: see **headset**

headset: a device consisting of one or two small audio reproducers connected to a headband for individual listening to audio sources. A headset with earpiece(s) and a microphone is called a headphone but the terms are often interchangeable.
F casque d'écoute; écouteurs

helical videotape recorder: see **video format**

heuristic approach: an exploratory approach to a problem using successive evaluations of trial and error to arrive at a final result.
F démarche heuristique

heuristic process: the solution of a problem by trial and error, but evaluating each step towards a final result.
F processus heuristique

HF: high frequency; a band of frequencies extending from 30 to 300 Khz.
F hautes fréquences

hidden curriculum: the informal and subtle ways in which a school mirrors and supports existing social values.
C *contents of education*
F contenu implicite de l'enseignement

hi-fi: see **high fidelity**

high-band standards: a videotape recording procedure using the 7, 8 to 10 megahertz carrier signal.
F normes à fréquences élevées

high-fidelity: an improvement in the system of recording and pressing disc recordings, now used to describe any recording without surface noise and a wide range of sound.
F haute-fidélité

high-level programme language: see **programming language**
F langage évolué

high-speed camera: camera specially designed to film at shutter speeds much higher than normal. High speed cameras with conventional intermittent film transport mechanisms allow filming up to about 500 frames per second. Beyond this speed highly specialized equipment is used, while speeds of over 100,000 fps. are possible.
F caméra grande vitesse

hiss: background noise of middle or high frequency which may originate in an amplifier, disc, line or tape.
F souffle; bruit de fond

holography: technique using a laser beam to record wave patterns on tape or film (holograms) which reconstruct to three-dimensional images complete with parallax.
F holographie

hook and loop board: a panel with a surface containing tiny nylon loops on which display materials, backed with tape strips having tiny nylon hooks, will intermesh and hold firmly.
F tableau en velcro

host: an entrepreneur or organization that provides access to a number of data bases through his/her own computer. Also known as 'information spinner' or 'on-line data service'.
F centre serveur; serveur de données

host computer: **1.** the primary or controlling computer within a distributed network, providing services such as computation, data base access or special programs and programming languages; **2.** a computer used to develop and translate programs that are then utilized by other computers or systems; **3.** a computer which provides services and/or guidance to users and/or satellite computers, terminals and other subsidiary devices.

F 1. 2. ordinateur hôte; 3. ordinateur hôte; serveur

howlround: see **feedback - 2**

hue: the attribute of colour reception that determines whether it is red, yellow, green, blue, purple or the like.

F teinte

hum: unwanted low frequency signal, generally from the power line.

F ronflement

human engineering: see **ergonomics**

hypnopedia: educational method based on suggestions made during sleep (for example, with the help of a loudspeaker placed near the sleeping person). Also called 'sleep learning'.

F hypnopédie

hypothesis: a testable propositional statement concerning phenomena of interest, involving a proposed relationship between two or more variables.

F hypothèse

Hz: hertz

F hertz

I

IC: see **integrated circuit**

ICEM: International Council for Educational Media.

F CIME

iconic sign: in semiotics, a sign is iconic to the extent that it has some perceptual resemblance (visual or acoustic) to the object, event or situation for which it is a sign. If the words 'cat' and 'meow' are both signs for the object cat, then 'meow' may be said to be more iconic than 'cat'.

C *analogy*
F signe iconique

iconography: **1.** illustration of subject by drawings or figures; **2.** study of these illustrations.

F 1. 2. iconographie

identification algorithm: a set of rules which, when applied in a prescribed sequence, make it possible to identify a given situation as one belonging to a certain class of situations.

F algorithme d'identification

IEC: International Electrotechnical Commission

F CEI

image: **1.** the individual's total conception of the world into which he or she fits his or her perception of events and interpretations of information input; **2.** the recreation of an object or scene by a lens.

F 1. 2. image

IMC: instructional media centre; see **educational media centre**

imitation: see **modelling**

impedance: resistance to the flow of alternating current; impedance is measured in ohms and often abbreviated as Z.

F impédance

implementation: putting an educational plan or idea into effect.

F exécution

incentives: external motivation to working in schools, e.g. consumable rewards for young children, marks for written work.

F récompenses; encouragements

incrust: see **superimposition**

independent study: an activity in which pupils, carrying on their studies without the requirement of formal classes, consult periodically with one or more staff members for direction and assistance and, frequently, work towards the completion of individual study projects.

C *autodidaxy; autonomy; individualized instruction; self-directed learning; self-instruction*

F travail indépendant; travail personnel

index: 1. an ordered reference list of the contents of a file or document together with references for identification or location of those contents; 2. in statistics, a variable or composite of variables employed to represent in quantitative form the changes in a trait.

C *menu*

F 1. index; 2. indice

indexing: providing a systematic analysis of the contents of materials arranged according to alphabetical, chronological, numerical, source or other chosen order.

F indexation

individualization: see **individualized instruction**

individualized instruction: instruction adapted to individual requirements. Should include, as appropriate, six basic and equally important elements: (a) flexible time frames; (b) diagnosis, remediation and exemption; (c) content options; (d) student evaluation – alternate forms and flexible times; (e) a choice of locations; (f) alternate forms of instruction. Also referred to as individualized teaching, individualized study/learning.

C *audio-tutorial method; autodidaxy; autonomy; independent study; personalized system of instruction; self-directed learning; self-instruction*

F enseignement individualisé; apprentissage individualisé

individually paced instruction: an instructional technique in which instruction is organized so that the learner may achieve objectives at a rate of his/her own choosing (not necessarily individualized).

C *pacing; self-assessment; self-pacing*

F enseignement à rythme individuel; apprentissage à rythme individuel

indicator: 1. a recording instrument; 2. in evaluation, a phenomenon used to draw conclusions concerning other phenomena; an indicator must be relevant, sensitive and readily available.

F 1. 2. indicateur

inductive learning: learning by the inductive method, that is by teaching based on the presentation to the learner of a sufficient number of specific examples to enable him/her to arrive at a definite rule, principle or fact. In programmed instruction this procedure of presenting first the examples and then the rule is called EGRUL.

C *RULEG*

F apprentissage par induction

informatics: the scientific, technological and engineering disciplines used in information handling and processing, their applications and their impact on society; sometimes referred to as 'computer science'.

F informatique

information: 1. the meaning assigned to data by known conventions; thus, 'data' are the marks, such as characters, signs, or symbols themselves, whereas the knowledge assigned to them is 'information'; 2. the amount of visual material on a given frame of film or the amount of audio-visual material on a given frame of film.

F 1. information; 2. information; charge d'information

information network: 1. generally more than two libraries, data banks or information centres interrelated by continuous transaction often in support of a common operation or service; **2.** the distribution of instructional and educational information by cable and/or microwave link between two or more institutions or organizations. The transmission may take the form of radio, television or computer data. Includes distribution of programmes by dial access and remote access systems.

F 1.2. réseau d'information

information network system: system which transmits both written and graphical information stored in a central computer for display on a domestic television set. The system may be one-way as in the case of CEEFAX, ORACLE and the broadcast form of TELIDON or may be a two-way interactive system, as in the case of PRESTEL (UK), ANTIOPE (France), CAPTAIN (Japan) and the interactive form of TELIDON (Canada).

C *Teleinformation; Télématique; Teletext*
F système d'information

information retrieval: the methods and procedures for recovering specific information from stored data.

F recherche de l'information

information retrieval service: see **host**

information spinner: see **host**

information technology: see **new information technology**

infrared photography: photography using film, either black-and-white or colour, which is sensitive to infrared light.

F photographie infrarouge

inlay: an intentional vignette in television.

F incrustation

innovation: 1. educational innovation: deliberate process of partial change leading either to a modification of the objectives of a particular educational practice or to a modification of the channels used to attain these objectives. Such innovation very often consists of adapting an educational situation to a change which has already taken place within or outside the education system, thereby making it possible to re-establish an equilibrium which has been upset; **2.** technological innovation: deliberate process of changing which may consist either in the appearance of a new technique or in a change in the principle on which an equipment functions. Cable television is based on a technical innovation (coaxial cables) but it also functions on a principle which is different from that of television.

F 1. innovation éducative; 2. innovation technologique

input: 1. the data to be processed; **2.** the device or collective set of devices used for bringing data into another device; **3.** a channel for impressing a state on a device or logical element; **4.** the process of transferring data from an external source to internal storage; **5.** the jack or device for inserting signals.

F 1. données en entrée; 2. organe d'entrée; 3. 4. 5. entrée

inputs: in evaluation, goods, services or other resources provided for an activity with the expectation of producing outputs and achieving the activity's objectives within a specified time frame.

C *evaluation; effectiveness; outputs*
F apports

input/output device: a unit that accepts new data, sends it into the computer for processing, receives the results and converts them into a readable form.

F organe d'entrée/sortie

inquiry method: an approach to learning in which a learner or group of learners search for an explanation of a problem. May be limited to reading 'to find out' but often involves the collection of empirical data. Usually based on a question or problem which does *not* have a single simple answer.

F méthode d'enquête

inquiry station: device or unit from which an information request is made.

F poste d'interrogation

insert: 1. close explanatory shot in a film or a TV programme, e.g. a letter, a clock face or a calendar; **2.** additional video tape, or film, added to previously completed material.

F 1. 2. insert

in-service teacher training: further training and retraining of educational personnel who have already received initial training.

F formation continue des enseignants

in-service training: education providing sustained further study enabling employed persons to improve skills and qualifications relating to their employment.

F formation en cours d'emploi

instruction: a set of characters (normally consisting of a command) which, when interpreted by the control unit, causes a data-processing system to perform one of its operations.

F instruction

instructional aids: devices which assist an instructor in the teaching-learning process by simply presenting supporting or supplementary information, usually intermittently.

C *instructional materials; educational media*

F auxiliaires d'enseignement

instructional developer: one who develops curriculum or teaching materials and related educational technology back-up.

F concepteur de programmes didactiques*

instructional development: a systematic approach to the design, production, evaluation and utilization of complete systems of instruction, including all appropriate components and a management pattern for using them; instructional development is larger than instructional product development, which is concerned only with isolated products, and is larger than instructional design which is only one phase of instructional development.

F mise au point de systèmes pédagogiques*

instructional film: film devised for use in teaching a particular subject.

C *educational film*

F film d'enseignement

instructional materials: generic term denoting all print and non-print materials used for teaching purposes.

F moyens d'enseignement

instructional media: see **educational media**

instructional module: an organized collection of learning experiences (usually in self-instructional form) assembled to achieve a specified group of related objectives, generally consisting of several hours to several weeks of instruction; may be called a mini-course if credit is given.

C *module*

F module d'enseignement; module d'apprentissage

instructional objectives: see **learning objectives**

instructional pathway: route in an instructional design along which the student is expected or chooses to proceed in order to reach a given instructional aim.

F cheminement pédagogique

instructional product: any material or group of materials replicable or able to be reproduced for instructional purposes.

F matériels didactiques

instructional programme: subject matter to be taught along with establishment of the teaching time for each subject matter, as well as the list of contents to be acquired — in other words, the required knowledge. The programme generally takes the form of administrative texts. A 'curriculum' is the organization of learning, in a particular discipline or at a given level. The purpose of the curriculum is to define the objectives of the learning, educational content and the methods and the materials to be employed. In the past, the term 'syllabus' was used to designate an instrument which served as a means for the educational institution to define the content of instruction (the programme) and its practical organization from the standpoint of learning activities.

F programme d'études

instructional strategy: the overall approach to instruction to be incorporated in the instructional system or instructional product; it includes the types of system operation, format, stimuli, responses, feedback, generalities, instances, difficulties, approach, presentation-organization, sequence, scope, size-of-step and pacing to be used.

F stratégie pédagogique

instructional system: an integrated group of programme components organized to accomplish specific learning objectives.

F système didactique

instructional technology: a sub-set of educational technology based on the concept that instruction is a sub-set of education. Instructional technology is a complex, integrated process involving people, procedures, ideas, devices and organization for analysing problems and devising, implementing, evaluating and managing solutions to those problems, in situations in which learning is purposeful and controlled.

F technologie de l'enseignement

instructional television - ITV: any television programme, broadcast or closed-circuit, developed specifically for instructional purposes; usually in conjunction with a specific course or set of lessons.

C *educational television; school television*

F enseignement télévisuel

instructional unit: see **module 3**

instrumental conditioning: see **operant conditioning, respondent conditioning**

integrated circuit - IC: a complete electronic circuit built into a single piece of semi-conductor material.

C *chip*

F circuit intégré

integrated curriculum: systematic organization of curriculum content and parts into a meaningful pattern.

F programme intégré

integrated experience approach: see **integrated teaching**

integrated services digital network—ISDN: any all-digital communication network that incorporates various voice, video, data and image transmission capabilities using common underlying facilities and interfaces.

F réseau numérique à intégration de services - RNIS

integrated teaching: an approach to instruction that involves the teacher in identifying as clearly as possible those responses, attitudes, concepts, ideas and manipulatory skills to be achieved by the student and then in designing a multifaceted, multisensory approach that will enable the student to direct his or her own activity to attain these objectives. The programme of learning is organized in such a way that students can proceed at their own pace, filling in gaps in their background information while omitting the portions of the programme which they have covered at some previous time.

F enseignement intégré

intelligence quotient - IQ: the quotient obtained by dividing mental development age by chronological age and multiplying by 100.

F quotient intellectuel

intelligence test: a standardized method of evaluation (group or individual) designed to measure an individual's ability to learn, to solve problems involving abstractions and to deal with new situations.

C *aptitude test*

F test d'intelligence

intelligent terminal: a computer terminal which is a computer in its own right

65

because of its inherant capabilities, e.g. memory; also called 'smart terminal'.

C *dumb terminal*

F terminal programmable; terminal intelligent

intelligent tutoring system: tutorial program based on an expert system so that the program understands and assesses students' responses and provides individualized learning strategies.

C *expert system; tutorial program*

F système tuteur intelligent

intensity: 1. the strength of a quantity; 2. the relative strength or amplitude of electric, magnetic, or vibrational energy; 3. the brilliance of an image on the screen of a cathode-ray tube.

F 1. 2. 3. intensité

interaction analysis: description and evaluation of communicative events occurring in a teaching situation, in particular, the way information is exchanged between teacher and students or among students in an organised learning situation.

F analyse d'interaction; analyse des interactions

interactive system: a system that allows two-way communications, with each part of the system affecting the others.

F système interactif

interactive video: an individualized learning system in which a random access videodisc player (or VCR) is linked to a microcomputer; the selection of pictures and video sequences varies according to user's responses. Sometimes wrongly used for 'videotex 2'.

F vidéo interactive

intercom system: a local communication system used, for example, for dialogue between control room and studio.

F interphone; intercommunication

interdisciplinary approach: way of organizing the curriculum as a whole or of teaching a particular course in such a way that traditional boundaries between disciplines are ignored and new relationships among them are established.

F approche interdisciplinaire

interface: 1. a shared boundary; the juncture between two or more systems or devices; 2. a device or programme that allows two different parts of a system to 'communicate' with each other.

F 1. 2. interface

interference: 1. an undesirable influence on a signal caused by other signals; 2. extraneous electronic impulses disrupting normal signal transmission.

C *noise*

F 1. brouillage; 2. interférence

interlaced scanning: a form of scanning in which the complete picture is explored by scanning along two or more sets of equidistantly spaced lines, each set being distributed over the whole picture area. The lines of each set are scanned sequentially and are located between the lines of the preceding and succeeding scans.

F balayage entrelacé

interlock: connection between two or more systems or parts of a system.

F couplage

intermediate: any film, other than a camera original, intended for use only in making duplicates, as a colour internegative, or duplicate positive or negative.

F film intermédiaire

intermediate objective: see **enabling objective**

intermediate technology: see **appropriate technology**

internal reinforcement: see **intrinsic motivation**

internegative: a colour duplicate negative.

F internégatif

interpreter: 1. a computer program that translates and executes each source language instruction before translating and executing the next one; **2.** a person who can translate one language into another as a speaker is speaking.

F 1. interpréteur; 2. interprète.

interpretive program: see **interpreter**

interruption: a break in a procedure in such a way that the normal flow can be resumed from the point of interruption.

F interruption

intrinsic meaning: see **denotation**

intrinsic motivation: the reward in a task which is intrinsic to the behaviour itself, without need for external reinforcers.

F motivation intrinsèque

intrinsic programming: a programming technique developed by Norman Crowder, characterized by relatively lengthy items, multiple choice questions and consistent use of branching.

C *branching; linear programming*

F programmation intrinsèque; programmation ramifiée

I/O device: see **input/output device**

IQ: see **intelligence quotient**

iris diaphragm: an adjustable diaphragm, usually incorporated into the structure of a lens barrel, designed to control the amount of light passing through a lens.

F iris

ISDN: see **integrated services digital network**

ISO: International Organization for Standardization

F Organisation internationale de normalisation

item: 1. in programmed instruction, a segment of material which the student handles at one time; may vary in size from a single incomplete sentence, question or instruction requiring a response up to a sizeable paragraph; **2.** in test construction, any single fact, part or unit that can be isolated for examination or measurement.

F 1. item; cadre; 2. item

item analysis: any one of several methods used in test validation or improvement to determine how well a given question or item discriminates among individuals of different degrees of ability or among individuals differing in some other characteristic.

F analyse d'item

item bank: set of test items classified according to content, level of difficulty, validity, reliability, etc.

F banque d'items

iterative process: a method of solving a problem by repeating a series of steps until the solution or a good approximation of it has been achieved.

F itération

ITU: International Telecommunications Union

F UIT

ITV: see **instructional television**

J

jack: the hole or opening in a device or connector to accept a matching plug and to feed power or signals into or out of it.

F jack; plot

jitter: a synchronization or projection fault leading to jerky and irregular displacement of the picture.

F gigue; sautillement (d'image); instabilité (d'image)

joiner: see **splicer**

joystick: a lever the motions of which control microcomputer graphics or the movement of a cursor on a VDU.

F manette; manche à balai

jump: 1. in motion pictures a discontinuity in the smooth action within a motion-picture scene, caused by momentary stopping and then starting the camera motor or by incorrectly removing a section of film within a scene during editing; **2.** to transfer program control in a computer to some statement other than the next consecutive instruction.

F 1. saut; 2. sauter; faire un branchement

K

K: a symbol standing for the number 1,024 or 2^{10} used in measuring the storage capacity of computers.

F K

Keller plan: see **personalized system of instruction**

keyboard: a set or panel consisting of an array of keys. Depressing a key causes the input of the specific character or symbol printed on the key.

F clavier

keypad: a telephone calling or coding device using keys instead of a dial.

F clavier à touches; clavier numérique

keypunch: a keyboard actuated device that punches holes in a card or tape to represent data for computer input.

F perforatrice à clavier

keypunching: transcribing alphabetical or numerical information into cards by manual keyboard punching of the data.

F perforation

keystone distortion: distortion of a projected image so that it is wider at the top than at the bottom.

F distorsion en trapèze

kinescope: 1. a film recording made from a TV programme on a picture-tube; **2.** see also **picture tube.**

F 1. kinescope; 2. tube image

kit: 1. a set of components for constructing something with instructions for putting them together; **2.** a package of materials and/or equipment which enables a teacher to conduct a learning activity or a group of related learning activities with one or a group of learners; **3.** a packaged set of materials to be used by an individual learner for mastering tasks either after teacher explanation or in self-training activities.

C *learning package*

F 1. kit; prêt-à-monter; 2. ensemble pédagogique; 3. matériel d'activité individuelle

L

laboratory: an area which has been equipped for special instructional purposes, e.g. science demonstrations and/or experiments, audiovisual practice or production, etc.

F laboratoire

laboratory work: a learning activity carried on by students in a laboratory designed for individual or group study of a particular subject-matter area, involving the practical applications of theory through observations, experimentation and research.

C *language laboratory*

F travail en laboratoire

lacing: the act of putting film or tape through the playing channel. This is the UK term; the USA term is:

C *threading*

F chargement (film, bande)

laminate: to stick a special transparent protective film to the image surface (or both surfaces) of a two-dimensional material. The process usually involves some type of acetate, vinyl or mylar film which has a transparent adhesive coating on one side.

F plastifier

LAN: see **local area network**

language: see **programming language**

language laboratory: a special facility used particularly in the aural-oral method of language teaching; often each learner has a separate booth connected with a central station which can receive his/her speech, record it for him/her to play back and also provide him/her other listening models of the language.

C *electronic classroom; audio-active-comparative laboratory/system*

F laboratoire de langues

large-screen television projector: see **television projector**

laser: acronym for 'light amplification by stimulated emission of radiation'. A device for the creation, amplification and transmission of a narrow, intense beam of coherent light. (A light wave of constant frequency and wave length.) Used for videodisc recording and playback and for communications.

F laser

laser printer: a high-speed printer system using a laser beam.

F imprimante à laser

latency: the time from the display of an instructional stimulus to the start of the student response.

F temps de latence

latent image: the invisible change caused by the action of light on the silver halide crystals in a photographic emulsion. A visible silver image is produced from the latent image when the emulsion is developed.

F image latente

Lavalier microphone: a small microphone on a chain or cord around the neck.

F micro-cravate

layout: a visualized plan for a display, poster, publication or other presentation. It is usually done in scale and with sufficient detail to indicate how the final product will appear.

F maquette de présentation

LCD: liquid crystal display.

F affichage à cristaux liquides

leader: 1. a section of plain tape or film that is added to the beginning, and possibly the end, of a magnetic tape or motion picture film for threading purposes; **2.** a person who can influence people so that they will

69

strive willingly toward the achievement of group goals.

C *trailer 1*

F 1. amorce; 2. leader

leakage: the undesired electric current that may flow from a device to or through an operator.

F fuite

learner-based education: education in which the content and the learning and teaching processes are determined by the needs and desires of the learners who participate actively in shaping and controlling them. It draws upon the learners' own resources and experiences.

C *competency based education; teacher centred; subject centred curriculum; student centred curriculum*

F éducation centrée sur l'apprenant*

learner-paced: see **self-pacing**

learner verification: proof offered by a programme or book producer that its use results in learning by the intended audience.

C *validation*

F preuve de succès d'apprentissage*

learning: see **concept learning; community-based learning; self-directed learning; individualized instruction; direct teaching/learning; problem-centred learning; programmed instruction.**

learning contract: a plan of instruction adaptable to individual differences, in which the course content is divided into a number of long-term assignments, each student receiving a contract and being allowed to proceed to the next contract upon completion of the previous one.

C *student contract*

F contrat pédagogique*; plan de travail individuel*

learning objective: precise statement indicating the performance expected of the learner in terms of specific skills and concepts.

C *enabling objective; performance objective; prerequisite objectives; terminal behaviour*

F objectif pédagogique

learning package: a collection of subject-related materials accompanied by special directions for learner use and for which there is a list of objectives and test items.

C *kit*

F ensemble pédagogique

learning resources: all of the resources (data, people and things) which may be used by the learner in isolation or in combination, usually in an informal manner, to facilitate learning; learning resources include messages, people, materials, devices, techniques and settings.

C *educational media*

F ressources éducatives; ressources pédagogiques

learning resources centre – LRC: see **educational media centre**

learning strategies: the dominant methods and general procedures used by learners and educators in order to attain the objectives of learning.

F stratégies d'apprentissage

learning style: the sum of the ways of problem solving, thinking and learning used habitually by an individual.

F mode d'apprentissage; style d'apprentissage

lecture: an activity in which the teacher gives an oral presentation of facts or principles, the class frequently being responsible for note taking. This activity usually involves little or no learner participation by questioning or discussion.

F cours magistral

LED: light emitting diode

F diode photoémettrice

legibility: term referring to the degree of the ease with which a text can be read in the sense of deciphered; physical readability.

F lisibilité*

lens: optical device used in forming an image by focusing rays of light (as in a camera or a projector).

C *zoom lens; coated lens; fresnel lens; telephoto lens; condensing lens; projection lens; anamorphic lens; wide-angle lens*

F objectif; lentille

lens angle: the horizontal or vertical angle of view of a lens as expressed in degrees.

F angle de champ

lens barrel: the cylindrical support in which a lens is mounted. Usually also includes a mechanical device to permit focusing.

F barillet de lentille

lenticular screen: a silver projection screen made with a series of ridges and hollows over the surface to control the distortion of reflected light.

F écran gaufré

lettering: the activity of applying letters and numbers to create text, titles or captions.

F lettrage

LF: low frequency; a band frequency extending from 3 to 30 Mhz.

F basses fréquences

library: a collection of organized information used for study and reference.

C *film library; tape library; educational media centre; polythèque; data bank*

F bibliothèque

lifelong education: the concept that education is not a once-for-all experience confined to the initial cycle of full-time education commenced in childhood, but a process that must continue throughout life. Life itself is a continuous learning process, but each person also needs specific opportunities for further and new education, both vocational and general, throughout life, in order that he may keep abreast of technical and social change, may adapt to changes in his own circumstances (marriage, parenthood, professional situation, old age, etc.) and may achieve his fullest potential for individual development. Lifelong education comprehends both an individual's intentional and incidental learning experiences.

F éducation permanente

lift: to record onto film, sound from discs, tapes, etc.

F repiquer

light board: see **lighting console**

light box: an illuminated transparent desk for animation work.

F boîte à lumière

light meter: see **exposure meter**

light patching board: see **lighting console**

light pen: an optical scanner that recognizes patterns of light and dark. Light pens are used with a cathode-ray tube screen to add, modify or delete information.

F photostyle; crayon lumineux

light video equipment: especially light portable video recording equipment, generally used for news gathering and amateur video recording.

F vidéo légère

lighting console: a console through which current for lights may be controlled or modified to achieve such functions as on-off, preset intensity and dimming.

F pupitre d'éclairage

lighting control board: see **lighting console**

limited rights: the author's rights as limited under copyright law (e.g. cases of free use, etc.) or the user's rights as partially transferred to him by the author.

F droits limités

line: 1. the electric supply system; **2.** one of the hundreds of horizontal lines used to

71

form a television image; **3.** a phrase in an actor's script; **4.** a single row of printed characters; **5.** the linkage between a computer and its terminals.

C *on-line; off-line*

F **1.** ligne électrique; **2.** ligne; trame; **3.** phrase de texte; **4. 5.** ligne

line frequency: the number of scanning lines traversed per second.

F fréquence de balayage horizontal; lignage; fréquence de trames

linear programming: a programming technique based on the principles of reinforcement theory, including active generation of responses, shaping of responses, repetition and immediate reinforcement. Set sequences of items present information in small units and require a response from the student at each step. Every student does each item in the programme, his progress differing only in the rate at which he proceeds through the sequence.

C *intrinsic programming*

F programmation linéaire

line up: adjust proper relationship of any elements: sound tracks, camera signals, etc., before production.

F aligner

lip synchronization: a recording of the speech of a person appearing in a motion picture so that the sound is heard at the same time as his lip movements are observed.

F synchronisation labiale

listening centre: 1. an audio distribution device to which headsets are or can be connected to enable more than one learner to hear an audio programme at the same time; **2.** an area where students listen to recorded materials.

F **1.** poste d'écoute; **2.** aire d'écoute

listing: a print-out or display of the statements of a computer programme.

F listage

live: a programme actually happening in real time. Not recorded or delayed.

F en direct (programme)

load: 1. a device that absorbs power and converts it into the desired form; **2.** to put information into the storage of a digital computer; **3.** to thread a film or tape into a machine, cassette or cartridge.

F **1.** chargeur; **2. 3.** charger

local area network—LAN: a network linking computing resources over a small area, e.g. a building or a campus.

C *custom network*

F réseau local

logic: mechanical or electronic device which can perform any one of the basic logical functions.

F logique (d'une machine)

log in/log out: the procedure by which a user initiates or ends a session on a time-sharing system.

F (log in, log out); procédure d'entrée/de sortie; ouverture/fermeture

logging in/out: see **log in/log out**

logging on/off: see **log in/log out**

logistics: all the resources and methods employed, e.g. for the organization of an educational activity.

F logistique

LOGO: a very simple interactive programming language used for educational applications and usually involving the generation of turtle graphics.

F LOGO

log out: see **log in/log out**

long-focus lens: a lens for photography of distant objects or for magnification.

F objectif à longue focale

long-playing disc/record: an audiodisc of about 12-inches diameter on which very fine grooves are cut in close proximity so as to permit 25 to 30 minutes listening on either side at $33^1/_3$ r.p.m. playing speed.

F disque longue durée; microsillon

loop: 1. a small amount of slack film used in motion pictures to give leeway in the threading of a projector; **2.** a closed path or any sequence of events in a computer programme that repeats itself, is closed back on itself, or connected back on itself.
C *film loop; tape loop*
F 1. (cinéma) boucle; 2. (informatique) boucle

loop film: a length of film joined into an endless band to facilitate constant repetition.
F film en boucle

loop projector: a projector, usually 8 mm, for use with film loops, enabling continuous and repetitive showing of a film sequence.
F projecteur pour film en boucle

loudspeaker: a device which converts electrical impulses into sounds. Loudspeakers may be in portable enclosures, permanently installed or built into other devices such as radios or television receivers.
F haut-parleur

low-band standards: a videotape recording procedure using the 5 to 6.8 megahertz carrier signal.
F normes à fréquences basses

low-cost technology: see **appropriate technology**

LP: long-playing disc/record.
F disque longue durée

LRC: learning resources, centre. See: **educational media centre**

LSI: large-scale integration; refers to the process of manufacturing large numbers of micro miniature electronic components on very small pieces ('chips') of semi-conductor material.
F intégration à grande échelle

luminance: a measure of brightness especially applied to television signals.
F luminance

luminosity: attribute of visual sensation according to which an area appears to emit more or less light. This is the term used in the United Kingdom; in the United States the term is:
C *brightness*
F luminosité

M

machine: see **teaching machine**

machine language: see **computer language**

machine run: see **run**

macrozoom lens: a zoom lens which is capable of focusing on very close objects.
F objectif à macro-zoom

magazine: 1. lightproof negative film containers of a film camera or a container for film, tapes, slides or filmstrips usually embodying a transport mechanism designed to supply or present the material for controlled exposure; **2.** a periodical for general reading containing articles on various subjects by various authors; **3.** a radio or television programme which continues in successive parts under the same main title and in a similar style.
F 1. magasin; 2. 3. magazine

magnetic board: a sheet of ferrous metal to which objects may be attached by means of magnets. This same surface may be coated with enamel or chalkboard paint and be used as a chalkboard or display board.
F tableau aimanté

73

magnetic disk: as used in computer systems, a flat circular plate with a magnetic surface on which data can be stored by selective magnetization of portions of the flat surface. Often in stacks in a container as a unit called a disk pack.

C *disk; floppy disk; hard disk*

F disque magnétique

magnetic film: a motion picture film base with sprocket holes which instead of being coated with photographic emulsion is coated with a magnetic oxide, upon which sounds may be recorded for playback.

F film magnétique

magnetic head: any component of audio or electronic video equipment which operates in contact with the iron oxide coating on magnetic film or tape, and which records sound, picks up sound for playback, erases sound, or records, plays back or erases video information.

F tête magnétique

magnetic recording: a method of recording information by impressing on a magnetic strip, film or wire, a succession of magnetic patterns representing the sequential wave patterns of the information being recorded.

F enregistrement magnétique

magnetic soundtrack: a soundtrack recorded on a strip of magnetic material which is coated on the edge of a print of a cine film.

C *optical sound track; COMOPT; COMMAG*

F piste de son magnétique

magnetic tape: a recording medium in the form of a ribbon, made of a non-magnetic base, coated with a magnetizable material in a suitable binder.

F bande magnétique

mainframe: 1. the fundamental portion, i.e. the portion that is the central processing unit and control elements of a computer system with large internal storage capacities; **2.** colloquial for big computers as opposed to mini-computers.

F 1. unité centrale; 2. (mainframe); gros ordinateur

main memory: see **storage**

main title: the name of the production, shown at the start of an audio-visual material.

F titre principal

mains: the electrical supply system in the United Kingdom.

F alimentation secteur; secteur

maintenance: activity intended to keep equipment (hardware) or programmes (software) in satisfactory working condition, including tests, measurements, replacements, adjustments, repairs, programme copying and programme improvement. Maintenance is either preventive or corrective.

F maintenance

management by objectives: a management technique which consists of the following major elements: (a) superiors and subordinates meet to discuss goals and jointly establish attainable goals for the subordinate; (b) the superior and subordinate meet again after the initial goals have been set to evaluate the subordinate's performance in terms of the pre-established goals.

F gestion par objectifs

markerboard: general term to include chalkboards, and other boards of various colours and materials for use with any kinds of markers or chalk.

F tableau

mark: the evaluation of a pupil's work by numerical means. This is the term used in the United Kingdom; the United States term is grade.

C *score*

F note

mass communication: a mode of non-personalized communication aimed at large non-specific audiences.

F communication de masse

mass media: generic term; those means of communication that reach large numbers of people at once with a common message – the press and printed text, film, radio, television – in contrast with means used for limited communication, as with groups of students (group media) or for communication between individuals or within a given institution (self-media).

C *audiovisual aid/materials; media; educational media; instructional media*

F moyens de communication de masse; moyens de communication sociale

mass storage: refers to large volume storage, on-line, and directly accessible to the central processing, arithmetical, logical or control unit of a computer; usually magnetic discs or tapes.

F mémoire de masse

master: the original or edited tape recording or film of a programme from which replicas (dupes or copies) are to be made; applies to audio (disc or tape) as well as video (film or videotape) recordings.

F original; matrice

master control room: the room in which all audio and/or video signals are assembled and processed.

F régie centrale

master file: a file that is used as an authority in a given job and that is relatively permanent, even though its content may change.

F fichier principal; fichier de base

mastery learning: educational strategy which assumes that all, or almost all, students can learn well and achieve effective mastery in a course, subject or even an entire curriculum at a high level of proficiency.

F pédagogie de la maîtrise

mat: see **matte**

matched action shot: the smooth continuation of action between two adjacent, related motion-picture scenes.

F plan de transition

matched groups: a procedure for assigning subjects to experimental and control groups which is meant to equate the groups. Subjects are usually matched on four or five variables. For each subject placed in one group, there must be another subject like him/her on the matching variables in the other group.

F groupes appareillés; groupes pairés

mathetics: a method of presenting information to be learned, particularly useful when multiple discriminations have to be made. The term is used by G.F. Gilbert to describe the systematic application of reinforcement theory to the analysis of knowledge and skills.

F mathétique

matrix: 1. a rectangular arrangement or organization of mathematical or other data which has x rows and n columns for easy understanding and comparisons; **2.** a mould in which type is cast or shaped.

F 1. matrice; 2. cliché

matrix printer: a printer in which each character is composed of a series of dots produced by a set of pens which moves across the paper. Also called 'dot matrix printer'.

F imprimante matricielle

matt: see **matte**

matte: 1. a mask used during printing to enable two separate images to be printed in succession on different areas of the same film; **2.** a card or metal mask placed in front of a camera to give such effects as looking through binoculars, through a key-hole, etc. The masks are placed in a matte box which secures to the front of the camera; **3.** a screen with a non-directional reflection pattern.

F 1. 2. cache; masque; 3. (écran) mat

MBO: see **management by objectives**

MCQ: see **multiple-choice question**

mean: the quotient obtained by dividing the sum of a set of scores by the number of scores; also called 'average' as opposed to 'median'.

F moyenne

mean square deviation: see **variance**

mean square error: see **variance**

measurement: process of obtaining a numerical description of the extent to which a person (or thing) possesses some characteristic. The term commonly applied to examining persons by giving some form of test.

C *docimologie; test; evaluation*
F mesure

media: 1. generic term for all of the forms and channels used in the transmission of information; 2. educational media or audio-visual media; 3. mass media.

F 1. 2. 3. médias

media-based instruction: any instructional technique based mainly on the use of audio-visual media.

C *computer-based instruction*
F enseignement fondé sur les médias

media-based instructional laboratory: an instructional space equipped with materials and equipment for learning – and especially self-learning – activities dependent upon educational media.

F laboratoire à apprendre

media centre: see **educational media centre**

media education: a means towards better understanding of the effects, roles and functions of the media for individuals and for society. In the 1950s it was referred to as 'screen education'.

F éducation aux médias

mediamobile: a truck, lorry or van specially designed and operated to distribute print and non-print materials. It serves both as a delivery unit and a satellite of a central learning resources centre.

F médiabus; (médiamobile)

median: the exact midpoint in a statistical distribution or set of scores as opposed to 'mean'.

F médian; médiane

mediated instruction: instruction which is conducted with communication rather than direct face-to-face interaction of the teacher with the student (e.g. by print, film, recording, telephone, radio, television or computer terminal).

F enseignement médiatisé

medium: means employed to impart and exchange information. Singular of 'media'.

F médium

memorization: committing to memory; learning by heart.

F mémorisation

memory: see **store**

memory card: in computer technology, an offline bulk storage memory consisting of a rectangular array of 960-bit positions on a card.

F carte à mémoire

memory span: the period of time during which retention of information occurs. May be 'short term' – limited to a few hours, or 'long term'.

C *span of attention*
F champ de mémoire; capacité d'appréhension

menu: a list of options presented by a computer program to a user.

C *index 1, command*
F menu

menu-driven program: a computer program that presents the user with a menu from which the section required at the time can be selected.

C *command-driven program*
F programme piloté par menu

message: an ordered selection from an agreed set of signs intended to communicate information.

F message

microcomputer: a complete small computer system, consisting of hardware and software, whose central processing unit consists of a single chip or a small number of chips.

C *mini-computer; mainframe*

F micro-ordinateur

microfiche: a sheet of microfilm, usually 4" by 6" (10 by 15 cm) containing multiple micro-images in a grid pattern which can be read with magnifying or projection devices.

F microfiche

microfilm: a generic term for photographic film on which are recorded micro-images. Most commonly used to denote microforms on reels or spools.

F microfilm

microfilm reader: see **microform reader**

microform: a generic term for materials — film or paper, printed or photographic — containing micro-images.

F microforme

microform reader: a rear-screen projection device for enlarging and viewing a translucent microform with the unaided eye. Includes microfilm readers, microfiche readers and combinations of these.

F lecteur de microfiches ou de microfilms

micro-image: photographic reproduction in a miniaturized format of such materials as printed pages, documents, drawings, publications.

F microimage

microphone: a device which converts sounds into electrical signals, usually for input into an amplification, mixing or sound recording system. Colloquial: 'mike'.

C *crystal microphone; dynamic microphone; cardioid microphone; condenser microphone; unidirectional microphone; omnidirectional microphone*

F microphone; micro

microprocessor: a single chip which contains the electronic circuitry necessary for digital arithmetic and logical operations used extensively in mini- and microcomputers.

F microprocesseur

microprojector: a device designed to enlarge and project microscopic transparencies such as microscope slides.

F microprojecteur

microteaching: a method of teacher training whereby teacher trainees gain simulated teaching experience with few students in small groups, and employing audio and/or video recording for playback and discussion.

C *autoscopie; minicourse; modeling*

F micro-enseignement

microwaves: electromagnetic waves of sufficiently short wavelength that practical use can be made of waveguide and associated cavity techniques in their transmission and reception.

F micro-ondes; hyperfréquences

microwave link: a radio system used for the point-to-point transmission of a television or audio signal thus avoiding long lengths of cable. Microwave links are limited to line of sight situations.

F liaison hertzienne; liaison par faisceaux hertziens

mike: see **microphone**

mimeo: see **mimeograph**

mimeograph: a type of rotary stencil duplicator.

F duplicateur ronéo

minicassette: trademark of an audiocassette.

F minicassette

minicomputer: a small, powerful, usually rugged and relatively inexpensive, general-purpose computer. Computers are often subgrouped as mainframe, mini- and

77

microcomputers according to the amount of storage they have (usually given in bytes), the number and kind of peripherals they use and the price range.

F mini-ordinateur

minicourse: **1.** a self-instructional package used in teacher training. Teaching skills are practised, as in microteaching. However, there is no supervisor present and the student-teacher works at his own pace following an individualized multi-media package; **2.** also, any short course on one topic or concept.

C *module, 1*

F 1.2. mini-cours*

mini-laboratory: a portable audio-active language laboratory.

F mini-laboratoire

mixer: 1. a device for combining several signals appearing simultaneously; **2.** a member of the sound crew who operates a mixing console.

F 1. mélangeur; 2. mixeur

mixing: a process for combining several signals appearing simultaneously from several sources into a single signal.

F mélange; mixage

mixing console: a desk grouping within the reach of a single operator all the controls required for mixing.

F pupitre de mélange; table de mixage

mixing desk: see **mixing console**

mock examination: an examination that is organized for its students by a school in order to simulate an external examination.

F examen blanc

mock-up: a representation of the real thing, constructed so as to emphasize a particular part or function of the real thing. It may be smaller or larger than the original, certain features may be made so as to give emphasis to functions or relationships.

F maquette de démonstration

mode: 1. a particular method of operating a computer; **2.** a statistical measure of the central tendency of a distribution, being the value or score at which the peak of the distribution occurs. See also 'mean' and 'median'.

C *conversational mode; tutorial mode*

F 1. 2. mode

model: 1. a conceptualization representing a real-life situation, procedure or ideal technique. It can take the form of an equation, a graphic analogue, a device or a narrative sequence; **2.** a reproduction of a real thing in an arbitrarily chosen scale.

F 1. modèle; 2. modèle; maquette

modeling: 1. in microteaching, refers to the use of teaching models (live or recorded) as a method of inducing behavioural change; **2.** an activity, frequently used for instruction in speech, in which the pupils listen to and observe a model as a basis upon which to practice and improve their performance; **3.** illumination from direction opposite to the key lights to give an illusion of the third dimension in TV.

F 1. imitation de maîtres modèles; 2. imitation de modèles; 3. éclairage d'ambiance

model school: a school in which approved methods of instruction may be observed by students or visiting educators, but in which there is no provision for practice teaching.

C *pilot school*

F école pilote

modem: an abbreviation of the words MOdulator-DEModulator. A device which enables data to be transmitted over telephone lines.

F modem

modular system: 1. any instructional package which is composed of self-contained elements, such that each can be studied as a complete unit; **2.** a piece of equipment with easy replacement or substitution of component parts.

F 1. 2. système modulaire

modulator-demodulator: see **modem**

modulate: vary the amplitude, frequency or phase of carrier wave with a signal.

F moduler

module: 1. an organized collection of learning experiences (usually in self-instructional form) assembled to achieve a specified group of related objectives; generally conceived of as constituting several hours to several weeks of instruction; may be called a minicourse if credit is given; **2.** a group of students following the same course of instruction in a flexible scheduling system; **3.** a unit of time in a flexible scheduling system; commonly varies in length from 15 minutes to one hour; **4.** a group of parts performing a specific function and assembled as a unit so that replacement is by unit rather than by part.

F 1. module d'enseignement; module d'apprentissage; 2. groupement d'élèves; 3. module de temps; 4. module d'équipement

modulation: a process whereby some characteristics of a carrier wave are changed or varied allowing transmission of usable audio and video impulses from one point to another. As information is added to the carrier, the amplitude or frequency changes proportionally to the amplitude of the modulation signal. The result is an amplitude modulated (AM) signal or a frequency modulated (FM) signal.

F modulation de fréquence (MF); d'amplitude (MA)

monitor: 1. assistant who helps a teacher carry out his/her duties, either by tutoring or by taking charge of small groups; **2.** student with a first degree who, under the responsibility of a professor, is in charge of supervising undergraduate students, especially for practical work; **3.** sometimes used to denote a non-qualified teacher; **4.** a device for displaying video signals on a cathode-ray tube, and connected to a transmission source (camera, videorecorder, computer terminal) by cable. Monitors generally have higher definition than domestic sets; **5.** to observe the picture shading and other factors involved in the transmission of a scene and the accompanying sound; **6.** a master loudspeaker used in an audio facility to listen to and evaluate an audio programme.

F 1. 2. 3. moniteur; assistant; 4. moniteur; écran de contrôle; 5. contrôler; surveiller; 6. haut-parleur de contrôle

monitoring: 1. an on-going quality check or appraisal of an activity or a system while it is actually in operation; **2.** the activity of following the progress of each learner as he moves through the sequence of instruction.

F 1. surveillance; suivi; 2. contrôle

monosemic message: a message which, as far as possible, tends towards a single meaning and with which only one form of educational application is possible.

C *polysemic message*

F message; monosémique

montage: a composite picture made up of several separate pictures.

F montage visuel

motion picture: a length of film, with or without a magnetic or optical sound track, bearing a sequence of images which create the illusion of movement when projected in rapid succession (usually 18 or 24 frames per second). Common motion picture sizes in instructional use are 16 mm, 8 mm, and super/single 8 mm. This is the term used in the United States; the United Kingdom term is:

C *film*

F film animé

motivation: 1. the internal factors that cause a person to act, the goals or purposes underlying an individual's behaviour; **2.** the practical art of applying incentives and arousing interest for the purpose of causing a pupil to perform in a desired way.

C *intrinsic motivation; extrinsic motivation*

F 1. 2. motivation

mount: to install equipment in position and condition for use.

F monter; assembler

mounting: the activity of attaching one surface or material to another surface or material in a process using heat and/or pressure and/or an intermediary paper or adhesive.

F assemblage; collage

mounting press: an electically heated press which applies heat and pressure for mounting and/or laminating flat graphics and photographic materials.

F presse de montage à sec

mouse: in computing, a device which is operated by rolling it over a surface in order to move text and illustrations, or a cursor, on a display screen.

C *light pen*

F souris

movie: see **motion picture**

multi-choice question: see **multiple-choice question**

multi-image show: the use of two or more separate images (usually projected) simultaneously in the same presentation.

F mur d'images

multimedia: 1. a term describing a single work designed to be presented through the integrated use of more than one medium (e.g. slide/tape presentation); **2.** in publishing, a term for all media other than print but particularly films, filmstrips, video, transparencies and recordings.

F 1. 2. multimédias

multimedia approach: methodology based on the principle that a variety of audio-visual media and experiences correlated with other instructional materials overlap and reinforce the value of each other. Some of the material may be used to motivate interest; others to communicate basic facts; still others, to clear up misconceptions and deepen understanding.

F approche multimédias

multimedia kit: see **multimedia package**

multimedia package: a collection of subject-related materials in more than one medium intended for use as a unit and in which no one medium is so clearly dominant that the others are dependent or accompanying.

F ensemble multimédias

multiple-choice question - MCQ: a kind of question, common in objective tests and branching programmes, to which there is more than one forced choice. Usually MCQs have four or five possible answers and incorporate distractors, i.e. wrong but plausible answers.

F question à choix multiple

multiple exposure: see **double exposure**

multiple image: see **ghost**

multiple track: 1. a provision within programmed instruction which allows students to pursue alternative subdivisions of the programme in terms of their successes or failures with earlier sections of the sequence; **2.** a recording process in which several longitudinal and parallel tracks are recorded on the same tape.

F 1. (enseignement programmé) itinéraire diversifié; 2. enregistrement multipiste

multiplex: an electronic device allowing the computer to be connected to several peripherals on a single channel.

F multiplexeur

multiplexer: 1. moveable mirror or prism set up in such a way that it can direct the image from slide projectors and film projectors into a television camera. Similar to film chain, but has additional sources; **2.** a device allowing several transmitters to be run in parallel on the same aerial without interaction.

F 1. 2. multiplexeur

multiplexing: 1. the process of transferring data from several storage devices operating at relatively low transfer rates to one storage device operating at a high transfer rate in such a manner that the high-speed device is not obliged to 'wait' for the low-speed units; **2.** the concurrent transmission of more than one information stream on a single channel.

F 1. 2. multiplexage

multiprocessor: one computer with several instruction and sequence control registers or a configuration with two or more central processors, one of which may control the others.

F multiprocesseur

multi-purpose room: a space designed or adapted specifically for two or more of the combined functions that might normally be served by a number of separate instructional spaces.

C *general-purpose space*

F salle polyvalente

multivariant analysis: general term for techniques of examining the relationship between several independent and dependent variables simultaneously.

F analyse multivariée

mute: see **silent film**

N

narration: the verbal comments made to accompany visual materials.

F commentaire

narrowcasting: distributing a programme or signal to a limited number or specially selected audience.

C *broadcasting*

F (narrowcasting); diffusion restreinte

natural language: a language whose rules reflect and describe current rather than prescribed usages (artificial language).

C *machine language*

F langage naturel

needs assessment: a systematic method of determining the educational needs and learning and social goals of a particular group or community.

F évaluation des besoins éducatifs*

negative entropy: see **negentropy**

negative picture/image: 1. an image, either black and white or colour, in the reverse of its normal appearance. Dark subject areas are light and light subject areas are dark, and in colour negative images, colours are represented by their complement; **2.** a piece of film with a negative image.

F 1. image négative; 2. négatif image

negative reinforcer: reinforcer that is meant to suppress a particular response or increase the frequency of escape behaviour.

F renforçateur négatif

negentropy: negative measure of disorder or a positive measure of order in a system that processes information, e.g. a learning system where entropy decreases as the assimilation of information proceeds.

C *entropy*

F négentropie

network: 1. a system of interconnected points, agencies, organizations or institutions which can distribute or interchange resources, energy or information; **2.** a group of radio or television broadcasting stations connected by relays or coaxial cable so that all stations may broadcast a single programme, originated at one point, simultaneously; **3.** two or more interconnected computers that perform local processing as well as transmit messages to one

81

another and/or to a central computer for updating information and/or processing inquiries.

C *information network*

F 1. 2. 3. réseau

network architecture: see **architecture**

new information technology—NIT: the application of electronic and other technologies, e.g., computers, communications satellites, fibre optics, videorecording, etc., to help produce, store, retrieve and distribute analogic or digital information.

C *telematics*

F nouvelles technologies de l'information— NTI

NIT: see **new information technology**

noise: 1. any unwanted disturbances superimposed upon a useful signal which tend to interfere with the information content of the useful signal; **2.** unwanted electrical energy or interference which may produce a snow-like pattern over a television picture or static in audio signals.

F 1. bruit; 2. souffle; bruit

noise level: see **signal-to-noise ratio**

non-book media: see **non-print materials**

non-print materials: materials which involve media other than the print medium (e.g. pictures, images, graphics, etc.). Many graphic materials are actually printed, but the term non-print has come to mean those materials which are not textual or book-like in nature. The terms media, non-print, and non-book are often used interchangeably.

C *printed materials*

F documents non imprimés

non-verbal test: a test in which the items consist of symbols, figures, numbers or pictures, but not words.

F test non-verbal

normal distribution curve: a bell-shaped curve representing a theoretical distribution of measurements that is often approximated by a wide variety of actual data. Scores are concentrated near the mean and decrease in frequency the further one departs from it.

F courbe de Gauss; courbe en cloche

norm-referenced test: a test which assesses the learner's performance in a given area in relation to that of some norm or reference group.

C *criterion-referenced test*

F test normatif (test à étalonnage normatif)

notation: in computer technology, a systematic or conventional method for representing information through the use of signs and symbols, such as numerals, alphabetic characters and special signs, and most commonly applied to number systems.

F notation

NTSC: National Television Standards Committee, colour video transmission system, used in the United States.

F NTSC

nuclearization: organizational and planning strategy of educational services (formal and non-formal) from the base upwards especially in Latin America. It aims at rationalizing resources and allowing maximum participation by the community in educational development.

F nucléarisation

O

OB: see **outside broadcast**

object language: the computer language or set of coded instructions into which a source language is translated by means of a compiler. Usually, object language and machine language are the same.

F langage résultant; langage objet

objective: 1. the desired outcome of an activity; **2.** detached, impartial, not influenced by personal feelings, prejudices or interpretations.

C *aim; goal; learning objective; educational objectives; performance objective*

F objectif

objective-based test: a test designed as far as possible to exclude the subjective element on the part of those taking it; and grading it by presenting a number of factual questions to be answered by one word or a check mark instead of verbal expression and organization of material.

F test objectif

objective lens: the main image-forming lens in a projector, or any optical system.

F objectif

octet: see **byte**

off-air recording: recording sound and/or images from a broadcast source.

F enregistrement d'une émission (radio ou télévision)

off-campus study: education carried on outside the formal school and higher education system.

F formation extra-universitaire

office automation: term designating the whole range of techniques and media tending towards the automation of office activities. Also called 'office technology'.

F bureautique

off-line: pertaining to the operation of a functional unit when not under the direct control of a computer.

F autonome; hors ligne; en différé

offprint: a section of a book or journal printed or reprinted for special distribution.

F tiré à part

off-screen – OS: not seen, but presumably not far from the action.

F hors champ

offset press: a printing press using photo-offset lithography, wherein the inked surface does not come into contact with the paper to be printed. Offset printing is the most common form of printing in instructional institutions.

F presse offset

OHP: see **overhead projector**

omnidirectional antenna: an antenna whose radiating properties at any instant are the same on all bearings.

F antenne omnidirective

omnidirectional microphone: a microphone equally sensitive in all directions.

F microphone omnidirectif

on-line: pertaining to the operation of a functional unit when under the direct control of the computer.

F en ligne; connecté; en direct

on-line data service: see **host**

on-the-air: in the process of broadcasting.

F à l'antenne; passage à l'antenne

opaque: impervious to the rays of visible light; not transparent or translucent.

F opaque

opaque projector: see **episcope**

open-circuit television: see **broadcasting**

open classroom: an instructional technique using a classroom setting to provide maximum freedom for the pursuit of students' interests. The classroom layout emphasizes a number of specialized interest areas rather than the usual student seating arrangement.

C *open school; open-plan school; open learning*

F classe ouverte*

open education: an approach to education where entry is not restricted by previous achievements. Not to be confused with 'open learning'.

C *open school; open university; open learning system*

F enseignement ouvert à tous; enseignement pour tous

open-ended: see **closed/open-ended**

open-ended activity: a type of learning activity in which the end result is not preconceived by the teacher or the learner. Usually refers to a certain type of experiment or inquiry. Often leads to further activities or experiments. Often the learner is guided by his own interests.

F travail libre

open-ended question: a semi-structured technique for probing associations connected with a specific area such as a sentence-completion test.

C *closed/open-ended; constructed response; multiple-choice question*

F question ouverte

open learning: a method of instruction in which according to their abilities and their needs the learners have a certain amount of direction in their studies, but also some autonomy of choice.

C *open classroom; open-plan school*

F pédagogie ouverte; méthodes ouvertes

open learning system: learning system accessible and available to all regardless of formal qualifications.

C *open school; open university*

F système d'enseignement ouvert

open system: see **closed system**

open-plan school: particular form of organization in certain elementary schools in order to break down the compartmentalization of subjects and class groups; especially apparent in architecture which is geared to a new mode of internal communication (assembly space, movable partitions, activity rooms, etc.).

F école à aire variable; école à plan flexible

84

open-reel: film or tape on a reel without a cassette or cartridge.

F sur bobine

open school: institution designed to offer adults access to education at the secondary and also at the tertiary level below that of higher education. No academic conditions for enrolment are imposed. Teaching is by correspondence, radio and television, or by face-to-face contact between teacher and student.

C *open university*

F école pour tous*

open university: a term originating in the United Kingdom and describing an institution designed to provide adults with access to higher education. All adults are eligible to enrol, regardless of formal academic qualifications. Teaching is by correspondence, radio and television, and may be supplemented by some face-to-face tuition and counselling.

F (open university); université ouverte

operant conditioning: a type of conditioning in which the emitted, rather than the elicited, behaviour of the organizer is reinforced, in contrast to respondent conditioning. Also referred to as 'instrumental conditioning'.

C *respondent conditioning*

F conditionnement opérant

operating system: 1. software which functions currently with user programs and controls their execution; **2.** in systems theory, a system or sub-system concerned with operating activities, i.e. those activities which directly contribute to the import, conversion and export processes which define the nature of the organization being described.

F **1.** système d'exploitation; **2.** système opératoire

operations research: the use of optimizing models; the use of mathematical models to reflect the variables and constraints in a situation and their effect on a selected goal; the application of scientific methods in a problem situation with a view to providing a quantitative basis to arrive at an optimum solution in terms of goals sought.

C *action research*

F recherche opérationnelle

optical disc: an audio or video disc which is read by an optical process.

F disque optique

optical fibres: bundles of tiny glass threads or fibres used to transmit signals.

F fibres optiques

optical printer: a kind of camera in the laboratory which allows variation of image from one film to another.

F Truca; tireuse optique

optical printing: printing carried out on a projection printer as distinguished from printing done on a contact printer.

F tirage optique

optical scanner: a device that optically scans printed or written data and generates their digital representations.

F lecteur optique

optical sound track: a photographic pattern on the side of a motion picture film which produces sound when projected onto a photo-electric cell connected to an amplifier and loudspeaker.

C *magnetic sound track; COMOPT; COMMAG*

F piste sonore optique

ORACLE: see **information network system**

organizer: see **advance organizer**

original: initial camera negative (or videotape recording before post-production).

F original

original negative: negative composed of original film exposed and processed to make up complete film.

F négatif original

original version: 1. primary source; **2.** print of film in the original language version as opposed to a dubbed version.

C *master*

F 1. version d'origine; 2. version originale

OS: see **off-screen**

outcomes: see **outputs**

outgoing profile: attitude which is expected from a student when he/she finishes a teaching/training sequence.

C *entry profile; post-test*

F profil de sortie

out of focus: descriptive of a distorted or fuzzy picture

F flou; pas au point

out of synchronization: see **synchronization**

output: information transferred from internal storage of a computer to output devices so as to produce output cards, tapes, business forms, etc.

F donnée de sortie; sortie

outputs: specific products in terms of type and magnitude which an activity can be reasonably expected to produce from the inputs provided and activities undertaken.

F produits

output power: the useful power or signal delivered by a circuit or device.

F puissance de sortie

outreach education: see **extension education**

outside broadcast — OB: 1. a programme originating elsewhere than in the studio of a broadcast. Also referred to as 'remote'; **2.** the broadcast description of an event in progress.

F 1. reportage (radio - télévision); 2. reportage en direct

over-exposed: film exposed longer than recommended or normal, usually unintentionally.

F surexposé

overflow: the condition arising when the result of an arithmetical operation exceeds the capacity of the storage place allotted to it in a digital computer.

F débordement; dépassement de capacité

overhead camera: a TV camera, generally fitted in a vertical position over an opaque screen lit from underneath used to read documents such as texts, maps, artwork and to scrutinize various objets. Also referred to as a 'TV-reader'.

F télélecteur

overhead projector—OHP: a projector placed in front of the viewers with a horizontal stage designed to project images from a slide or transparency through a lens and mirror system to a screen.

F rétroprojecteur

overlay: to dub one sound on top of another, e.g. traffic noise over speech.

F bruiter

overlay transparency: an additional transparency, attached to the frame or basic transparency of an overhead transparency. The overlay (or overlays) have information which further develops or enhances the information on the basic transparency.

F transparent à rabats

overt: see **covert/overt**

overt response: a response to a question in a test or a programme made by a student in some physical and observable way, e.g. by writing, drawing, using a tool, etc.

C *covert response*

F réponse manifeste

P

PA: see **public address**

pacing: 1. the act of directing the performance of an individual or class by indicating the speed to be achieved, in order to increase or decrease the rate of accomplishment; **2.** in programmed instruction, the rate at which the student proceeds through a given number of items; the usual procedure is self-pacing in which the student reads and responds at his/her own rate.

F 1. 2. rythme

package: a computer application designed for a particular purpose; it may require modification by the user.

C *applications program; learning package*

F progiciel

paddle: a hand-held control unit with a press button (or buttons) mainly used with computer games.

F télécommande

PAL: phase alternating line – British, Western European, etc., colour video system.

F PAL

pan: short for 'panorama', a shot in which the camera moves horizontally in a sweeping arc to take in a large area.

F panoramique

pan-and-tilt head: a camera mount which permits smooth rotation of the camera, both horizontally and vertically, and which may be attached to a tripod, dolly or clamp.

F plateforme pour panoramique horizontal et vertical

panel: 1. a section of material available to the student while she/he is working through more than one item; the section may include texts, diagrams, maps, globes, and laboratory equipment; **2.** a small group of persons having a purposeful conversation on an assigned topic with or without active participation by the audience; **3.** a board or surface on which instructions, switches, etc., are mounted.

F 1. bloc de matériel d'apprentissage*; 2. participants à une table ronde; plateau; 3. panneau

pan(ning) shot: see **pan**

pansemic: (of a word or picture) admitting almost anything signified.

C *monosemic message; polysemic message*

F pansémique

paper tape: a specially treated strip of paper on which a pattern of holes is punched.

F ruban perforé

parabolic antenna: an aerial with a reflector whose shape is that of a paraboloid of revolution or a parabolic cylinder. Also referred to as a 'dish antenna'.

F antenne parabolique

parabolic reflector microphone: a unidirectional concave dish-mounted microphone focussing distant sound waves without interference.

F microphone à réflecteur parabolique

paradigm: 1. a representation, a model of a theory, an idea or a principle; **2.** a pattern of procedure.

F 1. 2. paradigme

paradigmatic: paradigmatic is the opposite of syntagmatic. These terms designate two possible types of relationship between the elements of a message: elements are syntagmatic when they are present together in the message (AND); whereas they are known as paradigmatic when the element present in the message takes its meaning from other elements which are absent from the message (OR) (e.g. the colours of a flag, as opposed to the colours of traffic lights).

F paradigmatique

parallax: the difference between the vertical position of an object in a filmed scene as viewed through a viewfinder and that recorded on film through the camera lens.

F parallaxe

participatory method: educational method aimed at making the learner responsible for the acquisition of knowledge, by providing him or her with the conditions within which he or she will make discoveries for himself or herself. This method leads to the use of specific techniques such as local study projects, open essay topics, correspondence between schools, etc.

C *problem-solving approach*

F méthodes actives

part-time study: an administrative designation for learning engaged in by students who do not attend an educational institution on a full-time basis.

F étude à temps partiel

PASCAL language: a high-level, machine-independent language named after Pascal, a 17th century French philosopher and mathematician.

F PASCAL

password: a coded and often personalized recognition signal which a user inputs to a computer to gain access to the system.

F mot de passe

patch cord: a wire or cable with connectors or jacks on each end to connect one piece of equipment to another.

F cordon de liaison

pattern: 1. an interrelated, interwoven and virtually inseparable group or cluster of culture traits that, taken together, produce an established and typical result, such as a way of thinking, living or acting; **2.** the systematic arrangement of elements according to the regularities formed in the language.

F 1. pattern; structure; 2. pattern

pattern drill: in language instruction, an exercise using basic or model utterances in which several small and consistent changes in sound, form order and vocabulary are made repeatedly so as to promote the student's control over the specific grammatical (or other) structure involved.

F exercice structural

pattern recognition: automated scanning for recognition of characters and/or pictures.

F reconnaissance des formes

Pavlovian conditioning: see **respondent conditioning**

pay TV: form of television broadcasting, possibly incorporating a scrambler device, whereby the consumer only receives the signal in exchange for a payment or special license fee.

F télévision à péage

PBTE: see **performance-based teacher education**

peer teaching: a technique in which one or more learners provide instruction for a group of learners of the same age or placed in the same homogeneous grouping. The learners responsible for instruction have already mastered the content and skills being taught.

C *cross-age teaching*

F enseignement mutuel

peer tutoring: see **peer teaching**

perforations: the sprocket holes in the sides of motion-picture film which, together with the claw mechanism, aid the movement of the film through the camera or projector gate.

F perforations

performance: the actual behaviour emitted by a person or a group when given a task.

C *achievement*

F performance

performance-based instruction: a form of individualized, self-instructional teaching where the learners are not allowed to progress to the next stage of the learning programme until they have demonstrated competency or mastery of the present stage. Often the criterion of mastery is 100% success.

C *mastery learning*

F enseignement axé sur la performance*

performance-based teacher education – PBTE: teacher education placing stress on the explicit demonstration of performance as evidence of what the teacher knows and is able to do.

C *competency-based education*

F formation des enseignants fondée sur les résultats

performance (based) test: a test of capacity to achieve a desired result.

F test de performance; test centré sur la performance

performance objective: a definite learning specification; indicates in behavioural terms what a learner is expected to be able to do following exposure to instruction; under what conditions; and at what level of competence; also called 'behavioural objective'.

F objectif de performance; objectif comportemental

performance pitch: see **pitch**

performance right: the right to authorize presentation of a work by such action as playing, reciting, singing, dancing or projecting (either directly to the audience or by transmitting the presentation by broadcasting).

F droit d'interprétation ou d'exécution

peripheral equipment: 1. units or devices that are part of an entire data-processing system, but not actually part of a computer, e.g. an automatic typewriter functioning off-line, card sorter, reproducer, a forms burster, forms encoder and so forth; **2.** also any auxiliary equipment that may be connected, attached or used with a major piece of equipment.

F 1. périphériques; 2. accessoire

persistence: see **after image**

personalized system of instruction – PSI: instructional system or course structure developed in higher education. The system lays stress on the tutorial system, on the programming of instruction to suit the individual and on self-pacing by the student. Also referred to as 'Keller plan'.

C *individualized instruction; audio-tutorial method*

F système d'instruction personnalisé*

perspective: 1. audio-matching the apparent distance of a sound source; 2. the technique of drawing true resemblances of objects on a flat surface, as the objects appear to the eye, from any given distance; a representation of objects in perspective; 3. a point of view.

F 1. relief sonore; 2. 3. perspective

PERT - programme evaluation and review technique: a systematic timetabling and programming technique developed to measure, monitor and control the development and progress of a project or programme.

F méthode de PERT; méthode du chemin critique

phase reversal: a change in the aspect or characteristic of a signal.

F inversion de phase

phonograph: see **gramophone**

photocell: see **photoelectric cell**

photocomposing: 1. combining images by photographic means; 2. the photographic composition of text material by operating a keyboard.

F 1. 2. photocomposition

photocopy: a general term for copying, particularly electrostatic and wet-process copying.

F photocopie

photoelectric cell: a cell which is sensitive to light. In projectors, variations in light caused by the sound track are converted by the photocell into electric current which can be used as an audio signal.

F cellule photoélectrique

photograph: an image recorded on photographic or other opaque photosensitive material by photographic means.

F photographie

photography: the activity of operating a camera to record (usually on photographic film) the image viewed by the lens of the camera. Includes both technical and aesthetic considerations.

F photographie

photo-montage: montage in which photographic images are used (as in making a number of exposures on the same negative, projecting a number of negatives to make a composite print, or copying a picture consisting of cut and pasted prints).

F photomontage

photonovel: see **fotonovella**

photostat: photographic reproduction, usually enlarged or reproduced from the original to match available space in a layout.

F photocopie; reproduction photographique

pick-up arm: on a record player, a bar pivoting at one end and holding the pick-up head at the other end enabling the stylus tip to follow the groove in the surface of the disc.

F bras de lecture

picture: a specific item or material, a representation made on material, usually opaque by drawing, painting, photography or other graphic arts techniques, or the displayed television picture.

C *motion picture; picture tube*

F image

picture book: book for very young children consisting of pictures.

F livre d'images

picture negative: see **negative picture**

picture-phone: an experimental telephone which incorporates a television picture of the caller. Also called videophone.

F visiophone

picture tube: a cathode-ray tube specifically designed for the reproduction of television pictures.

F tube image

pilot: 1. an original or test programme, project or device; **2.** a low-level signal transmitted for receiver control purposes, e.g. automatic tuning control and automatic gain control.

F 1. pilote (programme, projet, matériel); 2. onde pilote

pilot light: an electric light usually used to indicate the position of a switch or circuit breaker, that a motor is in operation, or that the power is on.

F lampe témoin; voyant

pilot school: a school designed to pioneer on a small scale in the development or testing of an idea or educational programme in order to see if it is workable and warrants wider adoption.

C *experimental school; model school*

F école pilote

piracy: unauthorized duplication and distribution of programmes. Also called 'bootlegging'.

F piraterie (piratage)

pitch: the distance between the leading edges of two sprocket holes on motion picture film or filmstrip.

F pas de perforation

pixel: contracted form of picture element. The smallest picture element on a VDU screen.

F pixel

placebo effect: a term borrowed by education from medecine. Describes an effect obtained as a result of introducing a substance or activity to unaware subjects which will itself produce no effect in an experiment except to serve as a control in testing a substance or procedure to have positive effects.

F effet placebo

planning-programming-budgeting system – PPBS: strategy planning system and operational control process whose aim is to be most productive while facilitating the choice of resource distribution.

F système PPB; rationalisation du choix budgétaire

PLATO – programmed logic for automatic teaching operations: a large-scale computer-based education system developed at the University of Illinois since 1968. PLATO offers instruction from the collegiate level to the elementary school level.

F PLATO

playback: the reproduction of a signal (audio, video) that has previously been recorded.

F lecture

playback head: any device for reproduction of sound recorded by any of the media in common use.

F tête de lecture

plotter: a device used in conjunction with a computer to plot co-ordinate points in the form of a graph.

F traceur

plug: a connector or connecting device, usually at the end of a cord or cable which makes a connection by insertion into a jack or receptacle.

C *banana plug*

F fiche

point-to-point circuit: a radio link between two fixed stations.

F liaison point à point

polarized light: light which vibrates in one plane only; commonly found in reflections off most surfaces, except for chrome and other shiny metals.

F lumière polarisée

polysemic message: a message with multiple meanings which lends itself to a variety of pedagogic uses and applications.

C *monosemic message*

F message polysémique

(polythèque): French term for a multi-media library and a conventional library housed in the same place.

F polythèque

popping: sudden displacement of the centre of a slide due to expansion from heat.

F gondolage

population: a statistical term used in research referring to the larger group from which a sample is selected for study. The sample is studied and generalizations are made concerning the population from which the sample was taken by means of the process of statistical inference. The population is also referred to as the universe.

C *target population*
F *population*

portability: the ability of a computer program to be run on more than one computer system.

F *portabilité*

positive image: see **positive picture**

positive picture: an image in which the values of light and shade of the original subject are represented as they were in the original subject. In colour, the positive image also represents each colour of the original subject.

C *negative picture/image*
F *image positive*

positive print: projectible film with colour and/or tonal representation of original subject.

F *copie positive*

positive reinforcer: stimuli which tend to increase the frequency of operant behaviour.

F *renforçateur positif*

post-synchronization: recording a lip-synchronous sound which is recorded after film has been shot, either in the language used by the performers on in a foreign language. It fits the lip movements of the performers.

C *dubbing*
F *post-synchronisation*

post-test: the assessment made at the conclusion of instruction which determines the extent to which the learner has achieved the specified objectives.

C *pre-test; final test*
F *post-test; test de sortie*

poster: a large printed piece of paper or cardboard, often illustrated, posted to advertise or publicize something, e.g. health education posters.

F *affiche*

PPBS: see **planning-programming-budgeting system**

practical: part or fitting of a film studio set in the United Kingdom which may have to operate realistically, i.e. a door or window.

F *praticable*

practical period: a period spent at a place of work in which newly acquired practical skills are applied and initial experience in their use is gained.

F *stage pratique*

practicals: 1. individual experimental work, e.g. in physics or chemistry, also practical works; 2. manual activities, such as handicrafts, woodwork, etc. Not used in the United States.

F 1. *travaux pratiques;* 2. *travaux manuels*

practice exercise: 1. an activity in which pupils perform or work at a task repeatedly so as to acquire proficiency, as in 'practice maths', frequently used in combination as 'drill and practice'; 2. an activity in which pupils have opportunities to put to use those skills and knowledge previously learned through other instructional activities.

F 1. *exercice pratique;* 2. *pratique*

practice lesson: the class activities of one period of instruction conducted by a student teacher himself as part of the student teaching programme.

C *demonstration lesson; microteaching*
F *leçon d'essai*

practice school: an elementary or secondary school used by a teacher training institution to give students an opportunity to practise and observe teaching methods under the supervision of trained teachers.

F *école d'application; école annexe*

preamplifier: a device which increases the strength of a low-level or weak signal in a phonograph, projector or microphone before it is sent to the main amplifier.

F préamplificateur

pre-recorded: recorded or programmed in advance.

F pré-enregistré

prerequisite objectives: the statements specifying the prior skills and concepts necessary to undertake a particular learning task. (Also called entry level objective or entering behaviour.)

F prérequis

pressure plate: a mechanical component so arranged as to exert pressure on a film at a point in the film path where the film needs to be held in a rigidly prescribed position, as at projector or camera apertures. Usually a grooved, spring-loaded metal plate.

F cadre presseur

PRESTEL: see **information network system**

pre-test: the assessment made prior to instruction which determines the level of knowledge, skill and/or aptitude that a learner brings to instruction.

C *post-test*

F prétest; test d'entrée; test initial

preview: the viewing or review of an item, usually non-print, prior to purchase. Preview may be for the purpose of describing, annotating, reviewing, cataloging or preparing a presentation.

F visionnement préalable

primer: 1. an elementary schoolbook, particularly one for primary education; **2.** a typewriter with extra large type.

F 1. premier manuel; 2. machine à écrire à gros caractères

print: 1. a term sometimes used for a single, specific photograph, study print, art print or motion picture; **2.** a positive copy of a film made from a negative.

C *answer print; blueprint; first print; direct print; contact print; release print; positive print; reversal print*

F 1. épreuve; 2. copie

print media: see **printed materials**

print-run: the total number of copies of a publication printed.

F tirage

printed circuit: an electronic component in which the wiring circuit is printed on an insulating board.

F circuit imprimé

printed materials: generic term to denote textual or booklike materials (newspapers, magazines) and graphics used for education as opposed to audio-visual media and broadcast media.

C *non-print materials*

F documents imprimés; supports imprimés

printer: 1. an output device connected to a computer for printing out the results of data processing; **2.** a device used in photography through which an image-bearing film and a strip of unexposed film are run with light produced inside the printer passing through the image film then striking the unexposed film to form a latent image.

F 1. imprimante; 2. tireuse

printing: the activity of making an image (usually positive) on photographic paper from a piece of exposed and developed photographic film (usually negative). Includes contact printing, reducing, and enlarging on film as well as paper.

C *optical printing*

F tirage

printing frame: wood, metal or plastic frame in which a piece of sensitized paper is exposed behind a negative to produce a photographic positive print of the same size.

F chassis de tirage

printing paper: an opaque material used in photography, one surface of which is coated with a light-sensitive emulsion on which visual data and images can be recorded by exposure and subsequent processing.

F papier photographique

printout: the permanent record produced by a computer as the final product of a computation, a computer search, etc.

F copie papier; listage

problem analysis: the process of formalizing perceived (or identified) problems. It involves the activities of identifying relevant variables and specifying hypothetical relationships between/among those variables.

F analyse de problèmes*

problem-centred learning: a method of instruction by which learning is stimulated by the creation of challenging situations that demand solution. May be called discovery or heuristic learning.

F apprentissage centré sur les problèmes*

problem definition: see **problem analysis**

problem method: see **problem-centred learning**

problem-solving approach: a teaching and learning method whereby a topic is presented in terms of a problem to be solved, with all the necessary means and information at the student's disposal. The role of the teacher is to guide the learner to discover solutions for himself rather than to provide a ready-made answer.

C *heuristic process; inquiry learning*

F méthode de résolution de problèmes

process: a generic term that may include compute, assemble, compile, interpret, generate, etc.

F traiter

process evaluation: type of evaluation which provides periodic feedback to persons responsible for implementing plans and procedures.

C *formative evaluation; summative evaluation; product evaluation*

F évaluation des processus

processing: 1. treating an exposed film so as to produce positive images; **2.** a technique by which data to be processed must be coded and collected into groups prior to undergoing treatment.

F 1. traitement; 2. traitement de données

processor: 1. in a computer, a functional unit that interprets and executes instructions; **2.** in photography, a device in which photographic film or papers are automatically developed, fixed and sometimes washed and dried; also called a processing machine or film processor.

F 1. processeur; 2. machine à développer

producer: 1. in film and broadcasting industries, the person with financial and administrative responsibility for a production; **2.** in education, the person who is responsible for the content and form of a series of audio-visual programmes or materials.

F 1. 2. producteur

product evaluation: type of evaluation which measures and interprets the outcomes of an educational programme in relation to its enabling and/or terminal objectives.

C *process evaluation; summative evaluation*

F évaluation des produits

production centre: a facility specially equipped to prepare sound film or videotape programmes.

F centre de production

production manager: the executive who carries out detailed work under or for a producer.

F directeur de production

production schedule: a schedule of the sequence in which the shots for a film will be made, together with locations, crews, performers, equipment, transporation, and in some instances, alternative plans in case of bad weather.

F plan de tournage

productivity: an assessment of the effectiveness of a production process compared with the resources supplied to it.

F productivité

proficiency test: a test administered to students upon initial entry or at any subsequent time to measure the level of performance.

F test de capacité; test de rendement

prognosis test: test used to predict future success in a specific subject or field.

F test pronostique

program: an ordered list of instructions directing a computer to perform a desired sequence of operations

C *software*

F programme; logiciel

programme: 1. an organized set of activities, projects, processes or services which is directed towards the attainment of similar or related objectives; **2.** the materials used in programmed instruction; **3.** a term referring to the content of a medium and consisting generally of a message expressed in the terms and techniques of the medium, e.g. radio programme, television programme, theatre programme; **4.** a selection of films in a theatre or items on TV to be shown in one session.

F 1. 2. 3. 4. programme

programmed instruction: one self-educational method whereby the student, alone, at his own pace, works through material (on tape, film or in print) containing previously constructed sequences which lead him step-by-step to the desired goal through a specified set of responses. The programmed courses are arranged in such a way that each sequence must be mastered before the student may proceed to the next one.

F enseignement programmé

programmed learning: see **programmed instruction**

programmed logic for automatic teaching operations: see **PLATO**

programmed teaching: see **programmed instruction**

programmed tutoring: see **programmed instruction**

programmer: 1. a device which controls the operation or synchronization of sound reproduction and/or projection devices; **2.** a person who writes and documents computer programmes.

F 1. programmateur; 2. programmeur

programming language: an artificial language to give instructions to a computer, e.g. ADA, ALGOL, BASIC, FORTRAN, LOGO, PASCAL, etc.

F langage de programmation

progress chart: a chart showing actual performance in comparison with a pre-determined schedule or estimate of expected performance.

F courbe de performance

progression factor: causes of difficulty involved in the progress of learners that must be recognized in organizing a sequential course of training.

F facteur de progression

project: 1. a planned undertaking which is designed to achieve certain specific objectives within a given budget and within a specified period of time; **2.** a significant unit of instructional activity involving the study of a topic from a variety of angles over a given period of time and resulting in report or display of work.

F projet

project method: method requiring students individually, or in groups, to produce a thesis, a plan, a written or oral report or some other piece of work; the real objective lies in the learning and techniques used when producing it.

F travail sur projet

project training method: programmes combining classroom or vocational instruction with supervised and co-ordinated laboratory activities.

F méthode de formation intégrée

projection: the process of recreating an image on a screen.

C *front projection; back projection; still projection; daylight projection*

F projection

projection lens: a lens corrected for colour aberrations to suit the spectral sensitivity of the eye and the character of the light emitted by projection lamps. Used in a projector to recreate an image on a screen.

F objectif de projection

projection booth: a soundproof enclosure from whence films are projected so that the sound of the projector is not audible to the audience.

F cabine de projection

projector: a device for creating large images from slides, film or tape.

C *loop projector; slide projector; episcope; overhead projector; rear-screen projector; large-screen television projector*

F projecteur

projectual: see **transparency**

PROM – programmable read only memory: an internal storage device that can be permanently programmed by a computer user.

F mémoire morte programmable

promo: a generally short video tape production to promote pop music.

F vidéoclip

prompt: 1. a stimulus added to make the correct response more likely while the student is learning; it may be pictorial or verbal; **2.** a symbol that appears on the screen to let the user know that the computer is ready to pay attention to his commands; often called 'cue'.

F 1. indice; 2. clignotement; message de guidance; sollicitation

prompting: see **cueing**

property man: man responsible for the availability of all moveable items used in a set up (properties or props) and their subsequent lay-out and disposition.

F accessoiriste

props man: see **property man**

protected works: original intellectual works (of literary, scientific and artistic nature) enjoying protection under copyright law.

F œuvres protégées

protocol: formal set of rules governing the format, timing, sequencing and error control of message exchange within a communication system.

F protocole

protocol materials: a U.S. term for recordings of the performance of teachers and pupils in real-life classroom or other educational settings that are used for modelling in teacher training.

C *microteaching; modelling*

F *modèles; protocoles

PSI: see **personalized system of instruction**

psychomotor domain: part of Bloom's taxonomy of educational objectives including those objectives related to the manipulative or motor skill area.

C *cognitive domain; affective domain*

F domaine psychomoteur

(psychopédagogie): French term denoting an educational approach which gives a specific emphasis to the psychology of the child, or the adult.

F psychopédagogie

psycholinguistics: the study of the relations between communications or messages and the characteristics of the persons who communicate; specifically, the study of language as related to the general or individual characteristics of the users of language.

F psycholinguistique

public address – PA: an audio system to amplify sounds of speech or music; usually composed of one or more microphones, an amplifier and one or more loudspeakers. Some amplifiers are capable of receiving and amplifying music from tape recorders, gramophones or radios.

F sonorisation; sono

punch: 1. a device that will make holes to represent information in any medium in accordance with signals sent to it from another source, such as a computer, a communication link, or a human being through a keyboard; **2.** a hole in a data carrier or medium, such as tape, cards or sheets of paper, usually arrayed with other holes to represent information.

F 1. perforatrice; 2. perforation

punch card: a card into which hole patterns can be punched.

F carte à perforer

punched card: a computer card punched with a pattern of holes which represent data.

F carte perforée

punched tape: a tape on which a pattern of holes or cuts is used to represent data. The tape may serve as an input to a computer system, a telecommunications system, or a presentation programmer. Also a tape for controlling two or more projectors in a multi-image presentation.

F bande perforée

pupil: a member of a school who is undergoing a course of educational instruction.

C *learner; student*

F élève

push-pull: a type of electronic amplifier in which signals are simultaneously pushed and pulled to achieve high fidelity.

F symétrique

puppets: dolls with moveable arms, legs, etc., used in three-dimensional animation.

F marionnettes

Q

quad: see **quadruplex**

quadruplex: the designation given to professional broadcast videotape recorders currently in use because of the number of recording and playback heads (4) and their placement on the spinning headwheel transverse to the tape movement.

F quadruplex; magnétoscope à pistes transversales

quality control: the monitoring of a system so that adjustments can be made to correct differences between actual output performance (of system or components) and planned performance.

F contrôle de qualité

R

radio frequency – RF: in general, any frequency in the electromagnetic spectrum between the audio frequency and the infrared portion useful for radio and television transmission.

F fréquence radioélectrique

radio frequency amplifier: see **amplifier**

radio receiver: a device connected to an aerial or other source of radio signals in order to make available the required information content of the signals in some desired form.

F récepteur radioélectrique

radio set: see **radio receiver**

radiovision: an instructional media system presenting static visual media (usually slides or filmstrips) and sound. The sound portion is transmitted by radio, whilst visual materials are projected (or displayed) at the point of reception.

F radiovision

RAM – random access memory: see **direct access store**

random access: see **direct access**

randomize: assign individuals to experimental groups in a purely chance fashion.

F assigner au hasard

range finder: the camera attachment which indicates the distance from camera to subject, or sets a camera for proper lens focus.

F télémètre

raster: a grid on a VDU which divides the display into discrete elements (like a reference map).

F trame

rating: 1. the designated power and signal requirements for equipment; the nominal output power and quality of an electronic device; **2.** assessment of the performance of a student or a teacher.

C *grading; mark*

F 1. valeur nominale; capacité nominale; 2. appréciation; évaluation

ratio: see **aspect ratio; signal/noise ratio**

raw film: see **raw stock**

raw score: the first quantitative result obtained in scoring a test as opposed to standard score.

F score brut

raw stock: unexposed film.

F pellicule vierge

readability: a term referring to the degree of ease with which the reading and understanding of continuous textual material is possible.

C *legibility*

F intelligibilité; lisibilité

read only memory – ROM: see **read only store**

read only store: permanant storage which cannot be erased. A computer can read from it, but cannot write new information into it; it is an unchangeable storage.

F mémoire morte

reader: 1. see **optical reader; microform reader; 2.** a school textbook in the United Kingdom presenting selected pieces of prose and poetry.

F 1. lecteur; 2. livre de morceaux divers

reader-printer: viewing equipment for microforms (microfiche and microfilm) providing the option of printing selected pages from the microform.

F lecteur reproducteur

readiness curriculum: range of activities designed to help pupils to acquire the skills and awareness needed if they are to benefit subsequently from a vocationally oriented curriculum.

F pré-apprentissage

readiness test: a test designed to determine whether a would-be learner has the characteristics that he or she will need to cope satisfactorily with a particular course, etc.

F test de maturité spécifique; test de readiness

readout: soft copy output from a computer displayed on the screen of a VDU.

F affichage; lecture

realia: tangible objects, real items (as opposed to pictorial representations), used for instruction.

F objets

real time: expression referring to a system in which processing of data occurs virtually simultaneously with the event or events generating the data.

F temps réel

rear projection: see **back projection**

rear-screen projector: a device which projects the image, usually slides or film, onto the

97

back of a translucent screen, to be viewed from the front of the screen.

F projecteur pour écran translucide

receiver: see **radio receiver; television receiver**

F récepteur

reception: the receiving of a radio or television broadcast.

F réception

record: 1. a set of related data or words treated as a unit in a computer; **2.** a complete bibliographic entry including title, author and publisher; **3.** the activity of operating a recording device such as an audiotape recorder or videotape recorder to capture or preserve (or record) a presentation or programme; also called taping; **4.** another term for a phonograph record or audiodisc.

F 1. enregistrement; article; 2. dossier bibliographique; 3. enregistrer; 4. disque

recording studio: see **sound studio**

record player: a device consisting of a turntable with its driving system, a tone-arm and a pick-up head which reproduces sound from audio-discs.

F platine tourne-disque

recorded effects: sound effects which have been recorded for introduction into the master track during mixing with the idea of enhancing the illusion of reality in the finished presentation.

F effets pré-enregistrés

recorder: see **audiotape recorder; cassette recorder; videotape recorder**

recording: 1. action by which signals are suitably embodied in a material base; **2.** techniques whereby information is embodied in a material base with the aim of preserving it with a view to its subsequent reproduction; **3.** material base for signals after embodiment and, through extension, the signals themselves after reproduction; **4.** a generic term applied to audiotapes and audiodiscs.

C *sound recording; magnetic recording; videotape*

F 1. 2. 3. 4. enregistrement

recording head: the light valve or magnetic gap at which sound signals are converted into optical or magnetic tracks.

F tête d'enregistrement

recording level indicator: a device indicating signal level when recording.

C *VU meter*

F indicateur de niveau d'enregistrement

recording studio: see **sound studio**

reduction print: the print of a cine film made from a larger format master; usually a 8 mm print from a 16 mm master.

F copie en format réduit

redundancy: the characteristic of providing information which has already been given in another form. In information theory, the redundancy rate is the ratio of the units of a message which are not necessary (since they repeat units of information which are already present in the message) to the total number of units making up the message. Redundancy is used in communication transmission to control information at the receiving point.

F redondance

reel: a device, composed of a hub and two circular flanges on which magnetic tape or motion picture film may be wound.

C *supply spool; take-up spool*

F bobine

reference book: books such as dictionaries, encyclopaedias, directories, indexes and atlases which are compiled to supply definite items of information of varying extent and intended to be referred to rather than read through.

F livre de référence

referent: that which a sign refers to, or stands for, or denotes; used especially of a physical or imagined thing, event, quality, etc.

F référent

reflector: 1. any device used to redirect light (and/or energy) in a desired direction by reflection; **2.** in projection, a spherical mirror mounted behind the projection lamp to direct the rays of light from the back of the lamp forward through the lamp filaments, thus increasing the intensity of the illumination.

F 1. 2. réflecteur

reflex camera: a camera which has a mirror within the camera body so that the scene to be photographed is projected into the camera viewfinder.

F appareil à visée réflex

refresher course: activities intended to revise and renew previously learned attitudes, knowledge and skill patterns which have deteriorated through disuse.

F cours de recyclage

register: 1. a device inside the CPU that stores the smallest amount of usable information in a computer, with enough memory capacity for one or two bytes; **2.** variety in the language used for a specific purpose as opposed to a social or regional dialect.

F 1. registre; 2. niveau de langue

register board: a surface with two or more small vertical posts for holding paper, cardboard, or film materials all correctly aligned when more than one layer must be assembled for filming.

F plaque de fixation

regression analysis: general term for statistical techniques which employ a correlation in order to predict probable relationships.

F analyse de régression

reinforcement: a process in which some stimulus, presented immediately following a response, increases the rate at which the response is emitted in a standard situation or which increases the probability that the response will recur when the situation recurs.

C *negative reinforcer; positive reinforcer*

F renforcement

relay: 1. an electronically operated remote switch; **2.** to receive a signal and transmit to others.

F 1. relais; 2. relayer

release: distribution and exhibition of a production for general use.

F distribution; sortie

release print: a duplicate print of original audio-visual material prepared for general use.

F copie d'exploitation

reliability: 1. the characteristic of a measuring instrument or of a test which is certain to work in given conditions; **2.** the extent to which a measuring instrument or a test measures consistently whatever it sets out to measure. The consistency of the measurements depends upon the reliability of the instrument.

C *differential sensitivity; validity*

F 1. fiabilité; 2. fidélité

reliability coefficient: the coefficient of correlation between two forms of a test, between scores on two administrations of the same test, or between halves of a test, properly corrected.

F coefficient de fidélité

remake: new version of an old film or programme.

F remake

remedial class: small class of pupils who need special help to overcome some form of backwardness or to compensate for earlier inadequate learning.

F classe de rattrapage

remediation: 1. the activity of choosing and implementing further instruction (often in alternative formats) to help the learner master those skills not learned in the previous unit of instruction; **2.** instructional action taken because a learner has made an inappropriate response; remediation decreases the likelihood of an inappropriate response.

F 1. soutien; 2. correction

remote: see **outside broadcast**

remote access: access to an information system from a distance.

F accès à distance

remote control: control of any device from a distance by wires, sound, infrared or radio waves.

F télécommande

repeater (station): a combination of apparatus for receiving either one-way or two-way communication signals and delivering corresponding signals that are either amplified or reshaped or both.

F répéteur; ré-émetteur

replacement part: see **spare parts**

replication: the repetition of a research study under similar or slightly altered conditions to determine whether similar results are obtained.

F replication; reproduction; répétition

reprint: setting up type and printing again using a previous printing as 'copy' as distinct from manuscript 'copy'.

F réimpression

reprography: a general term to describe the techniques used for reproducing documents, photographs, printed matter, pictures, etc.

F reprographie

rerecording: 1. recording not from life, but from tapes, discs, etc.; 2. the transfer of sound from one medium to another, or to a unit of the same medium.

F 1. repiquage; 2. réenregistrement

resolution: 1. a measure of the ability to delineate image detail and picture detail; 2. ability of a TV system to reproduce and distinguish fine details on the screen. 'Vertical resolution' refers to the scanning lines seen on the screen. 'Horizontal resolution' refers to the number of variations within each scanning line and is variable according to the bandwidth used.

C *sharpness*

F 1. pouvoir de résolution; finesse; 2. définition

resource centre: see **educational media centre**

resources: see **learning resources**

resource(s)-based learning: an individualized student-centred learning system that relies mainly on self-study materials of various types often made available through a resource centre.

C *media based learning*

F *apprentissage fondé sur un travail personnel de recherche documentaire

respondent conditioning: the procedure by which a subject learns to respond to a new stimulus by associating it with a stimulus that originally elicited the desired response. Also referred to as 'classical conditioning' or 'Pavlovian conditioning'.

C *operant conditioning*

F conditionnement répondant

response: 1. any implicit or overt change in an effector organ (a muscle or a gland) consequent to stimulation; 2. the behaviour the learner emits following an instructional stimulus (usually a question or request to perform some activity); 3. the output signal resulting from a given signal applied to the input terminals of a network.

F 1. 2. 3. réponse

response analysis: analysis determining whether a learner's answer coincides with the answers anticipated by the person who formulated the educational programme. A specific process of analysis corresponds to each type of anticipated answer: number of words, answers to multiple-choice questions, etc.

F analyse de réponse

response analyser: see **student response system**

response frames: a frame in a computer-based learning or interactive video sequence that requires a response of the learner. Also called 'action frame'.

F cadre réponse; item de réponse

resource person: a person identified as a potential resource to a classroom group by reason of that person's special knowledge or experience. A person who has had special training and/or significant experience in the subject under consideration by a group and who serves the group by furnishing authoritative information when called upon to do so.

C *facilitator; leader; educational adviser; technical adviser*

F spécialiste (extérieur ou invité); consultant; conseiller technique; *personne ressource

retraining course: see **refresher course**

retrieval: operation by which items are selected from a collection – not only a library collection, but also any index or bibliography.

F recherche documentaire

retrieve: to find and select specific information in the record of a file storage.

F rechercher (une information)

reversal: see **reversal process**

reversal film: a film which, after exposure, is processed to produce a positive image on the same film.

F film inversible

reversal print: a film produced by a process which renders a positive image directly without the use of an intervening negative.

F copie inversible

reversal process: process rendering a positive image directly from the natural scene or from another positive without an intervening negative.

F inversion; procédé inversible

reverse action: action which goes backward on the screen.

F marche arrière

rewind: 1. the technique of returning the film or tape back on the reel after projection or taping; **2.** device, often built into recording or projection equipment, which allows the material to return to the supply reel.

F rembobiner; réenrouler; 2. rembobinage

rewinder: cutting room apparatus consisting of opposed spools or plates with turning gear, facilitating the winding up or the rewinding of films.

F réenrouleuse

RF: see **radio frequency**

rhythms: see **school work rhythms**

rights: creative or performance equities.

C *film rights; full rights; limited rights; author's rights; distribution right; performance right; copyright; credits; royalties; world rights*

F droits

role playing: an instructional technique involving a spontaneous portrayal (acting out) of a situation, condition or circumstance by selected members of a learning group who either assume overtly or imagine the part or function of another or others.

F jeu de rôles; jeu dramatique

rolling title: a device used to slowly move titles and/or written text containing too much material for one cartoon.

F déroulant

ROM: read only memory; see **read only store**

rotary magazine: a circular holder for slides for insertion into an automatic slide projector.

F carrousel

rote learning: learning in a purely mechanical way by the exercise of memory only and regardless of understanding.

F apprentissage par cœur

rough cut: the second step in editing a motion picture, on completion of which the length of scenes has been shortened somewhat but not necessarily to final length and action between adjacent scenes is not yet exactly matched.

F premier montage

round-table discussion: conference for discussion or deliberation by several participants often seated at a round table so that no precedence in rank can be indicated.

C *panel (2)*

F table ronde

routine: 1. a sequence of educational instructions or actions designed to carry out a single process or set of related processes; 2. a computer programme, or part thereof, that may have some general or frequent use.

F 1. procédure; 2. routine; programme; sous-programme

routing: 1. the systematic circulation of printed material or media among the staff or officers of an organization in accordance with their interests or needs; 2. the selection of paths through a network, for calls, sending data, or specific types of traffic.

F 1. diffusion interne; 2. acheminement

royalties: author's fee representing the author's share in the returns from the use of his works.

F redevances de droits d'auteur

RULEG: a technique for construction of programmed sequences in which the student is first presented with a general rule, principle, definition or the like (RUL) and then with an example (EG), including descriptions of physical events, theorems, statements of relationships between specific objects, etc. With EGRUL, the student is systematically introduced to examples (EG) of a concept before being lead to identify the principle or the rule (RUL) connecting them.

C *inductive learning*

F RULEG

rules method: see **RULEG**

rumble: an undesirable, low frequency sound, usually regular, which occurs in sound reproduction systems, particularly in phonograph systems.

F bourdonnement

run: in computer technology, the execution of one or several programmes which are linked to form one operating unit.

F passage en machine

running caption: see **rolling title**

running time: the amount of time taken to run from the beginning to the end of a film, tape or other recorded material.

F durée de projection; durée

rush print: quick print produced by a film laboratory of a master film to enable the production team to assess its acceptability.

F premiers positifs

rushes: daily printing of all scenes shot on a film production; used to select the best scenes for the final print. Also called 'dailies'.

F rushes

S

safety film: film which will not readily burn.

F film de sécurité; pellicule de sécurité

sample: 1. the group of individuals, events, situations or the like which will be involved in a study. The sample is always a part or a subset of a population; 2. a representative portion or item of material or equipment for testing.

F 1. 2. échantillon

sandwich course: a course in which periods of full-time instruction alternate with associated full-time industrial, professional or commercial experience.

F cours en alternance

satellite: see **distribution satellite; communications satellite; direct broadcast satellite**

satellite ground receiver: device for receiving signals from a satellite.

F récepteur de satellite au sol

satellite station: 1. separate television broadcast facility re-transmitting material of a near-by station to increase its local coverage; **2.** see **earth station**.

F 1. station satellite; 2. station au sol

scale: a system of marks in a pre-determined order at a known interval employed as an aid to measurements and comparison of various quantities.

F échelle

scanner: a device which automatically samples or interrogates the state of various processes, files, conditions or physical states.

F scanneur

scanning: systematic inspection of all parts of an area by a narrow beam of light or an electromagnetic radiation, e.g. the movement of the electron beam from top to bottom and from left to right on the television screen or in a TV camera.

F balayage; exploration

scenario: in technological forecasting, a systematic projection of likely future trends, problems and developments.

F scénario

scene: a single shot or group of shots combined to form one complete cinematographic idea and with continuous action in a given locale or setting.

F scène

scene shifter: see **grip**

scheduling: 1. the process of allotting or assigning equipment and/or materials and/or staff to fill specific requests; **2.** in radio, TV and similar telecommunications, the allotting or assigning to a programme or other transmission (such as an announcement or commercial) of a specific time period at which it will be transmitted.

C *flexible schedule*

F 1. affectation; 2. programmation

school achievement: 1. the school performance of a given population in a subject matter or at the end of a cycle; **2.** the result of school work undertaken by a student.

F 1. rendement scolaire; 2. résultat scolaire

school television: television programmes prepared primarily for use by schools; usually of an informational or instructional nature.

C *instructional television; educational television*

F télévision scolaire

school work rhythms: adjustment of school activities in relation to pupils' biological time (i.e. in relation to endocrine rhythms, growth rhythms, the rhythm of sleeping and waking, eating rhythms, etc.).

F rythmes scolaires

score: 1. music specially composed for a film; **2.** a number expressing the degree of success in a psychological or educational test; **3.** to correct or grade a test or performance.

C *raw score; mark; grading*

F 1. musique de film; 2. score; note; cote; 3. noter; coter

scrambled book: a programmed textbook format often adopted for branching programmes in which the pages or the paragraphs are not in the usual logical order and whose order of use is determined by the responses made by the reader to questions.

F livre brouillé

scrambler: equipment to modify the electric signals transmitted so that they are unintelligible until passed through a corresponding device at the receiving end.

F embrouilleur

scratch: 1. to put abrasion marks on a film unintentionally; 2. an abrasive mark; 3. to terminate a programme.

F 1. rayer; 2. rayure; 3. supprimer

screen: 1. a prepared surface – glass beaded, matte, metallic, lenticular or frosted – on which images are projected; 2. the surface of a CRT on which a picture is formed.

F 1. 2. écran

screen education: see **media education**

script: written text of a media production such as a motion picture, a slide/tape presentation, a television programme, or an audio-recording. Usually includes directions to the actors/narrators and those producing the presentation, as well as the actual text.

C *final shooting script; storyboard; synopsis; treatment*

F texte; découpage

script girl: recording clerk of all set action. This is the term in the United States; the term in the United Kingdom is:

C *continuity girl*

F scripte

scriptwriter: professional broadcast writer.

F scénariste

SECAM: colour video standard used by France and most Eastern European countries. Initials stand for SEquential Couleur A Mémoire.

F système SECAM

segue: see **cross fade**

selection: the process of choosing or specifying equipment and/or materials.

F sélection

self-assessment: evaluation method in which the learner makes his own evaluation as to whether he has reached mastery of a learning unit (often by passing a self-administered test) in order to proceed to the next assignment, or gives himself a rating or mark for his achievement, either in relation to a fixed standard or to other learners.

C *individually paced instruction; pacing; self-pacing*

F auto-évaluation

self-directed learning: a way of learning in which the learner takes responsibility for his own learning and is involved, to a greater or lesser degree, in making decisions about the nature of the learning and the way in which it is carried out: definition of objectives, choice of content and progression, selection of methods and techniques, fixing of location, times and place, and adoption of assessment procedures.

C *autodidaxy; autonomy; independent study; individualized instruction; self-instruction*

F apprentissage autodirigé

self-discipline: discipline freely established between members of a group without outside control or interference.

F autodiscipline

self-evaluation: see **self-assessment**

self-government: 1. collegiate administration and management of an educational institution by both staff and students or by delegated representatives of each group; 2. applied to adult education, this term, borrowed from the production sector, designates learners' responsibility for management, establishment of curricula, the choice and application of instructional methods in educational activities.

F 1. 2. autogestion

self-instruction: an instructional technique which involves the use, by students, of instructional materials (especially programmed instructional materials, learning packages and audio-tutorial systems) which include stimuli, provision for responses, feedback and testing so that the students can learn either without teacher intervention or with a minimum of teacher guidance. It is often erroneously considered a synonym for individualized instruction, but in reality self-instruction individualizes only the pace of instruction.

C *autodidaxy; autonomy; independent study; individualized instruction; self-directed learning*

F autodidaxie; auto-apprentissage

self-learning: see **self-instruction**

self-pacing: an arrangement in which the individual learner controls the rate at which he is presented with learning materials.

C *individually paced instruction; pacing; self-assessment*

F rythme individuel; autocontrôle de la progression

self-perception: the individual's perception of himself as a person.

F perception de soi

self-study materials: materials designed for use by a learner working on his own, sometimes as a reinforcement to a formal classroom programme or broadcast.

C *audiotutorial method; auto-instructional device; teaching machine*

F moyens pour apprentissage individuel

semantic differential: a procedure originally developed for measuring the meaning of concepts and used for attitude measurement.

F différenciateur sémantique

semantics: the science of meanings of words or other signs; the rules that describe the way signs relate to objects.

F sémantique

seminar: a short course or conference making extensive use of participative methods and devoted to the exclusive study of one subject with the object of furthering knowledge in that area.

F séminaire

semiotics: the systematic study of linguistic and non-linguistic signs. Its main sub-divisions are semantics, syntactics and pragmatics. Each of these, and so semiotics as a whole, can be pure, descriptive or applied. Pure semiotics elaborate a language to talk about signs; descriptive semiotics studies actual signs; applied semiotics utilizes knowledge about signs for the accomplishment of various purposes.

F sémiotique

sensitivity: the degree of response of an instrument or control unit to change in the incoming signal.

C *differential sensitivity; reliability; validity*

F sensibilité

sensitivity group: see **T-group**

sensitivity training: method of increasing quality and skills of inter-personal interaction through the use of group dynamics as a means of learning and re-education.

F éducation de la sensibilité

separate magnetic sound - SEPMAG: a magnetic sound-track recorded on a separate sprocketted tape, not on the edge of the picture film.

C *combined magnetic sound*

F son magnétique séparé; double bande

separate optical sound - SEPOPT: an optical sound-track on a separate film from the picture film.

C *combined optical sound*

F son optique séparé

separate track pulse: a signal on an audiotape, other than on the sound track, to control the visual presentation.

F topage

sepia: brownish colour typical of old photographs.

F sepia

SEPMAG: see **separate magnetic sound**

SEPOPT: see **separate optical sound**

sequence: 1. a section of an audio-visual material, more or less complete in itself, and made up of a series of related scenes; **2.** the order of presentation of aspects of the instructional programme, as within a grade, a course, or a series of grades or courses.

F 1. séquence; 2. progression

sequential access: access to items or information that depends on passing through a predetermined position or series of positions.

C *direct access*

F accès séquentiel

serial: a publication or a broadcast programme issued in successive parts, usually at regular intervals and, as a rule, intended to be continued over a certain period.

F feuilleton; série télévisée

serial access: see **sequential access**

series: 1. volumes, usually related to each other in subject matter, issued successively, generally by the same publisher, in a uniform style, and usually bearing a collective series title on the cover or title page; **2.** cell or battery connection that results in higher voltage; **3.** see 'serial'

F 1. collection; 2. montage en série

server: an information processor which provides supporting services and/or guidance to users and satellite processors terminals and other subsidiary devices, e.g. a file server, a printer server. Also called 'host computer'.

C *host*

F serveur; ordinateur hôte

service: as a verb, to conduct maintenance and repair activities.

F entretenir

service program: see **utility program**

set: 1. psychologist's term for a state of expectation or predisposition to behave in a certain way; **2.** in the United Kingdom, to give an examination or test; **3.** grouping of pupils of a particular are group according to ability in particular subjects; **4.** to adjust a device for some desired effect; **5.** a complete radio or television receiving apparatus; **6.** studio construction to suggest a real location.

F 1. disposition; 2. examiner; tester; 3. groupe de niveau; 4. régler; 5. récepteur radio ou télévision; 6. décor

setting: 1. the environment in which messages are received; **2.** the selected position of a moveable indicator; **3.** studio construction to suggest a real location; **4.** division of pupils into different groups according to ability in particular subjects.

C *streaming; tracking; ability grouping*

F 1. cadre; 2. réglage; 3. décor; 4. groupement par niveau

S/FX: see **sound effects**

sharpness: degree to which a picture shows fine detail. Also called resolution.

F finesse; netteté; définition

shoot: to make a camera shot or perform filming activity.

F tourner

shooting script: the orderly, written-down work plan of a film containing, shot-by-shot, the visual elements in one column and the audio material in the other. Also known as the 'screenplay'.

F découpage définitif

short film: a film under three thousand feet in length, i.e. thirty-three minutes playing time. In the United Kingdom it is also known as a short.

F court métrage

shot: 1. a single run of the camera; **2.** the smallest element of a motion picture within which spatial and temporal continuity is preserved.

F 1. 2. plan

shutter: the device in the camera and projector which closes off the taking of the picture while a new frame comes into place for the next exposure.

F obturateur

shutter-preferred: a camera in which the shutter speed is manually set and the aperture is automatically controlled.

F priorité à la vitesse

shutter speed: the interval between opening and closing of a camera shutter, measured in fractions of a second.

F vitesse d'obturation

side-effect: any effect – positive or negative – in addition to an intended or anticipated effect. Also referred to as 'unanticipated consequence'.

F effet second

sign: 1. any object or event – especially in action, or the direct result of an action – perceived as having a significance beyond itself; e.g. the blush of embarrassment, the slouched posture of fatigue or boredom; **2.** in semiotics, the association of a concept with an acoustic image or of a significant or designatum (what is referred to) with a sign vehicle or significator (which signifies).

F 1. 2. signe

signal: 1. sign communicated by one person to another in order to indicate that the time and place for a certain action are at hand; **2.** the physical quantity or impulse by which messages are transmitted.

F 1. 2. signal

signal strength: the amplitude of a signal at any particular point in time.

F intensité de signal

signal-to-noise ratio – S/N: at a specified point and for specified conditions, the ratio of the power of the wanted signal to that of the coexistant noise. The ratio is often expressed in decibels.

F rapport signal/bruit

silent film: film prepared or projected without a soundtrack.

F film muet

silk-screen printing: a printing technique that uses silk or a closely woven synthetic fabric stretched on a frame.

F sérigraphie

simulation: 1. the representation of features of the behaviour of a physical or abstract system by the behaviour of another system, e.g. the representation of physical phenomena by means of operations performed by a computer or the representation of a biological system by a mathematical model; **2.** a substitute system used in learning activities which makes the practice and materials as near as possible to the situation in which the learning will be applied; **3.** a learning process which involves pupils as participants in role presentations and/or games simulating real-life situations or environments.

C *dramatization; gaming; role playing*

F 1. 2. simulation; 3. jeu de simulation

simulation game: an instructional exercise or a program that includes all the essentials of both a game and a simulation.

C *gaming*

F jeu de simulation

simulator: an instructional device constructed to give safe and effective practice in handling the essential features of real equipment in a way that would be impossible with the equipment itself.

F simulateur

single concept film: a short motion picture (usually 8 mm or Super 8 mm, spliced in a continuous loop and encased in a cartridge) dealing with a single idea, skill or concept.

C *loop film*

F film monovalent; film court

single-frame exposure: exposing one frame at a time on a motion-picture film, as opposed to continuous exposure (8 frames per second or faster).

F prise de vues image par image

single-frame shooting: see **single-frame exposure**

single framing: see **single-frame exposure**

single system sound: see **sound-on-film**

single track: 1. see **track**; **2.** a common set of programmed materials which all subjects work through, there being no alternative programme, such as in the multiple-track situation.

F 1. monopiste; 2. itinéraire unique

SITE: acronym for Satellite Instructional Television Experiment. Experiment carried out in 1975-76 in India using an ATS-6 satellite for direct broadcast experiments using simple receivers in villages.

F SITE

skill: 1. ability acquired by observation, study or experience in mental and/or physical performance; **2.** an unusual level of performance.

F 1. 2. savoir-faire; capacité; compétence

Skinnerian programme: see **linear programming**

skip branching: a programmed learning technique where not all the frames are worked on. A student, on successful completion of one frame, may be 'skipped' ahead, missing out redundant material.

F programme à sauts

slant track: see **video-format**

slave station: in communication, a station which can be controlled automatically, usually from a distance.

F station asservie

sleep learning: see **hypnopedia**

slide: a transparent image (usually photographic) on film or glass intended for projection; actual image area may vary from micro-image to 3 $\frac{1}{4}$" by 4" (called a lantern slide).

C audioslide

F diapositive; vue fixe

slide changer: a device for positioning a series of slides accurately in a projector. May also be called a carrier, holder or magazine.

F passe-vues; panier

slide projector: a device for projecting slides or transparencies mounted in small frames, usually 2" by 2" (5 cm x 5 cm). Some models have provision for playing accompanying audiorecordings and may have automatic slide advance cued by a signal on the audiotape.

C diascope

F projecteur de diapositives

slide tape: see **tape slide**

slide viewer: a device equipped with a built-in magnifier or rear projection screen for viewing slides.

F visionneuse

slow motion: an effect achieved by running the camera at more frames per second than normal. When projected at normal speed, the motion seems to slow down on the screen.

C fast motion; time lapse

F ralenti

slow-scan television: television in which the video signal is compressed to a bandwidth suitable for transmission over telephone lines. Slow-scan television usually cannot reproduce moving images since it takes several seconds to recreate one picture.

F télévision à balayage lent

smart terminal: see **intelligent terminal**

S/N: see **signal-to-noise ratio**

snow: white spots in a television picture indicating a high random noise level.

F neige

socket: a part of a device with one or more holes for inserting something like a lamp, jack, or fastener, or connecting a plug.

F prise; douille

software: 1. generic term used to refer to materials (e.g., textbooks, films, sound recordings, filmstrips) as opposed to the equipment (hardware) used to play back the materials; **2.** set of programs, processes and rules and possibly documentation relating to operation of data processing systems.

C *categories of software*
  i) basic software – operating system, assembler, compiler, file manager, firmware, service programs;
  ii) software tools or utility software, authoring systems, editor, data base managers, spreadsheets, word processors;
  iii) applications programs or software packages, expert systems;
  iv) courseware: builders, drill and practice programs, intelligent tutor systems, interactive gaming, simulations, tutorial programs

F 1. (software); 2. logiciel

software engineering: the development of the various programming aids, internal programs and routines used to simplify programming and computer operations.

F génie informatique

software package: see **applications software, package**

software tool: see **utility software 2**

solid state: a term denoting various types of electronic components that convey or control electrons within solid materials (e.g. transistors, germanium diodes or magnetic cores).

F à semi-conducteur; transistorisé

sorter: an automatic device used to arrange punched cards or coded filmstrips in a predetermined sequence.

F trieuse

sound: see **combined optical sound; separate magnetic sound; separate optical sound; optical sound track; magnetic sound track; combined magnetic sound**

sound effects – S/FX: studio-created sounds incorporated in a programme to create an illusion of lifelike sounds.

F bruitage

sound fade: a gradual change from audible sound to no sound.

F fondu sonore

sound film: a film with synchronized, accompanying sound.

F film parlant; film sonore

sound head: the light box or magnetic head in a projector at which sound is picked up from optical or magnetic tracks.

F tête de lecture; tête sonore

sound level: the magnitude or amplitude of the signal level on a recorded or reproduced medium by comparison with a reference level.

F niveau sonore

sound-on-film: the recording of motion picture images and sounds simultaneously in synchronization on a single piece of motion picture film. Also referred to as 'simple system sound'.

F film avec piste son incorporée

sound-on-slide: see **audioslide**

sound page: an instructional media system involving separate pages of hardcopy with sound recorded on the back of each page. The page is placed on the top of a recording machine: the learner views the page and hears the sound. Also called 'audiopage'.

C *audiocard*

F page sonore

soundproof: 1. impervious to sound; **2.** to insulate so as to obstruct the passage of sound.

F 1. insonorisé; 2. insonoriser

sound recording: the activity of using a sound recorder and associated audio equipment to record sounds. Includes placement of microphones, mixing sounds, balancing sound levels, but not editing. Includes any dubbing and rerecording.

F enregistrement du son; prise de son

sound slide: see **audioslide**

sound studio: an area specially designed or adapted and equipped to record sound. The studio usually includes an acoustically treated area (with microphones) for the performance and a separate soundproof area for recording equipment and personnel. Also called 'recording studio'.

F studio d'enregistrement

sound track: the sound portion of a motion picture or videotape, although the term is sometimes applied to audiotapes to distinguish between the track containing the sound presentation and the track containing the synchronizing signal.

C *combined/separate magnetic sound; combined/separate optical sound.*

F piste sonore; bande son

source language: the original form in which a programme is prepared prior to processing by the computer.

F langage d'origine; langage source

source programme: a programme written in a source language.

F programme d'origine; programme source

source program: a program written in a source language.

F programme d'origine; programme source

span of apprehension: maximum number of objects which can be apprehended correctly simultaneously.

C *memory span*

F champ d'attention

span of attention: the length of time that an individual can concentrate on a given task without a break.

F durée d'attention

spare parts: replacement parts held in reserve for emergency use.

F pièces de rechange

speaker: see **loudspeaker**

special effects: any shot unobtainable by straightforward motion-picture shooting techniques. Into this category fall shots requiring contour matting, multiple-image montages, split-screens, vignetting, models and the like. The term also applies to explosions, ballistics effects and mechanical effects.

F effets spéciaux; trucage

special effects generator: a device which can electronically combine signals to produce such visual effects as split screens, wipes and sets. May be a separate unit or built into a console.

F générateur d'effets spéciaux

specimen: a sample or unit that is deliberately selected for examination, display or study and is usually chosen as typical of its kind.

F spécimen

speech analyser: electronic device enabling the use of human speech as a direct form of input.

F analyseur de parole

speech synthesizer: an electronic device which can generate human speech as a direct form of output.

C *synthetic speech*

F synthétiseur vocal

speeded-up: see **fast motion**

speeded-up cinematography: see **time-lapse cinematography**

speed-rating system: loosely, the exposure index of a film stock; the largest f-stop of a lens.

F indice de sensibilité

spirit duplicator: a duplication machine in which a paper master is brought into contact with a sheet of paper moistened with duplication fluid.

F duplicateur à alcool

splice: 1. to join two sections of film or tape using a film splicer or splicing block and cement or a special adhesive tape, e.g. hot, dry, or wet; **2.** a butt-joint in a magnetic tape or film held by means of a strip of adhesive material.

F 1. coller; 2. collure

splicer: a device used to join pieces of film or tape together.

F colleuse

split screen: special effect where two or more separate images appear on the screen at the same time.

F image composite; écran dédoublé

spool: see **reel**

spot brightness meter: a light meter which reads reflected light at a very narrow angle of acceptance.

F posemètre

spot exposure meter: see **spot brightness meter**

spot light: type of lighting instrument that produces narrow beams.

F projecteur ponctuel; projecteur à faisceau concentré

spot meter: see **spot brightness meter**

spreadsheet: a utility program that sets up an electronic spreadsheet in which the lines and columns are automatically calculated according to formulas chosen by the user. When one number is changed, the program will automatically change all the sums and multiples that are affected. Also called 'calc'.

C *toolkits; utility software*

F tableur; feuille de calcul électronique

sprocket holes: the perforations in the edges of a film.

F perforations

S-R: stimulus response

F S-R

stage: 1. a motion picture studio; **2.** an auditorium platform for performances.

F 1. plateau; 2. scène

stagehand: see **grip**

stand-by: ready, but waiting for performance or use.

F en attente

standard: 1. an agreed level of performance; **2.** technical specification for material and equipment established by various national and international standards organizations.

F 1. standard; 2. norme technique; standard

standard deviation: a measure of the deviation of a distribution from the arithmetical mean.

F écart type

standardize: to determine, by trying it out on a representative group of population, the norms of performance of a test or a measuring instrument and data on its reliability and validity, and to define the exact procedures to be used in testing and the method of scoring.

F étalonner

standard score: a score having a predetermined mean and standard deviation as opposed to raw score.

F note étalonnée

stencil duplicator: a paper duplicator in which ink is forced through a stencil to make copies.

F duplicateur à stencil

step-by-step: in programmed instruction breakdown of a subject into items.

F décomposition des items

stereo: see **stereophonic**

stereograph: a pair of opaque or transparent images (usually photographic) intended to produce a three-dimensional effect when viewed with stereoscopic equipment.

F stéréogramme

stereophonic: a term describing a sound reproduction system using two, or more, separate, discrete output signals.

F stéréophonique

stereoscope: an optical device with two lenses enabling each eye to see a separate image of essentially the same scene. The combined image seen by the two eyes gives the effect of three dimensions – as in normal binocular vision.

F stéréoscope

stereoscopic system: see **three-dimensional photography**

still frame: individual film or video tape frame held as continuous shot. Also called 'freeze frame'.

C *stop motion*

F image arrêtée

still picture: a picture without motion.

C *motion picture; graphic materials*

F image fixe

still projection: projection of filmstrips, slides or overhead transparencies.

F projection fixe

stock: 1. film raw stock; 2. stock footage; 3. travelling or short-term theatre presentation.

F 1. pellicule; film vierge; 2. métrage de pellicule; 3. répertoire

stock shot: photographic material (still or motion picture), accumulated in advance, which can be used in various programmes.

F plan d'archives

stop bath: a solution in which the chemicals stop the action of developer on exposed film.

F bain d'arrêt

stop lens: see **aperture**

stop motion: freezing a single frame of film or videotape into a still picture for as long as desired.

C *still frame*

F arrêt sur image

stop motion shooting: frame by frame cinematography.

F prise de vues image par image

storage: a functional unit into which data can be placed, in which they can be retained and from which they can be retrieved. This is the term used in the United Kingdom; the United States term is:

C *store*

F mémoire

store: 1. the action of placing data in a storage device; 2. the retention of data in a storage device.

F 1. mettre en mémoire; 2. stocker

storyboard: a series of sketches or pictures which visualize each topic or sequence in an audiovisual material to be produced; generally prepared after the treatment and before the script.

F scénario synoptique; conducteur image

streaming: refers to the various directions of specialization available at the secondary level in some education systems in which students are placed according to interest and ability; for example, general, classic, scientific, technical or vocational. This is the term used in the United Kingdom; the United States term is:

C *tracking; ability grouping*

F répartition en sections; répartition en filières

string: a sequence of alphanumeric characters in the storage of a computer.

F chaîne (de caractères)

stringout: the first step in editing a motion picture, on completion of which all scenes are of original camera length and have been spliced together in proper sequence.

F bout à bout

strip film: see **filmstrip**

stripe: a substandard magnetic track.

F piste étroite

striped film: cine film that carries a narrow strip of magnetic oxide down one edge on which a magnetic track can be recorded.

F film à piste couchée

strobe: illumination device that emits bursts of intense light at timed or regular intervals.
F stroboscope

stroboscopic effect: an unwanted effect created by the speed of objects during filming, e.g. wheels of a moving vehicle appearing to turn backwards.
F effet stroboscopique

structuring of content: a technique allowing programme segmentation into blocks of information or sub-routines of a total programme.
F structuration; structure

structuro-global: relating to a language learning theory initiated by Peter Guberina which emphasizes the structural working of the brain and the global apprehension of units of oral language in situations. The term is associated with a certain type of audio-visual method.
F structuro-global

student: 1. a person engaged in study; 2. a person undergoing a course of study in a university or other institution of higher education.
C *pupil; learner*
F 1. élève; 2. étudiant

student-centred curriculum: a systematic group of courses planned in terms of the student's needs, experience and interests and intended to develop his gifts and potentialities.
C *learner-based education; subject-centred curriculum; teacher-centred method*
F programme (d'études) centré sur l'étudiant*

student-centred learning: learning situation which involves student participation in goal setting.
F apprentissage centré sur l'étudiant*

student contract: particular arrangement whereby an individual student is enabled to handle a learning assignment in his or her own way and at his or her own pace without being rigidly governed by what the rest of the class is doing.
C *learning contract*
F travail individuel sur contrat*

student progress: movement of individuals or of groups through successive levels and forms of education.
F cursus scolaire

student response system: a type of teaching machine consisting of a given number (one per student) of individual multiple-choice units linked to a control console which provides an instantaneous display of the assessment of response. Also referred to as 'response analyser' and 'feedback classroom'.
F analyseur de réponses; station d'interrogation collective.

student-teacher contracting: instructional method which aims at developing the self-management abilities of the student by actively involving him/her in the decision-making process of what he/she learns.
F contrat de travail élève-professeur*

studio: a specially designed area for the production of radio and television programmes, broadcasts and/or recordings, motion pictures and photographs. Studios for production of different media differ significantly. Studios for a specific type of production (e.g. television) also differ considerably among locations and organizations.
C *sound studio*
F studio

study guide: a form of textbook specifically designed for the learner which is often used for written exercises; used in non-formal as well as formal education exercises.
C *teacher's guide*
F livre, cahier d'exercices

subject: 1. a branch of knowledge or study specially arranged and formulated for teaching; 2. an individual whose reactions or responses are studied.
C *subject matter*
F 1. discipline (d'étude); matière; domaine; question; sujet; 2. sujet

subject-centred curriculum: an arrangement of subjects and activities inside the school according to the logic of the subject matter

113

as opposed to the needs of the students' development.

C *student-centred curriculum*

F programme (d'études) centré sur la matière*

subject matter: a body of facts, understanding, processes, skills, values and appreciation related to a specific aspect of human activity and experience.

F matière

subliminal: of a stimulus which is perceived, but below the threshold of awareness.

F subliminal; infraliminaire

sub-routine: a routine that is part of another routine; a set of instructions placed aside as a whole in a specific part of a storage location to be called upon each time it is to be executed.

F sous-programme

subtitles: words, phrases or sentences that appear over a visual to explain, emphasize or clarify a point, or which translate recorded dialogue into a different language.

F sous-titres

success rate: the amount and nature of satisfactory accomplishment.

F taux de réussite

suggestopedy: a pedagogical system initiated by the Bulgarian, G. Lozanov, on the basis of his general theory of suggestology. The aim is to liberate (desuggest) the student from the tension created by social norms and stereotypes in order to increase his/her ability to mobilize reserve capacities (memory, intellectual activities) which are para-conscious.

F suggestopédie

summative evaluation: 1. evaluation intended to provide data for product validation **2.** evaluation oriented to consumer-administrator-teacher criteria and standards.

C *formative evaluation*

F 1. 2. évaluation sommative

super-eight film-S8: motion picture or filmstrip with larger images and smaller sprocket holes than the earlier 8 mm film.

F film super 8

superimposition: the technique of overlapping two or more pictures from different cameras.

F surimpression

superimposed sync pulse: a picture synchronizing pulse recorded on the regular sound track. May be audible or inaudible.

F impulsion de synchronisation

super 8: see **super-eight film**

supplementary film: a film that is offered in addition to the main film to supply additional information.

F film de complément

supply spool: see **delivery spool**

support material: material which provides the basis for a broader and more detailed utilization of the subject over and above accompanying documents specially designed as part of an audiovisual course or programme.

F documents d'appui; documentation complémentaire

switch: 1. a device for making, breaking or changing the connections in an electrical circuit; **2.** to change programmes or techniques.

F 1. commutateur; interrupteur; 2. commuter

switcher: 1. a device which allows selection of the television signals from any of several video sources such as a television camera, videotape recorder, or film chain; the term is sometimes used for similar audio units; **2.** in television, a person who operates a switcher chooses a single picture from between two or more cameras.

F 1. console image; 2. aiguilleur

switching system: an electronic device which controls the interfacing of one or more electronic terminals automatically with information or programme sources from stations in a remote access network.

F système de commutation

syllabus: outline of the elements of an educational course, presented in a logical order, or in one of increasing difficulty.

C *curriculum; contents of education; instructional program*

F programme détaillé

sync: see **synchronization**

sync generator: see **synchronizing pulse generator**

sync mark: see **synchronous mark**

synchronization: 1. the process of locking one element of a system into step with another; **2.** in television, the process of keeping the electron beam of the television receiver or monitor locked to (in synchronization with) the action of the scanning beam of the camera tube – generally called sync; **3.** exact alignment of sound and picture elements.

C *lip synchronization*

F 1. synchronisation; 2. accrochage; 3. synchronisation

synchronizer: table device for simultaneously editing film and soundtrack.

F synchroniseur

synchronizing pulse generator: equipment for regenerating the correct shape and amplitude of the sync signals from a partly mutilated video signal received, for example, from a long distance.

F régénérateur de synchronisation

synchronous: 1. a term applied to cameras or devices which are powered by a common generator; **2.** a mode of operation such that the execution of each instruction or each event is stepwise controlled by a clock signal.

C *asynchronous*

F 1. 2. synchrone

synchronous mark: a mark placed on the working leader of a strip of film to provide a reference point to which other strips of films may be synchronized. Also a mark placed on the frame in which clapsticks come together.

F marque de synchronisation

syndicate group: see **syndicate method**

syndicate method: in the syndicate method, a class is divided into groups of five or six which are required to write a joint report upon either the same or different topics. Each group, called a 'syndicate', works like a small committee instructed to inquire and report on a particular problem.

F travail par équipes*

synergy: a co-operative action where the total effect is greater than the sum of the individual effects.

F synergie

synopsis: brief description of the proposed content of a film or programme.

F synopsis

synthetic speech: human speech simulated by artificial means.

F parole synthétique

syntagmatic: see **paradigmatic**

F syntagmatique

systems analysis: the techniques of identifying components and interrelationships of a system and of identifying and studying problems in system design and functioning.

F analyse systémique

systems approach in education: method facilitating intervention in any given educational situation or organization (a lesson, programme, class, school, out-of-school activities, instructional system, educational broadcasting, etc.). Each situation or organization is considered as a system in itself, and its interaction with the environment is outlined. The procedure is based on a comprehensive and thorough description of the 'system' and its components, delineating the objectives, identifying the critical points, determining possible points for starting action and should result in developing strategies which take into account identified and supposed interactions between various elements, institutional levels and those who participate in the activities of the 'system'.

C *entry point; systems regulation; educational technology*

F approche systémique en éducation

systems regulation: in an education system, systems regulation is a process aimed at improving the operation and the outcomes of the system by adjusting action to aims and by harmonizing each component of the system with the system as a whole and with each of the other components and functions.

C *systems approach in education*

F régulation (de système)

S8: see **super-eight film**

T

tachistoscope: an apparatus for the very brief exposure of still visual stimuli used in the study of learning, attention and perception.

F tachistoscope

tag: one or more characters attached to a data item in a computer as a means of identification.

F étiquette

take-up spool: the spool or reel upon which the tape or film is wound during the recording or reproducing process.

C *reel*

F bobine réceptrice

talking book: a complete book recorded either on audiotape or on an audiodisc intended particularly for use by the visually handicapped.

F livre sonore; livre parlant; livre parlé

tape: 1. a thin strip or ribbon of material used as a linear storage medium. The tape may be reeled, spooled or contained in a cartridge or a cassette; it is usually magnetic, but sometimes paper; 2. to make a tape recording.

C *audio tape; video tape; leader (tape); magnetic tape*

F 1. bande; ruban; 2. enregistrer

tape cassette: a plastic container with a supply and take-up reel to allow easy placement and removal from a tape recorder.

F cassette

tape deck: a tape player without loudspeakers, usually fitted into a carrel or console and connected into a system.

F platine

tape format: the particular tape thickness, width, track configuration, speed, synchronizing pulse, container, etc., that distinguishes or identifies it.

F format de bande

tape library: an organized collection of tape recorded programmes.

F magnétothèque; bandothèque

tape loop: a length of tape joined head-to-tail for repetitive operation without rewinding.

F boucle (de bande magnétique)

tape recorder: see **audiotape recorder; videotape recorder**

tape/slide: a set of slides accompanied by an audiotape containing a sound track and sometimes a signal to project the next slide in the sequence Also called 'slidetape'.

F montage sonorisé

116

tape speed: the speed at which a tape moves past a fixed point.
F vitesse de défilement de bande

target audience: see **target population**

target population: that portion of the total learner population selected for exposure to a specific unit of instruction. This group is generally identified in terms of certain common social and/or learning characteristics.
F population cible

task analysis: in learning, an identification of the main skills to be acquired by the learner and the breakdown of these skills into their basic components. It indicates the performance and knowledge requirements for a particular skill.
F analyse des tâches

task force: a temporary organization or team made up of people with appropriate expertise, brought together to investigate and recommend a solution for a specific problem or proposal.
F groupe d'intervention; équipe spéciale

taxonomy (of educational objectives): structured set of educational objectives arranged according to a set of given criteria.
C *affective domain*
F taxonomie (des objectifs pédagogiques)

TBC: see **time-base corrector**

teacher-centred method: method of teaching that stresses the activities of teachers in directing learning, such as the lecture method and recitation.
C *student centred curriculum; subject centred curriculum*
F pédagogie centrée sur l'enseignant*

teacher(s) centre: organized centre for teachers to meet, discuss, find resources and develop materials, consult documentation.
F centre pédagogique

teacher's guide: an explanatory handbook for teacher use issued with a textbook or other teaching material. Sometimes contains a 'key' or answers to questions and problems in the textbook, or film, etc.
C *study guide*
F livre du maître

teacher's notes: see **teacher's guide**

teaching aids: see **instructional aids**

teaching film: see **instructional film**

teaching machine: a device which presents programmed materials and provides for reinforcement.
C *audiotutorial method; auto-instructional device; self-study materials*
F machine à enseigner

teaching materials: see **instructional materials**

team teaching: a type of instructional organization in which two or more teachers are given joint responsibility for all or a significant part of the instruction of the same group of students; the team may include such assistants as auxiliary aids or student teachers.
F enseignement en équipe

technical adviser: in media production, a person assigned by a client, or an authority hired by a studio to provide technical information.
F conseiller technique

technology: see **instructional technology; appropriate technology; educational technology**

telebroadcasting: see **broadcasting**

telecine: equipment for projection of film and slides for television.
F télécinéma

telecommunication: the transmission of information from one point to another by wire, radio or other electromagnetic systems.
F télécommunication

telecommunications satellite: see **communications satellite**

117

teleconference: a technique using a telephone conference call and related amplification equipment to allow individuals or groups at different locations to participate in a larger group conference; may also include video display devices such as electronic blackboards and other telewriting devices (video conference).

F téléconférence

telecopier: a device used in facsimile transmission for producing copies of documents at a distance.

F télécopieur

telelecture: an arrangement which brings a teacher or any lecturer to the classroom audience via regular telephone lines enabling the speaker to participate in several classes simultaneously at different locations; the installation may provide two-way communication between speaker and audience.

F télé-leçon*

teleinformatics: combined use of telecommunications and computer techniques in order to allow remote access to computer networks.

C *information systems; telematics*

F téléinformatique

telematics: contracted from *tele*communications and infor*matics*; term of French origin created to describe the grouping of computer and telecommunication technologies and equipment in one integrated system.

C *teleinformatics*

F télématique

telephone instruction: an instructional technique using telephone communication; includes tele-class, telelectures and telephone school-home instruction.

F enseignement par téléphone*

telephone school-home instruction: an arrangement which provides for two-way communication between a home-bound student and those in the classroom.

F enseignement par téléphone*

118

telephoto lens: a special lens attached to a camera for shooting distant objects.

F téléobjectif

teleprinter: a device resembling a typewriter which is connected to a telegraphic circuit. It can be used to transmit or receive and print out data. Also called 'teletypewriter' in the United States.

F téléimprimeur

teleprocessing: any processing of data using a combination of computers and data transmission facilities.

F télétraitement

teleprompter: equipment for showing scripts to a speaker while he is looking at the camera lens.

F télésouffleur

telerecording: see **transfer 1**

telesoftware: generic term for programs that can be loaded from one computer to another at a distance using videotex.

C *downloading*

F télélogiciel

Télétel: name of the French videotex system.

F Télétel

teletex: universal worldwide telecommunications standard enabling intercommunication between text terminals, including telex, word processors and some computers.

C *word processor*

F télétex

teletext: one-way data service using the spare transmission capacity of broadcast television signals to display pages of alphanumerical or graphical information on domestic television sets; also called broadcast videotex.

C *vertical interval; viewdata; videotex*

F télétext(e)

teletypewriter: see **teleprinter**

television: see **broadcast; cable television; school television; slow-scan television; open-circuit television; closed-circuit television; community antenna television; educational television; instructional television**

television monitor: see **monitor**

television projector: an electronic device that projects television images onto a screen, usually for viewing by groups of people.

F projecteur d'images télévisées; téléprojecteur

telewriter: a device which transmits (live or in real time) and displays handwriting and simple drawings over telephone lines. The device is often used in telelectures.

C *facsimile*

F téléscripteur; appareil de télé-écriture

telewriting: the use of telephone lines for live transmission of alphanumerical or graphic information (handwriting or drawing) for display on a television monitor or similar device.

F téléécriture

telex: an automatic exchange service provided for communication between subscribers using telegraphic equipment such as a teleprinter.

F télex

TELIDON: see **information network system**

tender: a formal request for bids on equipment, materials or services.

F appel d'offres

terminal: 1. the connectors, transformers and converter (if necessary) on the cable subscriber's set; **2.** a device by which data can be sent to or received from a computer system; for exemple, cathode-ray tube display, a graphics tablet, or a teletypewriter.

C *intelligent terminal*

F terminal

terminal behaviour: what the learner must be able to do or perform when he is demonstrating his mastery of the objective.

F comportement terminal

terminal objective: a statement specifying the skills and concepts the learner is expected to have acquired as a result of exposure to a particular sequence of instruction.

F objectif terminal

terrestrial station: see **earth station**

test: see **prognosis test; achievement test; proficiency test; formative evaluation; development testing; pre-test; post-test; final test; summative evaluation**

test card: see **test chart**

test chart: chart displaying geometrical patterns and fine details which is transmitted on television at specific times and enables the checking and adjustment of television receivers for picture size, symmetry, contrast, brightness, focus, definition and linearity. This is the term used in the United Kingdom; the term used in the United States is:

C *test pattern*

F mire

test film/tape: a special film or tape for evaluating the technical performance of equipment.

F film test; bande test

test pattern: see **test chart**

text processing: a computer procedure providing the capacity of editing and formatting text quickly and efficiently.

C *word processor; teletex*

F traitement de texte

textbook: a book dealing with a definite subject of study, systematically arranged, intended for use at a specified level of instruction, and used as a principal source of study material for a given course.

C *handbook; workbook*

F manuel scolaire; livre de classe

T-group: technique used in groups dynamics. The 'T' stands for training, the purpose being to increase students' sensitivity to how others perceive their behaviour and to develop diagnostic skills with reference to interpersonal behaviour. Also referred to as 'sensitivity group'.

F groupe de base; (groupe de sensibilisation)

thematic approach

F centre d'intérêt

thermal copier: a copying machine which exposes and develops images by infrared heat on special films and papers.

F thermocopieur

thermal process: a way of making paper or transparent copies of material with a machine and materials that rely on heat.

F procédé thermique; thermocopie

thesaurus: 1. a lexicon where words are grouped by ideas; 2. a structured collection of terms which is used to index documents.

F 1. dictionnaire analogique; 2. thesaurus

threading: see **lacing**

three-dimensional photography: photography having the illusion of depth and dimension. Also referred to as '3-D' and 'stereoscopic system'.

F photographie en relief; (procédé stéréoscopique)

threshold: 1. in psychology of perception, minimum value of a stimulus capable of producing a perceptible effect. Absolute threshold: minimum stimulus. Differential threshold: minimum difference between two stimuli, for which it is possible to perceive a variation; 2. in systems approach, the minimum value of a component which may show variation in terms of interaction or effect of an educational activity.

F 1. 2. seuil

throat microphone: see **Lavallier microphone**

tilt: move the camera vertically up or down.

F panoramique vertical

time-base corrector – TBC: an electronic device for improving the technical characteristics of a television signal from portable or non-broadcast type equipment so as to meet broadcast or high-quality standards.

F correcteur de base de temps

time channel: see **channel capacity**

time-lapse cinematography: the exposing of individual. motion-picture frames at a much slower rate than normal, for projection at normal speed; the method accelerates action. Also called 'speeded-up cinematography'.

C *slow motion*

F accéléré

time sharing: 1. the operation of a computer and its peripheral devices in a manner which permits many users to use the system simultaneously (or apparently simultaneously) and in such a way that each is (or can be) completely unaware of the use of the system by others; 2. the use of a device such as a studio or broadcast facility for two or more purposes during the same overall time interval, accomplished by interspersing component actions in time.

F 1. partage de temps; 2. en temps partagé

timing: see **grading**

title: see **main title; credits**

title caption: 1. the name or designation of a film; 2. any inscription contained in a film for the purpose of conveying information about the film, its message or its story to the viewer.

F 1. titre; 2. carton titre

tone: a steady, one frequency audio signal.

F tonalité

toolkit: colloquial term for 'utility software 2'.

F boîte à outils (logiciels)

topic: an identifiable segment of a unit of instruction.

F sujet; thème de travail

topic network: diagrammatic representation of the relationships between topics in a portion of curriculum or subject matter.

F réseau thématique

touch screen terminal: a terminal with a screen which is sensitive to touch.

F écran tactile

track: 1. the discrete path or area along a film, videotape, computer tape or audiotape on which a signal or data are recorded. An audiotape may have a number of tracks (usually 1, 2, 4, or 8) recorded upon it and these are described with such terms as: full track; single track; half-track; four-track; and eight-track; **2.** to keep account of various elements in a procedure; **3.** a pattern of subject organization or of course sequences in a school.

F 1. piste; 2. répertorier; 3. section

tracking: 1. an arrangement by which the frequency of resonance of one of a number of gauged tuned circuits is maintained at a constant difference from that of other circuits; **2.** see **streaming**; **3.** see **travelling**.

F 1. (dispositif d') accord décalé; 2. répartition en sections; répartition en filières; 3. prise de vues en travelling

trailer: 1. set of short extracts from a film to be exhibited to advise in advance; **2.** a length of a leader film/tape at the end of a motion picture film or a tape. Also called 'tail leader'.

F 1. bande de lancement; bande annonce; 2. amorce de fin; queue de bande

training: systematic practice in the performance of a skill.

C *drill*

F training

transcribe: to copy data from one storage medium to another with or without some form of translation. See also 'transfer 2'.

F recopier; transcrire

transcoder: an electronic system for transforming a TV signal from one colour standard to another.

F transcodeur

transducer: a device for converting electrical into magnetic or mechanical energy or vice versa.

F transducteur

transfer: 1. film copy of television picture tube image or vice versa; also recorded tape signal onto another tape, or onto negative film sound track; **2.** to convert from one medium to another; **3.** process whereby characters can be transferred onto a page from a plastic sheet – all the page setter has to do is to press lightly on the sheet and thus transfer the character required.

F 1. transfert; 2. transférer; 3. transfert

transformer: electric device for changing the voltage and current of an alternating circuit.

F transformateur

translate: to convert data from one language to another language without affecting the meaning.

F traduire

transmission copy: film copy to be broadcast.

F copie antenne

transmit: 1. to move data from one location to another, such as by reading or sensing the data at the source, moving it over a communication channel and storing it at the destination; **2.** to send out a signal either by radio waves or over a wire line.

F 1. transmettre; 2. émettre

transmitter: the broadcast equipment (in radio or television) necessary to generate, modulate and transmit signals through space from an aerial for reception within a predictable coverage area.

F émetteur

transparency: a generic term for visual materials intended to be viewed using transmitted rather than reflected light. The term includes slides and overhead transparencies.

F transparent

transponder: relay transmitter that shifts the frequency of relayed signals, without intermediate demodulation and remodulation.

F transpondeur; répéteur

travelling: in cinematography, following the action by moving the camera and/or its entire support. This is the term used in the United Kingdom; the United States terms are:

C *tracking; trucking*

F travelling

tray: a U.S. term for a slide magazine.

F panier

treatment: in media production, a written detailed statement to the media producer explaining the purpose, the audience for whom the production is designed, the time and cost parameters for producing, the type of material to be produced (i.e. film, slidetape, etc.), the overall instructional strategy and sequence to be followed, the objectives to be met, the content to be included and the story line, characters, setting, tone and approach.

C *synopsis*

F descriptif

treble: the upper range of frequencies in the audio spectrum.

F aigus

trial-and-error learning: finding out the best way to reach a desired result or a correct solution by trying out one or more ways or means and by noting and eliminating errors or causes of failure.

F essais et erreurs

trick film: film in which objects appear, change or disappear without apparent agency.

F film de trucage

tripod: an adjustable three-legged camera support, often braced and equipped with wheels.

F trépied de caméra

trolley: a small, wheeled stand or cart for holding and moving equipment.

F chariot

trucking: see **travelling**

tuner: an electronic device which receives and selects radio or television signals from an aerial and converts them into audio and/or television frequency signals which are sent to an amplification component or unit. Tuners may be built into receivers or may be separate units.

F (tuner); syntoniseur

tuning: adjustment of an electric circuit to obtain the desired effect.

F accord; réglage

turntable: a circular plate rotated by a driving mechanism and supporting a disc which is being used for reproduction or recording.

F platine; plateau

tutor: 1. a member of the instructional staff who instructs students usually on a one-to-one basis; **2.** in open learning systems, a person who mediates between learner and course materials; **3.** a teacher who has special responsibility for advising students.

C *facilitator*

F 1. tuteur; 2. moniteur; tuteur; 3. tuteur; conseiller; professeur principal

tutorial: an instructional session between a teacher and a single student (or a small group of students) in which face-to-face teaching and discussion can take place, often based on written material.

F leçon particulière; répétition; travaux dirigés

tutorial mode: 1. personal face-to-face teaching in a small tutorial group, the discussion between teacher or tutor and students often being based on written work by one or more of the students; **2.** in CAI, a mode of operation in which the computer determines the next sequence after analysis of the student's answer − as opposed to conversational mode.

C *conversational mode*

F 1. travail en direction d'études; 2. mode tutoriel

tutorial program/software: courseware that questions the learner, evaluates his/her responses and provides suggestions to aid him/her in knowledge and skill development.

C *drill and practice program; intelligent tutoring system*

F logiciel tuteur; tutoriel

tutoring: an activity in which instruction is provided to an individual learner by direct interaction in person with a teacher.

F tutorat; direction d'études

TV reader: see **overhead camera**

tweeter: a small loudspeaker, usually part of a speaker system, used to reproduce high-frequency sound.

F haut-parleur d'aigus

U

UHF: ultra high frequency.

F UHF; ondes décimétriques

U-matic: see **video format**

unanticipated consequence: see **side effect**

unconditional branch: a branch or jump out of the normal execution sequence in a computer programme which is executed regardless of conditions.

F saut inconditionnel

unconditional transfer: see **unconditionel branch**

underexposure: any adjustment of equipment which results in an insufficient amount of light reaching film exposed in a camera or a printer.

F sous-exposition

unidirectional microphone: a microphone which has a greater sensitivity to sound pickup in one direction than others.

F microphone unidirectif

unit: instructional unit, see **module 3**

university of the air: a university using mainly broadcasts as the medium of instruction to reach its students.

C *open university*

F université des ondes

university at a distance: university providing distance teaching for students, generally in employment, who only occasionally attend the university.

F téléuniversité; enseignement universitaire à distance

university without walls: university providing a considerable part of its teaching outside the university buildings and using mostly learning-at-a-distance methods.

C *open university; distance education*

F université sans murs

up-grading (course): course designed to prepare students or trainees for more highly qualified positions.

C *further training*

F cours de formation complémentaire

uplink: the device that sends signals to a satellite.

C *downlink*

F liaison terre-espace; liaison ascendante

up-time: time during which a machine is available for use or is used, and is not known to be malfunctioning.

F temps utilisable

user friendly: a term that describes computer hardware or software products or a com-

123

puter system that are easy for a non-specialist to understand and use.

F convivial

utilities: see **utility program 1**

utility program software: 1. program or set of programs prepared by the computer manufacturer generally as part of the operating system to perform routine operations such as sorting, indexing, assembling or merging. Also called 'service programs"; **2.** generic term to designate a category of general purpose applications programs such as spread-sheets, database managers and word processors, which can be used for instructional purposes and programs used to create other software such as graphic editors, courseware editors, authoring systems. Also known as 'software tools'.

C *applications program; toolkit*

F 1. programmes de service; utilitaires; 2. outils logiciels; logiciels outils

V

validation: the demonstration of the effectiveness of instructional products/systems by use of appropriate summative evaluation techniques.

C *field testing; developmental testing; learner verification*

F validation

validity: ability of a test or measuring instrument to measure what it claims to measure, e.g. ability of an intelligence test to really deal with intelligence and not with knowledge acquired through schooling.

C *reliability; differential sensitivity*

F validité

vanishing: the removal of more and more of the components of a specific chain of responses. The term is often used synonymously with fading, although the process of withdrawing prompts is not strictly parallel to the above process.

F évanouissement

variable focal length: see **zoom lens**

variance: 1. the difference between what has been expected or predicted and what actually occurs; **2.** extent to which measures deviate from the mean.

F 1. 2. variance

VCR: video cassette recorder: see **videotape recorder**

F magnétoscope à cassettes; cassettoscope

VDU: see **visual display unit**

velour paper: paper with a velvet-like backing used in preparing feltboard display materials.

C *flocking*

F papier floqué

version: see **original version**

vertical interval: the black border at the top and/or bottom of television frames used for synchronization and for transmitting teletext, captions and other coded information.

F intervalle de suppression de trame

VHF: very high frequency.

F VHF; ondes métriques

VHS: see **video format**

video: a term designating devices of communications systems used in origination, transmission or reception of visual information.

C *audio*

F vidéo

videocassette recorder—VCR: a device for visual recording (especially of television programmes) on to magnetic tape contained in plastic cassettes, as opposed to 'videotape recorder–VTR'.

F magnétoscope; magnétoscope de salon

videoconference: see **teleconference**

videodisc: a disc on which are recorded video and audio signals for television use. A videodisc requires a videoplayer compatible with the videodisc.

F vidéodisque

videodisc recording: see **videodisc**

video format: the technical considerations or standards that determine broadcast, reception, recording and reproduction compatibility and quality. Tape format may be ¼", ½", ¾", 1" or 2" width. Tape may be on or in an open reel, cassette or cartridge. Tape recording may be on slant or helical, transverse or longitudinal tracks. Colour may be encoded according to the NTSC, SECAM or PAL system. Beta or Betamax, Video 2000 (V-2000), VHS (video home system) and U-Matic denote proprietary composite recording and playback systems.

F format vidéo

video frequency: a frequency band extending from very low to very high frequencies, for example to several megacycles per second; more particularly, the frequency of the spectral components of the picture signal.

F vidéofréquence

videogame: a programmed video cassette which, used with an interactive console, permits the playing of games of psychomotor and/or cognitive skill.

F jeu vidéo

video monitor: see **monitor**

F écran de contrôle vidéo

video player: an electronic device which can playback images and sound from a video recording, either a videotape or videodisc. It does not record.

F vidéolecteur; lecteur vidéo

videophone: see **picture-phone**

F visiophone

video record: see **videodisc**

video signal: see **signal**

video system: see **video format**

videotape: a magnetic tape on which video and audio signals may be recorded.

C *video format*

F vidéobande; bande magnétoscopique

videotape recorder – VTR: equipment for recording and reproducing video and audio signals on magnetic tape, as opposed to a video cassette recorder-VCR.

C *video format*

F magnétoscope à bandes

videotex: 1. internationally agreed generic term for all cable and broadcast alphanumeric and graphic data systems using domestic video displays often incorrectly referred to as videotext; **2.** designates an interactive data service system, sometimes wrongly called interactive video, enabling the user to have access to alphanumeric and graphic information stored in a central computer on a domestic television set through a telephone network or cable link as opposed to one-way broadcast transmission (teletext).

C *teletext; information system*

F 1. vidéotex; 2. vidéotex; vidéographie interactive

videotext: 1. improprerly used for teletext; **2.** name of German or Swiss teletext system.

F vidéotext

view angle: the horizontal and vertical angle covered in the action field by a camera.

F champ de visée

viewdata: the original name for the PRESTEL service in the United Kingdom; see **teletext**.
C *information network system*
F (viewdata)

viewer: a device for enlarging film, filmstrips or slide images for individuals or small group use.
C *slide viewer*
F visionneuse

viewfinder: 1. the device on a camera by which one can view the field of action; **2.** small TV monitor on a television camera.
F 1. 2. viseur

viewing: 1. videotape playback; **2.** screening a film or other projected material.
F 1. 2. visionnement

visual aids: aids to communication which utilize the sense of sight, e.g. books, diagrams, flip charts, film, fixed models.
F auxiliaires visuels

visual display: display on a terminal unit of alphanumerical or graphical data.
F affichage

visual display unit—VDU: an input-output terminal for a computer giving a visual display of data by means of a cathode-ray tube.
F visu (n.f.); visuel; terminal à écran de visualisation

visual literacy: learned ability to interpret visual messages accurately and to create such messages.
C *media education*
F éducation visuelle

visual scanner: see **optical scanner**

visuals: collective term to include all materials such as graphics, pictures, motion pictures, etc.
F éléments visuels

vocational training: the systematic development of the attitudes, knowledge and skill pattern required for a job.
F formation professionnelle

voltage regulator: a manual or automatic device for providing constant electrical voltage for equipment.
F régulateur de tension

volume indicator: a device measuring the average amplitude of an electric signal which represents speech. Also called 'voice unit indicator'.
F V.U. mètre; vumètre

VTR: see **videotape recorder**

VU meter: volume unit meter: see **volume indicator**

V-2000: see **video format**

W

wall chart: see **chart**

waveguide: hollow metallic tube used to convey very high frequency waves.
F guide d'ondes

wave length: 1. measurable distance between wave points of like phase; **2.** used to designate the position of specific broadcast stations on a tuning dial.
F 1. 2. longueur d'onde

weather proofed: specially made, treated or enclosed for outdoor use.
F protégé contre les intempéries

weighted: having been assigned numbers indicating the relative importance or values of each of the items entering into the computation of a composite or statistic.
F pondéré

wet carrel: see **carrel**

wide-angle lens: a camera which permits a wider view of a subject and its surroundings than would be obtained by a normal lens from the same position.

F objectif grand angulaire

widescreen: screen with an aspect ratio whose width is greater in relation to its height than for the traditional format (3 to 2) of films.

F écran large

wipe: an optical effect in motion pictures or television in which a new scene seems to push the previous scene off the screen.

F enchaîné

wired television: see **cable television**

wireless: 1. term for radio in the United Kingdom; **2.** relating to radiotelegraphy, radiotelephony or radio.

F 1. 2. radio

wireless loop: a wire around the perimeter of a room or space to radiate a signal into special headphones.

F boucle magnétique

wireless microphone: a microphone which contains a small, short-distance transmitter and thus eliminates the use of a microphone cable.

F micro-émetteur

woofer: a loudspeaker designed to reproduce very low frequencies.

F haut-parleur de graves

word: a sequence or group of characters such as bits, treated as a unit and capable of being stored in one computer storage location.

F mot

word processing program: computer software for handling text material. Sometimes called 'word processor'.

F logiciel de traitement de texte

word processor—WP: 1. an integrated system incorporating a keyboard, VDU, microcomputer, store and printer that enables a text to be composed, edited, stored and printed in hard copy form; **2.** see 'word processing program'.

C *office automation*

F 1. unité de traitement de texte; 2. logiciel de traitement de texte

workbook: a study or learning guide for learners, often related to a particular textbook or to several textbooks; may contain exercises, problems, practice materials, directions for use, space for recording answers, and, frequently, means of evaluating work done.

C *handbook; textbook*

F livre d'exercices

workprint: an inexpensive copy of original motion-picture footage used during editing, and to which the original film is matched before duplicate copies are made.

F copie de travail

worksheet: a single page of workbook material for learners.

C *handouts*

F feuille d'exercices

workshop: 1. meeting that offers opportunities for persons with a common interest or problem to meet with specialists to receive first-hand knowledge and to undertake practical work; **2.** an intensive training course for adults of short duration and involving production of some kind; **3.** a maintenance or repair room.

F 1. 2. 3. atelier

world rights: the rights of the owner of copyright in a given work to authorize its use throughout the world.

F droits d'utilisation dans le monde entier

wow: a low-frequency fluctuation in the pitch of a transmitted or reproduced sound, usually caused by the regular variation in the angular velocity or speed of a turntable.

F pleurage

WP: see **word processor**

write: to record data in a storage device or on a data medium in a computer, e.g. place data on a magnetic tape.

F écrire

X

xerography: the activity of copying using a positive-to-positive electrostatic process utilising a light-sensitive, selenium-coated plate or drum which carries a positive electrostatic charge.

F xérographie; photocopie électrostatique

X-ray cinematography: see **cineradiography**

x-y plotter: see **graph plotter**

Z

zoom: a very slow changing of the focal length of the lens which has the effect of dollying in or out, but without moving the camera. On the screen, the image is progressively magnified as the action field becomes smaller (zoom in) or smaller as the lens zooms out.

F zoom; travelling optique

zoom lens: a camera lens of variable magnification (focal length) which permits a smooth change of subject coverage between distance and close-up without changing the camera position.

F objectif à focale variable; zoom

Bibliography

Aitchison, Jean. *Unesco thesaurus.* Paris, Unesco, 1977. 2 v.
Association for Educational Communications and Technology. *College learning resources programs: a book of readings.* Washington, D.C., 1977. 83 p.
Association for Educational Communications and Technology. *Educational technology: a glossary of terms.* Washington, D.C., 1979.
Canada. Department of Communications. Educational Technology Branch. *Educational technology glossary.* Ottawa, 1975.
Charp, S.; Hines, I.J. *Telecommunications fundamentals.* Arlington, VA, Bell of Pennsylvania, Bell Atlantic Company, 1985. 91 p.
Diamant, Lincoln. *The broadcast communications dictionary.* New York, Hastings House, 1974. 128 p.
Ellington, H.; Harris, D. *Dictionary of instructional technology.* London, Kogan Page; New York, Nichols Pub. Co., 1986. 189 p.
European Broadcasting Union. Technical Centre. *E.B.U. vocabulary for television tape-recording.* Brussels, 1972-73. (1st ed. December 1972, 131 p., 2nd ed. July 1973, 73 p., 1st complement November 1973, 8 p.)
Focal encyclopedia of photography. New York, Focal Press, 1965. 2 v.
Frank, Helmar, et al. *Begriffswörterbuch der kybernetischen Pädagogik.* Hannover, Heumann Schroedel, 1973. 234 p. (Paderborner Forschungsberichte, 1.)
Gibson, Janice T. *Psychology for the classroom.* Englewood Cliffs, N.J., Prentice-Hall, 1976. 563 p.
Harrod, Leonard Montagne. *The librarian's glossary of terms used in librarianship, documentation and the book crafts, and reference book.* 4th rev. ed. Aldershot, United Kingdom, Gower, 1982. 903 p.
Hills, P.J., ed. *A dictionary of education.* London, Routledge & Kegan Paul, 1982. 284 p.
International Electrotechnical Commission. Recording and reproduction of sound and video. *In: International electrotechnical vocabulary.* Geneva, 1975.
Jung, U., ed. *Das Sprachlabor: Möglichkeiten und Grenzen technischer Medien im Unterricht.* Königstein, Federal Republic of Germany, Scriptor/KNO, 1978. 200 p.
Kemp, Jerold E. *Planning and producing audiovisual materials.* San Francisco, Calif., Chandler Pub. Co., 1968.
Lewy, Arieh, ed. *Handbook of curriculum evaluation.* Paris, Unesco; New York, Longman, 1977. 306 p.
Meadows, A.J.; Gordon, M.; Singleton, A. *Dictionary of computing and new information technology.* 2nd ed. London, Kogan Page; New York, Nichols Pub. Co., 1984. 229 p.
Mehrens, William A.; Lehmann, Irvin J. *Measurement and evaluation in education and psychology.* New York, Holt, Rinehart and Winston, 1973.
Mercer, John, comp. *Glossary of film terms.* Rev. ed. Carbondale, Ill., University Film Association, Department of Cinema and Photography, Southern Illinois University, 1979.
Page, G. Terry; Thomas, J.B. *International dictionary of education.* London, Kogan Page; New York, Nichols Pub. Co., 1977. 381 p.
Poutnam, John F.; Chismore, W. Dale, comps. *Standard terminology for curriculum and instruction in local and state school systems.* Washington, D.C., National Center for Educational Statistics, 1970. 331 p. (State educational records and report series. Handbook, VI) (ERIC microfiche ED 048 510.)
Rowntree, D. *A dictionary of education.* London, Harper & Row, 1981. 354 p.
Schröder, K.; Finkenstädt, T., eds. *Reallexikon der englischen Fachdidaktik.* Darmstadt, Federal Republic of Germany, Wissenschaftliche Buchgesellschaft, 1977. XXII, 393 p.
Seibert, Ivan N. *A handbook of standard terminology and a guide for recording and reporting information about educational technology.* Washington, D.C., Association for Educational Communications and Technology; National Center for Educational Statistics, 1975. 178 p. (State educational records and reports series. Hand-

book, X) (ERIC microfiches ED 118091 and ED 125066.)

Sippl, C.J. *Computer dictionary.* 4th ed. Indianapolis, IN, Howard W. Sams, 1985. 562 p.

Titmus, Colin, et al. *Terminology of adult education/Terminologie de l'éducation des adultes/Terminología de la educación de adultos.* Paris, Unesco, 1979. 154 p. (Ibedata)

Unesco. *Evaluation terms: Unesco glossary.* Paris, 1979. 13 p. (BEP. 79/WS/8) (Unesco microfiche 80s0584.)

Unwin, Derick; McAleese, Ray, eds. *The encyclopaedia of educational media communications and technology.* London, Macmillan, 1978. 800 p.

Abbréviations

C = désigne un corrélat qui permet de cerner le terme.
A = traduction anglaise.
() = les entrées entre parenthèses n'ont pas d'équivalant dans l'autre langue.
* = une traduction approchée.

A

AA: voir **laboratoire audio-actif**

AAC: voir **laboratoire audio-actif comparatif**

abandon (scolaire – des études): situation des élèves ou des étudiants qui abandonnent leurs études avant d'avoir terminé une année scolaire ou un cycle d'études.

C *taux d'abandon*

A dropping out

abstract: voir **résumé analytique**

accéléré: prise de vues à une vitesse très inférieure à la normale, les images étant ensuite projetées à vitesse normale. Ce procédé permet d'accélérer la représentation d'un mouvement.

C *ralenti*

A time-lapse cinematography

accès: opération consistant à ranger une information dans une mémoire d'ordinateur, ou à l'en extraire.

C *terminal*

A access

accès automatisé à l'information: mode d'accès à une banque de données en composant un code sur un clavier ou un cadran.

A dial access information retrieval

accès direct: mode d'écriture ou de lecture des données indépendamment de leur emplacement dans une mémoire d'ordinateur.

A direct access

accès séquentiel: mode d'écriture ou de lecture des données dans des conditions qui dépendent à la fois de leur emplacement et des données extraites ou rangées auparavant dans la mémoire d'ordinateur.

A sequential access; serial access

accessoire: 1. objet et élément mobile d'un décor de théâtre, de cinéma ou de télévision; **2.** pièce d'équipement complémentaire d'un appareil audio-visuel; **3.** équipement pouvant être relié ou connecté à un équipement principal ou utilisé avec lui dans un système d'ordinateur.

A 1. properties; 2. accessory; attachment; 3. peripheral equipment

accessoiriste: technicien responsable de la fourniture de tous les objets et éléments mobiles (accessoires) nécessaires à une mise en scène, ainsi que de leur disposition sur le plateau.

A property man

accord: action de régler un circuit en vue d'obtenir le maximum ou le minimum d'une grandeur spécifiée telle que courant, tension, impédance, réactance, etc.

A tuning

accord décalé (dispositif d'): dispositif permettant de faire varier les fréquences d'accord de divers circuits faisant partie d'un même ensemble à commande unique en maintenant toujours entre elles les mêmes différences.

A tracking

accrochage: verrouillage du faisceau électronique d'un récepteur ou d'un moniteur pour qu'il demeure synchronisé avec le faisceau de balayage du tube de caméra.

A synchronisation

accumulateur: 1. dispositif qui emmagasine et restitue de l'énergie électrique; **2.** registre temporaire, situé dans l'unité arithmétique d'un ordinateur, qui permet de conserver des informations en vue d'effectuer toutes sortes d'opérations arithmétiques ou autres.

A 1. 2. accumulator

acétate (film, feuille, rouleau – d'): matière plastique transparente utilisée pour la fabrication des pellicules, des transparents pour rétroprojecteur et des cellulos d'animation.

A acetate (film, sheet, roll)

133

achromatique: qualifie un objectif spécialement conçu pour minimiser l'aberration chromatique.
A achromatic

acquis: 1. capital des connaissances, des expériences, des compétences et des qualités acquises et non innées; **2.** niveau de performance atteint par un sujet dans un domaine donné.
A 1. background; 2. achievement

acquisition: 1. document acquis par une bibliothèque ou un centre de ressources éducatives pour enrichir son fonds; **2.** acquisition de données: processus de collecte, généralement automatique, d'information en vue de leur traitement dans un ordinateur; **3.** connaissance qui vient augmenter les notions déjà assimilées par l'élève dans le cadre d'un programme d'études.
A 1. accession(s); 2. data acquisition; 3. knowledge; attainment

activités complémentaires: activités additionnelles et/ou activités d'approfondissement effectuées à la suite d'une leçon.
C *exploitation*
A follow-up activities

activités d'éveil: en France, à l'école élémentaire, et par opposition aux disciplines fondamentales, regroupement des disciplines telles que l'histoire, la géographie, les sciences d'observation, la morale, le dessin, le travail manuel, la musique. Sans exclure l'acquisition de connaissances, les activités d'éveil privilégient la formation de «compétences» et une préparation psycho-intellectuelle à une action ultérieure.
C *méthodes actives*
A (activités d'éveil)

activités dirigées: 1. occupations diverses à caractère éducatif (clubs d'histoire naturelle, d'astronomie, de cinéma, de langues vivantes) effectuées sous la conduite d'un enseignant dans le cadre d'un établissement scolaire; **2.** travaux et exercices donnés sur un thème, en application d'une ou plusieurs leçons. Au cours de ces activités, les élèves peuvent faire appel, en cas de difficulté, à des explications données par un enseignant ou un répétiteur.
C *méthodes actives; travail dirigé*
A 1. (extra-class) activities; 2. tutorials

activités libres: dans l'enseignement primaire, occupations individualisées dans lesquelles les élèves choisissent librement le sujet et les modalités de réalisation.
C *méthodes actives; travail autonome*
A free projects

ADA: langage de programmation évolué dérivé de PASCAL.
A ADA

adaptateur: élément (bague, cordon, fiche, jack) permettant l'interconnexion de deux ou plusieurs appareils.
A adapter (ring, cable, plug, jack)

adaptation: 1. modification d'un équipement en vue d'une utilisation spécifique; **2.** nouvelle version d'une œuvre, modifiée pour une exploitation ou une utilisation différente de celle pour laquelle elle a été originalement conçue ou produite; **3.** transposition d'une œuvre littéraire pour lui trouver des équivalents audiovisuels (droits d'adaptation); **4.** ensemble des activités par lesquelles un individu modifie ses conduites pour s'adapter à un milieu déterminé.
A 1. 2. 3. 4. adaptation

adresse: dans un système informatique, caractère ou groupe de caractères qui désigne un registre, une partie déterminée d'une mémoire, ou quelque autre origine ou destination de données.
A address

aérographe: vaporisateur de précision utilisé pour adoucir ou égaliser des tons ou des nuances dans les travaux d'art.
A airbrush

AF: audio-fréquence; voir **fréquence audio**

affectif: voir **domaine affectif**

affichage: 1. présentation visualisée d'informations alphanumériques ou graphiques sur un terminal d'ordinateur. On dit quel-

quefois aussi visualisation; 2. action de présenter des documents sur un panneau.
C *visuel; visualiser; tableau mural*
A 1. display; readout; 2. posting

affichage à cristaux liquides
A liquid cristal display

affiche: document grand format sur papier ou carton, souvent illustré, et placardé à des fins éducatives, informatives ou publicitaires.
C *tableau mural*
A poster

AFC - (automatic frequency control): voir **régulateur automatique d'accord**

AGC - automatic gain control: voir **commande automatique de gain**

agents pédagogiques: terme générique désignant les personnes intervenant d'une façon directe ou indirecte dans le processus pédagogique: enseignants, documentalistes, producteurs et techniciens de moyens d'enseignement, conseillers d'orientation, animateurs d'activités extrascolaires, etc.
A (agents pédagogiques)

agrandissement (photo): épreuve photographique réalisée à partir d'un négatif de dimensions inférieures par un procédé de projection.
C *gonflage*
A enlargement; blow-up

agrandisseur: appareil servant au tirage d'une image, habituellement à partir d'un négatif, par projection de l'image sur un matériau sensible à la lumière.
A enlarger

aides audiovisuelles: voir **moyens audiovisuels**

aiguilleur: technicien responsable du choix de l'image à partir de deux ou plusieurs caméras.
A switcher

aigus: zone supérieure des fréquences du spectre acoustique.
A treble

à l'antenne: en cours de diffusion.
A on-the-air

ALGOL - algorithm oriented language: langage de programmation évolué, algébrique et logique, utilisé avec de nombreux types d'ordinateur pour entrer des procédures numériques.
C *langage de programmation*
A ALGOL

algorithme: ensemble fini de règles déterminées servant à résoudre une classe de problèmes au moyen d'un nombre fini d'opérations ordonnées.
A algorithm

aligner: régler, avant une réalisation audiovisuelle, la mise en relation correcte de divers éléments comme par exemple les pistes son, les signaux de caméra, etc.
A to line-up

alimentation: montage électrique qui a pour fonction de fabriquer les tensions et courants nécessaires au fonctionnement d'un appareil électrique ou électronique.
A power supply

alimentation secteur: voir **secteur**

allure: voir **rythme**

alphanumérique: contraction des termes alphabétique et de numérique; jeu de caractères qui comprend à la fois des lettres de l'alphabet, des chiffres, des caractères d'espacement et habituellement une série de caractères spéciaux utilisés comme signes de ponctuation, etc.
A alphanumeric

ambiance: réverbération naturelle due, en particulier, au lieu où s'effectue un enregistrement sonore ou visuel.
A ambience

amorce: 1. ensemble d'instructions destinées à mettre en route l'exécution d'un programme par un ordinateur; 2. morceau de ruban non magnétique ou de pellicule non impressionnée monté au début et parfois à

135

la fin d'une bande magnétique ou d'un film animé, pour en faciliter le chargement.

A 1. bootstrap; 2. leader; trailer

amplificateur: appareil dans lequel le signal d'entrée, commandant une source d'énergie locale, fait apparaître un signal de sortie en général plus grand que lui et qui lui est lié par une relation pré-déterminée.

A amplifier

amplification: augmentation du volume d'un son.

A boost

ampoule: globe de verre dilaté vide d'air (ou rempli d'un gaz à faible pression) et contenant un filament incandescent pour l'éclairage électrique.

C *lampe; tube*

A bulb

analogie: 1. association ou ressemblance établies par l'imagination et traduites par le langage entre deux ou plusieurs objets de pensée différents par nature; 2. raisonnement qui conduit d'une ressemblance à une autre ressemblance; 3. ressemblance perceptive entre la chose représentée et ce qui sert à la représenter, par exemple entre un objet réel et sa photographie. On dit aussi iconicité.

C *signe iconique*

A 1. 2. 3. analogy

analogique: se dit par opposition à numérique, de la représentation de l'information à l'aide d'un phénomène physique variant de façon continue.

C *numérique*

A analog

analyse: objectif pédagogique ayant pour objet la décomposition d'un tout en parties constitutives et la mise en évidence de leur organisation et de leurs relations.

A analysis

analyse comparée: méthode faisant appel à la description, la classification et l'analyse de plusieurs systèmes, groupes ou autres ensembles, afin d'établir et d'évaluer des similitudes et des différences.

A comparative analysis

analyse comportementale: une des méthodes utilisées dans l'élaboration de programmes d'enseignement. On analyse d'abord les objectifs éducatifs visés en termes de comportements terminaux, puis on décrit la suite des comportements et des tâches intermédiaires que les élèves doivent être capables d'acquérir et d'effectuer avant d'atteindre les objectifs terminaux prévus par le programme.

A behavioural analysis

analyse contextuelle: analyse des significations dans leur liaison avec l'environnement ou les circonstances particulières où se produit un fait ou un événement.

A context analysis

analyse coût-bénéfices: forme spécialisée de l'analyse coût-efficacité qui permet de comparer des activités très différentes en exprimant tous les coûts et les avantages dans la même unité monétaire.

A cost/benefit analysis

analyse coût-efficacité: méthode d'analyse visant à déterminer les coûts et l'efficacité d'une activité, ou à comparer des activités analogues pour savoir laquelle permettrait d'atteindre le mieux les objectifs visés.

A cost/effectiveness analysis

analyse du contenu: technique utilisée pour décrire des messages complexes de façon à pouvoir les évaluer, consistant en une recherche systématique des éléments caractéristiques d'un message (par ex. d'un manuel scolaire ou d'un programme de télévision) en vue de dégager le contenu manifeste ou latent, les concepts, les tendances, les déviations.

A content analysis

analyse de public: étude systématique des caractéristiques des participants actuels ou potentiels à un programme radiophonique ou télévisuel en vue de connaître les faits dominants qui les concernent, tels que besoins éducatifs, conditions socio-économiques, facteurs géographiques, préférences en matière de loisir et d'études.

A audience analysis

analyse de régression: terme général décrivant des techniques statistiques qui utilisent une corrélation pour prédire des relations probables entre des variables.

A regression analysis

analyse de réponse: recherche de coïncidence entre une réponse fournie par un apprenant et les réponses anticipées par l'auteur d'un programme éducatif. A chaque forme de réponse attendue, réponse numérique, textuelle, réponse à une question à choix multiple, etc., correspond un processus spécifique d'analyse.

A response analysis

analyse des effets: techniques spéciales visant à déterminer, de manière objective et quantifiée, les effets qu'un contenu de communication particulier a produits. Les diverses techniques comprennent des tests d'information, des tests d'attitude et des interviews.

A effect analysis

analyse des tâches: dans le domaine de l'apprentissage, identification des principales capacités à acquérir par l'apprenant et décomposition de ces capacités en constituants de base. Ce type d'analyse définit les performances et connaissances nécessaires pour une capacité donnée.

A task analysis

analyse d'interaction, des interactions: description et évaluation des phénomènes de communication apparaissant dans une situation pédagogique, en particulier de la manière dont s'effectuent les échanges d'information entre enseignants et enseignés ou entre les enseignés eux-mêmes dans une situation d'apprentissage structurée.

A interaction analysis

analyse d'item: une des nombreuses méthodes utilisées pour la validation et l'amélioration des tests et qui servent à déterminer, entre autres, le pouvoir de discrimination d'une question ou d'un item donné entre des sujets possédant différents degrés de capacité ou entre des sujets différant entre eux par une autre caractéristique.

A item analysis

analyse factorielle: méthode de description des corrélations statistiques existant entre des tests en utilisant le plus petit nombre de facteurs possible, c'est-à-dire des données d'hypothèses comme, par exemple, le savoir-faire, la capacité ou les traits de personnalité, que l'on suppose présentes et déterminantes pour ces tests.

A factor analysis

analyse multivariée: terme général désignant les techniques d'examen des relations entre plusieurs variables indépendantes et dépendantes analysées simultanément.

A multivariant analysis

analyse systémique: processus d'identification des composants et des interrelations d'un système et d'identification et d'étude des problèmes liés à la conception et au fonctionnement de systèmes.

C *approche systémique; systémique*

A systems analysis

analyseur: dispositif procédant à l'échantillonnage ou l'interrogation automatiques de divers processus, fichiers, conditions ou états physiques.

C *scanneur*

A scanner

analyseur de parole: dispositif électronique permettant d'utiliser la parole humaine comme source d'entrée directe dans un ordinateur.

A speech analyser

analyseur de réponses: machine à enseigner comportant un système de réponses à choix multiple relié à un tableau de contrôle qui présente instantanément une analyse quantitative des réponses fournies. On dit aussi station d'interrogation collective.

A student response system; response analyser; feedback classroom

analyseur de vues fixes: voir **télécinéma**

andragogie: science et art de la formation des adultes. Le terme a été introduit pour distinguer cette discipline de celle de l'enseignement des enfants (pédagogie).
A andragogy

angle de champ: angle (horizontal ou vertical) sous lequel l'objectif voit la portion d'espace susceptible d'être enregistrée. Il s'exprime en degrés.
A lens angle

animateur: 1. personne responsable d'une activité d'animation. Le terme, employé d'abord dans le domaine socio-éducatif, pénètre progressivement dans le vocabulaire de l'école, du commerce et de l'industrie; **2.** personne qui prépare les objets ou dessins utilisés en animation pour le cinéma ou la télévision.
A 1. animator; facilitator; 2. animator

animation: 1. technique de production cinématographique donnant vie et mouvement apparents à de l'inanimé: objets, dessins, croquis, diagrammes et légendes; **2.** ensemble de méthodes pour faire participer activement les membres d'une collectivité à la vie (culturelle, sociale) du groupe.
C banc titre
A 1. 2. animation

animation globale: activités qui ont pour objet l'amélioration des conditions matérielles et sociales d'une communauté. Celle-ci, dans ce contexte particulier, désigne les habitants d'une localité urbaine ou rurale limitée dans son extension, où se rencontrent un sentiment d'identité de groupe et un ensemble d'intérêts communs. En principe, les habitants doivent être encouragés à prendre davantage de responsabilités dans les décisions qui les concernent et dans les activités en cours.
A community development

antenne: partie d'un ensemble d'émetteur ou d'une installation de réception radio-électrique, conçue en vue de rayonner ou de capter les ondes radio-électriques.
A aerial (UK); antenna (USA)

antenne centrale: dispositif ou ensemble de dispositifs permettant de capter des signaux d'émission de radio ou de télévision et de les transmettre sans distorsion à des récepteurs; comprend les antennes, les systèmes de distribution et les amplificateurs reliés au système.
A central antenna system

antenne communautaire: système de distribution réservé aux abonnés d'une zone géographique déterminée, qui consiste à capter par une antenne des programmes émis par une station ordinaire de radiodiffusion et à les retransmettre au moyen d'un système de télévision en circuit fermé.
A community antenna television

antenne omnidirective: antenne dont la force cymomotrice est sensiblement la même dans toutes les directions du plan horizontal à chaque instant.
A omnidirectional antenna

antenne parabolique: antenne constituée par un miroir en forme de paraboloïde de révolution (de cylindre parabolique).
A parabolic antenna

ANTIOPE – acquisition numérique et télévisualisation d'images organisées en pages d'écriture: service de télétext mis en œuvre en France à partir de 1976.
C Télétel
A ANTIOPE

AP: voir **laboratoire audio-passif**

appareil de lecture: voir **lecteur**

appareils: instruments et objets didactiques autres que les livres et les supports (films, logiciels). Il s'agit le plus souvent d'un assemblage de pièces ou d'organes formant un tout, mis en œuvre pour observer un phénomène, pour mettre en œuvre un programme ou pour prendre des mesures.
A apparatus

appareil à visée réflexe: appareil de prise de vues comportant un miroir dans le boîtier de sorte que l'image de la scène à photographier se trouve projetée dans le viseur.
A reflex camera

appareil photographique: appareil utilisé pour la réalisation de négatifs photographiques destinés à être tirés et présentés sous forme de photographies séparées.

C *caméra*

A camera

appel d'offres: demande officielle de soumission d'offres pour la fourniture d'équipements, de matériels et de services.

A tender

apports: biens, services, personnel et autres ressources fournis pour une activité en vue de produire des résultats et d'atteindre les objectifs de l'activité dans un délai déterminé.

C *produits; évaluation; efficacité*

A inputs

apprenant: toute personne engagée dans un processus d'acquisition de nouveaux savoir-faire, de nouveaux savoirs ou de nouvelles attitudes, soit en suivant un programme spécifique d'enseignement, soit en étant soumis à un ensemble aléatoire de stimuli.

C *élève; étudiant*

A learner

appréciation: mesure des performances d'un élève ou d'un professeur et attribution d'une valeur à ces performances.

C *notation; note; évaluation*

A rating

apprentissage auto-dirigé: forme d'apprentissage où l'apprenant assume la responsabilité de son propre apprentissage, et, en totalité ou en partie, intervient dans le choix des décisions concernant la détermination et la mise en œuvre de cet apprentissage: définition des objectifs, choix des contenus et progressions, sélection des méthodes et techniques, détermination des lieux, temps et rythmes, adoption du mode d'évaluation.

C *auto-apprentissage; autodidaxie; travail indépendant*

A self-directed learning

apprentissage centré sur l'apprenant*: situation d'apprentissage où l'étudiant participe à la détermination des objectifs, des contenus et de la démarche.

A student-centred learning

apprentissage centré sur les problèmes*: méthode pédagogique où l'apprentissage est stimulé par la confrontation à des situations présentant des défis à relever ou des problèmes à résoudre. Cette démarche s'apparente à la méthode d'apprentissage par la découverte et à l'approche heuristique.

A problem-centered learning

apprentissage en situation: terme généralement utilisé pour caractériser un processus d'apprentissage s'appuyant sur l'expérience réelle en situation vraie (non simulée): par exemple, apprendre les techniques de vente en travaillant dans un magasin.

A direct experience

apprentissage individualisé: voir **enseignement individualisé**

apprentissage par cœur: apprentissage effectué de manière purement mécanique et faisant appel uniquement à la mémoire et non à la compréhension.

A rote learning

apprentissage sur le tas: situation d'apprentissage où l'apprenant n'étudie pas en classe mais utilise plutôt les ressources qu'offre une communauté au niveau culturel, gouvernemental, économique et industriel, humain, documentaire, événementiel, institutionnel, logistique et matériel, comme motivation à, lieu de, et outils pour l'apprentissage. S'oppose à l'apprentissage scolaire.

A community-based learning

approche communicative: méthode d'enseignement des langues étrangères fondée sur l'utilisation d'un ensemble de techniques pédagogiques, de contenus de langue et de supports d'enseignement visant à l'acquisition, par les apprenants, d'une compétence de communication.

C *compétence de communication*

A communicative approach

approche heuristique: en pédagogie, approche exploratoire d'un problème utilisant les évaluations successives d'essais et d'erreurs pour arriver à un résultat final.

A heuristic approach

approche interdisciplinaire: agencement de l'ensemble du programme d'étude ou du contenu d'un ou de plusieurs cours de manière à établir des relations entre différentes disciplines au-delà des cloisons traditionnelles.

A interdisciplinary approach

approche multi media(s): méthodologie fondée sur le principe qu'un ensemble de moyens audiovisuels variés et d'activités diverses combiné à d'autres moyens d'enseignement favorise un recoupement bénéfique et un renforcement mutuel des qualités respectives de chacun des constituants.

A multimedia approach

approche systémique: méthodologie qui permet d'intervenir sur une situation pédagogique (une heure de cours, un programme, une classe, une école, une action d'animation, un système d'enseignement, un réseau de télévision) considérée comme un système et sur ses relations avec son environnement. Cette intervention repose sur la description de la situation, l'explicitation des objectifs, l'identification du ou des points critiques, la détermination du ou des points d'intervention, l'élaboration de stratégies tenant compte des interactions connues ou supposées entre les divers éléments et les différents niveaux institutionnels et acteurs qui déterminent cette situation.

C *analyse systémique; point d'entrée; point critique; régulation de système*

A systems approach

aptitude: ensemble de traits caractéristiques indiquant la capacité d'un sujet à acquérir un certain niveau dans un domaine donné.

A aptitude

aptitudes à communiquer: se réfère aux techniques employées pour réaliser une communication efficace et à la capacité d'utiliser ces techniques. Celles-ci peuvent être orales, écrites ou audiovisuelles.

A communication skills

arbre de décisions: technique de représentation d'un ensemble d'alternatives de décisions ou de résultats possibles; on affecte ensuite une valeur à chacun de ces choix et on détermine lequel permettrait d'atteindre au mieux un objectif pré-déterminé.

A decision tree

architecture: spécification des règles de composition qui régissent les éléments (matériels, protocoles, logiciels) d'un système informatique, d'un réseau de communication, d'une base de données.

C *configuration*

A architecture

archives: ensemble organisé de documents à conserver en raison, généralement, de leur intérêt historique, comme, par exemple, des écrits, des films, des bandes vidéo, etc.

A archives

archives cinématographiques: centre où sont conservés, à des fins d'étude et de recherche, des films et les documents imprimés qui leur sont associés.

C *cinémathèque*

A film archives

arrêt sur image: action d'arrêter le défilement continu d'un film ou d'une bande vidéo sur une image pendant un temps voulu.

A stop motion; freeze frame

ASA – American Standards Association; aujourd'hui American National Standards Institute: système de classification des sensibilités de pellicules. Ces indices de sensibilité sont généralement donnés selon une échelle arithmétique, par exemple le doublement de la sensibilité correspondant au doublement de la valeur numérique.

A ASA

ASCII - American Standard Code for Information Interchange: norme qui affecte une structure en unités d'informations binaires (bits) à chaque signe, symbole, chiffre, lettre, fonction, que l'on trouve sur un clavier.

A ASCII

assemblage: 1. en vidéo, opération consistant à mettre des plans généralement bruts (rushes) les uns après les autres. Pour le film, en emploie plutôt bout à bout; **2.** voir **collage.**

A 1. assembly; 2. mounting

assembler: 1. traduire en langage machine un programme écrit en langage symbolique (d'assemblage) en substituant des codes d'opérations et des adresses absolus aux codes d'opération et aux adresses symboliques; **2.** relier et connecter les éléments d'un équipement; **3.** voir **monter.**

A 1. 2. to assemble; 3. to mount

assembleur: programme propre à un ordinateur qui permet de traduire un programme écrit en langage d'assemblage symbolique (que l'homme peut lire et comprendre) en un programme machine (binaire) dont l'ordinateur peut exécuter les instructions.

A assembler

assigner au hasard: choisir au hasard les sujets qui feront partie d'un groupe expérimental.

A to randomize

assistant réalisateur: personne à qui le réalisateur confie certaines tâches qui doivent être effectuées au cours d'une production, mais qui peuvent l'être sans le contrôle direct du réalisateur.

A assistant director

asynchrone: mode d'opération d'un ordinateur dans lequel l'exécution de l'opération suivante est déterminée par un signal déclenché par la fin de l'opération précédente. S'oppose à synchrone.

A asynchronous

astigmatisme: défaut d'un objectif ne donnant pas d'un point une image ponctuelle.

A astigmatism

atelier: 1. réunion de personnes qui ont des intérêts ou des problèmes en commun, avec des experts pour recevoir des connaissances spécialisées ou pour faire des études pratiques; **2.** cours intensif de formation d'adultes de courte durée et impliquant une certaine forme de production; **3.** local de réparation ou d'entretien.

C *séminaire*

A 1. 2. 3. workshop

attache: lien plastique ou métallique utilisé pour relier les extrémités de rouleaux de pellicule sans les coller.

A clip

audio: 1. terme désignant des dispositifs ou systèmes de communication utilisés dans l'émission, la transmission ou la réception de l'information auditive (son); s'oppose à vidéo; **2.** plus spécifiquement, courants électriques correspondant au son ou à la partie sonore d'un programme transmis, enregistré ou reçu.

A audio 1. 2.

audio-carte: mince carte munie d'un morceau de ruban magnétique sur toute la largeur de sa partie inférieure. Le son enregistré sur le ruban a généralement une durée de 30 secondes ou moins. Un espace est prévu au-dessus de la bande pour des images ou des mots. Une audio-carte doit être enregistrée et lue sur un dispositif spécial.

A audiocard

audio-cassette: voir **cassette**

audio-conférence: voir **téléconférence**

audio-fréquence: voir **fréquence audio**

141

audiolingual: voir **méthode audio-linguale**

audio-oral: 1. voir **méthode audio-linguale**; 2. qualifie un ensemble de moyens ou de matériaux pédagogiques sans supports visuels et mettant l'accent sur les activités orales.

A 1. audio-lingual (method); 2. audio-oral

audiovisuel: ce qui a trait à la transmission de l'information par des procédés audio et/ou visuels.

A audio-visual

audiovisuel léger: par opposition aux mass médias tels que la radio ou la télévision qui exigent une infrastructure lourde, médias audiovisuels toujours à disposition de l'enseignant, tels que vues fixes, enregistrements sonores, disques.

A (audiovisuel léger)

auditoire encadré: groupes d'apprenants écoutant ou visionnant un programme de radiodiffusion encadrés par des moniteurs ou des animateurs.

A captive audience

auditorium: espace conçu et aménagé pour servir de lieu de réunion et comportant une scène incorporée et un plancher incliné ou des sièges fixes.

A auditorium

auteur: 1. personne composant des œuvres intellectuelles ou de création; 2. personne qui crée des logiciels didactiques (didacticiels) exécutables par un ordinateur; 3. voir 'langage auteur', 'système auteur'.

A 1. 2. author

auto-apprentissage: technique d'apprentissage impliquant l'utilisation, par les élèves, de matériaux d'apprentissage (particulièrement de matériaux d'enseignement programmé, d'ensembles pédagogiques et de systèmes audio-tutoriels) comportant des stimuli, un dispositif d'expression des réponses, un retour d'information et une procédure de validation, le tout permettant aux élèves d'apprendre soit sans l'intervention d'un enseignant, soit avec un minimum de guidage de la part de l'enseignant. Cela est souvent considéré, à tort, comme l'équivalent d'un enseignement ou d'un apprentissage individualisé, mais, en réalité, seul le rythme d'apprentissage est individualisé.

C *autodidaxie; autonomie; travail autonome*

A self-instruction/learning

autocorrection: voir **auto-évaluation**

autodidaxie: ensemble des situations d'apprentissage effectué par des apprenants en dehors d'un cadre éducatif formel. L'autodidaxie peut être «pure» ou assistée, individuelle ou de groupe, librement choisie ou imposée par les circonstances. A ne pas confondre avec Apprentissage auto-dirigé.

A autodidaxy

autodiscipline: discipline librement établie entre les membres d'un groupe, sans contrôle extérieur.

A self-discipline

auto-évaluation: méthode d'évaluation dans laquelle l'étudiant vérifie lui-même s'il a acquis la maîtrise d'une unité d'enseignement (souvent en passant un test qu'il se donne lui-même), et s'il peut entreprendre la tâche suivante, ou s'attribue une appréciation ou une note pour son travail sur la base des normes établies ou par rapport à d'autres apprenants.

A self-assessment; self-evaluation

autoformation: voir **auto-apprentissage**

autogestion: 1. administration et gestion collégiales d'une institution éducative par l'ensemble du personnel et des enseignés ou par des représentants délégués de chacune des catégories d'intéressés; 2. appliqué à l'éducation des adultes, ce terme emprunté au secteur de la production, désigne la prise en charge par les participants à une activité éducative de la gestion, de l'établissement des programmes, du choix et de l'application des méthodes.

A 1. 2. self-government

autonome: dans un système informatique se dit d'un matériel lorsqu'il fonctionne indépendamment de l'unité centrale de traitement.

C *en ligne; connecté*

A off-line

autonomie (dans l'apprentissage): selon le sens donné à ce terme, soit la capacité de prendre en charge son propre apprentissage, soit la libre conduite d'un apprentissage par un apprenant, soit le degré de liberté de l'apprenant par rapport aux contraintes d'une situation ou d'un environnement.

C *autodidaxie; travail autonome; enseignement/apprentissage individualisé; apprentissage auto-dirigé; auto-apprentissage*

A autonomy

autoscopie: utilisation surtout, mais non exclusivement, pour la formation des maîtres, d'enregistrements, généralement vidéo, en vue d'une analyse de son propre comportement dans une situation donnée.

C *micro-enseignement*

A autoscopy

auxiliaires d'enseignement: aides mises à la disposition d'un enseignant au cours du processus d'enseignement et d'apprentissage, et dont la fonction est seulement de présenter des informations annexes ou supplémentaires, généralement de façon intermittente.

C *moyens d'enseignement*

A instructional aids

auxiliaires visuels: auxiliaires de la communication faisant appel au sens de la vue, par exemple diagrammes, tableaux de papier, films, maquettes fixes.

A visual aids

B

baffle: voir **enceinte acoustique**

bague allonge: bague ou tube fileté qui permet de monter l'objectif à une certaine distance d'un appareil de prise de vues.

A extension tube

bain d'arrêt: solution où des composés chimiques arrêtent l'action du révélateur sur la pellicule photographique impressionnée.

A stop bath

bain de développement: liquide, solution chimique ou eau de rinçage utilisés dans le traitement des pellicules photographiques.

A development bath

BAL: voir **courrier électronique**

balance: dispositif de réglage des niveaux relatifs des canaux droit et gauche d'un système stéréophonique.

C *équilibrage*

A balance control

balayage: bombardement systématique de toutes les parties d'une surface par un étroit faisceau lumineux ou une radiation électromagnétique; par exemple, mouvement d'un faisceau électronique de haut en bas et de gauche à droite sur un écran cathodique ou à l'intérieur d'une caméra de télévision.

A scanning

balayage entrelacé: analyse ligne par ligne horizontale dans laquelle, pendant une période d'image, le balayage s'effectue sur des trames successives légèrement et régulièrement décalées dans le sens vertical.

A interlaced scanning

BALUN: voir **transformateur symétrique — dissymétrique**

banc titre: support réglage porteur d'une caméra de cinéma située à l'aplomb d'un plateau mobile horizontal muni d'un dispositif de repérage et de stabilisation, et sur lequel sont disposés les éléments à photographier. Le banc titre est utilisé pour la réalisation de dessins, schémas, et films

animés, et, parfois aussi, pour la réalisation de films fixes ou de diapositives.
A animation stand

bande: ruban étroit, enroulé sur une bobine, un noyau, contenu dans une cassette ou dans une cartouche, et qui sert au stockage d'informations.
A tape

bande amorce: voir **amorce**

bande audio: bande magnétique servant à l'enregistrement des signaux sonores. La bande audio est conditionnée en bobines, cassettes et cartouches.
C *piste sonore; piste audio; bande vidéo*
A audiotape

bande banalisée: voir **bande de fréquence banalisée**

bande CB: voir **bande de fréquence banalisée**

bande de fréquences: subdivision du spectre des fréquences radioélectriques qui désigne «la gamme des fréquences comprise entre deux fréquences limites». Ainsi la bande 8 correspond à la gamme de 30 à 300 MHz, c'est-à-dire aux ondes métriques. Abréviation: Bm, à substituer à l'ancienne notation THF (très haute fréquence) (en anglais VHF), maintenant déconseillée.
A band

bande de fréquence banalisée: bande de fréquence mise à la disposition du public dans des conditions déterminées pour exploiter à titre privé et avec des émetteurs de faible puissance diverses radio-communications. On dit aussi 'bande CB', 'bande banalisée'.
A citizen's band radio

bande de lancement: séquence de courts extraits d'un film projetés à l'avance, à titre d'annonce, avant sa programmation.
A trailer

bande dessinée – BD: 1. suite de dessins agencés en séquences et qui racontent une histoire quelquefois avec de courtes phrases de texte incorporées dans des bulles;

2. publication constituée de bandes dessinées.
C *dessin animé*
A 1. comic strip; 2. comic book

bande magnétique: support d'enregistrement à accès uniquement séquentiel constitué par un ruban flexible imprégné ou recouvert d'une couche sensible.
C *disque magnétique; disquette*
A magnetic tape

bande passante: la plus large bande de fréquences susceptibles d'être transmises par un canal ou par une voie de transmission.
C *largeur de bande*
A bandwidth

bande perforée: support d'information constitué par un ruban de papier ou de matière plastique comportant des configurations de trous ou d'encoches. La bande perforée peut être utilisée pour entrer des informations dans un ordinateur, un système de télécommunication ou pour contrôler un ou plusieurs projecteurs de diapositives dans une présentation à images multiples ou des machines-outils (machines-outils à commande numérique).
C *carte perforée*
A punched tape

bande son: voir **piste sonore**

bande test: voir **film test**

bande vidéo: voir **vidéobande**

banque de données: collection mise à jour systématiquement de données ou informations relatives à un domaine particulier mises à la disposition d'usagers déterminés qui peuvent les consulter au moyen de terminaux d'interrogation et de réponse.
A data bank

banque d'items: collection d'items de tests classés selon le contenu, le niveau de difficulté, la validité, la fiabilité, etc.
A item bank

barillet de lentille: support cylindrique sur lequel est monté un objectif de prise de vues. Il comprend aussi, généralement, un dispositif mécanique de mise au point.

A lens barrel

base de données: ensemble structuré de données accessible à plusieurs utilisateurs pour des travaux différents. Les bases de données sont structurées de façon à être utilisées par des programmes correspondant à ces applications différentes et de façon à faciliter l'évolution indépendante des données et des programmes.

A data bank

base de numération: nombre utilisé implicitement pour représenter des nombres en numération de position. En numération binaire, employant les chiffres 0 et 1, la base de numération est 2.

A base

BASIC - beginners all-purpose symbolic instruction code: voir **langage machine**

basses: zone inférieure des fréquences de spectre acoustique.

A bass

basses fréquences: voir **BF**

batterie: 1. série d'objets, d'appareils ou d'éléments reliés ou utilisés ensemble; **2.** groupement d'un certain nombre de piles ou d'accumulateurs servant à la production de l'électricité par des moyens chimiques. Les types les plus courants sont les batteries au carbone-zinc, au plomb-acide, à l'argent et les batteries alcalines; **3.** ensemble de tests possédant une certaine unité.

A 1. 2. 3. battery

bavure: quantité de matériau de moulage en excédent qui apparaît sur la tranche d'un disque pendant l'opération de moulage par compression.

A flash 1

BD: voir **bande dessinée**

betamax: voir **format vidéo**

BF: basses fréquences, ondes longues ou grandes ondes. Bande dans la gamme des fréquences de 30 à 300 kHz ou ondes kilométriques. Abréviation métrique: B.Km.

A LF - low frequency

biais: voir **erreur systématique**

bibliobus: bibliothèque itinérante, logée dans un camion ou une camionnette.

C *mediabus*

A bookmobile

bibliothèque: ensemble organisé de documents servant à des fins d'étude ou de référence.

C *cinémathèque; magnétothèque; médiathèque; polythèque; banque de données*

A library

bio-énergie: s'applique à des programmes et des méthodes qui visent à favoriser un développement harmonieux de la personnalité en tirant le meilleur parti des ressources vitales sur le plan corporel, le plan intellectuel et le plan affectif.

A bioenergetics

bit: contraction de *bi*nary digi*t* (chiffre binaire), unité binaire d'information. C'est l'unité d'information la plus petite dans un système de notation binaire. Utilisée pour mesurer la capacité de stockage d'une mémoire magnétique.

A bit

bleu: à l'origine, copies de dessins ou de plans obtenues par utilisation de ferro-prussiate donnant des épreuves sur fond bleu. Le terme est maintenant utilisé pour toutes les grandes copies de plans ou de dessins industriels reproduits par des procédés divers.

A blue print

bloc: groupe de bits ou de caractères transmis comme un tout et auquel est généralement appliquée une méthode de contrôle des erreurs.

A block

bobine: dispositif composé d'un noyau et de deux flasques circulaires qui sert à enrouler un film ou une bande magnétique.

A reel; spool

145

bobine débitrice: bobine à partir de laquelle la bande magnétique ou le film se déroule pendant l'enregistrement, la lecture ou une avance rapide.
A delivery spool

bobine réceptrice: bobine sur laquelle la bande magnétique ou le film s'enroule pendant l'enregistrement, la lecture ou une avance rapide.
A take-up reel/spool

bogue: défaut ou imperfection d'ordre mécanique, électrique, électronique ou logique dans un équipement ou dans son emploi ou bien erreur dans un programme codé.
A bug

boîte: conteneur en métal ou en plastique utilisé pour conserver un film ou une bande vidéo.
A can

boîte à lumière: pupitre éclairé et transparent utilisé en animation.
A light box

boîte à outils (logiciels): terme familier pour designer des outils logiciels.
A toolkit

boîte aux lettres—BAL: voir **courrier électronique**

boucle: 1. petite longueur de film non tendue, autorisant un certain jeu et facilitant le chargement dans le projecteur; **2.** en informatique ensemble d'instructions fermé sur lui-même qui se répète jusqu'à ce que certaines conditions soient remplies.
A 1. 2. loop

boucle (de bande magnétique): morceau de bande dont les deux extrémités ont été jointes l'une à l'autre, permettant ainsi de repasser la même bande en continu, sans rembobinage.
C *film en boucle*
A tape loop

boucle magnétique: câble faisant le tour d'une pièce ou d'un espace et diffusant un signal pouvant être capté par des écouteurs spéciaux.
A wireless loop

boucle sans fin: technique consistant à coller les deux extrémités d'un film très court (3 à 4 secondes), à disposer ce film dans un projecteur et à le projeter indéfiniment.
C *projecteur pour film en boucle*
A continuous loop

bout à bout: première étape du montage d'un film animé. Lorsqu'il est achevé, toutes les scènes tournées sont montées dans l'ordre, les unes à la suite des autres, avec leur longueur d'origine.
C *assemblage*
A stringout

(brainstorming): technique utilisée pour résoudre un problème demandant une solution originale. Elle consiste à présenter le problème à un groupe de personnes et à leur faire proposer autant de solutions qu'elles le peuvent dans un temps donné. L'accent est mis sur la proposition d'idées et non sur la critique des idées proposées. Le terme recommandé est remue-méninges.
A brainstorming

bourdonnement: bruit parasite, de basse fréquence, généralement régulier, pouvant survenir dans les systèmes de reproduction du son, particulièrement les électrophones.
A rumble

branchement: 1. en enseignement programmé, point de séparation où les apprenants sont dirigés en alternative vers des items différents selon leurs réponses à un item particulier. Une utilisation courante du branchement est celle des programmes intrinsèques où le branchement consiste en un item unique expliquant pourquoi une réponse particulière est incorrecte et renvoyant l'apprenant à l'item de départ pour un autre essai; **2.** en informatique, instruction qui spécifie que le choix de l'instruction suivante sera déterminé par le produit ou le résultat d'une opération arithmétique ou logique ou par l'information fournie par un indicateur; **3.** en informatique, modification du déroulement d'un ensemble d'instructions par commutation à l'endroit où apparaît une information prévue.

C *programmation intrinsèque; saut*

A 1. 2. branch; 3. branching

brouillage: en communication, trouble apporté à la réception d'un signal utile par des phénomènes indésirables, dus à la présence d'autres signaux ou de bruits se superposant à ce signal.

C *embrouilleur; interférence*

A interference

bruit: 1. dans la théorie de l'information, tout élément parasite s'ajoutant à un signal utile et tendant à interférer avec le contenu d'information de ce signal utile; **2.** brouillage parasite pouvant produire un effet de neige sur une image de télévision ou des perturbations dans des signaux sonores.

A 1. 2. noise

bruitage: sons produits en studio et intégrés à une réalisation audiovisuelle pour créer l'illusion de sons réels.

C *bruiter*

A sound effects

bruit de fond: 1. bruit ambiant existant dans toute situation et pouvant parasiter l'enregistrement que l'on désire effectuer. On a recours à l'insonorisation pour éliminer le bruit ambiant des studios d'enregistrement; **2.** signaux parasites produits à la sortie d'une voie de transmission en l'absence de tout signal utile, lorsque cette voie fonctionne dans des conditions normales d'utilisation.

A 1. background noise; 2. background noise; hiss

bruiter: superposer un enregistrement sonore sur un autre, par exemple des bruits de circulation sur une conversation.

A to overlay

bureautique: ensemble des techniques et des moyens utilisés pour automatiser les activités de bureau.

A office automation

bus: voie permettant d'acheminer des informations à partir de toute source et dans toute direction.

A bus

but: 1. objectif que l'on se propose d'atteindre, ou résultat que l'on s'efforce d'obtenir par la mise en œuvre délibérée, raisonnée et cohérente de divers moyens. Ce en quoi il se distingue des aspirations; **2.** substance, objet ou situation susceptible de satisfaire une exigence ou un besoin vers la satisfaction desquels s'oriente un comportement motivé; **3.** déclaration générale d'intention, expression des désirs et des attentes des concepteurs et/ou des utilisateurs d'un programme éducatif.

C *fins; objectifs de l'éducation*

A 1. aim, goal; 2. goal; 3. aim; goal

C

cabestan: axe entraîné par un moteur et réglant la vitesse de défilement de la bande magnétique devant les têtes d'un appareil enregistreur et/ou lecteur de bandes.

A capstan

cabine: 1. en radiodiffusion, petite pièce insonorisée d'où l'on peut adresser un message en direct au public; **2.** petite pièce insonorisée utilisée pour l'enregistrement des voix en cinéma ou vidéo; **3.** petit espace aménagé pour des activités d'apprentissage individuel comme, par exemple, les postes de travail dans un laboratoire de langues.

A 1. 2. 3. booth

cabine de projection: pièce insonorisée d'où les films sont projetés sur écran et construite de telle sorte que le bruit du projecteur ne soit pas perceptible pour les spectateurs dans la salle.

A projection booth

câble coaxial: câble de transmission constitué d'un certain nombre de conducteurs, isolés les uns des autres, et utilisés pour la transmission d'un signal ou de plusieurs signaux simultanément.

A coaxial cable

câblodiffusion: voir **télédistribution**

câblodistribution: voir **télédistribution**

cache: 1. feuille opaque utilisée au tirage pour permettre d'obtenir l'impression successive de deux images séparées sur deux parties différentes de la même pellicule; **2.** feuille de carton ou de métal que l'on dispose devant la caméra pour obtenir certains effets, par exemple, une scène observée à la jumelle ou par un trou de serrure, etc.

A 1. 2. matte

cadrage: 1. en projection cinématographique, ajustement du cadre de la fenêtre de projection ou réglage du système d'entraînement pour que l'image soit correctement centrée sur l'écran; **2.** centrage de la caméra de cinéma ou de télévision sur la scène à tourner.

A 1. 2. framing

cadran: 1. surface sur laquelle apparaissent des mesures ou indications numériques; **2.** disque, généralement pourvu d'un bouton ou d'une encoche, pouvant être tourné pour établir des connexions électriques ou régler le fonctionnement d'un appareil.

A 1. 2. dial

cadre: 1. environnement dans lequel des émissions radiodiffusées sont reçues; **2.** unité dans une séquence d'enseignement programmé (syn.: maille).

A 1. setting; 2. frame

cadre presseur: pièce mécanique exerçant une pression sur un film en un point où il est nécessaire de le maintenir fermement positionné, comme, par exemple, devant la fenêtre d'un projecteur ou l'ouverture d'un appareil de prise de vues. Elle se compose généralement d'une plaque de métal strié montée sur ressorts.

A pressure plate

cadreur: technicien chargé du maniement d'une caméra, de la mise au point ainsi que de la définition d'un champ de prises de vues pour composer l'image.

A cameraman

CAG: voir **commande automatique de gain**

caisson insonore: caisson permettant d'éliminer les bruits d'une caméra pendant un tournage.

A blimp

calculateur analogique: calculateur dans lequel on utilise essentiellement des représentations analogiques de données, c'est-à-dire des données représentées par une grandeur physique variant d'une façon continue et dont la valeur est directement proportionnelle à la donnée ou à une fonction appropriée de cette donnée.

C *ordinateur*

A analog computer

calculatrice: machine de bureau qui effectue les opérations arithmétiques et dont l'emploi exige l'intervention fréquente d'un opérateur humain.

A calculator

calculette: petite calculatrice de poche aux dimensions très réduites, grâce à l'emploi de circuits intégrés.

A pocket calculator

calendrier de travail: échelonnement des travaux dans le cadre d'une production audiovisuelle.

A breakdown

calque: voir **bleu**

caméra: appareil utilisé pour enregistrer l'image produite lorsque des rayons lumineux passent au travers d'un objectif ou d'une ouverture et viennent impressionner un support photosensible: **1.** anglicisme pour appareil photographique; **2.** caméra permettant de réaliser des films animés; elle sert au tournage de films sonores ou muets; **3.** appareil transformant des images optiques en signaux électriques pouvant être enregistrés sur magnétoscope et/ou restitués en images sur un moniteur de télévision.

A **1.** camera; **2.** motion-picture camera; **3.** video camera

caméra grande vitesse: caméra spécialement conçue pour filmer à des vitesses très supérieures à la normale et jusqu'à 100 000 images par seconde.

A high-speed camera

camescope: vidéocaméra avec enregistreur-lecteur incorporé.

A camcorder

canal:1. circuit de communication entre un émetteur et un ou plusieurs récepteurs; **2.** gamme déterminée de fréquences assignées à une station de radio ou de télévision pour la diffusion hertzienne ou par câble; **3.** voie qui permet l'acheminement de signaux et de données dans un ordinateur.

A **1. 2. 3.** channel

CAO: conception assistée par ordinateur

C *EAO*

A CAD; computer-assisted design

capacité: qualité ou état d'un sujet capable d'effectuer une tâche ou une activité

C *savoir faire*

A ability

capacité en voies: en télécommunication, quantité d'informations qu'un canal (espace) peut transmettre par unité de temps ou qu'un canal (temps) peut contenir.

A channel capacity

capacité nominale: voir **valeur nominale**

CAPTAIN: voir **système d'information en réseau**

caractère: lettre, chiffre, signe de ponctuation ou autre symbole représentant une information.

A character

cardioïde: configuration en forme de cœur caractéristique de la courbe de directivité d'un microphone directif.

A cardioid

caricature: dessin d'interprétation à caractère satirique ou exagéré dont le but est d'accentuer un aspect de ce qui est représenté.

A cartoon

carrel: 1. petite cabine ou pupitre isolé servant au travail individuel d'enseignants ou d'élèves; **2.** poste de travail pour apprenant comprenant un pupitre, une table ou une cabine normalisés et conçu pour permettre un travail plus efficace; qualifié de 'wet' (humide) lorsqu'il est pourvu d'équipements électroniques, et de 'dry' (sec) lorsqu'il ne l'est pas.

A **1. 2.** carrel

carrousel: panier circulaire s'adaptant à un projecteur automatique de diapositives.

A rotary magazine; carousel; tray (US)

carte: plaque directement enfichable dans un micro-ordinateur qui permet d'augmenter les capacités de mémoire ou de traitement du système de base.

A card

carte à fenêtre: voir **carte à microfilm**

carte à mémoire: mémoire autonome sous forme de carte rectangulaire offrant 960 positions de bits.

C *disquette*

A memory card

carte à microfilm: carte perforée ou codée comportant un microfilm.

A aperture card

carte à perforer: carte dans laquelle des configurations de trous peuvent être perforées.

A punch card

carte flash: carte fabriquée dans un matériau non-transparent (généralement carton ou plastique) et portant des mots, des chiffres ou des images. Ces cartes sont conçues pour être montrées un court instant aux élèves, soit à la main, soit à l'aide d'un appareil, et servent à des exercices de systématisation ou de discrimination.

A flash card

carte perforée: carte comportant des configurations de trous.

A punched card

carton titre: tout texte inséré dans un film et destiné à fournir des informations aux spectateurs sur le film, son contenu ou son histoire.

A title caption

cartouche: **1.** boîtier contenant une bande magnétique (ou un film) en forme de bande sans fin enroulée sur un seul noyau. Le système se déroule en boucle continue et permet une insertion/extraction rapide dans ou hors d'un appareil enregistreur-lecteur; **2.** informatique, boîtier contenant de la mémoire morte permettant à l'utilisateur de communiquer avec la mémoire centrale − cartouche de langage, de jeux, etc.

C *cassette*

A cartridge

casque d'écoute: dispositif composé d'un ou deux petits transducteurs acoustiques montés sur un serre-tête et qui a pour fonction de permettre l'écoute individuelle d'une ou plusieurs sources sonores. Un casque doté d'écouteurs et d'un microphone s'appelle un casque microtéléphone.

C *poste d'écoute*

A headset

cassette: boîtier contenant deux noyaux sur lesquels est enroulée une bande magnétique (ou un film) qui peut se déplacer d'un noyau à l'autre. Le système permet une insertion/extraction rapide dans ou hors d'un appareil enregistreur-lecteur.

C *cartouche*

A cassette

catalogage: **1.** description et établissement de la notice bibliographique d'une acquisition; **2.** établissement des notices d'un catalogue. Plus largement, toutes les opérations y compris la classification et le choix des vedettes matière, qui entrent dans l'établissement et la mise à jour d'un catalogue.

A 1. 2. cataloging

catalogue: liste méthodique d'articles, documents ou autres, qui est établie dans un ordre déterminé. Le catalogue permet d'enregistrer, de décrire et d'indexer, généralement de façon complète, les ressources d'un fonds.

A catalog

CCIR: comité consultatif international des radiocommunications.

A CCIR

CDI: voir **centre de documentation et d'information**

CEEFAX: voir **système d'information en réseau**

CEI: commission électronique internationale.

A IEC

cellule de mémoire: dans un ordinateur un ou plusieurs éléments de mémoire considérés comme un tout et habituellement désignés au moyen d'une adresse spécifique.

A storage cell

cellule photoélectrique: cellule senble à l'éclairement équipant, par exemple, les posemètres, certains systèmes d'alarme, etc. Dans les projecteurs de film à son optique, les variations de lumière issues de la piste sonore sont transformées par la cellule photoélectrique en courant électrique qui, amplifié, est envoyé au haut parleur.

A photoelectric cell

cellulo: morceau de plastique (cellophane) utilisé pour la réalisation de films animés ou de transparents superposables.

A cell

centre culturel: centre équipé de salles de réunions et d'exposition, d'une bibliothèque, d'une discothèque et d'ateliers.

C *réception collective*

A cultural centre

centre d'écoute: local aménagé pour l'écoute d'enregistrements sonores.

A listening centre

centre de documentation et d'information – CDI: en France, dans les collèges et les lycées, salle(s) où sont groupées les ressources éducatives pour les enseignants et les élèves.

C *centre pédagogique; médiathèque*

A learning resource centre

centre de production: organisme spécialement équipé pour la production de programmes audiovisuels (films ou documents vidéo).

A production centre

centre d'intérêt: thème pluridisciplinaire autour duquel s'organise un travail d'exploitation pédagogique pouvant durer plusieurs semaines.

C *activités dirigées; activités d'éveil; étude du milieu*

A thematic approach

centre pédagogique: organisation autonome disposant de locaux, de personnels, de documents et d'appareils, mise à la disposition des enseignants (de façon individuelle ou en groupe) à des fins de documentation, d'information et de formation.

A teacher's centre

centre serveur: voir **serveur**

centré sur: voir **éducation centrée sur l'apprenant, programme centré sur la matière, pédagogie centrée sur l'enseignant.**

chaîne: toute l'organisation administrative et technique qui va d'un émetteur de radiodiffusion au récepteur.

A programme

chaîne de caractères: terme d'informatique pour désigner une suite linéaire de caractères alphanumériques.

A string

chambre noire: endroit spécialement aménagé pour le développement des pellicules et épreuves photographiques. Il est protégé de la lumière et est doté d'une ventilation appropriée et d'un éclairage spécial pour l'exécution de travaux photographiques.

A dark room

champ d'attention: nombre maximum d'objets qu'un sujet peut percevoir à la fois de manière correcte.

C *champ de mémoire*

A span of apprehension

champ de mémoire: période de temps que peut embrasser un acte de mémorisation. Il peut s'étendre du court terme (quelques heures) au long terme.

A memory span

champ de visée: angle couvert par un appareil de photo ou une caméra pendant la prise de vues.

A view angle

changeur automatique: dispositif qui, couplé à deux projecteurs, éteint automatiquement l'un et allume l'autre pour assurer une projection continue, particulièrement dans le cas de films multibobines.

A automatic changeover

charge: 1. quantité d'électricité; 2. taux d'utilisation d'une machine à un moment donné.

A 1. 2. load

chargement: insertion d'un film ou d'une bande dans le couloir du dispositif d'entraînement.

A lacing (UK); threading (USA)

charger: 1. entrer des informations dans la mémoire d'un ordinateur; 2. disposer un film ou une bande dans un appareil, une cassette ou une cartouche; 3. action d'accumuler l'électricité dans une batterie ou un accumulateur.

A 1. 2. 3. to load

chariot: plateau monté sur roulettes servant à poser et à déplacer des équipements de cinéma.

A dolly

chariot automatique: mécanisme d'entraînement dans une imprimante qui permet une commande automatique de l'alimentation des espacements, de la tabulation et de la sortie du papier.

A carriage

châssis de tirage: châssis de bois, métal ou plastique permettant d'exposer une feuille de papier sensible derrière un négatif pour obtenir un tirage positif de mêmes dimensions.

A printing frame

chemin critique: voir **méthode du chemin critique**

cheminement pédagogique: itinéraire dans un programme d'enseignement qu'un apprenant est censé suivre ou choisit de suivre pour atteindre un objectif défini.

A instructional pathway

CIME: conseil international des moyens d'enseignement.

A ICEM

ciné-club: groupement de personnes qui s'associent pour visionner des films en dehors des circuits commerciaux qui, à l'occasion de la projection d'un film, participent à une discussion sur des thèmes reliés directement ou indirectement à cette projection.

A cineclub; filmclub

cinéma: 1. art ou technique de la réalisation de films (cinématographie); **2.** salle ou bâtiment servant à la projection de films (ciné).

A 1. cinematography; 2. cinema

cinémascope: nom commercial d'un procédé de projection de films sur grand écran. On utilise un anamorphoseur pour obtenir cet effet.

A cinemascope

cinémathèque: centre de dépôt de copies de films servant généralement au prêt mais aussi, dans certains cas, à l'étude et à la recherche.

C *archives cinématographiques*

A film library

cinérama: technique de projection utilisant trois films différents projetés sur écran large.

A cinerama

circuit feedback: circuit à l'intérieur d'un appareil électronique qui a pour fonction de réduire les distorsions.

A feedback

circuit fermé de télévision: voir **télévision en circuit fermé**

circuit imprimé: composant électronique consistant en un circuit imprimé sur une carte isolante.

A printed circuit

circuit intégré: composant télectronique constitué d'un ensemble de conducteurs et de semi-conducteurs intégrés dans un composant unique.

A integrated circuit

clap: voir **claquette**

claquette: appareil composé de deux pièces de bois articulées que l'on claque l'une contre l'autre. Le son produit sert de marque de synchronisation sur la piste son de chaque plan tourné au cours de la réaliation d'un film.

A clapper board

classe de rattrapage: classe constituée d'un petit groupe d'élèves qui ont besoin d'une aide particulière pour combler un retard spécifique ou compenser des insuffisances liées à un apprentissage antérieur.

A remedial class

classement: 1. organisation ou ensemble de procédés de classification ayant pour objet l'identification et la mise à disposition efficace de documents ou de données. Les systèmes de classement peuvent être séquentiels, alphabétiques, numériques ou codés de diverses manières; **2.** action de ranger les élèves dans un ordre de valeur résultant des notes obtenues dans un exercice ou dans un examen.

A 1. filing system; 2. ranking

clavier: dispositif ou tableau constitué d'une ou plusieurs rangées de touches; l'enfoncement d'une touche détermine l'entrée d'un caractère ou du symbole représenté sur cette touche.

A keyboard

clavier à touches: dans un appareil téléphonique, dispositif de codage sur touches remplaçant le cadran.

A keypad

cliché: 1. plaque sur laquelle est gravé en relief le texte ou l'image à reproduire; **2.** négatif photographique.

A 1. plate; block; matrix; 2. negative; photo

clignotement: 1. signal lumineux intermittent apparaissant sur l'écran pour indiquer à l'utilisateur que l'ordinateur est prêt à exécuter ses ordres; **2.** méthode pour attirer l'attention sur un message à l'écran en faisant scintiller les lettres.

A 1. prompt; 2. blinking

COBOL - common business oriented language: langage de programmation évolué destiné aux applications de gestion.

A COBOL

codage: 1. transformation selon un mode convenu entre des utilisateurs ou ensemble de règles clairement définies permettant de faire passer des messages d'un système dans un autre; **2.** processus psychologique par lequel une personne exprime son intention communicative sous forme d'un signal dans un système de communication donné, généralement un langage oral ou graphique mais parfois aussi gestuel; **3.** processus technique par lequel un message est transformé en signaux pouvant être transmis par un canal de communication.

C *décodage*

A 1. 2. 3. encoding

code: système de signes, purement conventionnel, destiné à la communication et tel que les unités prennent leur sens les unes par rapport aux autres. **1.** encoder: soumettre un ensemble de messages aux règles du code; **2.** décoder: déchiffrer un ensemble de messages avec l'aide du code.

A code; to encode; to decode

coefficient de fidélité: coefficient de corrélation entre deux versions d'un test, entre les résultats de deux passations d'un même test, ou entre deux moitiés d'un test, lorsque les épreuves sont correctement corrigées.

A reliability coefficient

cognitif: voir **domaine cognitif**

collage: fixation d'un document ou d'une surface unie sur un autre document ou une autre surface en utilisant pour cela une source de chaleur et/ou un moyen de pression et/ou un papier ou un adhésif intermédiaire.

C *montage à sec*

A mounting

collection: 1. recueil d'ouvrages, de publications ayant une unité; **2.** ensemble d'objets classés en vue de leur utilisation comme matériel pédagogique.

A 1. 2. collection

coller: raccorder deux morceaux de pellicule ou de bande à l'aide d'une colleuse ou d'une presse et de colle ou d'adhésif spécial. La collure peut se faire à chaud, à sec ou en milieu humide.

A to splice

153

colleuse: instrument utilisé pour raccorder deux morceaux de pellicule ou de bande.

A splicer

collure: assemblage bout à bout des parties de bande magnétique ou de pellicule au moyen d'un ruban adhésif.

A splice; join

combinatoire: terme emprunté aux mathématiques, à la logique et à la linguistique, qui désigne une stratégie d'emploi combiné de plusieurs moyens visant à compléter et renforcer mutuellement leur action pédagogique dans des circonstances déterminées.

C *approche multimedia*

A combinatoire

COMMAG: voir **piste de son magnétique**

commande: toute instruction donnée à un ordinateur.

C *menu*

A command

commande automatique de gain – CAG: dispositif incorporé dans un récepteur radiophonique afin de maintenir automatiquement la puissance de sortie à un niveau constant.

A automatic gain control

commande de voie de caméra: équipement du canal d'une caméra de télévision contenant la majeure partie des circuits électroniques. Il fournit à la caméra des signaux d'ordre et analyse les signaux provenant de la caméra. Il permet à l'équipement électronique abrité dans la caméra elle-même d'être réduit au minimum.

A camera control unit

commentaire: 1. texte d'accompagnement d'un film dit en voix hors champ; 2. description orale ou série de remarques accompagnant un film animé ou tout autre spectacle.

A 1. 2. commentary; narration

154

commentateur: personne qui dit un commentaire ou qui écrit ou compose un commentaire.

A commentator

communication: 1. ensemble des processus physiques et psychologiques par lesquels s'effectuent la mise en relation de deux ou plusieurs sujets et des échanges signifiants d'informations entre ces sujets, mettant en jeu des aspects cognitifs, affectifs, conatifs, en vue d'atteindre certains objectifs; 2. transmission d'une information entre un émetteur et un ou plusieurs récepteurs, par l'écriture, la parole, les gestes, les images, les systèmes de signes conventionnels ou les moyens audiovisuels et informatiques.

C *compétences de communication*

A 1. 2. communication

communication audiovisuelle: mode de communication ayant recours principalement à l'utilisation de messages audiovisuels.

A audio-visual communication

communication de masse: mode de communication non personnalisé s'adressant à de larges publics non ciblés.

A mass communication

communication sociale: voir **communication de masse**

commutateur: dispositif permettant d'établir, d'interrompre ou de changer les connexions dans un circuit électrique.

A switch

commutation (système de): dispositif électronique commandant, de manière automatique, l'interface d'un ou plusieurs terminaux électroniques et de sources d'information ou de programmes provenant de stations d'un réseau de téléconsultation.

A switching system

commuter: changer de programmes ou de techniques.

A to switch

COMOPT: voir **piste de son optique**

compact disc: voir **disque audio-numérique**

compatibilité: 1. possibilité d'harmonisation d'une ressource éducative avec d'autres pour ce qui est du contenu, format, etc.; **2.** possibilité pour un équipement d'une marque donnée d'être utilisé avec l'équipement d'une autre marque.

A 1. 2. compatibility

compétence: voir **savoir-faire; performance. 2.**

compétence de communication: savoirs et savoir-faire nécessaires pour utiliser au mieux le code et les règles linguistiques et para-linguistiques indispensables à la maîtrise efficace de la communication dans une situation donnée.

A communicative competence

(competency-based teacher education): application à la formation des enseignants de l'éducation axée sur la compétence.

C *éducation axée sur la compétence; pédagogie de la maîtrise*

A competency-based teacher education

compilateur: 1. personne qui rassemble ou met en forme des documents de sources diverses et les prépare à l'édition; **2.** logiciel qui traduit en langage machine avant l'exécution un programme écrit dans un langage de programmation évolué (langage d'origine).

A 1. 2. compiler

comportement initial: comportement d'un apprenant au début d'une séquence d'enseignement, et qui manifeste les compétences qu'il possède.

A entry behaviour

comportement terminal: ce que l'apprenant doit être capable de faire ou d'accomplir pour prouver qu'il a acquis ce qui avait été fixé comme objectif.

A terminal behaviour

composants: éléments d'un système.

A components

concepteur de programmes didactiques*: spécialiste qui élabore des programmes d'enseignement ou des matériaux pédagogiques ainsi que la stratégie éducative correspondant à leur utilisation.

A instructional developer

condensateur: 1. dispositif qui emmagasine ou arrête partiellement la circulation du courant électrique; **2.** voir **lentille condensatrice.**

A condenser; capacitor

conditionnement: procédure par laquelle un sujet apprend à répondre à un stimulus nouveau en l'associant à un autre stimulus qui a déclenché initialement la réponse souhaitée. Synonyme: conditionnement classique/Pavlovien.

A classical conditioning; Pavlovian conditioning

conditionnement opérant: type de conditionnement qui procède par le renforcement d'une réponse réussie émise par un sujet dans un environnement donné. Synonyme: conditionnement instrumental/Skinnérien.

A operant conditioning; instrumental conditioning

conducteur (image): ensemble de dessins ou photos illustrant chaque élément ou séquence d'une réalisation audiovisuelle avant sa production. Il est généralement établi après le descriptif et antérieurement au découpage.

A storyboard

configuration: description des éléments physiques (hardware), leurs connexions et leurs contraintes dans un système informatique donné.

C *architecture*

A configuration

connecté: voir **en ligne**

connotation: 1. somme des qualités impliquées par un terme; **2.** toute signification à laquelle renvoie le message dans son acception courante.

C *dénotation*

A 1. 2. connotation

conscientisation: terme inventé par Paolo Freire. Processus éducatif qui a pour objet d'aider une population analphabète vivant dans une situation très défavorisée à maîtriser son propre sort. On s'efforce d'éveiller la conscience de ce public, de développer chez lui une évaluation critique de sa situation, pour qu'il puisse intervenir pour la transformer. On emploie la méthode du dialogue pour préparer à l'action.

A conscientization

conseiller: étudiant plus âgé ou enseignant à même d'aider les jeunes élèves à maîtriser les matières d'étude mal assimilées ou à résoudre des problèmes personnels.

C *tuteur*
A tutor

conseiller pédagogique: 1. enseignant qui, en raison de ses aptitudes professionnelles et de son expérience pédagogique, est choisi pour assurer la formation pratique et le perfectionnement pédagogique des futurs enseignants; **2.** spécialiste du contenu et de la pédagogie dans une production audiovisuelle d'enseignement.

A 1. practice teacher; 2. educational adviser

conseiller scientifique: spécialiste du contenu dans une production audiovisuelle.

A scientific adviser

conseiller technique: spécialiste ou expert engagé par un producteur ou un studio pour fournir les informations techniques nécessaires à la réalisation d'un film, d'une émission de télévision ou de tout autre programme.

A technical adviser

console: ensemble des dispositifs matériels permettant de mettre en marche, arrêter et contrôler manuellement un processus de production audiovisuelle, ou le fonctionnement d'un ordinateur.

C *pupitre de commande*
A console; control; panel

console image: dispositif permettant la sélection des signaux de télévision provenant d'une des sources vidéo d'un système,

comme par exemple une caméra de télévision, un magnétoscope ou un télécinéma. On parle, parfois, de manière similaire, de console son pour la sélection de signaux provenant de plusieurs sources sonores.

C *pupitre de mélange*
A switcher

contenu implicite de l'enseignement: tout ce qui, dans un système scolaire, reflète et conforte, de manière indirecte et non-formalisée, les valeurs sociales existantes.

A hidden curriculum

contenu de l'éducation: désigne l'ensemble des savoirs, des savoir-faire, des valeurs, des attitudes, et des comportements harmonieux suscité par l'institution scolaire ou durant les activités extrascolaires. Le concept de contenus de l'éducation couvre à la fois les contenus enseignés, c'est-à-dire ceux qui font l'objet d'un programme explicite et les contenus latents proposés par la vie scolaire, les relations éducateur-élève, l'expérience du travail et l'ensemble des «messages» oraux, écrits et audiovisuels, que rencontrent les élèves.

A contents of education

continuité: progression méthodique d'une partie à une autre d'un programme de radiodiffusion ou de télévision d'après un plan préétabli pour produire un effet désiré.

C *enchaînement*
A continuity

contraintes: ensemble des déterminations institutionnelles, humaines, matérielles et techniques qui, dans un système donné, conditionnent la mise en œuvre d'une stratégie et la réalisation d'un objectif.

C *approche systémique; régulation*
A constraints

contraste: rapport entre les éléments clairs et foncés d'une image. Un contraste fort présente des opportunités extrêmes de clair et de foncé alors qu'un contraste faible joue sur des tons moyens.

A contrast

contrat pédagogique: plan d'étude adaptable aux différences individuelles des apprenants dans lequel le contenu du cours est divisé en un certain nombre de sections, chacune d'elles assortie d'un travail précis à effectuer nécessitant un temps assez long. Chaque élève s'engage à accomplir ces tâches au cours d'une période déterminée. La mise en œuvre du contrat suivant n'a lieu qu'après la réalisation du précédent.

C *système d'instruction personnalisé*

A learning contract

contrat de travail élève-professeur: méthode pédagogique visant à développer les capacités d'autodirection de l'étudiant en l'impliquant de manière active dans le processus des décisions concernant son apprentissage.

A student-teacher contracting

contretype: fac-similé négatif (contretype négatif) ou positif (contretype positif) d'un original servant à éviter d'avoir à utiliser cet original et permettant d'effectuer des travaux simultanés dans plusieurs laboratoires.

A dupe

contrôle: voir **surveillance**

contrôle (de la progression de l'apprenant): activité consistant à suivre la progression de chaque apprenant au fur et à mesure qu'il avance dans une séquence d'apprentissage. Le contrôle s'effectue par comparaison de la progression réelle avec la progression attendue, sans acte d'appréciation ni d'évaluation.

A monitoring

contrôle continu: méthode d'évaluation dans laquelle l'examen final est remplacé par une série de contrôles effectués à intervalles réguliers. Le contrôle continu qui a pour objet de réduire l'arbitraire d'une notation unique, permet ainsi de suivre le développement de l'étudiant et d'adapter les procédures d'enseignement.

C *évaluation formative*

A continuous assessment

contrôle de qualité: régulation d'un système permettant d'opérer des réglages pour corriger les différences entre la performance de sortie effective (du système ou de ses composants) et la performance attendue.

A quality control

contrôler: vérifier la correction de l'image et les autres signaux nécessaires à la bonne transmission d'une scène (son et image).

A to monitor

convergence: recherche rationnelle et systématique de la solution d'un problème qui consiste à rechercher la réponse la plus logique, la plus conventionnelle ou celle qui tend au conformisme.

C *divergence*

A convergent thinking

conversationnel: voir **mode dialogué**

convivial: qualifie les programmes interactifs qui disposent d'aides pour guider l'utilisateur.

A user friendly

copie: 1. tirage positif à partir d'une pellicule négative; 2. opération destinée à l'obtention simultanée d'un ou de plusieurs exemplaires de tout ou partie d'un programme enregistré (duplication); 3. travail écrit personnel rédigé par un élève.

C *document à copier*

A 1. print; 2. copying; 3. pupil script

copie d'antenne: copie d'un enregistrement sur film ou sur bande magnétique, spécifiquement destinée à la diffusion par un émetteur de radiodiffusion sonore ou de télévision.

A transmission copy

copie d'étalonnage: première copie combinée (image et son), tirée à partir d'un négatif et utilisée pour effectuer les corrections de couleur, densité, etc. La première copie d'étalonnage acceptable devient la première copie d'exploitation.

A answer print; check print

copie d'exploitation: contretype tiré à partir d'un document audiovisuel original et destiné à une exploitation générale.

A release print

copie de montage: assemblage non définitif des séquences d'images et des enregistrements sonores correspondants. Il sert au travail de montage.

A cutting copy

copie de travail: copie relativement peu coûteuse tirée à partir de l'original d'un film animé et utilisée au cours du montage. L'original sera mis ensuite en conformité avec elle avant le tirage d'autres copies.

A work print

copie directe: copie obtenue en une seule fois à partir de l'original.

A direct print; contact print

copie en format réduit: copie en format réduit d'un film animé faite à partir d'un original d'un format plus grand; généralement copie 8 mm faite à partir d'un original 16 mm.

A reduction print

copie inversible: copie obtenue par un procédé permettant de produire directement un positif sans passer par l'intermédiaire d'un négatif.

A reversal print

copie neuve: film neuf dont la couche de surface n'est pas encore stabilisée.

A green film

copie papier: voir **tirage papier**

copie par contact: voir **copie directe**

copie positive: film prêt à être projeté et possédant les couleurs et/ou les tons du sujet original.

A positive print

copie zéro: voir **copie d'étalonnage**

cordon de liaison: cordon ou câble muni de connecteurs ou de jacks à chaque extrémité, et servant à relier un appareil à un autre.

A patch cord

correcteur de base de temps: dispositif électronique destiné à améliorer les caractéristiques techniques d'un signal de télévision enregistré en rétablissant aux normes les signaux de synchronisation ligne et trame affectés par les fluctuations de vitesse du magnétoscope, ainsi qu'en compensant les pertes (drop-out), en les remplaçant par les lignes voisines, conservées en mémoire.

A time-base corrector

correction: 1. action de corriger des devoirs d'élève, des épreuves d'examen; 2. intervention pédagogique par laquelle sont indiquées à l'apprenant les réponses non appropriées ou les erreurs commises en vue d'une amélioration; dans l'enseignement programmé, la correction des fautes est immédiate afin de diminuer la probabilité d'apparition d'une réponse non appropriée.

C *(feedback)*

A 1. marking; 2. remediation

corrélation: existence d'une liaison apparente entre deux variables distinctes.

A correlation

côté émulsion: face d'une pellicule où se trouve la couche sensible.

A emulsion side

coupe: rupture intervenant toutes les fois que la caméra change de position ou qu'un plan nouveau apparaît à l'écran.

A cut

couper: 1. interrompre. Lorsque le réalisateur dit «coupez», il veut que la caméra s'arrête, la prise de vue étant terminée; antonyme: «moteur»; 2. supprimer une partie d'un programme radiodiffusé ou télévisé; 3. arrêter brusquement la transmission d'un programme de radio ou de télévision.

A 1. 2. 3. to cut

couplage: liaison entre deux ou plusieurs systèmes ou parties de système.

A interlock

158

coupleur acoustique: dispositif permettant de connecter un ordinateur à un appareil de téléphone et au réseau téléphonique.

A acoustic coupler

courant alternatif

A alternating current - AC

courant continu

A direct current - DC

courbe de Gauss: voir **distribution normale**

courbe de performance: courbe montrant la performance réelle de l'apprenant par rapport aux prévisions ou estimations de performances attendues.

A progress chart

courrier électronique: échange de messages par voie électronique entre utilisateurs d'un réseau informatique. Le message est enregistré dans une mémoire réservée à cet effet, la boîte aux lettres (BAL) électronique. On dit aussi 'messagerie électronique'.

A electronic mail

cours: 1. suite d'activités à caractère éducatif se rapportant à une matière d'enseignement organisées sur une base régulière et systématique en vue de faire acquérir aux élèves des notions durant une période déterminée à l'avance, par exemple une heure, une session de deux semaines, un trimestre scolaire normal, ou un semestre; **2.** indication du niveau scolaire.

A 1. course; 2. grade; level

cours accéléré: programme d'enseignement structuré, conçu pour répondre à des circonstances exceptionnelles dans le minimum de temps et en utilisant au maximum les ressources disponibles.

A crash course

cours en alternance: programme d'études organisé de telle façon que des périodes d'enseignement à plein temps alternent avec des périodes de travail professionnel continu.

A sandwich course

cours de recyclage: formation ayant pour but la mise à jour des connaissances rendue nécessaire par l'évolution de la science et de la technique.

A refresher course

cours par correspondance: voir **enseignement par correspondance**

court métrage: genre cinématographique: film de courte durée, généralement de type documentaire, traitant d'un sujet réel en dehors de toute fiction.

A short film

couverture (d'un émetteur): superficie de la zone de service d'un émetteur de radiodiffusion, ou population desservie par un émetteur.

A coverage

crayon lumineux: voir **photostyle**

crayon optique: voir **photostyle**

critère: 1. caractéristique ou mesure permettant de repérer d'autres caractéristiques qui font l'objet de l'examen ou de l'évaluation; **2.** niveau déterminé ou standard de réussite auquel on peut comparer le résultat de performances individuelles; **3.** ensemble de résultats ou de mesures qu'un test est supposé produire.

A 1. 2. 3. criterion

critérium: voir **critère**

curriculum: ensemble d'actions planifiées pour susciter l'instruction. Il comprend les définitions des objectifs de l'enseignement, les contenus (y compris l'évaluation), les matériels (y compris les manuels scolaires) et les dispositions relatives à la formation adéquate des enseignants.

C *programmes d'études*

A curriculum

curseur: signe mobile sur un écran de visualisation qui indique à l'utilisateur où va apparaître le caractère suivant.

A cursor

cursus (scolaire, universitaire): 1. progression d'un apprenant ou d'un groupe d'apprenants dans les niveaux et modes successifs d'éducation; **2.** ensemble des enseignements dispensés à un cycle donné du système éducatif et généralement sanctionnés par un examen final.

A 1. student progress; 2. university course

cuve à développer: grande cuvette pour développer les pellicules photographiques.

A developing tank

cybernétique: science constituée par l'ensemble des théories relatives aux communications et à la régulation entre l'être vivant et la machine. Elle étudie en particulier les systèmes qui comportent un mécanisme de feedback ou de rétroaction.

A cybernetics

D

dB: décibel

A decibel

débordement: dans un calculateur, événement survenant lorsque le résultat d'une opération arithmétique excède la capacité de stockage du registre ou de la zone mémoire dans lequel il doit s'inscrire.

C *dépassement de capacité*

A overflow

décalcomanie: voir **transfert à sec**

déclencheur souple: fourreau flexible avec câble intérieur utilisé pour actionner le mécanisme de prise de vues image par image ou le mécanisme de fonctionnement de certaines caméras de cinéma ainsi que l'obturateur d'appareils photographiques.

A cable release

décodage: processus par lequel on redonne à des symboles codés leur valeur ou leur information originales conformément au code utilisé

C *codage; code*

A decoding

décodeur: boîtier électronique permettant la restitution en clair d'informations ou d'émissions codées, notamment pour la télévision à péage.

A decoder

décomposition: en enseignement programmé, méthode de fragmentation en items d'un sujet à programmer.

A step-by-step technique

décor: dans un studio, construction ayant pour objet d'évoquer un environnement réel.

A set; setting

décorateur: technicien responsable de la conception des décors et de la fourniture des accessoires nécessités par le scénario.

A art director

découpage (texte): texte d'une réalisation comme, par exemple, un film, un montage sonorisé, une émission de télévision ou un enregistrement sonore; contient, généralement, en plus du texte, des indications pour les acteurs, les commentateurs et l'équipe de production.

C *découpage technique final; scénario; synopsis*

A script

découpage définitif: plan de tournage d'un film présentant, dans l'ordre et par plan, une description écrite des éléments visuels dans une colonne et des éléments sonores dans l'autre.

A shooting script

découpage technique final: découpage du scénario prêt à être tourné.

A final shooting script

dédié: se dit d'un ordinateur, d'un terminal ou d'une ligne consacrés à un usage particulier. On dit aussi exclusif, spécialisé.

A dedicated

définition: 1. fidélité de restitution du détail d'une image; **2.** degré selon lequel un système de communication reproduit les sons, les images ou les messages; **3.** fidélité avec laquelle les contours de découpage d'un circuit imprimé (conducteurs, inducteurs, etc.) sont reproduits par rapport à l'original ayant servi de modèle.

C *résolution*

A 1. resolution; 2. 3. definition

définition des objectifs: voir **détermination des objectifs**

dégradé: image allant du noir au blanc avec de nombreuses nuances de gris.

A continuous tone

degré de liberté: possibilité de déplacement ou de changement d'un élément (ou d'un composant) dans un système donné.

A degree of freedom

démarche inductive: stratégie d'enseignement fondée sur la présentation à l'apprenant d'un nombre suffisant d'exemples spécifiques pour lui permettre d'induire une règle, un principe ou un fait défini. En enseignement programmé, cette procédure consistant à présenter d'abord les exemples puis la règle, est appelée la méthode EGRUL (de l'anglais exemple + règle).

C *RULEG; méthode déductive*

A inductive learning

demi-image: image de film fixe dont la dimension est la moitié de celle de l'image standard 24 x 36 mm.

A half-frame

démonstration: activité dans laquelle un professeur ou un présentateur s'appuie sur des exemples, des expériences et/ou d'autres manipulations pour illustrer un principe ou montrer à un public comment faire quelque chose.

A demonstration

dénotation: terme de sémiologie pour désigner un ensemble ou une classe d'individus ou d'occurrences appartenant à une même conception ou désignés par un même terme.

C *connotation; message; monosémique*

A denotation

densité: 1. en général, compacité de la distribution spatiale sur un support de stockage comme un disque magnétique, une bande magnétique; **2.** pour une pellicule, degré d'opacité ou de transparence à la lumière.

A 1. 2. density

densité d'enregistrement: en informatique, nombre d'éléments binaires, de groupes d'éléments binaires ou de caractères susceptibles d'être enregistrés par unité de volume, de surface, ou de longueur, par exemple nombre d'éléments binaires rangés par millimètre sur une piste de bande magnétique.

A density

dépassement de capacité: voir **débordement**

dépouillement: avant le montage d'un film, planification de l'utilisation des plans, ou travail de réorganisation des scènes à partir de séquences de tournage non-ordonnées pour aboutir à l'ensemble final souhaité.

A breakdown

de réserve: voir **en attente**

déroulant: technique de banc-titre utilisée pour faire défiler lentement un générique et/ou un texte lorsque le contenu est trop important pour tenir sur un seul carton.

A rolling title

descripteur: mot ou locution contribuant à caractériser l'information contenue dans un document et à en faciliter la recherche.

A descriptor

161

descriptif: description écrite détaillée destinée au producteur, et donnant des informations sur l'objet de la réalisation, le public visé, les contraintes de temps et de coût, le type de document à produire (par exemple films, montage sonorisé, etc.), l'ordre à suivre, les objectifs à atteindre, le contenu à intégrer, les personnages, les décors, l'atmosphère et la perspective générale.

C *synopsis*

A treatment

de secours: personnel, équipement ou matériel supplémentaires disponibles en cas de besoin.

C *en attente*

A back-up

design: instructional design, terme créé par M.D. Merill pour désigner une opération consistant à spécifier ou produire des situations environnementales particulières de telle sorte que des changements déterminés se produisent dans le comportement de l'apprenant.

A instructional design

dessin animé: film réalisé en photographiant une série de dessins avec des procédés d'animation.

C *animation; film d'animation; bande dessinée*

A cartoon

détermination des objectifs: en pédagogie, opération consistant à définir en termes de comportement, l'ensemble des résultats attendus *a)* d'une activité pédagogique ou *b)* d'une action d'éducation.

C *buts; objectifs*

développement communautaire: ensemble des principes et des méthodes mis en œuvre pour encourager les habitants d'une communauté à s'intéresser et à participer, de manière responsable, à l'amélioration des conditions matérielles et sociales de cette communauté.

A community development

devoir: tâche, en général écrite, qui complète une leçon, un cours ou une série d'activités et que l'élève exécute en dehors des heures de classes avec pour but l'application de connaissances acquises à des fins d'assimilation et de contrôle.

A assignment

diagnostic: 1. dans l'approche systématique, démarche d'identification d'une situation (description des éléments et détermination des points critiques) en vue d'une intervention; **2.** processus de détermination des capacités existant chez un élève par une analyse de sa performance au cours d'une série hiérarchisée de tâches fondamentales dans une matière donnée comme les mathématiques ou la musique, en vue de lui faciliter l'apprentissage en lui assignant des tâches d'apprentissage appropriées à un niveau de rattrapage ou à un niveau avancé.

C *approche systémique*

A 1. 2. diagnosis

diagramme: 1. représentation moins fine et moins symbolique qu'un organigramme, incluant souvent des textes de description; **2.** représentation schématique d'une suite de sous-opérations à effectuer par l'ordinateur en vue de la résolution d'un problème.

C *graphique*

A 1. 2. diagram

dialogue: voir **mode dialogué**

diaphragme: dispositif contrôlant l'entrée de la lumière dans un appareil de prise de vues.

A diaphragm

diaphonie: mélange parasite de deux signaux audio ou vidéo séparés.

A crosstalk

diaporama: réalisation combinant des vues fixes (diapositives) et des enregistrements sonores sur bandes et destinée à une présentation ou une illustration le plus souvent automatisé, les projecteurs de vues fixes étant asservis à un magnétophone à plusieurs pistes.

A (diaporama)

diapositive: image transparente (généralement photographique) fixée sur pellicule ou sur verre et destinée à être projetée sur écran.

A slide

diapositive sonorisée: diapositive dont la monture ou le cadre spécial sert de support à un court enregistrement sonore. Les diapositives sonorisées nécessitent un projecteur spécial.

C *montage sonorisé*

A audioslide

diascope: appareil servant à visionner ou à projeter sur écran des vues fixes transparentes présentées sur verre ou sur film.

A slide projector

diazotypie: procédé de duplication consistant à placer un original translucide portant une image opaque ou absorbant la lumière entre une source de lumière ultraviolette et un papier ou film diazo qui est ensuite développé dans des vapeurs d'ammoniaque. Ce procédé est souvent utilisé dans la réalisation de transparents pour rétroprojecteurs.

A diazo process

dichroïque: caractérise un miroir ou réflecteur de lampe de projection conçu pour transmettre la chaleur et réfléchir la lumière. Ce dispositif est appelé aussi miroir froid.

A dichroic

dictionnaire analogique: lexique où les mots sont groupés par idées.

A thesaurus

didacticiel: en enseignement assisté par ordinateur, programme spécifique mettant en œuvre un processus d'enseignement.

C *imagiciel; ludiciel; exerciseur; tutoriel*

A courseware

différenciateur sémantique: technique mise au point, à l'origine, pour mesurer la signification de concepts et utilisée aussi pour évaluer des attitudes.

A semantic differential scale

diffusion: 1. action de répandre, de propager par exemple des idées nouvelles, etc.; **2.** transmission de messages par voie hertzienne; **3.** nombre moyen d'exemplaires d'une publication imprimée vendus ou distribués par d'autres moyens.

A 1. diffusion; 2. broadcasting; 3. circulation

diffusion interne: diffusion systématique de documents imprimés ou non à l'ensemble du personnel d'une organisation en fonction de ses intérêts ou de ses besoins.

A routing

diffusion restreinte: diffusion d'un programme de radio ou de télévision ou de signaux à un petit nombre de personnes ou à un public spécialement sélectionné.

C *radiodiffusion*

A narrowcasting

diffusion-transfert: méthode de fabrication de transparents pour rétroprojecteur consistant à exposer à la lumière un papier sensible placé contre le document original, puis à développer ce négatif au contact d'un positif dans une solution photographique.

A diffusion-transfer process

digital: anglicisme (digit = chiffre): voir **numérique.**

DIN: abréviation de Deutsche Industrie Normen, organisme de regroupement des normes allemandes. Les normes DIN s'appliquent à un grand nombre de produits y compris des éléments d'équipement comme les prises et les fiches.

A DIN

diode: dispositif électronique à semi-conducteur autorisant le passage du courant dans une seule direction.

A diode

diode photoémettrice

A light emitting diode (LED)

diorama: représentation d'une scène en trois dimensions.

A diorama

direct: voir **en direct; méthode directe**

directif: 1. autoritaire: voir **non directif; 2.** qui émet ou reçoit dans une seule direction; ('directionnel' est un terme déconseillé).

A 1. authoritarian; 2. directional

directivité: stratégie d'enseignement centrée sur le maître plutôt que sur l'étudiant.

A teacher-centred instruction

directeur de production: responsable de l'exécution détaillée du travail de production d'un film ou d'une émission sous la direction ou pour le compte d'un producteur.

A production manager

discipline: 1. branche de la connaissance ou domaine scientifique; **2.** ensemble spécifique de connaissances faisant l'objet d'un enseignement distinct; **3.** ordre qui règne dans une classe ou un groupe d'élèves.

C *autodiscipline*

A 1. discipline; 2. subject matter; 3. discipline

discipline d'éveil: voir **activités d'éveil**

discrimination: 1. capacité d'avoir des réactions diversifiées en réponse à des stimuli rencontrés précédemment et différant l'un de l'autre selon une ou plusieurs dimensions (définit un des types de capacité intellectuelle); **2.** finesse d'un test pour distinguer l'un de l'autre, avec le plus de précision possible, deux sujets ou deux objets.

A 1. 2. discrimination

discussion en petits groupes: technique d'animation ayant pour objet d'impliquer tous les membres d'un groupe important dans un travail entrepris en commun, en constituant un ou des petits groupes pour poursuivre, pendant une courte période et de manière non formelle, la discussion d'un sujet préalablement choisi.

A buzz group session

dispositif d'auto-instruction: dispositif d'apprentissage individuel. Comprend les régulateurs individuels de lecture, les équipements individuels de visionnement et d'écoute, les laboratoires de langues et autres machines à enseigner qui présentent des programmes de type verbal par l'intermédiaire de procédés variés, électroniques et mécaniques, de sorte que l'apprenant puisse donner sa réponse et soit informé de ses erreurs ainsi que de sa progression.

C *autonomie; travail indépendant; enseignement/apprentissage individualisé; apprentissage auto-dirigé; autodidaxie; auto-apprentissage*

A auto-instructional device

disque: plaque circulaire en matériau variable qui sert de support d'information.

A disk (computer); disc; record

disque audio: disque en matériau plastique sur lequel une information sonore est enregistrée et lue par un procédé mécanique.

C *vidéodisque*

A audiodisc

disque audio-numérique: minidisque métallisé sur lequel une information sonore est enregistrée sous forme de signaux numériques et lue optiquement par un faisceau laser. Le terme anglais «compact disc» désigne à la fois le disque et le lecteur qui lui est adapté.

A compact disc

disque compact: voir **disque audio-numérique**

disque longue durée: disque audio dont les sillons très fins sont gravés assez près les uns des autres pour permettre environ 25 à 30 minutes d'audition par face de 30 cm de diamètre pour un disque de 33 $\frac{1}{3}$ tours minute.

A long playing record/disc/disk

disque magnétique: élément de mémoire d'un ordinateur sous forme d'un disque plat, non flexible, recouvert d'une couche magnétique sur lequel peuvent être conservées un grand nombre d'informations (jusqu'à 600 millions de bits).

C *disquette*

A hard disk

disque optique: disque audio ou vidéo lu par un procédé optique.

C *disque audio-numérique*

A optical disc

disque souple: minidisque audio en matière plastique flexible.

A flexible record

disque vidéo: voir **vidéodisque**

disquette: élément de mémoire d'un ordinateur sous forme d'un disque magnétique souple de forme et de capacités réduites.

A floppy disk; diskette; floppy

distance focale: caractéristique d'un objectif: distance séparant le foyer d'un objectif de la surface sensible de la pellicule dans l'appareil lorsque la mise au point est faite sur l'infini.

A focal length

distorsion: 1. altération d'un programme audio ou visuel due aux dispositifs d'enregistrement, de transmission ou de reproduction; 2. voir **erreur systématique.**

A 1. distortion; 2. bias

distorsion en trapèze: qualifie la distorsion d'une image plus large au sommet qu'à la base.

A keystoned image

distracteur: réponse piège dans un item de test à choix multiple ou de test d'appariement, offrant une possibilité de choix logique mais incorrecte.

A distractor; decoy; foil

distribuer: 1. faire parvenir quelque chose (objets, marchandises, fluides, données) à des personnes différentes dans des endroits différents; 2. répartir d'une manière particulière selon un ordre donné; 3. exploiter une œuvre cinématographique.

A 1. to distribute; to deliver; 2. 3. to distribute

distributeur: 1. personne qui vend, loue, ou distribue un produit; 2. compagnie, organisme ou cinémathèque qui vend, loue ou distribue des films.

A 1. 2. distributor

distribution: 1. répartition et livraison de quelque chose à des destinataires différents; 2. ensemble des méthodes par lesquelles dans un réseau de transport d'information les messages sont amenés aussi près que possible de l'utilisateur; 3. ensemble des opérations qui vont du film achevé à sa projection en salle; 4. classement pour un effectif donné, d'un ensemble de mesures, de notes à des tests ou à des examens.

C *diffusion; exploitation*

A 1. 2. 3. 4. distribution

distribution artistique: ensemble des interprètes d'une œuvre et aussi liste des acteurs et des rôles apparaissant au générique d'un film ou d'un programme.

A casting; cast list

distribution des rôles: attribution des rôles à des acteurs dans une pièce ou un film.

A cast

distribution normale: distribution symétrique de notes par rapport à la moyenne, les notes se raréfiant à mesure que l'on s'en éloigne selon une équation mathématique. La représentation graphique de cette distribution revêt la forme d'une courbe en cloche ou une courbe de Gauss.

A normal distribution

distribution par câble: voir **télédistribution**

divergence: approche créative de la solution d'un problème qui consiste à rechercher des réponses multiples et originales; notion proche de celle de créativité.

C *convergence*

A divergent thinking

docimologie: science qui a pour objet l'étude systématique des examens, en particulier des systèmes de notation, et du comportement des examinateurs et des examinés.

A (docimologie)

document à copier: 1. document dactylographié ou document graphique avant composition ou photographie; 2. document préparé pour un traitement photographique ou, plus particulièrement, photomécanique.

A 1. 2. copy

documentaire (n.m.): film représentant des faits réels ou reconstitués comme, par exemple, un événement historique, la vie d'une personne, la façon de vivre d'un groupe ou d'une société, le déroulement d'un processus, etc.

A documentary film.

documentaliste: personne spécialisée dans la recherche, la sélection, le classement, la conservation et l'organisation de la documentation imprimée et audiovisuelle.

A documentalist

documentation automatique: ensemble des techniques de recherche et de sélection de l'information documentaire par l'intermédiaire d'un ordinateur.

C *recherche de l'information; recherche documentaire*

A automatic documentation

document(s) d'accompagnement: documents imprimés ou quelquefois audiovisuels accompagnant un moyen d'enseignement ou un programme audiovisuel afin de le présenter plus en détail et de spécifier son utilisation.

A accompanying document(s); accompaniments

document d'appui: document qui, au-delà des documents d'accompagnement, permet une exploitation plus large et approfondie d'un moyen d'enseignement ou d'un programme audiovisuel.

A support material

Dolby: procédé d'enregistrement et de reproduction du son permettant de réduire le bruit de fond sur les disques et les bandes magnétiques.

A Dolby system

domaine affectif: partie de la taxonomie des objectifs pédagogiques de Bloom englobant les objectifs qui décrivent les modifications de l'intérêt, les attitudes et les valeurs ainsi que les progrès dans le jugement et la capacité d'adaptation.

A affective domain

domaine cognitif: partie de la taxonomie des objectifs de Bloom englobant les objectifs qui traitent du rappel des connaissances (remémoration) et du développement des habiletés et des capacités intellectuelles.

A cognitive domain

domaine psychomoteur: partie de la taxonomie des objectifs pédagogiques de Bloom relative aux capacités motrices ou de manipulation.

A psychomotor domain

données: fait ou notion représenté sous forme conventionnelle destiné à faciliter son traitement soit par l'homme soit par des moyens automatiques.

A data

données d'entrée: données à traiter.

A input

données de sortie: information transférée depuis la mémoire interne aux organes de sortie d'un ordinateur en vue de produire des cartes, des bandes, des listages, etc.

A output

doublage: remplacement de la bande sonore originale d'un film par une bande provenant de l'enregistrement d'autres voix en une langue différente. Exemple: doublage d'un film italien en français.

A dubbing

double bande: présentation des images d'un film et du son correspondant en synchronisation sur deux bandes séparées, les enregistrements ayant été effectués sur des supports distincts et, généralement, avec des appareils différents.

A double track

double câble: procédé de doublement de la capacité de canaux, utilisant deux câbles disposés côte à côte pour transmettre des signaux différents.

A dual cable

double commande (appareil en): appareil commandé par deux mécanismes qui dépendent respectivement de l'élève et de l'instructeur; utilisé dans les formations pouvant présenter un danger.

A dual operation system; dual control system

double image: caractérise un film fixe dont les images ont deux fois la surface d'un film fixe de format simple (petit format).

A double frame

douille: pièce métallique à l'extrémité d'un fil électrique dans laquelle on fixe le culot d'une ampoule.

C *prise*
A socket

dramatisation: adaptation d'un texte de lecture, d'un conte, d'une fable, pour en permettre la représentation sous forme théâtrale ou audiovisuelle.

A dramatization

drill: voir **exercice d'automatisation**

droit d'auteur: 1. institution ou branche du droit; **2.** ensemble des droits accordés à un auteur en vertu de la législation nationale sur le droit d'auteur (peut être considéré comme un synonyme du terme «droits de l'auteur»).

C *droits de l'auteur*
A copyright

droit d'interprétation ou d'exécution: droit d'autoriser la présentation d'une œuvre par un moyen tel que l'exécution, la récitation, le chant, la danse ou la projection (soit directement à des auditeurs ou des spectateurs, soit en transmettant la présentation par la radiotélédiffusion).

A performance right

droit de mise en circulation: droit de mettre à la disposition du public en général ou de toute partie de celui-ci des exemplaires d'une œuvre (essentiellement par les circuits commerciaux appropriés).

A distribution right

droits d'adaptation cinématographique: droit exclusif de l'auteur d'une œuvre pré-existante d'en autoriser l'adaptation cinématographique.

A film rights

droits de l'auteur: droits accordés à un auteur en vertu de la législation sur le droit d'auteur à l'égard des œuvres qu'il a créées (généralement droits patrimoniaux et droits moraux).

C *droit d'auteur*
A author's rights

droits d'exclusivité: accord formel attribuant la totalité des droits de vente, location ou distribution d'une œuvre ou d'un produit pour une période spécifique.

A exclusive rights

droits d'utilisation dans le monde entier: droit du titulaire du droit d'auteur sur une œuvre déterminée d'autoriser son utilisation partout dans le monde.

A world rights

droits limités: droits de l'auteur tels qu'ils sont déterminés en vertu de la loi sur le droit d'auteur ou droits de l'utilisation tels qu'ils sont partiellement cédés à celui-ci par l'auteur.

A limited rights

droits sur une œuvre cinématographique: droits du titulaire du droit d'auteur sur une œuvre cinématographique (par exemple le droit de vendre et de mettre en circulation des exemplaires d'une œuvre, d'en autoriser la projection, la télédiffusion, etc.).

A film rights

duplicateur: appareil servant à reproduire un document graphique ou imprimé en un certain nombre d'exemplaires.

C *offset; reprographie*
A duplicator

duplicateur à alcool: duplicateur dans lequel un cliché papier est amené au contact d'une feuille de papier humectée à l'aide d'un liquide de duplication.
A spirit duplicator

duplicateur ronéo: sorte de duplicateur de stencils rotatif.
A mimeograph

duplicateur à stencil: duplicateur dans lequel l'encre est injectée dans les perforations d'un stencil pour produire des copies sur papier.
A stencil duplicator

duplication: réalisation d'une ou plusieurs copies à partir d'un original (bande, film, document, etc.).
C *copie*
A duplicating

durée: temps nécessaire pour faire défiler entièrement un film, une bande ou tout autre document enregistré.
C *durée de projection*
A running time

durée d'attention: période de temps pendant laquelle un sujet peut focaliser son attention sur une tâche donnée, c'est-à-dire sélectionner des informations dans l'environnement et réagir aux changements de stimulation en rapport avec cette tâche.
A span of attention

durée de projection: voir **durée**

dynamique de groupe: voir **dynamique des groupes**

dynamique des groupes: ensemble des facteurs qui soutiennent les interactions des individus à l'intérieur d'un groupe ainsi que le comportement des groupes eux-mêmes. L'étude de cette dynamique apporte un soutien théorique aux méthodes de groupe appliquées à l'instruction et à la formation.
A group dynamics

E

EAO: voir **enseignement assisté par ordinateur**

EBR — electron beam recording: voir **enregistrement par faisceau cathodique.**

écart type: mesure de l'écart d'une distribution par rapport à la moyenne arithmétique.
A standard deviation

échantillon: 1. groupe d'individus, d'événements, de situations ou d'autres éléments, pris en compte dans une recherche; un échantillon constitue toujours une partie ou une subdivision d'une population; **2.** éléments représentatifs d'un ensemble ou d'un équipement soumis à des tests.
C *contrôle de qualité*
A 1. 2. sample

échelle: suite continue de valeurs progressives dans lesquelles on situe les faits, les comportements ou les êtres particuliers pour les apprécier par rapport à un ensemble.
A scale

échelle d'attitudes: instrument d'évaluation quantitative destiné à mesurer les goûts et les aversions d'un sujet.
C *différenciateur sémantique*
A attitude scale

écho: répétition d'un son ou d'une image causée par la réflexion des ondes radioélectriques.
C *image fantôme*
A echo

écho d'image: voir **image fantôme**

éclairage d'ambiance: éclairage provenant d'une direction opposée à celle de l'éclairage principal et donnant l'illusion d'une troisième dimension.

A modeling

éclairage diffus: lumière adoucie par l'emploi de diffuseurs.

A diffuse lighting

école active: conception pédagogique fondée sur les principes de la pédagogie active tels qu'ils ont été définis notamment par Dewey, Freinet, Decroly, et visant à laisser aux élèves une très grande initiative dans l'élaboration des matières d'études. Les élèves se forment par un travail personnel ou de groupe répondant à leur intérêt propre.

A activity oriented education

école annexe: en France, ce terme désigne une école élémentaire ou maternelle, annexée ou proche d'une école normale d'instituteurs, où les élèves-maîtres s'exercent à la pratique de l'enseignement.

A practice school; laboratory school

école d'application: voir **école annexe**

école expérimentale: établissement scolaire rattaché à une institution de recherche et servant à réaliser des essais scientifiquement contrôlés de systèmes, de méthodes et techniques d'enseignement ou de formation du personnel.

C *école pilote*

A experimental school

école normale: en France, établissement public chargé de la formation des maîtres.

A teacher's college; teacher training college; normal school (USA); school of education (UK)

école ouverte: 1. dans la conception anglo-saxonne: école pour tous. Institution ayant pour fin d'offrir aux adultes un accès à des formes d'éducation situées au niveau secondaire et au niveau post-secondaire inférieur au niveau universitaire. Aucun titre académique n'est requis pour l'admission. L'instruction est assurée au moyen d'un enseignement par correspondance, par radio et télévision, ainsi que par des contacts personnels entre étudiants et professeurs; **2.** dans la conception française, organisation spécifique de certaines écoles élémentaires qui pratiquent l'étude du milieu et de l'environnement en faisant largement appel aux parents et aux habitants proches, recourent à une large concertation entre les enseignants afin de décloisonner les disciplines et les activités, et qui sont construites selon un modèle architectural spécifique (cloisons mobiles permettant de délimiter des aires très variables).

C *université ouverte; (open university); enseignement ouvert à tous*

A 1. open school; 2. open-plan school

école parallèle: expression introduite par le sociologue français G. Friedman, pour caractériser l'ensemble des informations, connaissances, valeurs, attitudes et modèles de comportement communiqués et transmis en dehors de l'école par les moyens de communication ou de masse, la presse, les bandes dessinées, la radio, le cinéma et la télévision.

A (école parallèle)

école pilote: établissement scolaire appliquant une innovation et accueillant des professeurs d'autres établissements en vue de leur initiation à des méthodes nouvelles.

C *école expérimentale*

A pilot school; model school

écouteur: voir **casque d'écoute**

écran: 1. surface sur laquelle sont projetées des images. Cette surface peut être perlée, mate, métallique, gaufrée ou dépolie; **2.** surface sur laquelle se forme une image électronique; **3.** cinéma (grand écran), par opposition à petit écran, qui désigne la télévision; **4.** en vidéotex désigne le contenu d'une page d'information présentée à l'écran, syn. page.

A 1. 2. screen; 3. cinema; 4. format

écran à bulles: écran qui utilise des bulles magnétiques pour la visualisation.

A bubble screen

écran aluminisé: voir **écran aluminium**

écran aluminium: écran de projection utilisant un revêtement d'aluminium comme surface réfléchissante.

A aluminium screen

écran cathodique: voir **tube à rayons cathodiques**

écran de contrôle: voir **moniteur (télévision)**

écran dédoublé: voir **image composite**

écran gaufré: écran de projection recouvert d'incrustations en relief d'une substance réfléchissant la lumière.

A embossed screen

écran large: écran de projection dont la largeur par rapport à la hauteur est supérieure ou plus grande que la normale.

A wide screen

écran lenticulaire: écran de projection argenté présentant, sur sa surface, une série géométrique de petites stries permettant de limiter la distorsion de la lumière réfléchie.

A lenticular screen

écran mat: écran à surface de réflexion non directive.

A matte

écran perlé: écran pour projection frontale recouvert d'une multitude de micro-perles de verre ou plastique; ce type d'écran présente un haut niveau réfléchissant et un angle de dispersion étroit.

A beaded screen

écran tactile: en informatique, dispositif d'entrée muni d'un écran qui reconnaît un pointage effectué au toucher.

A touch screen terminal

écrire: inscrire des données dans une mémoire d'ordinateur ou sur un support de données: par exemple, écrire sur une bande magnétique.

A to write

éditeur: programme utilitaire qui permet l'édition d'un fichier.

A editor; file editor

éditeur de didacticiels: outil logiciel d'aide à la création des didacticiels.

C *système auteur*

A courseware editor

édition: informatique: **1.** impression d'un ensemble de résultats en utilisant des formats permettant d'obtenir une certaine mise en page; **2.** construction ou modification d'un fichier de données ou de programmes.

A editing

(educational accountability): 1. théorie selon laquelle les enseignants et les systèmes scolaires peuvent être tenus pour responsables des progrès accomplis ou non par les élèves, et mesurés à l'aide de tests d'efficacité pédagogique par des organismes extérieurs au système; **2.** terme de technologie de l'éducation pour désigner la mesure dans laquelle la performance des élèves peut être attribuée à l'influence de l'enseignement plutôt qu'à des facteurs comme l'âge, la sélection, etc.

A 1. 2. educational accountability

éducation aux médias: activités éducatives visant à une meilleure compréhension des effets, rôles et fonctions des médias sur les individus et la société; s'appelait «éducation à l'écran» dans les années cinquante, car circonscrite à l'éducation au cinéma.

A media education

éducation axée sur la compétence: stratégie éducative fondée sur l'identification, la mise en évidence et l'apprentissage des connaissances, des capacités, des attitudes et des comportements nécessaires pour tenir un rôle particulier, exercer une profession ou mener une carrière déterminée. On dit quelquefois méthode compétentialiste.

C *pédagogie de la maîtrise; enseignement axé sur la performance*

A competency-based education

éducation centrée sur l'apprenant: stratégie éducative dans laquelle les contenus et les processus d'enseignement et d'étude sont déterminés par les besoins et les désirs des apprenants. Ceux-ci participent activement à l'élaboration et au contrôle des programmes. Ce mode d'éducation utilise les ressources et les expériences de ceux qui apprennent.

C *éducation axée sur la compétence; directivité; programme centré sur la matière; apprentissage centré sur l'étudiant; autogestion*

A learner-based education

éducation communautaire: activités organisées afin que les enfants et les adultes acquièrent un sens d'identification à leur communauté, en perçoivent les défauts et mettent en œuvre des modes de participation à des actions destinées à améliorer la qualité de la vie de cette communauté.

C *animation; conscientisation*

A community education

éducation compensatoire: éducation visant à fournir une formation générale à ceux qui, pour une raison ou une autre, soit ont reçu une instruction partielle, soit n'ont pas reçu d'instruction pendant la période normale de l'enseignement obligatoire.

A compensatory education

éducation de la sensibilité: méthode destinée à augmenter la qualité et la capacité des rapports interpersonnels par l'utilisation de la dynamique de groupe comme moyen d'apprentissage et de ré-éducation.

A sensitivity training

éducation permanente: concept selon lequel l'éducation n'est pas une opération limitée dans le temps et s'arrête à la fin de la scolarité à plein temps ou après des études supérieures, mais un processus qui doit se poursuivre tout au long de la vie. L'individu et la société ont besoin que chaque personne ait la possibilité de continuer à se perfectionner systématiquement, sa vie durant. Pour réaliser la pleine potentialité de ces expériences éducatives, il faut qu'il y ait intégration de toutes les étapes de l'éducation, pré-scolaire, primaire, secondaire, supérieure, formation continue (intégration verticale) et de toute la gamme de sortes d'éducation, générale, professionnelle, sociale, culturelle, intellectuelle, affective, physique (intégration horizontale). L'éducation permanente est conçue pour répondre aux problèmes soulevés par les changements rapides, technologiques, économiques et sociaux de la société contemporaine, par la complexité des rôles personnels et sociaux que chaque personne est appelée à remplir, et pour offrir une plus grande égalité de chances éducatives.

A lifelong education

effacer: démagnétiser électroniquement une bande, faire disparaître complètement l'enregistrement visuel ou sonore qui y était inscrit; éliminer tous les niveaux enregistrés antérieurement sur une bande pour pouvoir la réutiliser et en particulier supprimer les données qui figurent sur un support de données, ce qui le libère pour l'enregistrement de nouvelles données.

A to erase

effaceur total: dispositif permettant au même instant d'effacer la totalité d'un enregistrement.

A bulk eraser

effet Hawthorne: terme utilisé pour décrire une situation d'apprentissage où l'amélioration des résultats s'explique plus par l'introduction d'une technique nouvelle, c'est-à-dire par la nouveauté et l'intérêt qu'elle suscite, que par la valeur propre de la technique. Le nom provient d'expériences sur la stimulation de la productivité menées dans les usines de la Western Electric Company à Hawthorne, aux Etats-Unis.

A Hawthorne effect

effet Larsen: sifflement produit lorsque le son d'un haut-parleur est capté par un microphone dans un système de sonorisation.

A feedback

effet placebo: terme transposé du domaine de la médecine à celui de l'éducation. Il décrit l'effet obtenu en proposant à un sujet ou à un groupe témoin de sujets, à leur insu, un produit ou une activité qui sont en eux-mêmes dépourvus d'efficacité. Il est à prendre en compte dans les expériences destinées à tester l'efficacité d'un produit ou d'une activité dont on attend des effets positifs.

A placebo effect

effet second: tout effet, positif ou négatif, prévisible ou non prévisible, qui s'ajoute à un effet cherché ou attendu.

A side effect

effet secondaire: voir **effet second**

effet stroboscopique: effet parasite causé par la vitesse d'objets filmés en mouvement comme, par exemple, les roues d'un véhicule en marche qui semblent tourner à l'envers.

A stroboscopic effect

effets: selon le cas, effets sonores, effets visuels ou effets spéciaux.

A effects

effets pré-enregistrés: effets sonores enregistrés généralement pour être ajoutés ensuite, au montage, sur la bande son de la version définitive d'une production audiovisuelle afin de renforcer l'illusion d'authenticité.

A recorded effects

effets spéciaux: tout plan non réalisable par prise de vue directe. On trouve dans cette catégorie les plans nécessitant des effets de contour, les images multi-images, les images composites, l'utilisation de caches, l'emploi de maquettes et autres procédés. Le terme s'applique aussi aux plans d'explosions et aux effets balistiques et mécaniques.

A special effects

efficacité: mesure dans laquelle une activité atteint les objectifs qui lui ont été assignés.

A effectiveness

efficience: productivité du mode d'exécution d'une activité, c'est-à-dire mesure dans laquelle les apports ont été convertis en produits d'une façon satisfaisante. Par conséquent, alors que la notion d'efficacité se rapporte à la question générale de savoir si les objectifs d'une activité ont été atteints, la notion d'efficience se limite à la qualité de la gestion et à la productivité. Une activité pourrait être efficace sans être efficiente, si elle atteint ses objectifs alors qu'elle a été mal exécutée.

C *efficacité; évaluation; rendement*

A efficiency

égaliseur: dispositif complétant un système audio normal: il permet un réglage de la gamme de fréquences audibles plus fin (souvent octave par octave) que ne le permet un dispositif classique.

A equalizer

EIAJ: Electronic Industry Association of Japan.

A EIAJ

élaboration des programmes d'enseignement: processus d'organisation, d'agencement et de coordination des différents cours qui composent les programmes d'enseignement correspondant à différents niveaux de connaissance et de qualification. Ce processus comprend l'expérimentation, l'évaluation du contenu et de l'efficacité des programmes ainsi que la détermination des méthodes et matériels appropriés d'enseignement et d'apprentissage.

C *curriculum*

A curriculum development

électromagnétique: s'applique aux champs électriques et magnétiques créés par le déplacement d'électrons dans des conducteurs.

A electromagnetic

(electronic classroom): salle de classe pouvant être utilisée aussi comme laboratoire de langues. Elle est équipée d'une simple console maître et d'une série d'écouteurs ou d'un haut-parleur pour les élèves.

A electronic classroom

électrophone: ensemble électro-acoustique composé d'une platine tourne-disque, d'un système d'amplification et d'un ou plusieurs haut-parleurs incorporés ou détachables.

A gramophone (UK); phonograph (USA)

élément binaire : voir **bit**

élément de programme : en enseignement programmé, module distinct présentant une petite unité de base d'un programme.
A frame

élève : 1. personne inscrite dans un établissement d'enseignement ; **2.** écolier fréquentant un établissement d'enseignement élémentaire ou lycéen fréquentant un établissement d'enseignement secondaire.
C *apprenant ; étudiant*
A 1. student ; 2. pupil

embrouilleur : équipement modifiant des signaux électromagnétiques émis et les rendant inintelligibles jusqu'à leur passage dans un dispositif de décodage spécifique situé à l'endroit de réception.
A scrambler

émetteur : 1. dans la théorie de la communication, personne ou organisation qui est à l'origine, à la source d'un message ; **2.** matériel de radiodiffusion sonore ou de télévision qui permet de générer, de moduler et de transmettre dans l'espace, à partir d'une antenne, des signaux destinés à être captés dans une zone de réception définie.
C *récepteur*
A 1. communicator ; 2. transmitter

émettre : envoyer un signal électromagnétique par voie hertzienne ou par câble.
C *transmettre ; radiodiffusion ; distribution par câbles*
A to broadcast ; to transmit

émission : 1. transmission de signaux, image et son par ondes électromagnétiques ; **2.** ce qui est ainsi transmis.
C *transmission ; radiodiffusion ; programme*
A 1. broadcasting ; 2. broadcast

emploi du temps souple : organisation des horaires d'enseignement qui consiste à faire varier les effectifs en fonction des cours et permet de constituer des groupes qui se réunissent à intervalles variables pour des périodes variables.
A flexible schedule

émulsion : couche de la pellicule portant l'image.
A emulsion

en attente : se dit d'un équipement prêt à fonctionner ou à être utilisé à la demande.
C *de secours*
A stand-by

enchaîné : procédé qui donne l'impression qu'une image nouvelle chasse les précédentes de l'écran.
C *fondu-enchaîné*
A wipe

enchaînement : association, dans un ordre particulier, d'une série de réponses discriminables. La production de la première réponse sert de stimulus pour la suivante. Dans les exemples classiques de laboratoire, un renforcement est fourni à la fin de la chaîne de réponses.
A chaining

enceinte acoustique : coffre servant de logement au diffuseur d'un haut-parleur et conçu pour obtenir une bonne sonorité.
A baffle

encouragement : voir **récompense**

en direct : programme diffusé en temps réel, au moment même de sa réalisation. S'oppose à différé ou préalablement enregistré.
A live (programme)

en ligne : caractérise le mode d'exploitation d'un matériel qui fonctionne sous la commande directe de l'ordinateur.
C *autonome*
A on-line

enquête : voir **méthode d'enquête**

enregistrement : 1. ensemble des techniques permettant de fixer une information sur un support matériel en vue de sa conservation et de sa restitution ultérieure ; **2.** support matériel des signaux après fixation, et par extension les signaux eux-mêmes, après restitution ; **3.** terme générique appliqué aux bandes magnétiques et aux disques ;

173

4. en traitement automatisé, ensemble de données et de mots apparentés traités comme un tout.

A 1. recording; 2. 3. record, recording; 4. record

enregistrement d'une émission (radio ou télévision): enregistrement d'un programme radio ou télévision à partir d'une diffusion à l'antenne.

A off-air recording

enregistrement magnétique: technique d'enregistrement d'une information par l'impression, sur une bande, un film ou un fil magnétique, d'une succession de configurations magnétiques.

A magnetic recording

enregistrement multiple: procédé d'enregistrement qui utilise plusieurs pistes longitudinales parallèles entre elles sur une même bande.

A multiple track

enregistrement par faisceau cathodique: système de transfert d'une bande vidéo sur film assurant une bonne qualité de reproduction.

A electron beam recording

enregistrement du son: action d'enregistrer du son à l'aide d'un enregistreur et d'équipements annexes. Cette activité comprend le placement des microphones, le mélange des signaux et l'équilibrage des niveaux mais non les opérations de montage. Elle inclut aussi les repiquages et réenregistrements éventuels.

A sound recording

enregistrer: utiliser un appareil d'enregistrement tel qu'un magnétophone ou un magnétoscope pour capter ou conserver une séquence ou un programme.

A to record

enregistreur: terme générique désignant les appareils permettant d'inscrire une information sur un support matériel.

C *magnétophone; magnétoscope*

A recorder

enseignement à distance: mode d'enseignement qui n'implique pas la présence physique du maître chargé de le donner à l'endroit où il est reçu ou dans lequel le maître n'est présent qu'à certains moments ou pour des tâches spécifiques. Les communications enseignants-enseignés se font principalement par recours à la correspondance, aux imprimés, aux divers médias audio-visuels, à l'informatique, à certains regroupements.

A distance education

enseignement alterné: voir **cours en alternance**

enseignement assisté par ordinateur—EAO: technique d'enseignement ou d'apprentissage qui consiste à utiliser un ordinateur, dont les terminaux sont mis à la disposition des étudiants, pour présenter des programmes didactiques. L'emploi de l'ordinateur peut constituer une des composantes d'un système multimédias.

C *enseignement géré par ordinateur; enseignement généré par ordinateur; enseignement informatisé; informatique*

A computer assisted instruction; computer assisted learning

enseignement à rythme individuel: technique d'enseignement permettant d'organiser les activités de telle sorte que l'apprenant peut atteindre les objectifs fixés en suivant un rythme de son choix (non nécessairement individualisé).

C *enseignement individualisé; auto-évaluation; rythme individuel*

A individually paced instruction

enseignement axé sur la performance*: forme d'auto-enseignement individualisé dans lequel les apprenants ne peuvent accéder à l'étape suivante du programme d'apprentissage que s'ils font la preuve qu'ils ont assimilé ou maîtrisé le contenu de l'étape précédente. Souvent, le critère de réussite est fixé à 100%.

C *pédagogie de la maîtrise*

A performance-based instruction

enseignement collectif: modalité d'organisation pédagogique visant à enseigner les mêmes choses pendant le même temps à un même groupe d'élèves.

C *pédagogie de groupe; enseignement individualisé*

A group instruction

enseignement didactique: méthode d'enseignement mettant l'accent sur les règles, principes, modes de conduite et directives, qui sont généralement présentés directement à l'élève par une autre personne.

A didactic teaching

enseignement direct: enseignement qui s'effectue dans une situation pédagogique de face à face entre enseignant et élève.

C *enseignement à distance; enseignement médiatisé; méthode directe*

A direct teaching

enseignement en équipe: type d'organisation pédagogique comprenant des enseignants et leurs élèves, et dans lequel deux enseignants, ou plus, ont la responsabilité commune de tout ou d'une grande partie de l'enseignement dispensé à un même groupe d'élèves; l'équipe peut inclure, pour l'assister, des auxiliaires ou des élèves-maîtres.

A team teaching

enseignement en grand groupe: voir **enseignement collectif**

enseignement fondé sur les médias: voir **enseignement médiatisé**

enseignement généré par ordinateur: utilisation d'un ordinateur comme moyen d'organisation, de sélection et/ou de production de matériels pédagogiques visant à faciliter l'apprentissage. Ne s'applique pas aux procédures où l'apprenant se trouve en interaction directe avec l'ordinateur.

C *enseignement géré par ordinateur*

A computer-developed instruction

enseignement géré par ordinateur: utilisation de l'informatique en éducation, non pour un enseignement direct, mais pour la gestion du processus pédagogique, à l'exclusion de la gestion administrative des établissements. Les principales applications sont: la gestion des cursus, l'orientation des élèves, la notation, les emplois du temps, la gestion des ressources didactiques, l'individualisation des programmes, le suivi d'élèves dans les systèmes d'enseignement à distance, le diagnostic et l'autocontrôle.

A computer-managed instruction

enseignement individualisé: type d'enseignement adapté aux besoins individuels, par opposition à l'enseignement collectif. Il doit, en principe, tenir compte de six facteurs fondamentaux d'égale importance: (a) emploi du temps souple; (b) diagnostic, soutien spécifique et possibilité de sauts; (c) choix offert entre divers contenus; (d) évaluation diversifiée de l'élève sans contrainte de temps; (e) choix des lieux d'apprentissage; (f) possibilité de pédagogie différenciée.

C *autodidaxie; autonomie; apprentissage auto-dirigé; auto-apprentissage; enseignement à rythme individuel; travail indépendant; travail personnel*

A individualized instruction

enseignement informatisé: terme générique pour désigner toute technique d'enseignement utilisant un ordinateur.

A computer-based instruction

enseignement intégré: conception pédagogique exigeant que l'enseignant identifie aussi clairement que possible les réponses, attitudes, concepts, idées et capacités motrices que l'élève doit acquérir, puis conçoive une approche multiforme et multisensorielle permettant à l'élève d'orienter son activité pour atteindre ces objectifs. Le programme d'apprentissage est organisé de telle manière que les élèves peuvent progresser à leur propre rythme, comblant au fur et à mesure les lacunes, tout en ayant la possibilité de sauter les parties du programme qu'ils ont déjà assimilées lors d'un apprentissage antérieur.

A integrated teaching

enseignement médiatisé: enseignement fondé sur le recours aux médias par opposition à l'enseignement direct. Il s'effectue, par exemple, en utilisant des documents imprimés, des films, des enregistrements, des liaisons téléphoniques, des émissions de radio-télévision ou des terminaux d'ordinateurs.

A *mediated instruction; media-based instruction*

enseignement mutuel: mode d'organisation de l'enseignement dans lequel l'encadrement des apprenants n'est pas assuré par un enseignant mais par d'autres apprenants, en général du même âge et appartenant au même groupe, et qui ont déjà atteint les objectifs d'apprentissage visés. Ces moniteurs ne dispensent pas un enseignement de base, mais aident les apprenants qui, par ailleurs, disposent d'autres documents didactiques ou bénéficient d'un enseignement de rattrapage.

A *peer teaching*

enseignement mutuel inter-niveaux: mode d'organisation par lequel l'enseignement ne s'effectue pas par l'intermédiaire d'un enseignant mais par celui d'autres apprenants, généralement plus âgés, qui ont déjà acquis les contenus ou maîtrisé les compétences à enseigner.

A *cross-age teaching*

enseignement ouvert (à tous): système d'enseignement conçu principalement pour ceux qui n'ont pu ou ne peuvent fréquenter un établissement traditionnel d'enseignement, ou ne disposent pas des diplômes requis pour y être admis.

C *école ouverte; université ouverte*

A *open education*

enseignement par correspondance: forme d'enseignement à distance fondée essentiellement sur l'envoi d'imprimés et sur des échanges de correspondance entre enseignants et enseignés.

C *enseignement à distance*

A *correspondence instruction*

enseignement par groupes de niveau: voir *groupe de niveau*

enseignement par téléphone: 1. tout système d'enseignement utilisant la communication par téléphone et notamment les techniques de téléleçon, de téléconférence et les liaisons téléphoniques entre le domicile et l'école de l'élève; **2.** procédé permettant à un élève retenu chez lui de communiquer avec sa classe par l'intermédiaire du téléphone.

A 1. *telephone instruction;* 2. *telephone school-home instruction*

enseignement périscolaire/péri-universitaire: activités de formation menées par des institutions éducatives à l'intention d'un public extérieur au corps des étudiants régulièrement inscrits. Elles peuvent comprendre des cours de courte durée, des cours radiodiffusés ou télévisés, un enseignement par correspondance, des conférences, des ateliers ou la fourniture de conseils.

A *extension education*

enseignement programmé: méthode d'auto-instruction permettant à l'étudiant de travailler seul et à la cadence de son choix, à l'aide d'un équipement pédagogique (fiches, enregistrements, diapositives, films, etc.) comportant des séquences préalablement construites pour le conduire à l'objectif visé, étape par étape, au moyen d'une série de réponses spécifiques. Les cours programmés sont agencés de manière telle que l'étudiant doit maîtriser une séquence avant de pouvoir passer à la suivante.

C *enseignement assisté par ordinateur*

A *programmed instruction*

enseignement télévisuel: système d'enseignement utilisant essentiellement la télévision comme moyen de communication éducative.

C *télévision éducative; télévision scolaire*

A *instructional television*

ensemble multimédias: ensemble à finalité éducative constitué par un tout cohérent dans lequel chaque média pris isolément a une fonction spécifique et a une position et un rôle déterminé par rapport à ceux des autres.

A multimedia package

ensemble pédagogique: 1. ensemble de documents et/ou d'équipement intégrés en un module d'enseignement et qui permet à un enseignant de mener une série d'activités pédagogiques avec un élève ou un groupe d'élèves; **2.** documents pédagogiques d'autoformation conditionnés ensemble, portant sur le même sujet, accompagnés d'instructions spécifiques à l'usage de l'apprenant et contenant une liste d'objectifs à atteindre ainsi qu'une série d'items de test. On dit aussi matériel d'activité individuelle et trousse pédagogique.

A 1. kit; 2. kit; learning package

en temps partagé: utilisation d'une installation telle qu'un ordinateur, un studio, ou un centre de radiodiffusion à deux ou plusieurs fins, dans le même intervalle de temps, par un système d'alternance des interventions dans le temps.

C *partage du temps*

A timesharing

entraînement: apprentissage d'une tâche fondé sur la répétition méthodique d'un certain nombre de comportements ou d'opérations. S'emploie surtout en éducation physique, en formation professionnelle, mais aussi pour des opérations intellectuelles ou pour la préparation d'une épreuve.

A training

entraînement mental: méthode de formation à la pensée réfléchie, fondée sur l'analyse de situations vécues et sur des procédures répétitives et contrôlées de construction d'opérations intellectuelles surtout employée dans l'éducation des adultes.

A creative thinking development

entrée: 1. jack ou dispositif permettant de faire entrer des signaux dans un appareil; **2.** processus de transfert d'une mémoire externe à la mémoire interne d'un ordinateur; **3.** canal à traiter par un ordinateur en relation avec une entrée ou les données et états correspondants; **4.** en indexation, toute vedette unique ou vedette identifiée dans un index; elle peut s'accompagner de subdivisions, de modificateurs et/ou d'autres références.

C *apports; sortie; données d'entrée*

A 1. 2. 3. input; 4. access

entretenir: assurer un service d'entretien et de réparation.

A to service

entropie: 1. en thermodynamique, grandeur qui permet d'évaluer la dégradation de l'énergie dans un système, c'est-à-dire la quantité d'énergie non disponible; **2.** dans la théorie de l'information, l'entropie mesure le bruit ou les erreurs aléatoires qui arrivent au cours de la transmission de signaux ou d'un message.

A 1. 2. entropy

épidiascope: appareil de projection permettant de projeter à la fois des documents opaques et des vues transparentes.

A epidiascope

épiscope: appareil destiné à la projection de documents opaques et d'objets à surface plane éclairés en réflexion.

A episcope (UK); opaque projector (USA)

épreuve: terme parfois utilisé pour désigner une photographie particulière, un tirage d'étude, un travail d'art ou un cliché d'un plan de film.

A print

épreuve contact: tirage photographique, de même dimension que le négatif, obtenue en exposant à la lumière les positifs et négatifs (pellicule ou papier) disposés ensemble.

A contact print

équilibrage: dans un système audio, l'équilibrage est atteint lorsque le son diffusé par les haut-parleurs s'approche au maximum de l'ambiance originale du lieu où s'est effectué l'enregistrement.

A balance

équipe: ensemble de personnes travaillant à la réalisation de tel ou tel aspect d'un film, par exemple équipe de prise de vues, équipe de prise de son, etc.

A crew

équipement : 1. tout ce qui sert à pourvoir une personne, un local, une institution des choses nécessaires à une activité déterminée. Dans le domaine de l'éducation, ce terme désigne l'ensemble des biens durables (appareils, machines, matériels, mobiliers) portés à l'inventaire d'un établissement ; **2.** par opposition à matériel ou programme, désigne les installations et les appareils : par exemple, équipement audiovisuel, équipement scientifique.

C *matériel ; moyens d'enseignement ; (hardware) ; (software)*

A 1. 2. equipment

équipement scolaire et universitaire : ensemble des constructions, installations et matériels nécessaires au fonctionnement des diverses institutions d'enseignement et d'éducation.

A educational facilities

ergonomie : étude scientifique fondée sur l'anatomie, la physiologie et la psychologie, des conditions d'adaptation réciproque de l'homme et de son travail, de l'homme et de la machine. Dans le domaine de l'éducation, l'ergonomie concerne la relation entretenue par l'apprenant (ou les apprenants) et l'éducateur (ou les éducateurs) avec leurs occupations, l'équipement et les auxiliaires utilisés dans le processus d'enseignement et d'apprentissage, leur environnement de travail et d'étude, et l'organisation socio-temporelle et spatiale de leur travail.

A ergonomics

ergot de sécurité : petite languette ou lamelle à l'arrière d'une cassette qui peut être cassée pour prévenir tout nouvel enregistrement sur la piste correspondante.

A breakout lug

erreur systématique – distorsion : erreur qui affecte toutes les observations dans le même sens mais pas nécessairement de façon égale. On dit aussi biais.

A bias

essais et erreurs : en pédagogie, procédé de découverte de la meilleure manière d'atteindre un résultat souhaité ou de résoudre un problème par tâtonnements successifs et par l'élimination systématique des erreurs ou des causes d'échec.

A trial-and-error learning

essai général : essai expérimental d'équipements ou de programmes d'ordinateur.

A dry run

estimation : 1. jugement de valeur porté dans un domaine qualitatif ; **2.** essai d'évaluation par approximation ; **3.** valeur particulière (ou statistique) calculée sur un échantillon particulier.

C *appréciation ; évaluation*

A 1. estimation ; 2. 3. estimate

estompage : en enseignement programmé, retrait progressif des indices dans une séquence d'items didactiques. Les séquences commencent normalement par des items à forte densité d'indices et s'achèvent par des items terminaux dépourvus d'indices. Le terme est parfois utilisé comme synonyme d'évanouissement.

A fading

étalonnage : 1. modification subjective des intensités de lumière et des filtres de couleurs au tirage pour obtenir un positif équilibré à partir d'un négatif qui ne l'est pas ; **2.** action d'étalonner un test ou un instrument de mesure.

A 1. grading ; (USA : timing) ; 2. standardization

étalonner : appliquer un test ou plus généralement un instrument de mesure à un groupe de référence en vue d'élaborer des normes statistiques.

C *note étalonnée*

A to standardize

étiquette : dans un système informatique, information particulière, liée à une donnée ou à un ensemble de données qui permet de la repérer et de l'identifier.

A tag

étude à temps partiel : désignation administrative pour une formation suivie par des étudiants qui ne sont pas inscrits à plein temps dans une institution éducative.
A part-time study

étude de faisabilité : étude visant à déterminer dans quelle mesure une stratégie est applicable, un projet réalisable.
C *faisabilité*
A feasibility study

étude du milieu : organisation synthétique d'activités permettant aux élèves d'appréhender et de connaître leur environnement proche, et impliquant une convergence de l'enseignement de disciplines telles que la géographie, l'économie, l'histoire, la biologie et la physique.
A environmental studies

étudiant : personne inscrite dans un établissement d'enseignement supérieur.
C *élève*
A student

évaluation : 1. terme générique pour désigner l'ensemble des opérations d'appréciation, de contrôle et de mesure d'un résultat, d'une stratégie, d'un système, d'une personne, etc. ; **2.** processus visant à délimiter, obtenir et réunir l'information utile pour juger des alternatives de décision, à contrôler l'efficacité de l'exécution d'une activité et à juger après coup de son intérêt ; **3.** voir **appréciation.**
C *évaluation formative; évaluation sommative; examen critique; apports; contrôle*
A 1. 2. evaluation ; 3. rating

évaluation concomitante : voir **évaluation sommative**

évaluation des besoins éducatifs : méthode systématique d'estimation des besoins éducatifs et des buts éducatifs et sociaux d'un groupe ou d'une communauté.
A needs assessment

évaluation des processus : type d'évaluation fournissant un feedback périodique aux responsables de la mise en œuvre des plans et des procédures.
C *évaluation formative; évaluation sommative; évaluation des produits*
A process evaluation

évaluation des produits : type d'évaluation mesurant et interprétant les résultats d'un programme d'éducation par rapport aux objectifs intermédiaires et/ou terminaux.
C *évaluation des processus; évaluation sommative*
A product evaluation

évaluation formative : 1. évaluation de programmes d'enseignement quand ils sont encore en cours de mise au point ; **2.** évaluation ayant pour objet de fournir des données utiles à la révision de matériels d'enseignement ; **3.** évaluation effectuée à l'intérieur et tout au long du processus de conception et de réalisation d'une production, d'un cours ou d'un programme et qui permet une rétroaction.
C *contrôle continu; évaluation sommative*
A 1. 2. 3. formative evaluation

évaluation sommative : 1. évaluation dont le but est de fournir des données pour une validation de programmes et matériels d'enseignement ; **2.** évaluation orientée vers des critères et des normes faisant intervenir les usagers, les administrateurs et les enseignants ; **3.** évaluation finale considérée hors de tout processus de rétroaction ou de feedback.
C *évaluation formative*
A 1. 2. 3. summative evaluation

évaluer : voir **examiner**

évanouissement : 1. diminution temporaire du niveau moyen des signaux électromagnétique due à des variations dans le temps des conditions de propagation ; **2.** en enseignement programmé, réduction progressive des éléments d'une chaîne spécifique de réponses. Le terme est souvent utilisé comme synonyme d'estompage, qui désigne le processus de diminution des indices.
A 1. fading ; 2. vanishing

éveil: voir **activités d'éveil**

examen: 1. opération d'analyse et d'évaluation d'une activité, d'un projet, d'un dispositif ou d'un matériel; **2.** épreuve complexe visant l'appréciation des connaissances et des capacités des élèves ou des étudiants et déterminant soit l'attribution d'un diplôme, soit le passage d'un niveau ou d'un cycle d'études à un autre.

A 1. assessment; 2. examinations

examen blanc: simulation d'un examen public organisée par une institution d'enseignement, par ex.: bac blanc.

A mock examination

examen critique: processus de quantification ou de qualification des performances d'un individu, d'un groupe, d'un dispositif ou d'un matériel.

C *examen préalable; évaluation*

A assessment

examen préalable: évaluation critique de la pertinence, de la faisabilité et de l'efficacité potentielle d'une activité ou d'un projet avant que soit prise la décision de l'exécuter ou de lui accorder une aide.

C *examen critique*

A appraisal

examiner: 1. analyser et juger, de manière critique et concluante, la nature, la signification, la dimension ou la valeur de quelque chose; **2.** faire passer un examen ou un test.

A 1. to assess; 2. to set

exercice d'automatisation: exercice systématique et répétitif lié à une activité d'apprentissage et ayant pour but d'aider à acquérir et à fixer un point particulier ou un savoir-faire spécifique.

A drill

exercice pratique: activité dans laquelle les élèves effectuent une tâche ou un travail dans un domaine donné de manière répétée, afin d'acquérir une compétence; on y associe souvent un entraînement («répétition et entraînement»).

A practice exercise

exercice structural: en enseignement des langues, exercice faisant appel à des énoncés modèles ou canoniques dans lesquels des changements partiels mais consistants au niveau des sons, de l'ordre des éléments et du vocabulaire sont effectués de manière répétée pour aider l'élève à acquérir la maîtrise de la structure spécifique (grammaticale ou autre) qu'il pratique.

A pattern drill

exerciseur: voir **programme d'exercices**

expérimentation sur le terrain: expérimentation à grande échelle de la version quasi définitive d'un ensemble de matériels pédagogiques, effectuée à l'extérieur ou en dehors d'un centre de production, pour déterminer les défauts généraux et/ou la viabilité et l'utilité finale de l'ensemble ou pour en mesurer l'efficacité, les coûts et les potentialités.

A field testing

exploitation: voir **distribution 3**

exploitation en duplex: mode d'exploitation suivant lequel la transmission est possible simultanément dans les deux sens de la voie de télécommunication.

C *multiplex*

A duplex operation

exploitation pédagogique: ensemble des activités et exercices suggérés et proposés à l'enseignant – et/ou ensemble des activités menées par l'enseignant – en vue de faciliter l'intégration d'un document relativement long et complexe (une émission de radio, de télévision, un film...) dans la progression pédagogique.

A follow-up activities

exposition: 1. présentation en un lieu déterminé et pendant une certaine durée d'objets et/ou de documents groupés autour d'un thème dans une perspective d'ensemble; **2.** quantité de lumière passant par l'objectif et impressionnant la pellicule sensible.

A 1. exhibit; 2. exposure

extinction: élimination ou réduction progressive de l'ampleur ou de la fréquence d'une réponse conditionnée lorsqu'il y a suppression du renforcement. Le terme s'applique à la fois au conditionnement classique et au conditionnement opérant.

A extinction

extra-muros: enseignement extra-muros: enseignement donné hors des murs de l'université grâce au recours à la correspondance et à divers médias; étudiants extra-muros: étudiants faisant leurs études hors des murs de l'université grâce à divers processus de communication éducative à distance.

A extra-mural

F

facilitateur: personne qui peut, grâce à ses connaissances et à son expérience, aider un élève dans sa démarche de formation.

C *animateur; tuteur*

A facilitator

fac-similé: 1. reproduction exacte d'un document original; 2. en télécommunication, document obtenu par télécopie.

C *télécopie*

A 1. 2. facsimile

faire un branchement: voir **sauter**

faisabilité: caractère de ce qui est réalisable en fonction des ressources et des possibilités techniques.

C *étude de faisabilité*

A feasibility

faisceau: 1. ensemble de rayons électromagnétiques, lumineux ou électroniques, issus d'une même source et contenus à l'intérieur d'un cône déterminé ou d'un lobe de rayonnement; 2. région de l'espace contenant l'ensemble de ces rayons électromagnétiques.

A 1. 2. beam

(feedback): information-retour. Dans un système physique, biologique ou humain, désigne la réaction de l'élément récepteur qui parvient à l'élément émetteur et qui constitue pour ce dernier une information sur l'effet produit.

C *réponse; retour d'écoute; rétro-action*

A feedback

fenêtre: endroit où sont placés les transparents sur un rétroprojecteur; ouverture rectangulaire ou carrée devant laquelle se présentent les diapositives ou les images d'un film dans un projecteur.

A aperture

fermé/ouvert: qualifie un message (une question, un récit, un film) en fonction des possibilités d'interprétation, de réponse qu'il permet. Film fermé, film qui ne permet qu'une interprétation; item fermé, item dont les réponses ont été précodées.

C *monosémique; polysémique; question ouverte; système fermé/ouvert*

A closed/open ended

fermeture d'une session: voir **ouverture/fermeture d'une session**

fermeture en fondu: voir **fondu**

feuille de calcul électronique: voir **tableur**

feuilleton: publication ou émission de radio ou de télévision présentée en épisodes successifs, d'ordinaire à intervalles réguliers, et, conçue, en règle générale, pour se poursuivre pendant un certain temps.

A serial

fiabilité: caractéristique d'un équipement, d'un instrument de mesure ou d'un test qui fonctionne de manière sûre dans des conditions déterminées.

C *fidélité; sensibilité; validité*

A reliability

fibres optiques: ensemble de miniscules fils ou fibres de verre utilisés pour la transmission de signaux.

A optical fibres

fiche: 1. connecteur ou dispositif de connexion, généralement placé à l'extrémité d'un cordon ou câble, la connexion étant effectuée par insertion, avec ou sans verrouillage, dans la prise correspondante; **2.** feuille ou carton sur laquelle on inscrit des renseignements en vue d'un classement.

C *fiche banane*

A 1. plug; 2. card

fiche auto-corrective: dans la pédagogie Freinet, matériel pour le travail individualisé constitué par un ensemble des fiches proposant des exercices de difficulté progressive ainsi que des fiches-réponse.

A work card with answer key*

fiche banane: fiche électrique à un seul conducteur. La fiche mâle est terminée par une extrémité en métal fondu ou équipée d'un dispositif faisant ressort pour assurer un bon contact avec la fiche femelle.

A banana plug

fichier: dans un système informatique, ensemble de données compact et structuré habituellement conservé sur un élément de mémoire comme un disque. Les fichiers ne font pas partie des programmes, mais sont accessibles pour consultation pendant l'utilisation d'un programme.

A file

fichier auto-correctif: voir **fiche auto-corrective**

fichier principal: en informatique, fichier de référence contenant les informations de base nécessaires à une application et en particulier les tables d'accès aux autres fichiers.

A master file

fidélité: degré selon lequel un instrument de mesure ou un test mesure de manière constante ce qu'il est censé mesurer.

C *fiabilité; sensibilité; validité*

A reliability

filament: conducteur filiforme qui peut être rendu incandescent par le passage d'un courant électrique.

A filament

filières: désigne les différentes séries de programmes susceptibles d'être offertes par l'enseignement secondaire, séries vers lesquelles sont orientés les élèves en fonction de leurs intérêts et aptitudes; par exemple: filière générale, classique, scientifique, technique ou professionnelle.

C *groupement selon les aptitudes*

A streams (UK); tracks (USA)

film: 1. pellicule photosensible servant à la prise de vues photographie ou cinématographique; **2.** œuvre cinématographique, voir **court métrage; documentaire; film animé.**

A 1. film; stock; 2. film (UK); motion picture (USA)

film amorce: voir **amorce**

film animé: pellicule d'une certaine longueur, avec ou sans piste sonore magnétique ou optique, servant de support à une séquence d'images produisant une illusion de mouvement lorsqu'elles sont projetées à cadence rapide (généralement 18 ou 24 images par seconde). Les formats les plus courants des films animés éducatifs sont 16 mm, 8 mm et super 8 mm.

C *dessin animé; film fixe; film d'animation*

A film (UK); motion picture (USA)

film annonce: voir **bande de lancement**

film à piste couchée: film ayant, sur le côté, une mince bande d'oxyde magnétique sur laquelle on peut enregistrer une piste magnétique.

A striped film

film avec piste sonore incorporée: enregistrement d'images cinématographiques animées et du son synchrone correspondant sur un seul et même film.

A sound-on-film

film cinématographique: voir **film animé**

film couleur: voir **pellicule couleur**

film court: voir **film monovalent**

film d'animation: film produit par un procédé d'animation.

C *animation; film de trucage; dessin animé*
A animated film; cartoon

film de banc titre: film réalisé à partir d'images fixes, généralement en utilisant des effets spéciaux.

A filmograph

film de complément: 1. film additionnel conçu pour apporter des informations complémentaires à celles contenues dans un film principal.; **2.** petit film précédant le film principal dans un programme.

A 1. supplementary film; 2. second feature

film d'enseignement: film produit essentiellement à des fins pédagogiques.

C *film éducatif*
A teaching film; instructional film

film de long métrage: film dépassant 48 minutes ou comportant plus d'une bobine. Le terme est parfois utilisé abusivement pour désigner tout film de fiction.

A feature film

film de présentation: film ne montrant que les éléments essentiels du film original.

A abstract

film de sécurité: pellicule dont le support est difficilement inflammable et combustible.

A safety film

film de trucage: film avec effets spéciaux, par exemple lorsque des objets apparaissent, se modifient ou disparaissent sans cause apparente...

C *film d'animation; effets spéciaux*
A trick film

film documentaire: voir **documentaire**

film doublé: voir **doublage**

film éducatif: au sens large, tout film utilisé en contexte éducatif pour l'enseignement de savoir-faire, de faits, de concepts, d'attitudes et de valeurs. Au sens étroit, film scolaire.

A educational film

film en boucle: une certaine longueur de film dont les extrémités sont collées ensemble, formant ainsi un ruban sans fin permettant un défilement continu.

C *film monovalent*
A loop film

film en cartouche: film animé, monté en boucle et contenu dans un boîtier, pour déroulement continu sans rembobinage.

A cartridge film

film en couleur: film réalisé en utilisant une pellicule couleur.

A colour film

film exposé: état d'une pellicule après son passage dans une caméra ou une tireuse et avant le développement des images latentes dont elle est le support.

C *surexposition; sous-exposition*
A exposed film

film fixe: morceau de pellicule d'une certaine longueur servant de support à une série ordonnée d'images fixes, en 18 x 24 mm ou 24 x 36 mm, projetées une par une. La plupart des films fixes sont en 35 mm, mais certains sont en 16 mm en moins.

A filmstrip

film impressioné: voir **film exposé**

film intermédiaire: voir **tirage intermédiaire**

film inversible: film qui, après exposition, est traité pour donner un positif sur la même surface.

A reversal film

film magnétique: support de film animé muni de perforations et recouvert, à la place d'émulsion photographique, d'un oxyde magnétique permettant l'enregistrement et la lecture des sons.

A magnetic film

film monovalent: film animé court (généralement de format 8 mm ou super 8 mm, monté en boucle et conditionné en cassette) exposant une seule idée, un seul savoir-faire ou un seul concept. On dit aussi film court.

A (single) concept film; loop film

film muet: film réalisé ou projeté sans piste son.

A silent film

film parlant: film animé avec son synchrone correspondant.

A sound film

film sonore: voir **film parlant**

film super 8: film animé ou fixe présentant des images plus grandes et des perforations plus petites que les premiers films 8 mm.

A super 8 film

film test, bande test: film ou bande spécialement conçu pour évaluer les performances techniques d'un équipement.

A test film/tape

filtre: 1. élément fait de verre teinté ou traité ou d'une autre substance transparente et ayant pour fonction de modifier la quantité, la couleur ou la composition de la lumière impressionnant la pellicule; **2.** dispositif électronique servant à limiter ou à contrôler les réponses de fréquences.

A 1. 2. filter

finalités: voir **fins**

finesse: voir **définition 1.**; **pouvoir de résolution**

fins: buts ultimes, énoncés en termes généraux, d'une action éducative ou d'un apprentissage. Ces buts sont généralement relatifs à l'épanouissement de la personne ou au développement de la société.

C *but; objectif*

A aims

(fisheye): objectif à très courte distance focale permettant de prendre des photographies avec un très grand angle de champ.

A fisheye

flannellographe: voir **tableau de feutre**

flash: 1. lampe émettant une lumière brève mais intense permettant de prendre des instantanés; **2.** information importante transmise en priorité.

A 1. 2. flash

flashcard: voir **carte flash**

flash électronique: dispositif d'éclairage par procédé électronique produisant une lumière brève mais intense servant à éclairer un objet à photographier. Beaucoup de ces dispositifs sont portatifs et peuvent se fixer sur l'appareil photo lui-même.

A electronic flash

flasque: disque circulaire situé sur l'un ou les deux côtés d'un noyau pour maintenir ou guider une bande ou un film.

A flange

flocage: procédé consistant à pulvériser des fibres textiles ou des particules diverses sur du carton afin de le rendre adhésif sur un tableau de feutre.

C *papier floqué; tableau en velcro*

A flocking

flou: 1. image caractérisée par une absence de finesse, de définition ou de luminosité; **2.** absence de mise au point.

A 1. blurred; 2. out of focus

focale: voir **foyer; objectif à focale variable; objectif à longue focale**

fonds: contenu d'une bibliothèque ou d'un centre de ressources éducatives.

A collection

fondu: 1. apparition progressive d'une image à partir du noir (ouverture en fondu) ou disparition progressive vers le noir (fermeture en fondu); **2.** dans un système audio, abaissement volontaire progressif du volume sonore. Voir aussi fondu enchaîné, fondu sonore.

A 1. fade; 2. shunt

fondu enchaîné: en mixage son, film et télévision, abaissement progressif du niveau d'une source avec, simultanément, augmentation progressive de celui d'une autre.

A cross fade

fondu sonore: passage progressif d'un signal sonore audible au silence.

A sound fade

format: 1. dimensions caractéristiques d'un support de message (livre, film, bande magnétique, etc.); 2. disposition des données sur un support d'information indépendamment de leur codage (syn. structure de données).

A 1. 2. format

format de bande: caractéristiques telles que l'épaisseur, la largeur, le nombre et la disposition des pistes, la vitesse, l'impulsion de synchronisation, le conditionnement, etc. servant à distinguer ou à identifier les bandes.

C *largeur de bande; format vidéo*

A tape format

format de l'image: en photographie, rapport de la largeur à la hauteur d'une image rectangulaire.

A aspect ratio

formation continue des maîtres: le terme désigne les activités de formation destinées au perfectionnement et au recyclage des personnels de l'éducation qui ont déjà reçu une formation initiale.

A in-service teacher training; continuing teacher education

formation continuée des maîtres: voir **formation continue des maîtres**

formation (initiale) des maîtres: ce terme désigne la formation tant générale que professionnelle fournie aux futurs enseignants dans les centres de formation.

C *formation continue; école normale*

A teacher education; pre-service teacher training

formation en cours d'emploi: formation fournie à des personnes engagées dans une activité professionnelle ayant pour objet d'améliorer les capacités et les qualifications reliées à l'emploi.

A in-service training

formation extra-universitaire: formation en dehors du système universitaire institutionnel.

C *extra-muros*

A off-campus study

formation professionnelle: formation ayant pour objet de développer les attitudes, les connaissances et les compétences requises pour l'exercice d'un emploi ou d'un métier.

A vocational training

formatage: opération de préparation d'un disque magnétique qui consiste à délimiter des secteurs pour lui permettre de recevoir des données.

A formatting

format vidéo: spécifications techniques ou standards déterminant la compatibilité et la qualité de diffusion, réception, enregistrement et reproduction des bandes vidéo. Le format de bande peut être de ¼, ½, ¾, 1 pouce ou 2 pouces. La bande peut être présentée sur bobine ou conditionnée en cassette ou en cartouche. L'enregistrement peut être fait sur pistes obliques ou hélicoïdales, transversales ou longitudinales. La couleur peut être codée selon les procédés NTSC, SECAM ou PAL. Les appellations BETA ou BETAMAX, VHS (Video Home System), Video 2.000 (V 2.000) et U-MATIC désignent des systèmes combinés d'enregistrement et de lecture commercialement brevetés.

A video format

fortran: (FORmula TRAnslation); langage de programmation évolué très utilisé pour les applications numériques.

A FORTRAN

foyer: point optique où les rayons lumineux traversant l'objectif se recoupent pour donner une image nette.

C *distance focale*

A focus

fréquence: 1. oscillation d'une onde ou d'un signal exprimée en hertz, autrefois en «cycles par seconde». La fréquence est ainsi utilisée pour définir tout courant ayant une périodicité régulière comme un courant alternatif; **2.** nombre d'occurences d'un phénomène par rapport à un ensemble.

A 1. frequency; 2. proportion

fréquence audio: fréquence appartenant à la partie de la bande des fréquences audibles utilisée pour la transmission ou la reproduction des sons. Le terme basse fréquence est déconseillé.

A audio-frequency

fréquence de balayage horizontal: nombre de lignes parcourues par un spot analyseur ou synthétiseur pendant une seconde.

A line frequency

fréquence de trame: voir **fréquence de balayage horizontal**

fréquence radio-électrique: toute fréquence du spectre électromagnétique inférieure aux fréquences optiques. C'est une fréquence utile pour la transmission vidéo ou télévision.

C *micro-onde; hyperfréquence*

A radio frequency (RF)

fréquence vidéo: bande de fréquences s'étendant depuis les fréquences très basses jusqu'à des fréquences très élevées, par exemple plusieurs mégahertz; en particulier, fréquences des composantes spectrales du signal d'image.

A video frequency

fuite: courant électrique parasite pouvant s'établir entre un appareil et un opérateur ou passer par cet opérateur.

A leakage

futurologie: voir **prospective de l'éducation**

G

gain: 1. dans un système, rapport de la sortie à l'entrée, les deux grandeurs étant exprimées dans la même unité; **2.** rapport de deux grandeurs réelles ou complexes, de même nature mesurées respectivement à la sortie et à l'entrée d'un amplificateur ou d'un récepteur. Exemples: gain en puissance, gain en tension, gain en courant.

A 1. 2. gain

généralisation: processus selon lequel les résultats obtenus avec des sujets particuliers ayant fait l'objet d'une recherche spécifique peuvent être étendus valablement à une population beaucoup plus grande.

A generalization

générateur de caractères: dispositif électronique permettant d'afficher des caractères alphanumériques sur un écran de télévision.

A character generator

générateur d'effets spéciaux: dispositif permettant de combiner électroniquement des signaux pour produire des effets visuels comme ceux d'images composites, d'apparition ou d'effacements par volet et de compositions diverses. Il peut se présenter sous forme d'une unité indépendante ou être incorporé à une console.

A special effects generator

génération: terme désignant une copie ou un contretype d'un film ou d'une bande. L'original constitue la première génération. Une copie à partir de cet original est de seconde génération. Une copie de la première copie est de troisième génération, et ainsi de suite.

A generation

génération d'images: production de tracés par un ordinateur sur un écran cathodique.

A generation

générique: liste des noms des personnels ayant participé à la réalisation d'un programme radio ou télévisé ou d'un film.
C *déroulant*
A credits

génie informatique: conception, réalisation et validation des systèmes informatiques.
A software engineering

genlock: voir **verrouilleur du générateur de synchronisation**

gestionnaire de données: outil logiciel ayant pour fonction la gestion automatisée d'une base de données.
C *système de gestion de base de données*
A data base manager; data base management program

gestionnaire de fichiers: programme utilitaire appartenant au système d'exploitation d'un ordinateur et qui permet un traitement aisé des différents fichiers.
A file manager; file management program

gestion par objectifs: technique de gestion participative dans laquelle supérieur et subordonnés identifient ensemble leurs buts communs, définissent chacun des principaux domaines de responsabilité individuelle en termes de résultats escomptés et utilisent ces objectifs préétablis comme guide pour gérer une unité et évaluer leur contribution réciproque.
C *pédagogie par objectifs*
A management by objectives

gigue: déplacement saccadé et irrégulier de l'image visible dû à un défaut du système de synchronisation ou de projection.
A jitter

gondolage: déplacement soudain du centre d'une diapositive en raison d'une déformation causée par la chaleur.
A popping

gonflage: procédé utilisé pour obtenir des copies de film de format supérieur à partir d'une pellicule de format inférieur; par exemple: gonflage de copies 16 mm en 35 mm, pour salles de spectacle.
C *agrandissement*
A blow up

gradateur: dispositif servant à contrôler l'intensité d'une lumière.
A dimmer

graphe: représentation graphique d'une fonction ou d'un ensemble de relations par un ensemble de points appelés sommets et d'arêtes ou d'arcs joignant ces sommets.
A graph

graphique: mode de représentation géométrique des résultats statistiques.
C *diagramme*
A graph; chart

grain: particules chimiques élémentaires développées formant une image sur une pellicule. Si ces particules sont de très petites dimensions, la définition de l'image est très bonne et on dit que la pellicule a un grain fin.
A grain

griffe d'entraînement: mécanisme d'entraînement du film vers le bas, dans une caméra de cinéma ou un projecteur, qui fait descendre une seule image à la fois, tandis qu'un obturateur masque l'opération. Le résultat donne une illusion de mouvement.
A claw

grille des programmes: répartition horaire des programmes de radio et de télévision.
A programme schedule

groupe de base: technique utilisée en dynamique de groupe. Elle a pour objet de rendre les participants plus sensibles au fait qu'autrui perçoit leur comportement d'une façon différente de la leur, et de développer leurs capacités de diagnostic en matière de comportement interpersonnel. En général, les participants à un groupe de base ne se connaissent pas à l'avance, et surtout ne sont pas en relation permanente entre eux.

C *groupe de diagnostic*

A training-group; T-group; sensitivity group

groupe de contrôle: voir **groupe témoin**

groupe de diagnostic: technique utilisée en dynamique de groupe, qui consiste à travailler sur un certain nombre de problèmes communs à des personnes qui sont normalement en relation entre elles.

A therapy group

groupe de discussion: voir **groupe de diagnostic**

groupement selon les aptitudes: répartition des élèves en des groupes homogènes, à des fins d'apprentissage ou d'enseignement, en fonction de la mesure de certaines capacités.

C *groupe de niveau*

A ability grouping

groupes appareillés: technique d'affectation de sujets dans un groupe expérimental et un groupe témoin, ayant pour but la constitution de groupes équivalents. Les sujets sont généralement appareillés en tenant compte de quatre ou cinq variables. A chaque sujet affecté dans un groupe, correspond un sujet analogue dans l'autre groupe, établissant une correspondance de sujet à sujet, selon les mêmes variables.

A matched groups

groupes pairés: voir **groupes appareillés**

grue: terme générique pour tout dispositif en forme de grue permettant de suspendre un microphone, une caméra et, parfois, du matériel d'éclairage.

A boom; camera crane

guide d'ondes: tube métallique creux utilisé pour la transmission d'ondes de très hautes fréquences.

A wave guide

groupe de niveau: regroupement d'élèves, en général d'un même niveau et/ou d'une même classe, selon leurs compétences dans certaines matières.

A ability group; set; setting

groupe de sensibilisation: voir **groupe de base**

groupe d'intervention: formation ou équipe temporaire constituée de personnes possédant des compétences appropriées et réunie pour rechercher et proposer une solution à un problème particulier ou aux difficultés liées à un projet spécifique.

A task force

groupe expérimental: ensemble des sujets d'un échantillon, présumés être les seuls à posséder les caractéristiques de la variable indépendante, ou les seuls à faire l'objet du traitement expérimental.

C *groupe témoin*

A experimental group

groupe témoin: échantillon constitué de la même façon que le groupe expérimental mais non soumis à l'expérience. La comparaison entre l'évolution des deux groupes permet de mesurer l'efficacité de l'expérience.

A control group

groupement par niveau: voir **groupe de niveau**

H

habileté: voir **savoir-faire**

halo: 1. image parasite qui entoure sur une pellicule celle normalement produite par l'objectif; **2.** tache parasite sur la surface sensible, due à la réflexion d'un excès de rayons lumineux sur la partie dorsale du support de la pellicule; **3.** zone sombre d'un tube image entourant une zone brillante saturée.

A 1. 2. 3. halation

(hardware): mot emprunté au vocabulaire américain de l'informatique; en français «matériel»; **1.** ensemble des éléments physiques employés pour le traitement des données; **2.** ensemble des appareils et équipements.

C *équipement; matériel; (software)*

A 1. 2. hardware

haute fidélité − hi-fi: technique très performante d'enregistrement, de conservation et de reproduction des sons principalement musicaux, reproduisant fidèlement les sons originaux.

A high fidelity (hi-fi)

hautes fréquences: voir **HF**

haut-parleur: appareil transformant des impulsions électriques en sons. Les haut-parleurs peuvent être montés dans des enceintes acoustiques ou être intégrés ou incorporés à d'autres appareils comme des récepteurs de radio ou de télévision.

A loudspeaker

haut-parleur d'aigus: petit haut-parleur généralement incorporé à une enceinte et servant à reproduire les hautes fréquences.

A tweeter

haut-parleur de contrôle: haut-parleur principal d'un système audio servant à écouter et à vérifier la qualité d'un programme.

C *moniteur*

A monitor

haut-parleur de graves: haut-parleur conçu pour reproduire de très basses fréquences.

A woofer; boomer

heuristique: voir **approche heuristique**

HF: ondes courtes, hautes fréquences; bande dans la gamme de fréquences entre 3-30 Mhz qui correspond aux ondes décamétriques. Abbréviation métrique, B.dam.

A high frequency; hf

hi-fi: voir **haute-fidélité**

holographie: technique utilisant de la lumière cohérente obtenue par laser pour photographier sur bande ou film des sujets restitués en trois dimensions avec parallaxe, les hologrammes étant observés en lumière cohérente ou non.

C *laser*

A holography

hors champ: qui n'apparaît pas à l'écran mais qui est supposé n'être pas éloigné du lieu de l'action.

A off screen (USA)

hyperfréquences: radio fréquences suffisamment élevées pour permettre l'emploi de techniques telles que celles des guides d'ondes et des cavités: les fréquences les plus basses correspondantes sont de l'ordre du gigahertz.

A microwave frequency

hypnopédie: méthode d'enseignement fondée sur des suggestions exercées au cours du sommeil (par exemple à l'aide d'un diffuseur placé près du dormeur).

A hypnopedia

hz: hertz

I

IA: voir **intelligence artificielle**

iconicité: voir **analogie 3.**

iconographie: 1. diverses représentations d'un sujet; **2.** étude de ces représentations.

A iconography

image: 1. représentation inversée sur un miroir d'un objet qui s'y réfléchit; **2.** représentation d'un sujet ou d'une scène sur un support quelconque, écran, papier, pellicule; **3.** ensemble des lignes horizontales décrites au cours d'une analyse complète d'une image transmise électroniquement;

Glossaire français – image arrêtée

4. une vue d'un film (ou d'un film fixe);
5. représentation mentale d'une réalité en l'absence de l'objet qui lui a donné naissance; 6. représentation analogique d'une réalité par exemple: symbole, allégorie, métaphore.

C *arrêt sur image; analogie*

A 1. image; 2. picture; 3. 4. frame; 5. 6. image

image analogique: représentation visuelle de l'information à l'aide d'un phénomène physique variant continuellement et qui correspond par conséquent aux caractéristiques traditionnelles de la perception.

C *image numérisée*

A analog image

image arrêtée: image prise dans un film animé ou une bande vidéo et gardée en plan continu.

C *arrêt sur image*

A still frame

image composite: effet spécial où deux ou plusieurs images séparées apparaissent ensemble sur l'écran.

A split screen

image digitale: voir **image numérisée**

image fixe: image immobile obtenue par un procédé de projection fixe (diapositive, film fixe, transparent) par opposition au film et à la télévision.

C *projection fixe*

A still picture

image fantôme: défaut d'une image visible se manifestant par l'apparition d'une ou plusieurs images décalées par rapport à l'image normale, correspondant à des signaux retardés par un phénomène d'écho prenant naissance soit au cours de la propagation, soit dans les appareils de la voie de transmission.

C *écho*

A ghost

image latente: modifications invisibles causées par l'action de la lumière sur les cristaux d'halogénénure d'argent d'une émulsion photographique. Une image argentique visible est ensuite obtenue, par développement, à partir de cette image latente.

A latent image

image négative: image en noir et blanc ou en couleur dont l'aspect est l'inverse de ce qui est photographié. Aux zones sombres du sujet correspondent des zones claires et aux zones claires des zones sombres. Dans le cas d'images négatives en couleur, les couleurs sont représentées par leurs complémentaires.

A negative picture/image

image numérisée: par opposition à une image analogique, représentation des données de l'information visuelle sous une forme codée, discontinue au moyen de caractères ou de chiffres pour en faciliter la transmission. Nécessite un décodage à la réception.

A digital image

image par image: technique consistant à filmer avec arrêt après chaque image ou à faire un montage vue par vue.

A single frame; stop motion

image positive: image photographique sur laquelle les valeurs des zones claires et sombres du sujet original sont représentées comme sur cet original. En couleurs, l'image positive représente aussi chaque couleur du sujet.

A positive picture/image

imagiciel: didacticiel d'illustration graphique servant à la manipulation des formes et l'exploration de concepts géométriques, utilisé pour dessiner des figures.

A *builder; electronic blackboard

imitation de maîtres modèles: en micro-enseignement, utilisation de modèles fournis par des enseignants praticiens, présentés directement ou sous forme d'enregistrements, comme méthode d'induction de changements de comportements.

A modeling

imitation de modèles: technique fréquemment employée dans l'enseignement de la langue orale, où les élèves écoutent et étudient un

190

modèle qui sert ensuite de base à leur pratique et à l'amélioration de leur performance.

A modeling

impédance: inertie opposée par un système à la circulation d'un courant alternatif. L'impédance, mesurée en ohms, est souvent représentée par la lettre Z.

A impedance

imprimante: dans un système d'ordinateur, organe qui fournit les données de sortie sous forme imprimée.

A printer

imprimante à laser: imprimante à grande vitesse utilisant un faisceau laser.

A laser printer

imprimante matricielle: imprimante dans laquelle les caractères sont formés à partir d'une matrice d'aiguilles.

A matrix printer; dot matrix printer

impulsion de synchronisation: dans un montage sonorisé, signal de synchronisation de l'image, enregistré sur la piste son ordinaire. Peut être audible ou non.

C *synchronisation*
A (superimposed) sync pulse

incidents critiques: voir **technique des incidents critiques**

incrustation: procédé de substitution d'une partie d'une image vidéo par une autre.

A inlay

indexation: analyse systématique du contenu de documents classés selon un ordre alphabétique, chronologique, numérique, selon la source ou selon tout autre mode déterminé.

A indexing

indicateur: 1. instrument servant à fournir des mesures ou des indications; **2.** phénomène qui permet de témoigner de l'existence d'un autre. Peut servir d'instrument d'évaluation. Un indicateur doit être pertinent, sensible et facilement disponible.

A 1. 2. indicator

indicateur de niveau d'enregistrement: dispositif indiquant le niveau du signal à enregistrer.

C *vu-mètre*
A recording level indicator

indice: 1. indication volontaire ou non, mettant sur la voie de la solution d'un problème; **2.** coefficient caractéristique des variations dans l'espace ou dans le temps d'une grandeur directement observable ou d'un certain nombre de grandeurs simples considérées comme représentatives d'un ensemble qui ne peut pas être observé directement.

A 1. cue; clue; prompt; 2. index

indice d'écoute: pourcentage de tous les récepteurs en marche réglés sur une chaîne ou une station de radiodiffusion donnée parmi celles qu'ils peuvent capter.

A audience share

indice de pose: valeur numérique affectée à une pellicule par le fabricant indiquant la sensibilité relative de cette pellicule et permettant de déterminer le réglage de l'appareil photographique (ouverture et vitesse).

A exposure index; speed rating

indice de sensibilité: voir **indice de pose**

individualisé: voir **enseignement individualisé**

induction: voir **méthode inductive**

infographie: application de l'informatique à la représentation graphique et au traitement de l'image.

A computer graphics

information: 1. séquence de signaux correspondant à des règles de combinaison précises, transmise entre un émetteur et un récepteur par l'intermédiaire d'un canal qui sert de support physique à cette transmission; ce qui est transmis; **2.** charge d'information d'un message visuel, quantité d'information visuelle dans une image donnée; **3.** message communiqué au public par les mass-media; **4.** dans un système informatique, élément de connaissance susceptible d'être représenté à l'aide de conventions pour être conservé, traité ou communiqué.

A 1. 2. information; 3. news; 4. information

information en retour: voir **rétroaction, (feed-back)**

information parasites: informations non désirées et dénuées de signification dans la mémoire d'un ordinateur.

A garbage

informatique: 1. science du traitement rationnel, notamment par machines automatiques, de l'information considérée comme le support des connaissances humaines et des communications dans les domaines technique, économique et social; **2.** matière d'enseignement.

C *traitement automatique de l'information*

A 1. computer science; informatics; 2. computer studies

informatique éducative: terme générique désignant l'ensemble des utilisations éducatives de l'informatique (initiation informatique, EAO, enseignement informatisé, enseignement de l'informatique).

A computer education

infraliminaire: voir **subliminal**

innovation éducative: processus intentionnel de changement partiel aboutissant soit à une modification des objectifs d'une pratique éducative, soit à la modification des voies et moyens permettant d'atteindre ces objectifs. Très souvent, l'innovation consiste dans l'adaptation d'une situation éducative à un changement qui a déjà eu lieu dans ou hors d'un système éducatif et permet ainsi de rétablir un équilibre qui s'est trouvé rompu.

A educational innovation

innovation technologique: changement technologique qui peut consister soit dans l'apparition d'une technique nouvelle, soit dans le changement du principe de fonctionnement d'un appareillage. La télévision par câble repose sur une innovation technique (les câbles coaxiaux) mais aussi sur un autre principe de fonctionnement que la télévision ordinaire.

A technological innovation

insert: 1. plan rapproché dans un film ou un programme de télévision qui fournit une information en montrant par exemple une lettre, le cadran d'une horloge ou un calendrier; **2.** séquence filmée insérée dans un programme de télévision en direct et plus généralement bande vidéo, film ou enregistrement venant s'ajouter à un document déjà réalisé.

A 1. insert; cut-in; 2. insert; clip; film insert

insonorisé: rendu insonore par isolation.

A sound-proof

instabilité d'image: voir **gigue**

institutionnel: voir **pédagogie institutionnelle**

instruction: consigne exprimée dans un langage de programmation qui déclenche une opération ou une série d'opérations dans un système de traitement de l'information.

A instruction

(instructional development): systématisation de la conception, production, évaluation et utilisation de systèmes complets d'enseignement, regroupant tous les composants nécessaires avec un schéma directeur pour leur utilisation. La mise au point de systèmes pédagogiques est une activité plus large que la mise au point de matériels pédagogiques qui ne concerne que des éléments isolés, et plus large également que le seul design qui ne constitue qu'une phase de la réalisation de systèmes pédagogiques.

C *design*

A instructional development

intégration à grande échelle: s'applique au procédé de fabrication en grandes séries de micro-composants électroniques montés sur de très petits supports («puces») faits de matériau semi-conducteur.

A large-scale integration

intégré: voir **circuit intégré**

intelligence artificielle: ensemble de techniques utilisées pour essayer de réaliser des automates adoptant une démarche proche de la pensée humaine.
C *système expert*
A artificial intelligence

intelligibilité: degré de facilité de compréhension d'un message.
C *lisibilité*
A readability

intensité: 1. force relative ou amplitude d'une énergie électrique, magnétique ou vibratoire; 2. quantité d'électricité traversant un conducteur pendant l'unité de temps (seconde), se mesure en ampères; 3. brillance d'une image sur un écran cathodique.
A 1. 2. 3. intensity

intensité de signal: amplitude d'un signal en un instant déterminé.
A signal strength

interactif: qualifie les matériels, les programmes ou les conditions d'exploitation qui permettent des actions réciproques, en mode dialogué avec des utilisateurs ou en temps réel avec des appareils.
C *mode dialogué; vidéotex*
A interactive

interface: 1. limite commune à deux ensembles ou appareils; 2. dispositif ou programme de jonction entre deux matériels ou logiciels leur permettant d'échanger des informations par l'adoption de règles communes, physiques ou logiques.
A 1. 2. interface

interférence: phénomène résultant de la superposition de deux ou plusieurs oscillations ou ondes cohérentes de même nature et de fréquences égales ou voisines.
C *brouillage*
A wave interference

interférences basses fréquences: forme d'interférence ayant pour effet de produire une raie mince se déplaçant verticalement ou horizontalement sur l'image.
A glitch

internégatif: négatif tiré à partir d'une copie positive d'un négatif original.
A internegative

interphone (système d'intercommunication): réseau téléphonique intérieur permettant une communication orale, par exemple entre la régie et un studio.
A intercom; intercommunication system

interprète: personne pouvant traduire une langue dans une autre au rythme de la parole.
A interpreter

interpréteur: programme d'ordinateur en langage binaire qui traduit et exécute chaque instruction du langage d'origine d'un programme, avant de traduire et d'exécuter l'instruction suivante.
A interpreter

interrupteur: voir **commutateur**

interruption: suspension dans l'exécution d'un programme d'ordinateur réalisée de façon à en permettre la reprise.
A interruption

intervalle de suppression de trame: bord noir au sommet et/ou au bas des images de télévision utilisé à des fins de synchronisation et de transmission d'informations de télétexte, de légendes et d'autres messages codés.
A vertical interval

intra-muros: enseignement intra-muros: enseignement donné à l'intérieur d'une université; étudiants intra-muros: étudiants dont la scolarité se déroule dans les locaux de l'université.
A intra-mural

intrants: voir **apports**

intrinsèque: voir **programmation intrinsèque, motivation**

inversion: suite d'opérations permettant d'obtenir directement un positif photographique par traitement approprié, sans passage par un négatif.
A reversal process

inversion de phase: changement de l'aspect ou de la caractéristique d'un signal.

A phase reversal

invisible/observable: 'invisible' qualifie tout comportement ou stimulus non directement observable, c'est-à-dire appartenant au domaine mental, cognitif ou interne, ou se situant au-dessus du seuil de la perception; 'observable' qualifie tout comportement ou stimulus directement saisissable par la perception auditive ou visuelle.

C *latent/manifeste; sublimal*

A covert/overt

iris: diaphragme réglable, monté généralement dans le système de barillet de lentille, et destiné à contrôler le faisceau lumineux traversant l'objectif d'un appareil de prise de vues.

A iris; diaphragm

ISO: Organisation internationale de normalisation

A ISO

item: 1. unité distincte dans un ensemble organisé, objet d'observation; 2. élément d'un test faisant l'objet d'une notation distincte; 3. élément d'une séquence d'enseignement programmé. La dimension d'un item peut varier d'une seule phrase ou question à compléter, ou instruction à suivre pour accomplir une tâche fixée, jusqu'à la taille d'un gros paragraphe.

C *analyse d'item; banque d'items; cadre; séquence*

A 1. 2. item; 3. item; frame

itération: en informatique, méthode de résolution de problèmes consistant à répéter des algorithmes d'exécution jusqu'à ce que la solution ou une bonne approximation ait été trouvée.

A interactive process

itinéraire diversifié: en enseignement programmé, disposition particulière d'un programme permettant aux élèves, en fonction de leur taux de réussite ou d'échec dans la série d'items de la séquence précédente, d'être orientés vers des sous-programmes différents du même ensemble, proposés en alternatives.

C *branchement*

A multiple track

itinéraire unique: en enseignement programmé, parcours identique effectué par tous les apprenants à partir des matériaux proposés, à la différence de l'itinéraire diversifié.

A single track

J

jack: prise femelle d'un appareil ou d'un connecteur pouvant recevoir une fiche mâle correspondante et permettant l'entrée ou la sortie d'une source d'alimentation ou de signaux.

A jack

jeu de rôles: technique pédagogique faisant appel à la représentation verbale ou non verbale (mise en scène) d'une situation, circonstance ou événement par des apprenants choisis dans un groupe qui prennent le rôle ou la fonction d'une autre ou d'autres personnes.

C *psychodrame*

A role playing

jeu de simulation: activité spécialement conçue pour donner aux participants l'occasion d'être confrontés à certains aspects de la vie réelle. Elle fait intervenir un groupe de joueurs, un ensemble de règles, une série d'actions permises, une période de temps donnée et un cadre général où se situe l'ensemble.

A gaming

jeu vidéo: cassette vidéo programmée qui, utilisée avec une console interactive, permet de se livrer à des jeux d'adresse, de réflexion ou éducatifs sur un récepteur de télévision.

A video game

K

K : symbole représentant le nombre 1024 ou 2^{10}, utilisé pour mesurer la capacité de mémoire d'un ordinateur.
A K

kinescope : enregistrement sur film d'images vidéo.
A kinescope

kit : ensemble comprenant les éléments nécessaires à la construction d'un objet donné ainsi que les instructions de montage correspondantes.
A kit

L

laboratoire : salle équipée spécialement pour des utilisations pédagogiques spécifiques comme, par exemple, des expériences et/ou des démonstrations scientifiques, des leçons ou des productions audiovisuelles, etc.
A laboratory

laboratoire à apprendre : espace à vocation pédagogique, doté de matériels et d'équipements audiovisuels et informatiques facilitant la mise en œuvre d'activités d'apprentissage (et particulièrement d'auto-apprentissage) dépendant de moyens d'enseignement.
A media-based instructional laboratory

laboratoire audio-actif − AA : laboratoire de langues permettant l'écoute d'un stimulus sonore pré-enregistré et de la réponse fournie par l'élève mais non l'enregistrement de cette réponse.
A audio-active laboratory

laboratoire audio-actif comparatif − AAC : laboratoire de langues équipé d'un système au moyen duquel l'élève peut écouter un stimulus sonore pré-enregistré, y répondre durant les intervalles interposés, s'il en existe, entendre simultanément sa réponse à l'aide d'un combiné écouteur-microphone (casque) et enregistrer cette réponse pour la comparer ensuite au stimulus pré-enregistré.
A audio-active comparative laboratory

laboratoire audio-passif − AP : laboratoire de langues ne permettant que l'écoute du stimulus sonore pré-enregistré.
A audio-passive laboratory

laboratoire (de développement et tirage) : service ou centre spécialisé dans le développement et le tirage de pellicules impressionnées.
A film laboratory

laboratoire de langues : salle équipée d'un ensemble de magnétophones reliés à une console centrale et utilisés pour l'apprentissage de langues.
C *electronic classroom*
A language laboratory

lampe : 1. appareil d'éclairage ; 2. ampoule électrique ; 3. tube fluorescent ; 4. tube électronique.
A 1. lamp ; 2. bulb ; 3. fluorescent tube ; 4. lamp

lampe à arc : lampe fournissant une lumière très intense produite par une décharge électrique en arc entre deux électrodes.
A arc lamp

lampe-éclair : lampe ou ampoule photographique de grande intensité lumineuse commandée électriquement ou manuellement. Elle ne possède qu'un temps d'illumination limité et ne peut être ré-utilisée.

A flash bulb

lampe excitatrice: lampe qui éclaire la piste son d'un film et transforme les signaux qu'elle lit en énergie électrique, laquelle est diffusée par des haut-parleurs sous forme de musique, effets sonores et/ou dialogue.

A exciter lamp

lampe témoin: témoin lumineux électrique qui a généralement pour fonctions d'indiquer la position d'un commutateur ou d'un interrupteur, ou de signaler qu'un moteur marche ou qu'un appareil est sous tension.

A pilot light

langage auteur: langage de programmation très proche du langage naturel qui permet à un utilisateur de créer ses propres programmes.

C *système auteur*

A authoring language

langage d'assemblage: langage de programmation symbolique dont les instructions doivent être traduites en langage machine par un assembleur.

C *assembleur*

A assembly language

langage d'origine: langage qui sert à écrire un programme avant son traitement par l'ordinateur.

A source language

langage de programmation: langage artificiel destiné à l'écriture de programmes exécutés par un ordinateur, par ex.: ADA, ALGOL, BASIC, FORTRAN, LOGO, PASCAL, etc.

A programming language

langage machine: langage lié à l'ordinateur dont toutes les instructions sont des instructions machine.

C *langage de programmation*

A computer language

langage naturel: langue parlée ou écrite ordinaire par opposition aux langages artificiels ou formels qui sont des langages de programmation.

A natural language

langage objet: voir **langage résultant**

langage résultant: langage ou série d'instructions dans lesquelles le langage d'origine est traduit par le compilateur. Souvent synonyme de langage machine.

A object language

large bande: expression adjectivale utilisée pour décrire des équipements ou des systèmes pouvant être porteurs d'une large gamme de fréquences ou de canaux et voies.

A broadband

largeur de bande: différence entre la fréquence la plus haute et la fréquence la plus basse d'une bande passante.

C *bande passante*

A frequence range; dynamic range

largeur de film: format d'une pellicule de film: 8 mm, S 8 mm, 16 mm, 35 mm, etc.

C *format*

A gauge

laser - light amplification by stimulated emission of radiation: appareil pouvant produire, sous forme d'impulsions ou en continu, une onde lumineuse, de fréqueur et longueur d'onde constantes, utilisée, entre autres, pour l'enregistrement et la lecture de vidéodisques et pour certaines communications.

A laser

latent/manifeste: distinction introduite par la psychanalyse mais qui intervient aussi dans l'analyse de contenu et la sémiotique. Le contenu LATENT est l'ensemble des spécifications qui sont progressivement dégagées par le travail de l'analyse et qui, dans certains cas, contredisent les spécifications apparentes. Le contenu MANI-

FESTE est l'ensemble des significations qui s'offrent explicitement.

C *invisible; observable*
A covert/overt

LCD: voir **affichage à cristaux liquides**

leader: dans un groupe, personne capable d'en influencer d'autres pour qu'elles collaborent activement et volontairement à la réalisation des objectifs du groupe.

A leader

learning: terme utilisé en français avec un sens plus précis qu'apprentissage : acquisition d'un comportement nouveau par répétition d'actes de même nature.

A learning

leçon de démonstration: voir **leçon modèle**

leçon d'essai: leçon conduite durant un stage de formation professionnelle pratique par un élève-enseignant sous la supervision d'un enseignant expérimenté ou le contrôle d'un formateur.

C *micro-enseignement*
A practice lesson

leçon modèle: leçon conduite par un enseignant expérimenté et pleinement compétent à l'intention d'élèves-enseignants pour illustrer un cours théorique ou servir de modèle à imiter.

C *micro-enseignement*
A demonstration lesson

lecteur: dispositif permettant de lire des microformes ou de reproduire des sons ou des images enregistrés sur un support magnétique ou par un procédé optique.

A reader

lecteur de microfiches ou de microfilms: dispositif de rétroprojection permettant le grossissement et l'observation à l'œil nu de microformes transparentes. Il comprend les lecteurs de microfilms, de microfiches ou d'ultrafiches, et la combinaison de ces divers lecteurs.

A microform reader

lecteur de son: dispositif optique ou tête magnétique d'un projecteur ayant pour fonction de lire le son enregistré sur les pistes optiques ou magnétiques.

A sound head

lecteur optique: dispositif qui utilise un procédé optique pour reconnaître des formes (et en particulier des caractères écrits ou imprimés) et générer des signaux analogiques ou digitaux qui peuvent entrer dans un ordinateur.

A optical scanner

lecteur-reproducteur: appareil de visionnement de microformes (microfiches et microfilms) permettant aussi l'impression de certaines pages choisies de ces microformes.

A reader printer

lecture: 1. restitution sous leur forme initiale de signaux enregistrés; 2. extraction d'une information dans une mémoire ou sur un support quelconque.

A 1. playback; 2. read-out

légende: texte explicatif accompagnant les images d'un document audiovisuel.

C *titre; carton titre*
A caption

lentille condensatrice: lentille ayant pour fonction de concentrer sur une petite surface le flux de rayons lumineux provenant d'une source lumineuse comme, par exemple, une lampe de projection.

A condensing lens

lentille de fresnel: système optique à grande ouverture comprenant une lentille centrale et diverses couronnes prismatiques permettant d'obtenir un faisceau lumineux homogène de grand diamètre, utilisé dans les phares marins, par exemple. La fenêtre d'un rétroprojecteur est constituée de ce type de lentille.

A fresnel lens

lettrage: composition de textes, titres ou légendes à l'aide de lettres et de chiffres.
C *transfert*
A lettering

liaison: communication régulière assurée entre deux points, par exemple par téléphone ou par câble.
A link

liaison espace-terre/terre-espace: transmission de signaux d'un satellite à la terre (trajet/liaison descendante) ou de la terre vers le satellite (trajet/liaison montante).
A down-link/uplink

liaison hertzienne: système de radiodiffusion utilisé pour la transmission point à point d'un signal de télévision ou d'un signal radio, évitant ainsi l'utilisation de grandes longueurs de câble. Les liaisons hertziennes par hyperfréquences sont limitées au cas de transmission en ligne de visée directe.
A microwave link

lignage: voir **fréquence de balayage horizontal**

ligne: 1. système de fils ou de câbles transportant des signaux ou de l'énergie électrique; **2.** liaison entre un ordinateur et ses terminaux; **3.** rangée de caractères imprimés; **4.** l'une des centaines de lignes horizontales constituant une image de télévision.
C *liaison; connecté; en ligne; autonome*
A 1. 2. 3. 4. line

lisibilité: 1. degré de facilité de perception visuelle des lettres et des textes manuscrits ou imprimés ou des images; **2.** degré de facilité de compréhension d'un message (on dit aussi intelligibilité).
A 1. legibility; 2. readability

listage: document en continu produit par une imprimante d'ordinateur.
A listing

livre: volume imprimé non périodique d'au moins 49 pages (au-dessous, on dira brochure).
C *manuel scolaire; document d'accompagnement; manuel*
A book

livre brouillé: en enseignement programmé, livre servant de support à un programme à branchement. A chaque item, selon la réponse faite, le lecteur est renvoyé à des pages différentes, à des items différents. Il effectuera ainsi un itinéraire plus ou moins long.
A scrambled book

livre de classe: voir **manuel scolaire**

livre de référence: livre de la catégorie des dictionnaires, encyclopédies, annuaires, index ou atlas, c'est-à-dire fournissant des informations, par rubriques, et destiné à être consulté plutôt que lu d'un bout à l'autre.
A reference book

livre d'exercices: livre, souvent associé à un ou plusieurs manuels, qui propose des exercices, des problèmes, des indications d'activités et des instructions pour l'élève, et, fréquemment, des éléments permettant d'évaluer le travail effectué. En général, la présentation typographique prévoit des espaces pour permettre aux élèves d'inscrire la réponse.
C *manuel; manuel scolaire*
A workbook

livre d'images: livre illustré pour les tout jeunes enfants.
A picture book

livre du maître: livre d'explications à l'usage de l'enseignant, accompagnant un manuel ou tout autre ensemble pédagogique. Il contient parfois une 'clef' donnant les réponses aux questions ou exercices proposés dans le manuel, le film, etc.
A teacher's guide/notes

livre parlant: livre enregistré intégralement soit sur bande magnétique audio, soit sur disque audio, et spécialement destiné aux aveugles ou aux handicapés visuels.
A talking book

livre parlé: voir **livre parlant**

livre sonore: voir **livre parlant**

logiciel: ensemble de programmes, procédés et règles et, éventuellement, de la documentation, relatifs au fonctionnement d'un ensemble de traitement de l'information.

C *catégories de logiciels:*

   i) *logiciels de base* — *système d'exploitation, programmes de service ou utilitaires, assembleur, compilateur, gestionnaire de fichiers, microprogrammes;*
   ii) *logiciels outils* — *éditeur, gestionnaire de données, système auteur, système de gestion de base de données, tableur, traitement de texte;*
   iii) *logiciels d'application ou progiciels* — *système expert;*
   iv) *logiciels d'enseignement ou didacticiels* — *imagiciels, ludiciels, programmes d'exercices, programmes tuteurs, simulations, système tuteur intelligent.*

A software

logiciel d'application: ensemble des programmes conçus pour des applications particulières et pour lesquelles l'utilisateur doit fournir ses propres données par opposition au système d'exploitation qui régit le fonctionnement de l'ordinateur; syn. de progiciel.

A application(s) program

logiciel d'enseignement: voir **didacticiel**

logiciel d'exercices: voir **programme d'exercices**

logiciel d'exploitation: voir **système d'exploitation**

logiciel de service: voir **programme de service**

logiciel outil: terme désignant des programmes d'application générale comme les tableurs, les logiciels de traitement de texte, les gestionnaires de données, qui peuvent être utilisés à des fins pédagogiques mais n'ont pas été conçus à cet effet, ainsi que des programmes d'aide à la création d'autres logiciels — éditeurs, éditeurs graphiques, systèmes auteur, etc. A ne pas confondre avec les utilitaires ou programmes de service.

C *boîte à outils*

A utility software

logiciel tuteur: voir **programme tuteur**

logique (d'une machine): dispositif mécanique ou électronique pouvant effectuer l'une des fonctions logiques de base.

A logic

logistique: ensemble des moyens et des méthodes mis en œuvre pour l'organisation d'une pratique ou d'une activité éducative.

A logistics

LOGO: langage de programmation très simple, utilisé notamment pour des applications éducatives.

A LOGO

longueur d'onde: 1. distance mesurable entre des points d'onde de même phase; **2.** terme utilisé pour indiquer la position de stations de radio spécifiques sur un cadran de syntonisation.

A wave length

ludiciel: logiciel de jeu interactif à fin pédagogique.

A interactive educational game

lumière d'ambiance: éclairage obtenu par un projecteur ou une rampe de projection, et qui illumine une zone spécifique sans éblouissement ni reflet.

A flood light

lumière parasite: voir **taches lumineuses**

lumière polarisée: lumière dont les vibrations ne s'effectuent que dans un plan; c'est partiellement le cas des réflexions ordinaires sur la plupart des surfaces excepté celle du chrome et des autres métaux brillants.

A polarized light

luminance: mesure de brillance d'une image de télévison.

A luminance

luminosité: attribut de la sensation visuelle selon lequel une surface paraît émettre plus ou moins de lumière.

A luminosity (UK); brightness (USA)

199

M

MA — modulation d'amplitude: voir **modulation**

machine à développer: appareil dans lequel les pellicules ou papiers photographiques sont automatiquement développés, fixés, et, parfois lavés et séchés.
A processor

machine à enseigner: appareil desservant un ou plusieurs postes de travail permettant à des individus ou à de petits groupes une activité de renforcement ou un auto-apprentissage à partir de la présentation de documents programmés.
C *enseignement programmé; enseignement assisté par ordinateur; méthode audio-tutorielle; dispositif d'auto-instruction*
A teaching machine

machiniste: ouvrier qui s'occupe des changements de décor et de divers équipements sur un plateau de tournage.
A grip

macrozoom: voir **objectif macro à focale variable**

magasin: boîtier étanche à la lumière, protégeant le film négatif dans une caméra de cinéma; aussi, boîte de protection de films, bandes, diapositives ou films fixes, généralement munie d'un dispositif assurant la présentation régulière et contrôlée du contenu pendant la prise de vues ou l'enregistrement.
A magazine

magazine: 1. périodique d'intérêt général, contenant des articles sur des sujets variés écrits par différents auteurs; 2. programme de radio ou télévision constitué de séquences successives mais groupées sous le même titre général et réalisées dans le même style.
A magazine

magnétocassette: voir **magnétophone à cassette**

magnétophone à bande: appareil mixte d'enregistrement et de lecture utilisant une bande magnétique comme support d'enregistrement. Une ou plusieurs pistes peuvent être utilisées sur cette bande selon le type d'appareil.
A audiotape recorder

magnétophone à cassette: magnétophone qui n'enregistre et ne lit que des cassettes.
A cassette recorder

magnétoscope: appareil d'enregistrement et de lecture de signaux vidéo et audio sur une bande magnétique ou une vidéocassette.
A videotape recorder; videocassette recorder

magnétoscope à pistes transversales: voir **quadruplex**

magnétothèque: collection ordonné de programmes enregistrés sur bande.
C *vidéothèque*
A tape library

maille: voir **cadre 2.**

maintenance: ensemble d'actions tendant à prévenir ou à corriger les dégradations d'un matériel ou d'un logiciel afin de maintenir ou de rétablir sa conformité aux spécifications.
A maintenance

maîtrise: voir **pédagogie de la maîtrise**

mallette pédagogique: voir **ensemble pédagogique**

manche à balai: dispositif de commande à plusieurs degrés de liberté servant à déplacer le curseur d'une visu. On dit aussi 'manette' ou 'poignée'.
C *télécommande*
A joystick

manifeste: voir **latent/manifeste**

manuel: 1. ouvrage sur un sujet spécialisé, présentant souvent une vue d'ensemble simple mais complète; **2.** livre scientifique ou technique écrit avant tout à l'intention de praticiens pour leur servir d'ouvrage habituel de référence ou de révision.

C *manuel scolaire; livre d'exercices*

A 1. 2. handbook

manuel scolaire: livre spécialement conçu pour présenter la base d'un cours correspondant à un niveau donné, et traitant d'une partie délimitée du programme d'études de ce niveau (une discipline par exemple).

C *manuel; livre d'exercices*

A textbook

maquette: reproduction en trois dimensions à une échelle donnée, arbitrairement choisie, d'un objet réel (appareil, machine, bâtiment, etc.) ou d'un phénomène réel. On dit aussi modèle.

A model

maquette de démonstration: modèle représentant un objet réel, et spécialement conçu pour mettre en évidence certains aspects ou certaines fonctions de la réalité à laquelle il renvoie. Ce type de maquette peut être plus petit ou plus grand que l'original et certains aspects peuvent être accentués pour mieux faire apparaître des fonctions ou des relations particulières.

A mock-up

maquette de présentation: modèle permettant de visualiser un projet de présentation, d'affiche, de publication ou de toute autre réalisation analogue. Une telle maquette est généralement faite à l'échelle et avec assez de détails pour donner une idée de l'apparence du produit final.

A layout

marche arrière: inversion du mouvement sur l'écran.

C *trucage; effets spéciaux*

A reverse action

marionnettes: figurines utilisées dans l'animation tridimensionnelle.

A puppets

marquage: imprégnation d'une image sur le tube analyseur d'une caméra, due à une lumière extrêmement brillante ou à une mise au point de la caméra sur une image très contrastée, pendant un temps trop long.

A burn-in

marque de fin de bobine: petit point ou autre signe disposé dans le coin supérieur droit d'une image repère située près de la fin d'une bobine de film pour indiquer au projectionniste qu'il faut changer de bobine.

C *signal d'avertissement*

A changeover cue

marque de synchronisation: marque faite au montage sur l'amorce d'une longueur de pellicule pour fournir un point de repère, pour la synchronisation d'autres morceaux de film. Aussi, marque placée sur l'image correspondant à la fermeture complète des claquettes.

A synchronous mark

masque: voir **cache**

masse critique: seuil à partir duquel un effet devient perceptible ou se trouve modifié d'une manière significative.

A critical mass

mass media: voir **moyen de communication de masse**

matériel: 1. par opposition à personnel, désigne l'ensemble des objets, instruments et machines nécessaires pour réaliser une activité ou utilisés dans un service ou une exploitation; **2.** pour l'enseignement, lorsqu'il est opposé à équipement, désigne les programmes et les documents; **3.** dans un système d'ordinateur, ensemble de machines ou d'organes qui servent au traitement de l'information par opposition au logiciel qui désigne les programmes.

C *équipement; moyens d'enseignement; (hardware)*

A 1. equipment; 2. materials; 3. hardware

matériel didactique: 1. ensemble des objets et appareils destinés à faciliter les activités d'enseignement et/ou d'apprentissage; 2. tout produit, ou ensemble de produits, conçu à des fins pédagogiques et pouvant être multiplié ou reproduit.

A 1. instructional media; 2. instructional product

matériel scolaire: mobiliers, instruments et moyens d'enseignement utilisés dans les établissements d'enseignement.

C *moyens d'enseignement*

A instructional equipment and materials

mathétique: terme utilisé par T. F. Gilbert pour décrire l'application systématique de la théorie du renforcement à l'analyse de savoirs et de savoir-faire. Méthode de présentation de l'information à acquérir particulièrement utile lorsque des discriminations multiples doivent être effectuées.

A mathetics

matière: domaine de connaissance ou d'étude, particulièrement lorsqu'il est organisé et mis en forme à des fins d'enseignement.

A subject

matrice: 1. tableau rectangulaire ou carré composé de lignes et de colonnes dont l'intersection définit des cases à l'intérieur desquelles figurent des données mathématiques ou autres; 2. empreinte qui sert de moule pour la fabrication de clichés; 3. empreinte qui sert de moule pour le pressage de disques; 4. voir **original**.

A 1. 2. 3. matrix; 4. master

média(s): 1. terme générique pour toutes les modalités de transmission de messages; 2. s'emploie comme équivalent de moyens d'enseignement ou de moyens imprimés ou audiovisuels.

A 1. 2. media

médiabus: véhicule aménagé en médiathèque qui dessert un secteur déterminé.

C *bibliobus*

A mediamobile

médiamobile: voir **médiabus**

médian: valeur qui divise une série de valeurs ordonnées en deux parties égales. S'oppose à moyenne.

A median

médiane: voir **médian**

médiathèque: centre ou service qui abrite une collection intégrée de ressources éducatives que l'on peut soit emprunter, soit consulter sur place, grâce à un équipement spécial.

C *centre de documentation et d'information; polythèque*

A educational media center

médium: singulier de médias. De moins en moins utilisé en ce sens. On dit de plus en plus *un* média.

A medium

mélange: voir **mixage**

mélangeur: dispositif permettant de combiner plusieurs signaux émis simultanément.

A mixer

MEM: mémoire morte.

A read only store

membrane: feuille d'un microphone sensible à la pression acoustique du son ou cône d'un haut-parleur reproduisant le son.

A diaphragm

mémoire: dans un ordinateur, unité fonctionnelle qui peut recevoir, conserver et restituer des données codées.

A storage; memory

mémoire à cassettes: mémoire magnétique dans laquelle les données sont conservées par enregistrement magnétique sur la surface d'une bande magnétique contenue dans une cassette ordinaire.

A cassette storage

mémoire auxiliaire: dans un ordinateur, toute mémoire qui s'ajoute à la mémoire principale, telle que mémoires à disques, à bandes magnétiques, ou tout autre type de mémoire.

C *mémoire*

A auxiliary store/storage

mémoire de masse: mémoire externe de très grande capacité, directement accessible aux organes centraux d'un ordinateur et qui se présente habituellement sous la forme de disques ou de bandes magnétiques.
A mass storage

mémoire externe: élément de mémoire extérieure à l'ordinateur (bande magnétique, disque magnétique, cartes perforées) et à laquelle l'ordinateur ne peut avoir accès que par l'intermédiaire de canaux d'entrée et sortie.
A external store/storage

mémoire morte – MEM: mémoire qui n'est accessible qu'en lecture et dont le contenu, fixé lors de la fabrication, ne peut plus être modifié. C'est une mémoire permanente.
A read only store

mémoire morte programmable: mémoire qui n'est accessible qu'en lecture et qui peut être programmée à l'aide d'un matériel spécifique. A l'issue de cette opération, le contenu ne peut plus être modifié.
A PROM

mémoire principale: désigne la mémoire centrale de traitement d'un ordinateur.
A main storage

mémoire tampon: mémoire auxiliaire employée pour compenser une différence de débit des informations ou un décalage dans l'arrivée des signaux entre divers organes d'un ordinateur, le plus souvent entre la mémoire et les organes d'entrée. La mémoire tampon a pour fonction de réunir et retenir les données pour les transmettre à l'unité de traitement quand nécessaire.
A buffer

mémoire vive – MEV: mémoire dont le contenu peut être modifié en usage normal et qui sert souvent à conserver des informations à titre provisoire. Il s'agit le plus souvent d'une mémoire non permanente dont le contenu est perdu lorsque l'alimentation électrique est coupée.
A direct access store

mémorisation: 1. fait d'apprendre par cœur;
2. voir **mise en mémoire.**
A 1. memorization; 2. storage

mention de réserve: le fait de citer, de mentionner l'origine et le nom de l'auteur d'une œuvre que l'on utilise.
A credit

menu: liste de commandes et des options offertes à l'utilisateur par un logiciel.
C *commande; programme piloté par menu*
A menu

message: sélection ordonnée constituée d'un certain nombre de signes choisis dans un ensemble conventionnel et ayant pour objet de communiquer de l'information.
A message

message audiovisuel: message empruntant un support visuel et sonore.
A audio-visual communication

message de guidage: informatique, message guidant l'utilisateur d'un programme et sollicitant une réponse.
A prompt

messagerie électronique: voir **courrier électronique**

mesure d'audience: nombre de points obtenus ou pourcentage attribué à un programme de radio ou de télévision, cette valeur étant établie à partir de la proportion estimée d'auditeurs ou de téléspectateurs suivant l'émission par rapport au nombre total de foyers équipés de radio ou de télévision.
C *indice d'écoute*
A audience rating

méthode: ensemble de moyens mis rationnellement en œuvre afin de parcourir sans errements les étapes successives d'un processus d'apprentissage d'une connaissance ou d'une habileté donnée. La méthode pédagogique diffère de la technique pédagogique car elle implique nécessairement un plan d'action orienté vers la réalisation d'un ou de plusieurs objectifs tandis que la technique est un procédé ou un ensemble de procédés particuliers.
A method

méthode(s) active(s): par opposition aux méthodes traditionnelles, terme générique qui caractérise l'ensemble des méthodes fondées sur les intérêts des élèves et destinées à la formation de leur personnalité. Les méthodes actives font appel à l'initiative personnelle et aux talents d'exploration de l'enfant à travers des techniques de groupe: utilisation d'ateliers; correspondance scolaire; journal scolaire; coopérative scolaire; sortie, enquête, etc.

C *activité d'éveil; activités dirigées; activités libres; étude du milieu*

A activity learning/method; participatory learning

méthode audiolinguale: méthode d'enseignement des langues étrangères qui définit les langues comme un ensemble d'habitudes que l'on peut acquérir par des exercices de répétition et un surapprentissage; écouter et parler constituent les deux aptitudes essentielles, lire et écrire venant ensuite.

C *méthode audiovisuelle*

A audiolingual method

méthode audiovisuelle: méthode d'enseignement des langues étrangères fondée sur l'utilisation de la représentation audiovisuelle de situations (dialogues enregistrés, illustrés par des images correspondantes, généralement sur films fixes) pour communiquer le sens des formes linguistiques. Le recours à la langue maternelle est proscrit, et la présentation et la pratique des éléments de langue s'effectuent surtout de manière orale.

C *méthode audiolinguale; structuro-global*

A audio-visual method

méthode compétencialiste: voir **competency-based teacher training; éducation axée sur la compétence**

méthode d'apprentissage par la découverte: découverte de principes ou de notions par un apprenant qui généralise des expériences sans recevoir d'instruction d'une autre personne.

C *approche heuristique; méthode de résolution de problèmes*

A discovery learning method

méthode d'audio-instruction: système d'apprentissage multimédias à rythme individuel comprenant des leçons enregistrées sur bandes magnétiques accompagnées de matériaux didactiques et de fiches pour travail personnel en carrel.

C *dispositif d'auto-instruction; machine à enseigner*

A audiotutorial method

méthode déductive: méthode de raisonnement ou de présentation qui part de principes généraux ou de portée universelle et aboutit à des applications particulières de ces principes et à une validation des conclusions déduites.

C *RULEG*

A deductive method

méthode de formation intégrée: organisation d'un processus de formation combinant dans une perspective de complémentarité fonctionnelle, divers moyens: enseignement théorique de type académique, expériences de laboratoire contrôlées et coordonnées, activité professionnelle.

A project training method

méthode de la découverte: voir **méthode d'apprentissage par la découverte**

méthode de la redécouverte: méthode utilisée dans l'enseignement scientifique et technologique selon laquelle l'apprenant est placé dans les conditions de la découverte d'un phénomène, d'une invention ou d'un appareil. Cette méthode recourt généralement aux principes de la méthode inductive et de la méthode déductive.

A discovery learning method

méthode de PERT: voir **PERT**

méthode de résolution de problèmes: méthode qui consiste à présenter les sujets d'enseignement comme des problèmes à résoudre en fournissant à celui qui apprend toute l'information et les moyens nécessaires à cet effet. Dans cette méthode, le rôle de l'enseignant consiste essentiellement à aider celui qui apprend à découvrir les solutions par lui-même plutôt qu'à fournir les réponses a priori.

C *approche heuristique*

A problem-solving approach

méthode de RULEG: voir **RULEG**

méthode des cas: méthode de formation dans laquelle un groupe utilise la description écrite d'un fait, d'un événement ou d'une situation comme base de discussion et d'analyse de théories, de concepts et de phénomènes de la vie réelle.

A *case study method*

méthode des projets: dans l'enseignement individualisé, organisation des activités d'apprentissage à partir d'un projet choisi par l'apprenant, visant à le familiariser avec les notions de programmation (fiches) et de planification (contrat), à fournir un contenu concret à l'enseignement et à soutenir l'intérêt de l'apprenant aux divers apprentissages envisagés, tout en favorisant son adaptation à la vie.

C *travail sur projet*

A *project method*

méthode directe: méthode d'enseignement des langues étrangères qui privilégie, dans la présentation et les activités proposées, l'utilisation de la langue étudiée elle-même.

C *enseignement direct*

A *direct method*

méthode directive: méthode pédagogique dans laquelle le travail de l'élève est largement orienté, dirigé et guidé par le maître, et qui ne laisse aucune initiative à l'élève.

C *non directivité*

A *directed teaching*

méthode du chemin critique: détermination du cheminement critique, c'est-à-dire, d'une séquence d'événements et d'activités reliés entre le début d'un projet et sa fin et qui nécessite le temps le plus bref. Cette méthode montre le temps le plus court dans lequel le projet peut se réaliser et elle est utilisée comme instrument de planification.

A *critical path method*

méthode du cours magistral: méthode d'enseignement où le professeur présente oralement les phénomènes ou les principes à étudier pendant que, généralement, les élèves de la classe prennent des notes. Ce type de pédagogie n'autorise guère ou pas du tout de participation active des élèves sous forme de questions ou discussions.

A *lecture method*

méthode heuristique: voir **approche heuristique**

méthode inductive: méthode utilisée principalement dans l'enseignement des sciences, avec des élèves débutants, selon laquelle on part des expériences et de leurs conclusions pour parvenir à l'énoncé des lois et des principes. Cette méthode suit une démarche inverse de celle de la méthode déductive.

C *méthode d'apprentissage par la découverte*

A *inductive teaching*

méthode structuro-globale: voir **structuro-global**

métrage: 1. longueur d'un film exprimée en mètres; 2. une certaine quantité de pellicule.

A 1. *footage*; 2. *stock*

metteur en scène: voir **réalisateur**

mettre au point: 1. régler un appareil de prise de vues ou de projection pour obtenir une image de netteté maximale; 2. en informatique, détecter, localiser, éliminer les erreurs de programmation.

C *bogue*

A 1. *to bring into focus*; 2. *to debug*

MEV: mémoire vive.

A *direct access store*

MF: 1. modulation de fréquence – voir **modulation**; 2. abréviation anglaise: ondes moyennes ou ondes hectométriques; voir **bande de fréquence**.

A 1. *FM*; 2. *MF*

micro: voir **microphone**

microcinématographie: technique de réalisation cinématographique où l'on utilise, pour les prises de vues, une caméra de cinéma couplée à un microscope.

A *cinemicrography*

microcopie: copie photographique transparente d'un document assez réduite pour ne pouvoir être lue qu'avec un agrandisseur.

A microcopy

micro-cravate: petit microphone fixé sur une chaînette ou un cordon passé autour du cou.

A Lavalier microphone

micro-émetteur: microphone muni d'un petit émetteur de courte portée permettant ainsi de se passer d'un câble de liaison de microphone.

A wireless microphone

micro-enseignement: méthode de formation d'enseignants par laquelle les élèves-maîtres enrichissent leur expérience pédagogique dans des situations de simulation, avec un petit nombre d'élèves répartis en petits groupes. Ces sessions peuvent donner lieu à des enregistrements audio et/ou vidéo qui sont ensuite analysés et discutés.

C *autoscopie; mini-cours; imitation de maîtres modèles; leçon d'essai; leçon modèle*

A microteaching

microfiche: feuille de microfilm, généralement de 10 x 15 cm (4 x 6 pouces) contenant de nombreuses micro-images disposées sur une grille et conçue pour être lue au moyen d'un appareil d'agrandissement ou de projection.

A microfiche

microfilm: terme générique pour tout film transparent servant de support à une série de micro-images. Désigne souvent un rouleau ou une bobine de microformes.

A microfilm

microforme: terme générique pour tout document, film ou papier, imprimé ou photographique, contenant des micro-images.

A microform

micro-image: reproduction photographique en format miniaturisé de documents tels que des pages imprimées, des dessins ou autres publications.

A micro-image

micro-ondes: voir **hyperfréquences**

micro-ordinateur: ordinateur dont l'unité centrale de traitement est constituée d'un seul microprocesseur ou d'un petit nombre de microprocesseurs.

C *microprocesseur; mini-ordinateur; ordinateur; calculatrice*

A microcomputer

microphone: appareil transformant les ondes sonores en énergie électrique en vue de les amplifier, enregistrer ou transmettre.

A microphone

microphone à réflecteur parabolique: microphone unidirectif fixé sur un réflecteur concave et destiné à capter sans brouillage des ondes sonores éloignées.

A parabolic reflector microphone

microphone électrodynamique: terme générique pour des microphones fonctionnant selon des principes électrodynamiques, à savoir microphones à bobine mobile ou à ruban.

A dynamic microphone

microphone électrostatique: type de microphone où les ondes sonores occasionnent des variations de la capacité d'un condensateur. Ce condensateur fait partie d'un circuit électrique et l'énergie sonore est ainsi transformée en tension électrique.

A condenseur microphone

microphone omnidirectif: microphone d'une sensibilité égale dans toutes les directions.

A omnidirectional microphone

microphone piézoélectrique: microphone utilisant un cristal piézoélectrique comme transducteur.

A crystal microphone

microphone unidirectif: microphone possédant une plus grande sensibilité d'enregistrement dans une direction que dans les autres.

A unidirectional microphone

microprocesseur: plaquette de dimension très réduite (puce) sur laquelle sont rassemblés tous les circuits électroniques nécessaires à l'exécution de fonctions arithmétiques ou logiques.

A microprocessor

microprogramme: ensemble d'instructions internes à une machine enregistrées dans la mémoire morte.

C *logiciel*
A firmware

microprojecteur: appareil conçu pour agrandir et projeter des transparents de préparations microscopiques comme des lames de microscope.

A microprojector

microsillon: voir **disque longue durée**

minicassette: nom déposé d'une marque d'audiocassettes.

A minicassette

mini-cours*: module d'auto-enseignement utilisé pour la formation des maîtres. Comme dans le cas du micro-enseignement, le but cherché est de développer des savoir-faire pédagogiques. Mais il n'y a pas de conseiller présent et l'élève-maître travaille à son rythme propre en utilisant un ensemble multi-média individualisé.

A minicourse

mini-laboratoire: laboratoire de langues audio-actif portatif.

A mini-laboratory

mini-ordinateur: ordinateur universel de petite taille, moins puissant, habituellement plus rustique et relativement moins onéreux qu'un ordinateur normal. On distingue le micro, mini et maxi ordinateurs en fonction de la capacité de mémoire qu'ils offrent, de leur vitesse de traitement, du nombre et du type de leurs équipements périphériques et de leur coût.

C *ordinateur*
A minicomputer

minitel: terminal télématique de faible coût permettant un raccordement au service vidéotex en France.

C *Télétel*
A minitel

mire: image de contrôle composée de dessins géométriques très précis; diffusée à des moments définis, elle sert à effectuer un certain nombre de vérifications et de réglages sur les récepteurs de télévision : dimension de l'image, symétrie, contraste, luminosité, mise au point, définition et linéarité.

A test chart/card (UK); test pattern (USA)

mise au point: obtention d'une image de netteté maximale par réglage des dispositifs optiques ou électroniques d'un appareil de prise de vues.

A focus

mise au point automatique: dispositif permettant une mise au point automatique autocommandée dans un appareil de prise de vues.

A autofocus

mise au point de systèmes pédagogiques: voir **(instructional development)**

mise en mémoire: action d'introduire des données dans une mémoire.

A store (USA); storage

mixage: combinaison en un seul signal de signaux provenant simultanément de plusieurs sources.

A mixing

mixage son: mélange électronique de deux ou plusieurs sources sonores sur piste mono ou stéréo.

A audio mix

mixeur: technicien du son responsable d'un pupitre de mélange.

A mixer

mode: 1. forme particulière sous laquelle se présente une action; 2. forme particulière d'exploitation d'un ordinateur.

A 1. mode; manner; 2. mode

mode conversationnel: voir **mode dialogué**

mode d'apprentissage: ensemble de méthodes qu'emploie de préférence quelqu'un pour organiser sa pensée, acquérir des connaissances ou résoudre des problèmes.

A learning style

mode dialogué: mode d'exploitation dans lequel l'utilisateur est en communication directe avec l'ordinateur et peut obtenir immédiatement réponse à ses questions.

C *interactif; enseignement assisté par ordinateur; mode tutoriel*

A conversational mode

modèle: 1. en sciences, objet concret ou système de relations qui sert à représenter, observer, étudier et prédire le comportement d'un autre objet ou d'un phénomène qui présente une structure analogue, mais qui est moins facile à étudier ou à manipuler.; **2.** type d'énoncé caractérisé par une certaine structure phonologique ou morpho-syntaxique proposé à des élèves pour être imité et reproduit.

C *analogie; maquette; exercice structural*

A 1. model; 2. pattern

mode tutoriel: enseignement assisté par ordinateur: mode d'exploitation dans lequel la machine présente un enseignement suivi d'exercices. L'analyse de la réponse détermine la séquence suivante.

A tutorial mode

modem: abrégé de 'modulateur-démodulateur'. Dispositif qui permet la transmission des données par l'intermédiaire d'une ligne téléphonique.

A modem

modulaire: qualifie un élément ou un composant qui peut s'articuler avec un autre pour former un ensemble et/ou qui se présente sous forme de module.

A modular

modulation: procédé par lequel on change ou modifie certaines caractéristiques d'une onde porteuse pour permettre la transmission d'impulsions audio ou vidéo utilisables d'un point à un autre. En ajoutant de l'information à la porteuse, l'amplitude ou la fréquence changent proportionnellement à l'amplitude du signal de modulation. On obtient ainsi un signal modulé en amplitude (MA) ou modulé en fréquence (MF).

A modulation

modulation (d'amplitude) — MA: voir **modulation (de fréquence)**

modulation (de fréquence) — MF: voir **modulation**

modulateur-démodulateur: voir **modem**

module: 1. élément ou unité que l'on peut combiner avec d'autres éléments ou unités analogues (modulaire); **2.** unité de programme d'enseignement se présentant sous forme d'un ensemble organisé d'activités, de documents et/ou d'appareils permettant de réaliser une partie définie et délimitée d'un programme plus vaste.; **3.** unité de temps à l'intérieur d'un emploi du temps organisé de manière souple dont la durée varie généralement de 15 minutes à une heure; **4.** ensemble de pièces ou d'appareils dont la combinaison permet d'assurer une même fonction spécifique et qui sont réunies en une seule unité fonctionnelle de sorte que le remplacement, en cas de besoin, s'effectue au niveau de l'unité plutôt que de chacune des pièces.

A 1. module; 2. instructional module; 3. 4. module

moduler: faire varier l'amplitude, la fréquence ou la phase d'une onde porteuse avec un signal.

A to modulate

moniteur: 1. enseignement primaire. Enseignant sans qualification, appartenant au corps des auxiliaires. Dans l'enseignement secondaire général et technique, adjoint d'un professeur, se chargeant, sous la responsabilité de ce dernier, d'encadrer de petits groupes d'élèves pour diverses activités, en général manuelles ou pratiques; **2.** enseignement supérieur. En France, personne qui, durant la partie expérimentale d'un cours, aide le professeur à monter et réaliser une manipulation ou une expérience (quel que soit son statut administratif); **3.** dans l'enseignement mutuel, élève assurant des fonctions d'enseignement ou de soutien d'enseignement pour des élèves du même âge ou du même groupe; **4.** dispositif relié à une source de transmission (caméra, magnétoscope, terminal d'ordinateur) par l'intermédiaire d'un câble de connexion, permettant de visionner des images vidéo, notamment à des fins de contrôle. Synonyme: écran témoin, écran de contrôle.

A 1. monitor; assistant teacher; 2. assistant (UK); aide (USA); 3. peer tutor; 4. monitor

monosémique: se dit d'un message qui, dans la mesure du possible, tend à n'avoir qu'une seule signification et qui n'entraîne qu'une seule forme d'application pédagogique.

C *polysémique; pansémique*

A monosemic

montage: 1. activité de sélection et de mise en ordre de séquences imprimées, sonores, vidéo ou filmiques pour composer une suite continue et ordonnée; **2.** choix et assemblage des plans d'un film; **3.** combinaison de deux ou plusieurs enregistrements sonores en enregistrement complexe par réenregistrement.

A 1. editing; 2. cutting; 3. dubbing

montage à sec: fixation d'un cliché sur son carton de support au moyen d'un adhésif de montage à sec et d'une presse chauffante.

C *collage*

A dry mounting

montage électronique: méthode suivant laquelle le montage de bandes vidéo est effectué par réenregistrement sans coupure matérielle des bandes, en maintenant la continuité de toutes les pistes.

A electronic editing

montage en série: assemblage de piles ou d'accumulateurs permettant d'obtenir un voltage supérieur.

A series

montage final: dernière étape du montage d'un film: une fois cette opération effectuée, les scènes ont la longueur désirée et les raccords entre les scènes se trouvent mis en place.

A final cut

montage sonorisé: jeu de diapositives accompagné d'une bande magnétique audio sur laquelle se trouve une piste sonore et, parfois aussi, un signal de pilotage commandant la projection de la diapositive suivante dans la série.

A tape/slide (slide/tape) presentation

montage visuel: image composite faite de plusieurs images séparées.

A montage

monter: installer un équipement de sorte qu'il soit prêt à fonctionner.

A to mount

monteur/monteuse: personne responsable du montage de films.

A editor

monture à baïonnette: type de monture pour objectif ou lampe de projection comportant deux ergots. L'objectif ou la lampe sont insérés dans la monture et un système de blocage les maintient en place.

A bayonet mount

mot: groupe de caractères, par exemple des bits, considéré comme une unité et susceptible d'être stocké dans une cellule de mémoire d'ordinateur.

A word

mot d'entrée: en indexation, mot initial ou premier d'une entrée à plusieurs mots; mot qui détermine l'entrée toute entière.

A access term

motivation: 1. ensemble des phénomènes dont dépend la stimulation à agir pour atteindre un objectif donné; **2.** mise en œuvre, en vue de stimuler un apprentissage donné, d'éléments affectifs ou d'intérêts.

A 1. 2. motivation

motivation extrinsèque: utilisation de récompenses extérieures à l'action elle-même pour stimuler un comportement donné.

A extrinsic motivation

motivation intrinsèque: récompense d'une tâche à effectuer qui est intrinsèque au comportement lui-même, et ne nécessite pas de renforcement extérieur.

A intrinsic motivation

moyenne: quotient obtenu en divisant la somme d'un ensemble de nombres par leur nombre. S'oppose à médian, médiane.

A mean

moyens audiovisuels: type d'auxiliaires pédagogiques conçus pour une projection visuelle et/ou une reproduction sonore, à l'exclusion des livres.

C *moyens d'enseignement; auxiliaires d'enseignement*

A audio-visual materials/aids

moyens de communication de masse: terme générique désignant les moyens de communication touchant un large public à la fois lors de la diffusion du message: par exemple, la presse, le livre ou le document imprimé, le film, la radio, la télévision. Ils s'opposent aux moyens employés pour une communication limitée, par exemple avec des groupes restreints d'élèves ou une communication entre des individus ou à l'intérieur d'une institution donnée.

C *moyens audiovisuels; médias; moyens d'enseignement*

A mass media

moyens de communication sociale: voir **moyens de communication de masse**

moyens d'enseignement: 1. ensemble de documents, quel qu'en soit le support (imprimé, bande sonore, visuelle, audiovisuelle, disquette...) utilisés à des fins pédagogiques; **2.** tous documents et équipements didactiques utilisés dans les établissements d'enseignement.

C *équipement; matériel; médias*

A 1. instructional materials; 2. educational media

moyens graphiques: terme générique désignant tous les documents qui représentent une réalité par l'intermédiaire d'une symbolisation visuelle, parfois accompagnée de mots tels que dessins, affiches, diagrammes, organigrammes, etc.

A graphic materials

moyens visuels: terme générique pour désigner tous les documents tels que dessins, photos, films animés, etc.

A visual material; visuals

multigraphié: voir **polycopie**

multi-images: association de deux ou plusieurs images séparées (généralement projetées) présentées ensemble. Une présentation multi-images n'est pas, d'ordinaire, la combinaison de deux images provenant d'une même source.

C *mur d'images*

A multi-image

multi média (adj.): **1.** désigne la combinaison de plusieurs médias associés de manière complémentaire (par exemple diapositives et bande son) dans une présentation pédagogique ou un module d'enseignement; **2.** terme utilisé par les éditeurs pour tous les moyens d'enseignement autres que les documents imprimés, en particulier les films animés, les films fixes, les bandes vidéo, les transparents et les disques.

A multi-media

multiplet: chaîne d'éléments binaires (bits) adjacents traitée comme un tout, par exemple, octet, sextet, groupes composés de 8, de 6 bits, et utilisée habituellement pour représenter une lettre ou un chiffre.

C *bit; octet*

A byte

multiplex: système qui permet de diffuser en direct des émissions provenant de plusieurs lieux différents.

A multiplex

multiplexage: 1. dans un système d'ordinateur, opération consistant à transférer des données provenant de plusieurs dispositifs de mémoire, opérant à vitesse de transfert de sorte que le dispositif le plus rapide ne soit pas contraint à «attendre» les plus lents; **2.** transmission conjointe de plusieurs courants d'information sur le même canal.

A 1. 2. multiplexing

multiplexeur: 1. dispositif électronique permettant à l'ordinateur d'être connecté à plusieurs périphériques en n'utilisant qu'une seule voie de transmission; **2.** miroir ou prisme mobile conçu de telle façon qu'il puisse transmettre l'image provenant de projecteurs de diapositives et de projecteurs de films à une caméra de télévision. Il constitue un dispositif semblable au télécinéma, mais avec des sources supplémentaires; **3.** dispositif permettant de mettre en parallèle sur une même antenne plusieurs émetteurs en évitant toute réaction entre eux.

A **1.** multiplex; **2. 3.** multiplexer

multiprocesseur: ordinateur qui possède plusieurs organes de calcul associés à une seule mémoire centrale.

A multiprocessor

multivision: spectacle caractérisé par la projection simultanée ou successive sur plusieurs écrans.

A multiscreen show

mur d'images: projection simultanée de plusieurs images sur un même écran.

A multi-image show

musique de film: musique spécialement composée pour un film.

A score

N

nanoréseau: terme utilisé pour désigner en France dans les écoles un réseau local en ligne constitué par la connexion de plusieurs micro-ordinateurs de type personnel utilisés comme postes de travail avec un micro-ordinateur de type professionnel gérant la bibliothèque de logiciels et les échanges dans le réseau.

A local area network; *nanoréseau

(narrowcasting): voir **diffusion restreinte**

NB: noir et blanc.

A BW – black and white

négatif: voir **image négative**

négatif combiné image et son: négatif de film comportant le montage image et le son correspondant en parfaite synchronisation.

A composite negative

négatif déposé: négatif de film mis en dépôt et enregistré dans un laboratoire de tirage.

A deposited negative

négatif image: négatif ou film comportant seulement le montage image.

A picture negative

neige: présence, sur une image de télévision, de nombreuses petites tâches blanches qui dénotent un niveau élevé de parasitage.

A snow

niveau de langue: utilisation spécifique et répertoriée d'une langue donnée caractérisée par des marques sociolinguistiques identifiables au niveau lexical, morphosyntaxique, phonétique, etc. On dit aussi registre de langue.

A register

niveau de lecture: perspective dans laquelle un message (conte, récit, film, etc.) est interprété.

A interpretation level

niveau d'information: degré d'information d'un individu dans une matière donnée.

A information level

niveau d'instruction: niveau atteint dans les degrés successifs d'un système éducatif.

A instructional level

niveau scolaire: ensemble des acquisitions réalisées par un élève par comparaison au programme scolaire correspondant normalement à son âge.

A school level

niveau sonore: valeur du niveau du signal sur un support enregistré définie par comparaison avec le niveau de référence.

A sound level

non directivité: 1. méthode pédagogique ou thérapeutique centrée non sur le contenu à transmettre, ou la tranformation à opérer, mais sur la personne en tant que telle. Elle repose sur l'écoute et l'acceptation d'autrui tel qu'il est. A ne pas confondre avec le laisser-faire qui est un des modes possibles d'exercice de l'autorité (C. Rogers); **2.** méthode libérale dans la gestion d'une classe, laissant beaucoup d'initiative aux élèves, par opposition à l'attitude autoritaire.

C *centré sur l'enseignement; centré sur la matière; méthode active; méthode directive*

A 1. client centred approach; 2. democratic attitude

norme: 1. règle ou modèle déterminé, servant de référence pour porter des jugements de valeur ou rendant compte du fonctionnement d'un système; **2.** état conforme à la majorité des cas. Plus particulièrement, niveau de développement ou de performance que la majorité voire la totalité des membres d'un groupe devrait atteindre pour satisfaire à un critère; **3.** formule qui définit un type d'objet, un produit fabriqué, un procédé technique.

C *moyenne; test normatif; standard*

A 1. norm; 2. norm; standard; 3. standard

normes (techniques): liste, établie par un organisme officiel, qui a une valeur obligatoire ou de recommandations, de l'ensemble des spécifications qu'une catégorie de produits et de matériels ou de procédés doit présenter pour répondre aux besoins des utilisateurs de façon efficace et rationnelle, et notamment à certaines exigences de qualité.

A standards

normes à fréquences basses: normes de fonctionnement d'un magnétoscope utilisant un signal porteur de 5 à 6,8 mégahertz.

A low-band standards

normes à fréquences élevées: normes de fonctionnement d'un magnétoscope utilisant un signal porteur de 7,8 à 10 mégahertz.

A high-band standards

notation: 1. appréciation d'un travail scolaire par l'emploi d'une note chiffrée ou de symboles divers; **2.** méthode systématique et conventionnelle pour représenter des données par l'utilisation de signes et de symboles tels que les chiffres, des lettres et des signes spéciaux.

A 1. marking; grading; 2. notation

note: expression chiffrée de l'appréciation d'un travail d'élève.

C *score*

A mark (UK); grade (USA)

note étalonnée: note dérivée située par rapport à une moyenne et un écart type prédéterminés; s'oppose à note brute.

C *score brut*

A standard score

noter: 1. mesurer ou évaluer les résultats d'un test de performance; **2.** donner une appréciation chiffrée à un travail d'élève.

A 1. to score; 2. to rate; to mark

nouvelles technologies de l'information — NTI: mise en œuvre de technologies récentes, telles que les ordinateurs, les fibres optiques, les satellites, l'enregistrement vidéo, etc., pour produire, stocker, rechercher et distribuer l'information sous forme analogique ou numérique.

C *télématique*

A new information technology – NIT

noyau: petite bague circulaire de plastique sur laquelle est enroulé un film.

A core

NTI: voir **nouvelles technologies de l'information**

NTSC: système de transmission de télévision couleur utilisé aux Etats-Unis (National Television Standards Committee).

A NTSC

nucléarisation: stratégie d'organisation et de planification des services de l'éducation formelle et non formelle à partir des communautés de base, particulièrement répandue en Amérique latine. Elle vise à rationaliser les ressources et à permettre une participation maximale de la collectivité au développement de l'éducation.

A nuclearization*

numération binaire: système de numération de base 2 utilisé pour le codage en informatique (par opposition à la numération décimale qui utilise la base 10).

A binary number system

numérique (adj.): se dit, par opposition à analogique, de la représentation de données ou de grandeurs physiques au moyen de caractères en chiffres et aussi de systèmes, dispositifs ou procédés employant ce mode de représentation discontinu.

C *analogique; disque audio-numérique*

A digital

numérisation: conversion d'un signal analogique en signal numérique porteur de la même information.

A digitizing

numéro de bord: série de numéros correspondants imprimés à intervalles réguliers sur le bord de l'original d'une pellicule cinématographique et sur celui de la copie de travail de sorte que, après montage, on puisse faire correspondre l'original et la copie.

A edge number

O

objectif: 1. but spécifique d'une activité; 2. système optique servant à la formation d'images par focalisation des rayons lumineux dans un appareil de prise de vues, un projecteur ou tout autre système.

C *lentille condensatrice; lentille de Fresnel; zoom*

A 1. objective; 2. lens

objectif à focale variable: objectif d'un appareil de prise de vues possédant un dispositif de variation de la distance focale, offrant ainsi la possibilité d'un passage graduel d'un plan éloigné à un gros plan du même sujet, sans changer la position de l'appareil.

C *zoom*

A zoom lens

objectif à longue focale: objectif capable d'agrandir l'image et servant à photographier des sujets éloignés.

C *téléobjectif*

A long-focus lens

objectif anamorphoseur: système optique utilisé soit comme objectif de prise de vues, pour transformer par anamorphose une grande image en une image de format standard de film, soit comme système de projection, pour agrandir une image «écrasée» en lui restituant sa largeur initiale.

A anamorphic lens

objectif anastigmatique: objectif traité optiquement, à la fabrication, pour corriger l'astigmatisme.

A anastigmatic lens

objectif comportemental: voir **objectif de performance**

objectif de performance: degré spécifique d'apprentissage indiquant, en termes de comportement, ce qu'un apprenant est censé faire à la suite d'un enseignement reçu, les conditions dans lesquelles il peut le faire, et le niveau de compétence dont il doit pouvoir faire preuve.

A performance objective

objectif de projection: optique utilisée dans un projecteur pour reconstituer l'image projetée sur un écran. Il a été corrigé contre les aberrations de couleurs pour pouvoir correspondre à la sensibilité spectrale de

213

l'œil et à la caractéristique de la lumière émise par les lampes de projection.

A projection lens

objectif grand angulaire: objectif d'un appareil de prise de vues dont l'angle de champ est supérieur à celui d'un objectif standard.

A wide-angle lens

objectif intermédiaire: objectif pédagogique qui n'est pas poursuivi pour lui-même et qui constitue un passage obligé sur le chemin qui conduit à un objectif terminal.

A enabling objective

objectif macro à focale variable: zoom permettant la mise au point sur des sujets très rapprochés.

C *macrozoom*

A macrozoom lens

objectif médiateur: voir **objectif intermédiaire**

objectif pédagogique: définition précise de la performance attendue d'un apprenant en termes de capacités et savoirs spécifiques.

C *objectif de l'éducation; objectif de performance; pré-requis; comportement terminal; domaine affectif; domaine cognitif; domaine psychomoteur; détermination des objectifs*

A learning objective

objectif terminal: définition des savoirs et savoir-faire que l'apprenant est censé avoir acquis à la fin d'une séquence spécifique d'enseignement.

C *test pronostique; test de rendement; test de connaissances; test de capacité; évaluation formative; pré-test; post-test*

A terminal objective

objectif traité: optique dont la surface est recouverte d'une couche spéciale pour diminuer les reflets et augmenter ainsi le passage de la lumière.

A coated lens

objectifs de l'éducation: résultats concrets que l'on espère obtenir en un temps donné par la mise en œuvre de stratégies et la visée d'objectifs clairement définis, pour répondre à certains problèmes existants et aux besoins résultant du développement du système éducatif ainsi qu'aux besoins sociaux de la communauté.

A educational objectives

observation: 1. activité perceptive, généralement méthodique en vue d'acquérir la notion claire d'un objet, d'un phénomène, ou d'une série d'événements; 2. technique d'examen d'un sujet ou d'un phénomène à l'aide de moyens d'investigation et d'études appropriées.

A 1. 2. observation

observation dirigée: observation guidée ayant pour but d'améliorer l'étude, la compréhension et l'évaluation de ce qui est observé.

A directed observation

obturateur: dispositif d'un appareil de prise de vues ou d'un projecteur qui ferme l'appareil après chaque image tandis qu'une autre section de la pellicule est positionnée pour l'opération suivante.

A shutter

obturateur à rideau: mécanisme d'obturation surtout utilisé dans les appareils réflex.

A focal axis shutter

octet: multiplet de 8 bits. Il constitue la plus petite unité adressable dans certains systèmes de traitement des données.

A byte

œuvres protégées: œuvres de l'esprit originales (de nature littéraire, scientifique et artistique) jouissant de la protection en vertu de la législation sur le droit d'auteur.

A protected works

offset: 1. procédé d'impression par report; 2. presse offset.

A 1. offset process; 2. offset press

onde hertzienne: voir **fréquence radioélectrique**

onde pilote: oscillation (onde) périodique sinusoïdale émise à faible niveau en vue de permettre à la réception une commande automatique de gain ou d'accord.
A pilot wave

onde porteuse: onde électromagnétique transmise, rendue porteuse de signaux ou d'impulsions audio ou vidéo par modulation.
A carrier

opaque (adj.): qui ne laisse pas passer les rayons lumineux, par opposition à transparent ou translucide.
A opaque

open university: voir **université ouverte**

opérateur de prise de vues: voir **cadreur**

optique (système): voir **objectif 2.**

ORACLE: voir **système d'information en réseau**

ordinateur: machine de traitement de l'information susceptible d'effectuer à grande vitesse de nombreuses opérations arithmétiques ou logiques sans intervention d'un opérateur humain au cours de l'exécution. Les ordinateurs sont classés, selon la capacité de leur mémoire interne, en gros, mini et micro ordinateurs.
C *calculateur analogique; micro-ordinateur; mini-ordinateur; calculatrice*
A computer

ordinateur hôte: 1. dans un réseau, l'ordinateur principal qui contrôle tout le système et assure des fonctions communes telles que calcul, accès à des bases de données ou traduction de programmes; **2.** ordinateur qui prépare des programmes qui seront utilisés par un autre ordinateur ou un autre système; **3.** dans un réseau, l'ordinateur qui dessert un certain nombre de machines dans un travail de transmission de données. On dit aussi serveur.
A 1. 2. host computer; host; 3. host computer; server

ordinateur universel: ordinateur capable de traiter tous les problèmes par opposition aux ordinateurs spécialisés.
A general-purpose computer

organe arithmétique: voir **unité arithmétique**

organe d'entrée/sortie: unité qui reçoit des données nouvelles, les envoie à l'ordinateur pour traitement, reçoit la réponse et la communique sous une forme lisible.
A input/output (I/O) device

organigramme: 1. représentation graphique de la définition, analyse ou solution d'un problème ou du fonctionnement d'un système, accompagnée de symboles représentant les opérations, le flux des données et les équipements; **2.** visualisation graphique du système logique d'un programme d'informatique. (Synonyme: ordinogramme).
C *schéma fonctionnel*
A flow chart

organisateur avancé: texte court placé avant un ensemble important de connaissances à acquérir au cours d'un apprentissage. Il sert de guide pour les points principaux de cet ensemble sans se substituer à lui en tant que source première d'apprentissage.
A advanced organizer

organisation de la classe: ensemble de dispositions particulières prises par un enseignant pour organiser les activités éducatives en fonction des objectifs pédagogiques, de la méthode d'enseignement choisie, de la spécificité des différents acteurs du groupe-classe (enseignant et enseignés), et des contraintes et des ressources existantes.
A class management

Organisation internationale de normalisation — ISO
A International Organization for Standardization

orientation tendancieuse: point de vue intentionnel ou non, exprimé dans un film ou un programme.
A bias

original: document photographique, filmique, sonore ou bande vidéo initiale, par opposition à toute copie ou reproduction.
A master; original version

outil-logiciel: voir **logiciel outil**

ouvert: voir **fermé**

ouverture: 1. diamètre d'ouverture du diaphragme, chaque position d'ouverture correspondant à une graduation; **2.** extrémité ouverte d'un cornet, d'un réflecteur ou d'un appareil analogue.

A 1. 2. aperture

ouverture en fondu: voir **fondu**

ouverture/fermeture d'une session: procédure de début ou de fin d'une session de travail en temps partagé dans un système de traitement de l'information.

A log in; log out

P

(package): terme d'informatique (Français: progiciel) désignant, par extension, un ensemble de programmes ou de documents conçus de façon à traiter un problème défini et délimité, et pour répondre aux besoins d'une grand nombre d'utilisateurs. Utilisable en situation d'enseignement collectif ou individuellement.

C *ensemble multi média; ensemble pédagogique; kit*

A learning package

page sonore: moyen d'enseignement comportant des pages de papier fort dont le verso porte un enregistrement sonore. La page peut être placée sur la platine d'un appareil lecteur-enregistreur: l'élève regarde cette page en écoutant le son.

A sound page

PAL — phase alterning line: système de télévision couleur utilisé dans certains pays d'Europe Occidentale.

A PAL

panneau électrique: terme générique s'appliquant à de nombreux dispositifs utilisés pour des tests, des exercices ou des démonstrations. Il comprend, généralement, un circuit électrique déclenchant un timbre, une cloche ou un signal lumineux lorsque des boutons de contact ou des commutateurs appropriés sont pressés ou actionnés en réponse à une question ou à des documents visuels apparaissant sur un tableau.

A buzz board

panel: 1. groupe social sélectionné en vue de répondre régulièrement à des questions d'enquête d'opinion; **2.** réunion-débat entre un petit groupe d'experts devant un auditoire plus important.

C *table ronde*

A 1. panel; 2. panel discussion

panier (de diapositives): voir **passe-vues**

panoramique: 1. rotation de la caméra autour de son axe dans le plan horizontal; **2.** plan obtenu grâce à ce mouvement.

A 1. 2. pan

panoramique vertical: 1. rotation de la caméra autour de son axe dans le plan vertical; **2.** plan obtenu grâce à ce mouvement.

A 1. 2. tilt

pansémique: caractère d'un signifiant qui, à la limite, admet n'importe quel signifié.

C *monosémique; polysémique*

A pansemic

papier floqué: carton mince sur lequel ont été pulvérisées des fibres afin de le rendre adhésif sur une surface de feutre.

C *flocage*

A velour paper

papier photographique: papier opaque dont un côté est enduit d'une couche d'émulsion photosensible, sur laquelle les images viennent se fixer par exposition et traitement approprié.

A printing paper

cadence plus ou moins rapide, perceptible par l'œil.

C *scintillement*

A flicker

paradigmatique: paradigmatique s'oppose à syntagmatique pour désigner l'un des deux types de relations possibles entre les éléments d'un message; des éléments sont syntagmatiques quand ils sont coprésents dans le message *(et)* alors qu'ils sont dits paradigmatiques lorsque l'élément présenté dans le message prend une signification par rapport à d'autres absents du message *(ou)* (les couleurs d'un drapeau par opposition aux feux de circulation).

A paradigmatic

paradigme: 1. exemple type; 2. modèle de conjugaison.

A 1. 2. paradigm

parasite: perturbation, le plus souvent brusque et aléatoire, ne correspondant à aucun signal intentionnel, qui vient troubler le fonctionnement d'un appareil électromagnétique.

A disturbance

parallaxe: différence entre la position verticale d'un objet filmé telle qu'elle est perçue dans le viseur et telle qu'elle est fixée sur la pellicule par l'intermédiaire de l'objectif de prise de vues.

A parallax

parole comprimée: enregistrement de la parole qui a été accéléré par un procédé électronique (compresseur de son), sans augmentation ni diminution de hauteur.

A compressed speech

parole synthétique: simulation de la parole humaine par des moyens artificiels.

A synthetic speech

partage de temps: technique d'exploitation d'un même ordinateur par plusieurs utilisateurs qui exécutent simultanément, en mode dialogué, chacun à son propre rythme, des travaux indépendants.

A time-sharing

pas de perforation: distance entre les bords d'attaque de deux perforations sur un film fixe ou animé.

A pitch

pascal: langage de programmation évolué nommé d'après Blaise Pascal, philosophe et mathématicien français du 17e siècle.

A pascal language

passage de film: programmation d'un film dans une salle d'exploitation.

A run; showing

passage en machine: voir **passage machine**

passage machine: soumission d'un travail à un ordinateur.

A run

passe-vues: dispositif permettant la mise en place d'une série de diapositives dans un appareil de projection.

A slide changer; tray

pattern: groupe ou faisceau de traits culturels reliés les uns aux autres, entrelacés et virtuellement indissociables qui, en tant qu'ensemble, forme une structure typique et reconnue comme, par exemple, un mode de pensée, de vie ou d'action.

A pattern

pédagogie centrée sur l'élève: voir **programme centré sur l'élève**

pédagogie centrée sur l'enseignant: pédagogie mettant l'accent sur les activités de l'enseignant dans la direction de l'apprentissage, comme, par exemple, le cours magistral ou la récitation de leçons.

C *centré sur l'étudiant; centré sur la matière; non directivité*

A teacher-centred method

pédagogie de groupe: stratégie éducative fondée sur le principe de la participation active des membres du groupe d'apprenants à la conception et à la détermination des procédures d'apprentissage (souvent utilisée dans l'éducation des adultes).

C *méthodes actives; enseignement collectif; pédagogie en groupe*

A group learning; (group-centered instruction)

pédagogie de la maîtrise: stratégie éducative fondée sur le fait que tous les élèves d'une classe sont à même de maîtriser, dans leur très grande majorité, une unité d'enseignement ou d'apprentissage, à condition de bénéficier d'une aide suffisante et de disposer d'assez de temps pour surmonter les difficultés rencontrées, ce qui suppose nécessairement une organisation rigoureuse de l'enseignement.
A mastery learning

pédagogie de soutien: mise en œuvre d'une aide aux élèves qui sont en difficulté dans certaines parties du programme.
A remediation; remedial teaching

pédagogie différenciée: démarche qui cherche à mettre en œuvre un ensemble diversifié de moyens et de procédures d'enseignement et d'apprentissage afin de permettre à des élèves d'âges, d'aptitudes, de comportements, de savoir-faire hétérogènes, mais regroupés dans une même division ou classe, d'atteindre par des voies différentes des objectifs communs ou en partie communs.
C *pédagogie de la maîtrise*
A adaptive teaching

pédagogie en groupe: procédure pédagogique particulière centrée sur l'utilisation à des fins d'apprentissage et de maturation personnelle des interactions qui se manifestent au sein du groupe (notamment des apprenants), des dimensions affectives du vécu et de l'impact des échanges interpersonnels (utilisés en éducation spéciale, en rééducation, et aussi en éducation des adultes).
C *dynamique des groupes; pédagogie institutionnelle; pédagogie de groupe*
A group instruction

pédagogie institutionnelle: stratégie éducative fondée sur la transformation des relations de l'ensemble des acteurs dans un établissement d'éducation (du concierge au directeur) et sur la modification des règles de l'institution plus que sur celle des modalités de transmission des connaissances.
C *non-directivité; dynamique des groupes; pédagogie de groupe*
A (pédagogie institutionnelle)

pédagogie ouverte: démarche pédagogique qui s'adapte aux possibilités et aux besoins des élèves et leur laisse une grande marge d'autonomie dans le cadre d'orientations générales. Ne pas confondre avec «enseignement ouvert».
C *autonomie; travail autonome*
A open learning

pédagogie par objectifs: effort d'organisation pédagogique poursuivi par un enseignant pour définir les objectifs de son action en termes comportementaux.
C *objectif pédagogique*
A behavioural instruction

pellicule: support d'une émulsion photographique.
A film

pellicule à double perforation: pellicule présentant des perforations sur ses deux bords.
A double perforation stock/film

pellicule couleur: pellicule avec plusieurs couches d'émulsions sensibles à toutes les couleurs du spectre.
A colour film

pellicule de sécurité: voir **film de sécurité**

pellicule vierge: pellicule cinématographique non-impressionnée.
A raw stock

pensée convergente/divergente: voir **convergence, divergence**

perception de soi: image de lui-même qu'a un individu en tant que personne.
A self-perception

perchiste: voir **preneur de son**

perfectionnement: 1. formation complémentaire ou supérieure dans un domaine d'activité où on a déjà acquis une certaine compétence; 2. classes de perfectionnement. Enseignement pour les inadaptés.
C *formation continue*
A 1. further training; 2. special education

perforateur: dispositif de sortie d'un système informatique qui perfore sur un ruban de papier ou une carte des informations sous une forme codée ou en clair.

A puncher

perforation(s): 1. trous perforés dans un support de données appropriées (carte, ruban, etc.) selon une configuration déterminée pour mémoriser des informations; **2.** opération consistant à transcrire des informations alphanumériques sur des cartes ou des rubans en perforant des trous avec une perforatrice; **3.** trous de dimension et de forme normalisée, disposés sur les bords d'une pellicule.

A 1. punch; 2. key punching; 3. sprocket holes; perforations

perforatrice: 1. machine à clavier, connectée ou non à un ordinateur permettant de perforer des cartes ou un ruban de papier selon un code donné; **2.** opératrice de saisie de l'information qui transcrit des informations codées sur un support mécanographique ou magnétique à l'aide d'une machine à clavier.

A 1. punch; puncher; keypunch; 2. punch operator

performance: 1. accomplissement d'une tâche selon un mode imposé; **2.** niveau atteint par un individu pour une tâche donnée.

A performance

périphériques: appareils ou unités qui font partie d'un système de traitement de l'information, mais distincts de l'unité centrale de traitement et pouvant assurer des communications avec l'extérieur ou des services supplémentaires.

C *imprimante; visuel*

A peripheral equipment

persistance rétinienne: sensation visuelle survenant après que le stimulus extérieur déclencheur a cessé d'opérer.

A afterimage; persistence of vision

PERT: technique consistant à définir de manière systématique une programmation et un calendrier d'exécution afin de mesurer, contrôler et diriger le déroulement et la progression d'un projet ou d'un programme.

A PERT (programmed evaluation and review technique)

perte de niveau: affaiblissement brusque et important de niveau du signal lu par une tête magnétique.

A dropout

phonographe: voir **électrophone**

phonothèque: établissement dans lequel sont réunis et conservés les documents enregistrés constituant les «archives de la parole».

A sound archives

photo: voir **photographie 3.**

photocomposition: ensemble des méthodes de composition par photographie donnant directement sur film des textes prêts pour le montage.

A photocomposing

photocopie: 1. terme général pour la copie de documents, particulièrement celle effectuée au moyen de procédés électrostatiques et de tirage humide; **2.** copie photographique d'un document.

C *xérographie*

A 1. photocopy; 2. photocopy; photostat

photographie: 1. procédé technique permettant d'obtenir une image durable des objets par l'action de la lumière sur une surface sensible; **2.** technique et art de prendre des images photographiques; **3.** image obtenue par ce procédé. (Photo n.f. synonymes cliché, épreuve, diapositive).

A 1. 2. photography; 2. photograph; picture; still

photographie en relief: photographie donnant une illusion de profondeur et de volume.

A three-dimensional photography

photographie infrarouge: prise de vues cinématographique utilisant une pellicule noir et blanc ou couleur sensible à la lumière infrarouge.

A infrared photography

219

photomontage: montage où l'on combine des images photographiques (soit par superposition d'un certain nombre de prises sur le même négatif, soit par projection de différents négatifs pour faire un cliché composé, soit par composition d'une image faite d'épreuves découpées ou collées).

A photomontage

photoroman: histoire racontée sous forme d'une suite de photographies accompagnées de textes brefs ou de légendes.

C *bande dessinée*

A fotonovella

photostyle: dispositif d'entrée d'un ordinateur muni d'une cellule photo-électrique. Les photostyles peuvent être pointés sur un écran cathodique pour ajouter, corriger ou effacer des informations. Se dit aussi «crayon lumineux», «crayon optique».

A light pen

photothèque: collection d'archives photographiques.

A picture archives; photo/stills library

pièces de rechange: pièces gardées en réserve pour remplacer un objet ou un élément identique soit usé, soit défectueux.

A spare parts

pile: **1.** générateur d'électricité produisant du courant par une action thermique ou chimique; **2.** élément de base d'une batterie électrique.

A 1. battery; 2. cell

pile de disques: assemblage de disques magnétiques utilisés pour conserver des données, et généralement amovible.

A disk pack

pile sèche: pile voltaïque dont les composants sont fixés au moyen d'un absorbant.

A dry cell

pilote (adj.): (classe, programme, projet, matériel, recherche, etc.) qui peut servir d'exemple, qui utilise de nouvelles méthodes, qui montre la voie.

A pilot

piratage: voir **piraterie**

piraterie: reproduction et distribution de programmes sans autorisation ni permission, en infraction au droit d'auteur; on dit aussi «piratage».

A piracy; bootlegging

piste: trace séparée continue sur un film, une bande vidéo, une bande d'ordinateur ou une bande magnétique audio, servant de support à l'enregistrement de signaux ou de données. Une bande magnétique audio peut avoir un ou plusieurs pistes d'enregistrement (généralement une, deux, quatre ou huit). On parle alors de pleine piste ou piste unique, demi-piste, quatre pistes et huit pistes.

A track

piste de son magnétique – COMMAG: Piste sonore enregistrée sur une mince bande enduite d'une couche magnétique et située sur le bord de la pellicule d'un film animé.

C *piste de son optique*

A combined magnetic sound track

piste de son optique – COMOPT: piste disposée latéralement sur la pellicule d'un film animé et portant un signal photographique transformé en son lorsqu'il est lu par une cellule photo-électrique reliée à un amplificateur et un haut-parleur.

C *piste de son magnétique*

A combined optical sound track

piste élève: sur une bande magnétique utilisée avec un magnétophone audio-actif-comparatif, piste servant de support à l'enregistrement de l'élève.

C *piste maître*

A student track

piste étroite: piste magnétique de largeur réduite.

A stripe

piste magnétique couchée: voir **piste de son magnétique**

piste maître: sur une bande magnétique utilisée avec un magnétophone audio-actif-comparatif, piste servant de support au stimulus sonore pré-enregistré de référence.

C *piste élève*

A master track

piste optique: voir **piste de son optique**

piste sonore: 1. partie d'une pellicule filmique ou d'une bande vidéo servant de support au son; **2.** sur une bande magnétique, partie contenant l'enregistrement sonore par opposition à celle contenant le signal de synchronisation.

A 1. 2. sound track

pixel: plus petite surface homogène constitutive d'une image enregistrée définie par les dimensions de la maille d'échantillonnage.

A pixel

placebo: voir **effet placebo**

plan: 1. projet élaboré comportant une suite ordonnée d'opérations; sert en particulier comme instrument de planification; **2.** représentation schématique d'un objet ou d'un lieu; **3.** ce qu'une caméra enregistre en continu sans s'arrêter; **4.** élément constitutif minimal d'un film animé conservant la même unité de lieu et de temps.

A 1. 2. plan; 3. 4. shot

planche contact: voir **épreuve contact**

plan d'archives: document photographique conservé en prévision de réalisations ultérieures et pouvant être utilisé dans diverses productions.

A stock shot

plan de tournage: descriptif spécifiant l'ordre de réalisation des séquences d'un film, les lieux de tournage, les équipes, les acteurs, l'équipement, les moyens de transport, et, parfois aussi, les séquences de remplacement en cas de mauvais temps.

A production schedule

plan de transition: plan permettant d'assurer une continuité harmonieuse de l'action filmique entre deux scènes voisines, reliées l'une à l'autre.

A matched action shot

plan d'études: organisation de l'enseignement dans les différentes matières; liste détaillée des contenus de l'enseignement.

C *curriculum; contenus de l'enseignement; programme d'études*

A syllabus; curriculum guide

plan focal: plan perpendiculaire à l'axe d'un objectif où les rayons lumineux sont focalisés. Pour obtenir une image nette, la surface sensible de la pellicule dans l'appareil doit être positionnée dans le plan focal de l'objectif.

A focal plane

planification de l'éducation: processus impliquant un effort méthodique et rationnel de sélection des meilleures alternatives possibles, ainsi qu'une programmation plus ou moins contraignante des diverses activités à mettre en œuvre en vue de promouvoir le développement de l'éducation; elle établit des rapports entre les moyens et les objectifs à atteindre.

A educational planning

planification d'éléments contingents: préparation prévisionnelle d'un ensemble de programmes, plans ou alternatives permettant de répondre aux éléments imprévus ou incertains pouvant intervenir dans un dispositif opérationnel.

A contingency management/planning

plastifier: recouvrir un document graphique en deux dimensions (sur le côté image ou sur les deux côtés) d'un mince film protecteur transparent.

A to laminate

plateau: 1. scène équipée pour la prise de vues; **2.** ensemble des participants à un débat radiotélédiffusé; **3.** voir **platine (tourne-disque).**

A 1. floor; 2. live show; 3. turntable

plate-forme pour panomarique horizontal et vertical: support de caméra permettant une rotation sans à-coup de la caméra dans le plan horizontal et vertical. Il peut être monté sur un trépied, un chariot ou un dispositif de fixation.

A pan-and-tilt head

platine (de magnétophone): enregistreur-lecteur de bandes ou de cassettes sans amplificateur ni haut-parleur. Généralement utilisé comme élément d'un studio ou d'une chaîne hi-fi.

A tape deck; cassette deck

platine (tourne-disque): ensemble comprenant un plateau circulaire et son système d'entraînement, un bras et une tête de lecture, utilisé pour la lecture des disques audio.

A turntable

PLATO: système d'enseignement assisté par ordinateur, mis au point à l'Université d'Illinois, aux Etats-Unis, en 1968, et offrant des programmes de l'école primaire jusqu'à la formation professionnelle.

A PLATO - programmed logic for automatic teaching operations

pleurage: déformation du son transmis ou reproduit, due à une variation ou à une diminution de la vitesse de défilement du support.

C *scintillement*

A wow

point à point: liaison mettant un jeu deux interlocuteurs ou deux groupes et deux seulement, par opposition au multipoint, ou à la diffusion hertzienne.

A point to point

point d'accès: dans un réseau informatique, poste ou emplacement à partir duquel un utilisateur peut accéder au réseau pour entrer ou sortir des données.

A access point

point d'entrée: élément d'un système sur lequel on décide d'intervenir de manière privilégiée parce que, du fait de sa sensibilité et de son interconnexion avec les autres éléments du système, il permet d'agir sur l'ensemble. Exemple: intervenir sur la structure d'un examen pour entraîner en chaîne un changement des programmes d'enseignement, de l'attitude des enseignants, des élèves, etc.

C *approche systémique en éducation*

A entry point

polarisation: procédé utilisé en enregistrement magnétique, et consistant à superposer au signal à enregistrer un signal sinusoïdal haute fréquence (40 à 120 kHz), destiné à linéariser la courbe d'aimantation du matériau magnétique.

A bias

polycopie: reproduction non-photographique d'un document original en deux dimensions, en passant par l'étape intermédiaire de la composition d'une matrice ré-utilisable d'où l'on tire des copies multiples.

A duplicating

polysémique: se dit d'un message possédant plusieurs significations et se prêtant donc à diverses applitions et utilisations pédagogiques.

C *monosémique; pansémique; fermé/ouvert*

A polysemic

polythèque: réunion dans un même local d'une médiathèque et d'une bibliothèque.

A (polythèque); multimedia library*

pondéré: Affecté de coefficients proportionnels à l'importance relative de chacun des divers éléments entrant dans l'élaboration d'un calcul ou d'une statistique.

A weighted

population: en statistique, ensemble des individus ou unités qui satisfont à une définition commune et constituent la collectivité étudiée. C'est à partir de la population que l'on construit l'échantillon.

A population

population cible: 1. public particulier auquel on destine un message, un programme ou une activité spécifique; 2. partie de la population totale des apprenants choisie pour recevoir un module spécifique d'enseignement. Ce groupe est généralement défini par un certain nombre de caractéristiques communes de milieu social et/ou d'apprentissage.

A 1. 2. target population/audience

portabilité: aptitude d'un programme à être utilisé sur des systèmes informatiques de types différents.

A portability

porteuse: voir **onde porteuse**

pose: exposition de la surface sensible d'une pellicule à l'action de rayons lumineux.

A exposure

posemètre: dispositif servant à mesurer la lumière incidente ou réflechie par l'objet à photographer et donc le temps de pose.

A exposure meter

positif combiné image/son: positif comprenant les images et la piste sonore.

A composite print; married print

poste d'écoute collective: appareil de diffusion du son sur lequel on peut brancher plusieurs casques permettant ainsi à plusieurs élèves d'écouter un même enregistrement sonore en même temps.

A listening centre

poste d'interrogation: terminal d'utilisateur dont la fonction essentielle est de permettre l'interrogation d'un ordinateur.

A inquiry station

postsonorisation: ajout, à un film, d'éléments sonores de toute nature non enregistrés au moment du tournage.

A dubbing

postsynchronisation: synchronisation labiable effectuée après le tournage d'un film, soit dans la langue des acteurs, soit dans une autre langue en respectant les mouvement des lèvres des acteurs.

C *synchronisation*

A post-synchronization; dubbing

post-test: mesure faite après la fin d'un enseignement et évaluant le degré de ce qui a été atteint par l'apprenant dans les objectifs spécifiés par rapport au niveau d'entrée et par rapport au test de fin d'apprentissage. Quelquefois utilisé comme équivalent de test final.

C *pré-test; test final; profil de sortie*

A post-test

pouvoir: voir **capacité**

pouvoir de résolution: mesure de la capacité de définition du détail d'une image.

A resolution

PPBS: voir **rationalisation des choix budgétaires**

praticable: partie ou élément de décor qui doit pouvoir fonctionner comme dans la réalité; exemple: porte ou fenêtre.

A practical (UK)

préamplificateur: dispositif augmentant la force d'un signal de faible niveau ou puissance dans un électrophone, projecteur, microphone ou autre appareil, avant de l'envoyer à l'amplificateur principal.

A preamplifier

préapprentissage: ensemble d'activités, souvent organisées de façon très souple, proposées à des élèves ou à des adolescents, en vue de leur faire acquérir un ensemble de pré-requis (appréhension du monde social et professionnel, bases en mathématiques, en expression orale et écrite...) indispensables pour qu'ils puissent ensuite suivre avec profit un cycle organisé d'études professionnelles.

A readiness curriculum

préenregistré: enregistré ou programmé à l'avance.

A pre-recorded

prémagnétisation: voir **polarisation**

premier contretype: contretype réalisé directement à partir de l'original.

A first generation duplicate

premier montage: deuxième étape du montage d'un film. Lorsqu'il est effectué, la longueur des scènes se trouve un peu raccourcie, mais pas nécessairement comme dans la versioin finale, et les raccords précis entre les scènes ne sont pas encore définitivement mis en place.
A rough cut

première exclusivité: première distribution et présentation d'un film dans une large zone d'exploitation.
A first release

premier positif: copie d'un film tirée rapidement par un laboratoire à partir de l'original pour permettre à l'équipe de production de juger de son acceptabilité.
C *rushes*
A rush print

preneur de son: technicien chargé d'effectuer la prise de son à l'aide d'un microphone monté à l'extrémité d'une perche. On dit aussi perchiste.
A boom man (USA); boom operator (UK)

prérequis: connaissances et savoir-faire préalables nécessaires pour entreprendre un apprentissage particulier.
C *profil d'entrée*
A prerequisite

présentateur: personne présentant ou animant une émission.
A presenter; host; speaker

présentation: action de présenter un film à un public
A screening; showing

presse de montage à sec: presse chauffée électriquement et fournissant la chaleur et la pression nécessaires au montage et/ou à la plastification de documents graphiques et photographiques plats.
A mounting press (dry)

PRESTEL: voir **système d'information en réseau**

prêt à monter: voir **kit**

prétest: mesure faite avant un enseignement et évaluant le niveau de connaissance, de savoir-faire et/ou d'aptitudes qu'un apprenant possède au moment d'aborder l'apprentissage. On dit aussi test d'entrée.
C *post-test; test final*
A pretest

preuve de succès d'apprentissage*: preuve, présentée par un réalisateur de matériel pédagogique ou un auteur d'ouvrage, que l'utilisation de ces documents comme outils de travail offre une possibilité d'apprentissage efficace pour le public auquel ils s'adressent.
C *validation*
A learner verification

priorité à la vitesse: caractéristique d'un appareil photographique où l'exposition est choisie manuellement et l'ouverture du diaphragme réglée automatiquement.
A shutter preferred

priorité au diaphragme: caractéristique d'un appareil photographique où l'ouverture du diaphragme est choisie manuellement et l'exposition réglée automatiquement.
A aperture preferred

prise: contacteur électrique, chacune des deux parties du dispositif: 1. bouton isolant portant deux fiches ou prises mâles; **2.** Socle isolant muni de deux douilles ou prises femelles.
C *douille*
A 1. plug; 2. socket

prise de courant: voir **prise**

prise de son: voir **enregistrement du son**

prise de vues: 1. action de filmer un plan avec une caméra; **2.** le plan ainsi filme.
A 1. shooting; filming; 2. take

prise de vues image par image: exposition d'une pellicule avec arrêt après chaque image, par opposition à une exposition en mouvement continue (8 images par seconde ou plus).
A stop motion shooting; single frame exposure

procédé stéréoscopique: voir **photographie en relief**

processeur: dans un ordinateur, unité fonctionnelle qui interprète et exécute des instructions.

A processor

producteur: 1. au sens professionnel de l'industrie cinématographique et de la radiotélévision, le responsable administratif et financier d'une production; **2.** le responsable du contenu et de la forme d'une série de documents ou programmes audiovisuels éducatifs.

A 1. 2. producer

producteur exécutif: directeur administratif qui ne produit pas de films lui-même directement mais supervise le travail de l'équipe de production.

A executive producer

production: ensemble des opérations nécessaires à la réalisation d'un film, d'une émission, etc.

A production

production convergente/divergente: voir **convergence, divergence**

productivité: mesure de l'efficacité d'un processus de production par rapport aux moyens qui lui sont affectés.

A productivity

produits: résultats particuliers – qualitatifs ou quantitatifs – que l'on peut raisonnablement attendre d'une activité, étant donné les apports fournis et les efforts déployés.

C *apports*
A outputs

profil: représentation (graphique ou non) traduisant des résultats obtenus à diverses épreuves.

A profile

profil d'entrée: ensemble des capacités ou comportement nécessaires avant de commencer un apprentissage.

C *prétest; prérequis*
A entry profile

profil de sortie: ensemble de capacités ou comportement attendus une fois un apprentissage achevé.

C *post-test*
A outgoing profile

profondeur de champ: distance, dans une scène à photographier, entre le point de netteté le plus rapproché et le point de netteté le plus éloigné de l'appareil photographique.

A depth of field

profondeur de foyer: dans un appareil photographique, distance entre l'objectif et la pellicule qui assure l'obtention d'une image nette du sujet photographié. A ne pas confondre avec la profondeur de champ.

A depth of focus

progiciel: ensemble complet et documenté de programmes d'ordinateur conçu pour être fourni à plusieurs utilisateurs en vue d'une même application.

A package; applications software

programmateur: dispositif commandant les diverses opérations ou la synchronisation d'un appareil de reproduction du son et/ou de projection d'images.

A programmer

programmation: 1. affectation ou assignation d'un moment précis de diffusion à une émission ou à tout autre programme (annonce, message, publication, etc.); **2.** organisation dans le temps des programmes audiovisuels; **3.** élaboration et codification de la suite des opérations orientées vers la réalisation d'un programme d'ordinateur; **4.** phase du processus de planification qui consiste à sélectionner et déterminer les priorités et à organiser les cibles, les projets et les activités dans le temps en fonction des ressources; **5.** séquence d'enseignement programmé.

A 1. scheduling; 2. 3. 4. 5. programming

programmation en chaîne: en enseignement programmé, technique de programmation où la bonne réponse à un item n'est pas présentée seule, mais est incluse dans le texte de l'item suivant. Les items consécutifs sont ainsi étroitement reliés par la nécessité de répéter, dans le nouvel item, le ou les mots-clés dégagés dans l'item précédent. La réponse à un item devient donc une partie du stimulus de l'item suivant.

A conversational chaining

programmation intrinsèque: technique de programmation mise au point par Norman Crowder et caractérisée par des items relativement longs, des questions à choix multiple et l'emploi systématique de branchements. Le cheminement est déterminé par les réponses de l'élève alors que dans la programmation linéaire, elle est fixée par le programmeur. On dit aussi programmation ramifiée.

C *branchement*

A intrinsic programming; branching

programmation linéaire: technique de programmation fondée sur les principes de la théorie du renforcement de Skinnner, comportant la production active de réponses, la mise en forme de ces réponses, la répétition et le renforcement immédiat. Des séquences définies d'items présentent des petites unités d'information et sollicitent une réponse de l'élève à chaque étape. Chaque élève étudie tous les items du programme, sa progression n'étant différente de celle des autres que par le rythme auquel il avance dans la séquence.

C *programmation intrinsèque*

A linear programming

programmation ramifiée: voir **programmation intrinsèque**

programme: 1. annonce des diverses parties d'un spectacle ou d'une cérémonie; **2.** suite définie d'actions, de projets, de processus ou de services visant à atteindre un résultat déterminé; **3.** détail des matières qui constituent l'enseignement durant l'année scolaire pour une classe donnée ou sur lesquelles porte un examen ou un concours; **4.** ensemble des instruction données à un ordinateur qui vise à l'exécution d'un ensemble précis d'opérations en vue d'une application donnée; **5.** en enseignement programmé, suite ordonnée d'éléments de connaissance aussi fins que possible et rangés selon une progression méthodique, présentés sur un support approprié (fiche, livre, machine); **6.** ensemble des émission diffusées par une station ou leur organisation en série et partant une émission de radio ou de télévision.

C *curriculum; plan d'études; programme d'enseignement; programme d'études*

A 1. 2. programme; 3. syllabus; 4. program; 5. 6. programme

programme à sauts: technique d'enseignement programmé où l'on n'étudie pas toutes les séries d'items. Si un élève réussit une séquence donnée, il peut effectuer un «saut» en avant dans le programme sans passer par une séquence d'éléments redondants.

A skip branching

programme centré sur la matière: organisation des sujets d'étude et des activités selon la logique des matières étudiées et non selon les besoins de développement des élèves; s'oppose au programme centré sur l'étudiant.

A subject-centred curriculum

programme centré sur l'élève: ensemble organisé de cours, systématiquement structuré en fonction des besoins de l'élève, de son expérience et de ses intérêts, et ayant pour objet de développer ses dons et ses potentialités.

A student-centred curriculum

programme d'application: voir **logiciel d'application**

programme d'éducation: terme administratif pour désigner un plan d'action en matière d'éducation. La portée d'un programme peut être très vaste, par exemple programme de formation des enseignants au niveau national ou réduite aux activités d'une institution.

C *programme pédagogique*

A educational programme

programme d'enseignement: texte décrivant, pour tout ou partie du système scolaire, les orientations du plan d'enseignement: philosophie d'ensemble, lignes d'action, buts, objectifs, matières d'études, ressources et activités. Le champ d'application peut être large, englobant l'enseignement au niveau national, ou restreint, unité ou thème d'enseignement.

C *curriculum; programme d'études; plan d'études; contenus de l'éducation*

A curriculum guide; programme

programme d'études: détermination des disciplines à enseigner et établissement, pour chaque discipline, du nombre d'heures d'enseignement et de la liste des contenus à acquérir, c'est-à-dire des connaissances exigées. Un programme d'études prend généralement la forme de textes administratifs. Une «progression» (ou «curriculum») est l'organisation de l'apprentissage, dans une discipline ou à un niveau donnés. Le curriculum cherche en effet à déterminer les objectifs d'apprentissage, les contenus, les méthodes et les matériels éducatifs. On utilisait autrefois le terme «plan d'études» («syllabus») pour désigner un instrument qui tenait à la fois d'une liste établie par l'institution éducative des contenus de l'enseignement (c'est-à-dire le programme) et de leur organisation pratique du point de vue de l'apprentissage (le curriculum).

C *curriculum; plan d'études; programme 3.; programme d'enseignement*

A instructional programme

programme d'exercices: didacticiel conçu pour répéter des données de base en vue de faire acquérir et de fixer un apprentissage spécifique. On dit aussi «exerciseur».

C *programme tuteur*

A drill and practice program

programme de service: programme destiné non à traiter l'information, mais à faciliter l'emploi d'un ordinateur, par ex.: vidage de mémoire, duplication d'une pile de dossiers. On dit aussi «utilitaire».

A service program; utility software

programme d'origine: programme d'ordinateur écrit en langage d'origine.

A source program

programme informatique: voir **logiciel**

programme intégré: organisation systématique du contenu et des diverses parties d'un programme d'enseignement à l'intérieur d'un ensemble fonctionnel.

A integrated currculum

programme outil: voir **logiciel outil**

programme pédagogique: par opposition à programme budgétaire, document définissant la vocation et la structure d'un établissement d'enseignement à construire.

A educational specifications

programme piloté par menu: type de programme très utilisé dans l'EAO (enseignement assisté par ordinateur) qui présente à l'utilisateur des options permettant de choisir telle ou telle partie du programme.

A menu-driven program

programme tuteur: didacticiel qui questionne l'élève et évalue ses réponses et fournit de nouvelles suggestions. On dit aussi «tutoriel».

C *système tuteur intelligent*

A tutorial program

programmeur: personne qui écrit les programmes d'ordinateur et établit leur documentation.

A programmer

programme utilitaire: voir **programme de service**

progression: ordre de présentation des divers éléments d'un programme d'enseignement à l'intérieur d'un niveau ou d'un cours ou d'un ensemble de niveaux.

A sequence

projecteur: 1. appareil permettant de projeter des images à partir de diapositives, de films ou de bandes; **2.** dispositif optique qui projette les rayons d'une source lumineuse en faisceau parallèle (fam. «projo»).

C *visionneuse*

A 1. projector; 2. projector; light

projecteur à faisceau concentré: voir **projecteur ponctuel**

projecteur de diapositives: appareil permettant de projeter des diapositives ou de petits transparents montés sur cadres, généralement de 50 mm x 50 mm. Certains projecteurs sont équipés pour la reproduction des enregistrements sonores; dans certains cas, un signal enregistré sur la bande son déclenche l'avance automatique des diapositives.

A slide projector

projecteur de films fixes: appareil permettant de projeter des films fixes (généralement en 35 mm) et pouvant donc normalement projeter une série d'images fixes de petit ou de grand format. Certains projecteurs sont équipés pour la reproduction des enregistrements sonores; certains modèles sont pourvus d'un dispositif d'avance automatique piloté par l'enregistrement sonore.

A filmstrip projector

projecteur d'images télévisées: appareil électronique qui projette des images électroniques sur un écran, généralement pour un visionnement collectif, ou pour une projection en plein air. On dit aussi téléprojecteur.

A television projector; large-screen television projector

projecteur double bande: projecteur de films utilisant deux bandes séparées, l'une pour l'image, l'autre pour le son, la synchronisation étant assurée grâce aux perforations.

A double system projector

projecteur ponctuel: type d'appareil d'éclairage envoyant un faisceau lumineux étroit.

A spot light

projecteur pour film en boucle: projecteur utilisé avec des films en boucle, généralement 8 mm ou S8, et permettant de faire défiler indéfiniment une même séquence filmée.

C *boucle sans fin*

A loop projector

projecteur vidéo: voir **projecteur d'images télévisées**

projection: 1. reconstitution d'une image sur un écran; 2. mécanisme par lequel un sujet attribue à «l'autre» (une personne, une image, une situation) des qualités, des sentiments, des attitudes qui lui sont propres, mais qu'il ignore ou refuse de reconnaître. Certains matériaux neutres favorisent les comportements projectifs.

A 1. 2. projection

projection fixe: projection de films fixes, diapositives ou transparents.

A still projection

projection frontale: projection optique d'une image envoyée sur un écran à partir d'un point situé du même côté que le spectateur.

A front projection

projection par reflexion: voir **projection frontale**

projection par transparence: 1. projection d'images sur un écran translucide placé entre le projecteur et les spectateurs; 2. effet obtenu en disposant dans un studio des acteurs devant un grand écran translucide sur lequel est projeté un décor.

A 1. back projection (UK); rear projection (USA); 2. background projection

projection plein jour: système de projection qui, par un procédé ou par un autre, permet d'obtenir sur l'écran une image assez brillante pour être vue même si la lumière ambiante est très intense. On utilise généralement un dispositif de rétroprojection, mais parfois aussi des systèmes de projection frontale avec des écrans et/ou des sources de lumière spéciaux.

A daylight projection

projet: 1. entreprise planifiée, unité de gestion, visant à atteindre certains objectifs spécifiques dans le cadre d'un budget donné et au cours d'une période fixée; **2.** activité pratique et signifiante, à valeur éducative, visant un ou plusieurs objectifs de compréhension précis. Elle implique des recherches, la résolution de problèmes et, souvent, l'utilisation et la manipulation d'objets concrets. Une telle activité est planifiée et menée à bien par les élèves et l'enseignant dans un contexte naturel et «vrai».

A 1. 2. project

projet éducatif: projet d'une équipe qui s'est mise d'accord sur un style de pédagogie, des objectifs, des méthodes.

A curriculum proposal

prolongateur: câble utilisé pour prolonger le câble d'alimentation d'un appareil électrique lorsque celui-ci est situé à une certaine distance d'une source d'énergie.

A extension cord

propriété artistique: voir **droit d'auteur**

prospective de l'éducation: à la différence de la prévision, la prospective est une investigation méthodique du futur à partir d'une approche qui privilégie les changements et la nouveauté tout en évitant, au contraire de la futurologie, une rupture entre le passé et le futur. Dans le domaine de l'éducation, la prospective dégage alors les faits porteurs d'avenir souvent encore peu perceptibles, mais qui sont susceptibles d'avoir des répercussions profondes et étendues sur l'évolution et signale par là-même les décalages déjà existants entre les contenus de l'éducation et le développement des sociétés.

A future studies on education

protégé contre les intempéries: spécialement conçu, traité ou conditionné, pour un usage extérieur, par tout temps.

A weather-proofed

protocole: 1. ensemble de conventions définissant les règles qui permettent à deux appareils ou à deux systèmes de coopérer; **2.** n.pl. enregistrement de situations didactiques à des fins de formation. On dit aussi «modèles».

A 1. protocol; 2. protocol materials

prototype: premier exemplaire d'un objet destiné à être testé avant d'être produit en série.

A prototype

psychodrame: utilisation de la technique du jeu dramatique pour aider l'individu à exprimer indirectement des sentiments et des attitudes qu'il peut ne pas être à même d'exprimer directement et pour aider les membres d'un groupe à manifester, pratiquer et encourager des compétences de communication interpersonnelle.

C *jeu de rôles*

A dramatization

psycholinguistique: étude des relations entre les communications ou les messages et les caractéristiques des sujets communicants; plus spécifiquement, étude du langage dans sa relation avec les caractéristiques générales ou individuelles des utilisateurs du langage.

A psycholinguistics

psychopédagogie: approche pédagogique fondée sur la connaissance psychologique de l'enfant et de l'adulte.

A (psychopédagogie); educational psychology*

puce: composant électronique sous forme d'un microsupport à plaquette, habituellement de silicium, qui sert de support à des circuits électroniques intégrés.

A chip

puissance de sortie: puissance utile ou signal utile fourni par un circuit ou un dispositif.

A output power

pupitre: voir **console**

pupitre d'éclairage: dans un studio, pupitre commandant l'alimentation et le réglage des éclairages, en particulier les opérations d'ouverture, de fermeture, de pré-réglage et de variation d'intensité.

A lighting control board; light board; light patching board

pupitre de commande: partie d'un ordinateur qui permet à un opérateur de communiquer avec le système. Le pupitre de commande comporte des panneaux lumineux, des clefs, des interrupteurs et tous les circuits permettant une communication homme-machine.

A control console

pupitre de mélange: pupitre groupant à la portée d'un même opérateur tous les organes de commande et de contrôle nécessaires au mélange des signaux de modulation.

A mixing console

pupitre de mélange vidéo: voir **console image**

pupitreur: spécialiste chargé de la mise en route, de la conduite et de la surveillance des installations d'un système de traitement électronique de l'information (pupitre de commande et autres unités périphériques).

A console operator

push-pull: voir **symétrique**

Q

QCM: voir **question à choix multiple**

QI: voir **quotient intellectuel**

quadruplex: désignation donnée à des magnétoscopes professionnels 2 pouces encore utilisés, en raison du nombre de têtes d'enregistrement et de lecture (quatre) et de leur disposition sur le disque porte-têtes rotatif, transversale par rapport au sens de défilement de la bande.

A quadruplex

question à choix multiple – QCM: type de question fermée fréquemment utilisée dans les tests objectifs et les programmes à branchements, posée de telle façon que le sujet doit opérer un choix parmi plusieurs réponses qui lui sont proposées. Généralement, un QCM offre quatre ou cinq réponses possibles et inclut des distracteurs, c'est-à-dire des réponses fausses mais apparemment correctes.

C *distracteur*

A multiple-choice question

question à réponses précodées: voir **question fermée**

question fermée: question posée de telle façon que le sujet ne peut fournir qu'une seule réponse ou doit choisir entre plusieurs réponses dans une série limitée et définie.

A closed question

question ouverte: question à laquelle le sujet répond en construisant sa réponse. C'est donc un outil de recherche semi-directif qui permet d'observer les associations mises en œuvre dans un domaine particulier. Exemple: test de complètement de phrases.

A open-ended question

quotient intellectuel – QI: quotient obtenu en divisant l'âge mental par l'âge chronologique et en multipliant par 100.

A intelligence quotient

R

raccord (image): plan – généralement court – destiné à faciliter le passage d'un plan à un autre.

A continuity shot

raccord sonore défectueux: défaut dans la continuité de la bande son généralement dû à un défaut de collure.

A bloop

radio: 1. abrégé de radiodiffusion sonore; 2. «radio» plus substantif: qui fonctionne au moyen de la radio, par exemple radio-club, radio-téléphone.

A 1. 2. radio; (wireless, USA)

radiocinématographie: radiographie filmée faisant appel à plusieurs techniques, spécialement celle des intensificateurs d'images.

A cineradiography

radiodiffuser: émettre et transmettre par radiodiffusion.

C *émettre*

A to broadcast

radiodiffusion: émission et transmission radioélectriques par ondes hertziennes d'un programme ou d'un signal susceptibles d'être captés par tous les récepteurs radio ou télévision situés à l'intérieur de la zone couverte par une station d'émission.

C *diffusion restreinte; (narrowcasting)*

A broadcasting

radio éducative: utilisation de la radio à des fins éducatives, formelles ou non formelles.

C *radio scolaire, télévision scolaire, télévision éducative, enseignement à distance*

A educational radio

radiofréquence: voir **fréquence radioélectrique**

radio scolaire: ensemble des programmes de radio destinés aux élèves des écoles.

A school radio; school broadcasting

radiotélévision scolaire – RTS: ensemble des services chargés d'assurer la préparation, l'animation, la réalisation et l'exploitation pédagogique des émissions de radio et de télévision à usage d'enseignement.

A school broadcasting service

radiovision: moyen d'enseignement présentant des images statiques, généralement diapositives ou films fixes, accompagnées de son. La partie sonore est transmise par radio tandis que les images sont projetées – ou présentées – sur le lieu de la réception.

A radiovision

RAF: voir **régulateur automatique de fréquence**

ralenti: effet obtenu en faisant fonctionner une caméra à une vitesse de prise d'images-seconde supérieure à la normale. A la projection, le mouvement apparaît ralenti sur l'écran.

C *accéléré*

A slow motion

rallonge: voir **prolongateur**

RAM: random access memory: voir **mémoire vive**

ramification: voir **branchement**

rapport: 1. quotient de deux grandeurs de même nature; 2. compte rendu d'une activité.

A 1. ratio; 2. report

rapport d'aspect: voir **rapport des dimensions**

rapport des dimensions: rapport de la largeur à la hauteur d'une image rectangulaire.

A aspect ratio

rapport signal-bruit: rapport de la puissance du signal utile en un point spécifié de la voie de transmission, à la puissance du bruit (signal brouilleur) mesuré au même point dans des conditions de fonctionnement spécifiées. Ce rapport est souvent exprimé en décibels.

A signal-to-noise ratio

rationalisation des choix budgétaires: système de planification stratégique et procédé de contrôle opérationnels visant à atteindre la meilleure productivité tout en facilitant le choix des répartitions des ressources. On dit aussi système plan programme budget; système PPB.

A planning-programming-budgeting system

rayure: marque, en forme de raie, causée par frottement, sur une pellicule ou un disque.

A scratch

rayures d'enroulement: rayures de la pellicule causées par une traction sur l'extrémité libre d'un rouleau.

A cinch marks

réalisateur: perrsonne responsable de la réalisation d'un film, d'une émission ou d'un enregistrement et dirigeant toutes les phases de sa production.

A director

réalisation: ensemble des opérations nécessaires pour passer d'un projet, d'un scénario à un film, une émission ou un enregistrement.

A production

rebobineuse: voir **réenrouleuse**

récepteur: 1. celui qui reçoit un message émis (lecteur, auditeur, spectateur); **2.** voir récepteur radio ou télévision.

C *émetteur*

A 1. recipient; 2. set

récepteur radio ou télévision: poste de radio ou de télévision permettant la réception d'émissions radiodiffusées.

C *moniteur 4*

A set

réception: fait de recevoir une émission radiodiffusée.

A reception

réception collective: visionnement ou écoute d'un programme qui s'effectue dans un centre social ou culturel.

A community viewing/listening

recherche action: 1. type de recherche effectuée sur le terrain pour mettre en œuvre de nouveaux savoir-faire ou de nouvelles méthodes et résoudre les problèmes avec application directe en situation éducative; **2.** type de recherche caractérisée par l'engagement subjectif du chercheur et l'apparition d'interactions multiples entre le programme de recherche (ou le chercheur) et l'objet de la recherche. On dit aussi recherche participative.

C *observation; recherche sur le terrain*

A 1. action research; 2. action research; participatory research

recherche de l'information: ensemble de méthodes et de procédures ayant pour effet d'extraire, de données rangées dans la mémoire d'un ordinateur, les informations concernant un sujet déterminé.

A information retrieval

recherche documentaire: opération par laquelle des éléments précis sont extraits d'un fonds documentaire, non seulement d'un fonds de bibliothèque, mais aussi d'un index ou d'une bibliographie.

A retrieval

recherche opérationnelle: technique de la préparation des décisions qui procède de la mathématisation des facteurs essentiels entrant en jeu dans les problèmes d'organisation militaire, économique, éducative.

C *analyse de système; approche systémique*

A operations research

recherche participative: voir **recherche action 2.**

recherche sur le terrain: 1. recherche ayant pour but l'étude intensive de l'arrière-plan général, du statut et des interactions avec l'environnement d'un individu, d'un groupe, d'une institution, d'un organisme ou d'une communauté; **2.** recherche conduite en situation réelle ou sur un chantier éloigné.

A 1. 2. field research

recompense: encouragement extérieur au travail scolaire comme par exemple des friandises pour de jeunes enfants, des notes validant le travail écrit, etc.

A incentive

reconnaissance des formes: dans un système d'ordinateur, balayage automatique effectué en vue de la reconnaissance de caractères et/ou d'images.

A pattern recognition

redécouverte: voir **méthode de la redécouverte**

redevances de droits d'auteur: rémunération versée à l'auteur et représentant sa participation aux profits tirés de l'utilisation de son œuvre.

A royalties

redondance: caractère de ce qui apporte une information déjà donnée sous une autre forme. En théorie de l'information, le taux de redondance est le rapport entre les unités d'un message non nécessaires qui répètent des unités informatives déjà présentes dans le message et l'ensemble des unités qui constituent le message. La redondance est utilisée dans la transmission de la communication pour assurer le contrôle de l'information au point de réception.

A redundancy

réémetteur: ensemble d'équipements permettant de recevoir des signaux de télécommunication à sens unique ou à double sens et de produire des signaux correspondants qui sont soit amplifiés soit remodelés soit les deux.

A repeater (station)

réenrigstrement: enregistrement, par une méthode quelconque, sur un support d'enregistrement, de tout ou partie d'un programme déjà enregistré.

A rerecording

réenrouler: voir **réembobiner**

réenrouleuse: appareil utilisé dans les salles de montage: il se compose de deux bobines ou plateaux symétriques et d'un dispositif d'enroulement et permet le bobinage et le réembobinage des filsm.

A rewinder

feférent: ce à quoi un signe linguistique renvoie ou ce qu'il représente ou dénote; utilisé spécialment à propos d'un objet matériel ou imaginé, d'un événement, d'une qualité, etc.

A referent

réflecteur: 1. tout dispositif destiné à réorienter par réflexion la lumière et/ou l'énergie dans une direction donnée; **2.** en projection, miroir sphérique monté derrière la lampe de projection et servant à diriger vers l'avant les rayons lumineux provenant de l'arrière de la lampe en les faisant repasser par les filaments, ce qui augmente ainsi l'intensité de l'éclairement.

A 1. 2. reflector

réflex: voir **appareil à visée réflexe**

réflexe: type de réponse élémentaire et involontaire liée à une structure organique déterminée.

C *réponse*
A reflex

régénérateur de synchronisation: appareil reconstituant la forme et l'amplitude correctes des signaux de synchronisation d'un signal d'image complet plus ou moins déformé, par exemple par une transmission à grande distance.

A synchronizing pulse generator

régie: 1. administration chargée de l'organisation matérielle d'un spectacle; **2.** local ou espace spécial où sont traités les signaux provenant d'une unité de production. Une petite régie s'appelle aussi une cabine de commande.

A 1. production management; 2. control room

régie centrale: local où arrivent et sont regroupés pour traitement tous les signaux audio et/ou vidéo.

A master control room

régisseur de plateau: assitant du réalisateur responsable des activités d'un plateau de film ou de télévision.

A floor manager

registre: mémoire située dans l'unité de traitement d'un ordinateur dotée d'une capacité de mémoire très petite, souvent limitée à un ou deux mots.

A register

registre cumulatif: répertoire (dossier, classeur, rapport, etc.) conçu pour recevoir des documents additionnels de même nature que ceux déjà réunis. Il fournit un registre de classement étalé dans le temps.

A cumulative record

registre de langue: voir **niveau de langue**

réglage: 1. positionnement précis d'un indicateur mobile; **2.** voir **accord 1.**

A 1. adjustement; control; setting; 2. tuning

régler: positionner précisément les commandes d'un appareil pour obtenir un certain effet.

A to set

régulateur automatique de fréquence, (d'accord) = RAF: dispositif incorporé à un récepteur radioélectrique pour compenser automatiquement les variations de la fréquence porteuse du signal incident ou de la fréquence de l'oscillateur local.

A automatic frequency control

régulateur de tension: dispositif à commande manuelle ou automatique assurant une tension électrique constante pour l'alimentation d'appareils.

A voltage regulator

régulation (de système): dans un système éducatif, processus continu visant à améliorer le fonctionnement et les résultats par l'ajustement des actions aux finalités et par l'harmonisation de chaque sous-système avec le système lui-même et avec chacune des autres parties.

C *approche systémique en éducation*

A systems regulation

réimpression: composition et impression utilisant les mêmes caractères et la même disposition qu'un tirage précédent qui sert alors de «copie»; à distinguer de la première «copie» faite avec le manuscrit.

A reprint

relais: commutateur télécommandé électroniquement.

A relay

relation maître-élèves: rapports affectifs qui s'établissent entre enseignants et enseignés dans une situation éducative.

A teacher-student relationship

relayer: recevoir un signal et le retransmettre.

A to relay

relief sonore: effet obtenu par l'adaptation acoustique en fonction de la distance apparente d'une source sonore.

C *stéréophonie*

A perspective

remake: nouvelle version d'un film ou d'un programme ancien.

A remake

rembobinage: dispositif souvent incorporé à un appareil d'enregistrement ou de projection et permettant le retour rapide d'une bande ou d'un film de la bobine réceptrice à la bobine débitrice.

A rewinding

rembobiner: opération consistant à redisposer un film ou une bande sur la bobine d'origine après une projection, un enregistrement ou une lecture.

A to rewind

remue-méninges: voir **brainstorming**

rendement: voir **efficience**

234

rendement scolaire : ensemble des performances scolaires d'une population donnée dans une discipline ou dans un sous-système éducatif. A ne pas confondre avec résultats scolaires.

C *niveau d'instruction*

A school achievement

renforçateur : dans un conditionnement, stimulus introduit après une réaction afin d'en modifier la force, la rapidité ou la fréquence.

C *renforcement*

A reinforcer

renforcement : processus psychologique spontané ou provoqué, dans lequel un stimulus, présenté immédiatement après une réponse, augmente le taux d'occurrence de cette réponse en situation normale ou augmente la probabilité de reproduction de cette réponse lorsque la situation se reproduit.

C *renforçateur; conditionnement*

A reinforcement

renforcement négatif : processus tendant à diminuer la fréquence d'un comportement erroné en le faisant suivre d'une sanction.

A negative reinforcement

renforcement positif : processus tendant à augmenter la fréquence d'un comportement correct en le faisant suivre d'une récompense.

C *conditionnement opérant*

A positive reinforcement

répartiteur : panneau regroupant des terminaisons de fils ou de câbles et assurant les interconnexions appropriées.

A distribution frame

repérer : préparer un document audiovisuel pour être lu ou visionné de sorte que, à l'utilisation, il soit synchronisé avec les autres éléments de présentation ou de diffusion.

A to cue

répertorier : garder une trace des divers constituants d'un processus.

A to track

répéteur : voir **transpondeur**

repiquage : transfert d'un enregistrement sonore ou vidéo d'un support à un autre, généralement de disque à bande, de bande à bande ou de bande à film. Se dit aussi de l'enregistrement d'une émission de radio ou du son d'une émission de télévision.

A re-recording

réponse : 1. terme générique correspondant à toute réaction automatique, spontanée ou intentionnelle ; 2. signal que l'on obtient à une sortie d'un réseau en fonction du signal appliqué à l'entrée de ce même réseau.

C *réflexe*

A 1. 2. response

réponse implicite : voir **réponse invisible**

réponse indépendante du contexte : réponse qui n'est pas influencée par les mots ou les éléments du contexte immédiatement antérieur ou postérieur. S'oppose à réponse dépendante du contexte.

A context-free answer

réponse invisible : comportement ou réponse non détectable par un observateur. Un tel comportement ne peut être déduit qu'à partir de l'observation de comportements ultérieurs ou de l'introspection du sujet.

C *réponse manifeste; latent/manifeste*

A covert response

réponse libre : reponse librement élaborée et non choisie parmi un ensemble de réponses proposées, comme dans les questionnaires à choix multiple. On dit aussi réponse ouverte.

A constructed response

réponse manifeste : réponse à une question dans un test ou un programme exprimée de façon matérielle et observable, par exemple par l'écriture, le dessin, l'emploi d'un outil, etc.

C *réponse invisible; latent/manifeste*

A overt response

réponse ouverte: voir **réponse libre**

reportage: programme de radio ou de télévision réalisé en dehors d'un studio.

A outside broadcast

reportage en direct: reportage réalisé sur le lieu de l'événement et au moment où il se produit.

A live coverage

report optique: opération consistant à reporter sur une pellicule cinématographique le son d'un film, à partir d'un original, sur bande magnétique perforée de 35 mm ou 16 mm.

A optical transfer

reproduction sonore: voir **lecture**

reprographie: ensemble de techniques qui permettent de reproduire un document au moyen d'un rayonnement calorique, électrique, gazeux, lumineux.

A reprography

réseau: 1. système constitué d'un ensemble de points, centres, institutions ou organismes reliés entre eux et pouvant distribuer ou échanger des ressources, de l'énergie ou de l'information; **2.** groupe de stations émettrices (radio ou télévison) reliées entre elles par un système de relais ou de câbles coaxiaux leur donnant ainsi la possibilité de diffuser toutes le même programme simultanément à partir d'un point donné du système.

C *réseau d'information; réseau local*

A 1. 2. network

réseau d'information: 1. ensemble généralement constitué de plusieurs banques de données ou centres d'information reliés les uns aux autres par un système d'échanges constants et fonctionnant souvent dans le cadre d'un système ou d'un service commun; **2.** distribution d'informations pédagogiques et éducatives utilisant une liaison par câble et/ou liaison hertzienne entre deux ou plusieurs centres ou organismes. La transmission peut se faire par radio, télévision ou moyens informatisés. Ce type de système comprend aussi la mise à disposition de programmes par accès automatisé et téléconsultation.

C *système d'information en réseau*

A 1. 2. information network

réseau local: connexion de deux ou plusieurs ordinateurs entre eux de façon à permettre à la fois un traitement local des données et la transmission des informations à un autre ordinateur et/ou à un ordinateur central.

C *nanoréseau*

A local area network; custom network

réseau numérique à intégration de services — RNIS: réseau de communication entièrement numérisé, utilisant des infrastructures communes pour la transmission de messages de divers types (téléphone, télécopie, vidéo, données informatiques, etc.).

A integrated services digital network–ISDN

réseau thématique: diagramme représentant les relations entre les thèmes d'une partie de programmes d'enseignement ou de matière à enseigner.

A topic network

résolution: pour une image, degré de restitution des détails fins.

C *définition*

A sharpness; resolution

responsabilité éducative: voir **educational accountability**

ressources éducatives: ensemble des informations, appareils, objets et documents qu'il est possible à un individu ou à un groupe de mettre en œuvre pour faciliter l'apprentissage et/ou l'appropriation d'informations. Les ressources éducatives peuvent inclure les personnes (enseignants ou autres) à même d'aider l'individu ou le groupe.

A learning resources

résultats scolaires: résultats du travail scolaire d'un élève.

A school achievement

résumé analytique: résumé présentant l'essentiel du contenu d'une publication.

A abstract

retour d'écoute: circuit par lequel on assure le retour des signaux de modulation au studio de production en vue de régler son intervention dans le déroulement du programme.

A feedback circuit

retour d'écoute différé: retour d'écoute de l'enregistrement élève dans un laboratoire de langues audio-actif-comparatif n'intervenant qu'à la fin d'une batterie d'exercices; s'oppose au retour direct dans un laboratoire audio-actif-comparatif-correctif où l'élève peut immédiatement comparer sa production à la bonne réponse (réponse maître).

A delayed feedback

retransmission: diffusion nouvelle ou diffusion sur un autre réseau.

A retransmission; rebroadcasting

rétroaction: 1. utilisation d'une partie des éléments de sortie d'un système pour modifier automatiquement les éléments d'entrée ou le fonctionnement du système; **2.** action en retour des corrections et des régulatioins d'un système de traitement de l'information sur le centre de commandes; **3.** dans les méthodes d'autocorrection, information fournie sur la validité d'une réponse ou d'un résultat en vue de leur amlioration (feedback).

C *feedback; autocorrection; régulation de système*

A 1. 2. 3. feedback

rétroprojecteur: appareil placé devant les spectateurs et permettant, à l'aide d'un système optique, de projeter sur un écran des documents transparents placés sur une plage de projection horizontale.

A overhead projector

révélateur: solution où des composants chimiques rendent l'image visible en agissant sur les sels d'argent d'une pellicule qui a été exposée à la lumière et modifiée par elle durant la prise de vues.

A developer

RF: radio-fréquence; voir **fréquence radioélectrique**

RNIS: voir **réseau numérique à intégration de services**

ROM: read only memory; voir **mémoire morte**

roman photo: voir **photoroman**

ronflement: signal parasite basse fréquence provenant généralement du câble d'alimentation.

A hum

routage: organisation de l'acheminement des documents imprimés et audiovisuels par le réseau postal ou tout autre système.

A dispatching

routine: 1. habitude d'agir ou de penser toujours de la même manière; **2.** programme ou partie de programme d'ordinateur qui peut avoir un emploi général ou répété.

A 1. 2. routine

ruban perforé: bande de papier spéciale où se trouve découpée une configuration de trous.

A punched paper tape

RULEG: technique de construction de séquences d'enseignement programmé consistant à présenter d'abord une règle, une loi, une définition ou tout autre principe à valeur générale, symbolisé par RU, puis des exemples (descriptions de phénomènes physiques, théorèmes, énoncés de relation entre des éléments spécifiques, etc.) symbolisés par EG. A l'inverse, la technique EGRUL procède par la présentation systématique d'exemples, EG, avant d'amener l'élève à l'identification du principe ou de la règle, RU, qui les soustend.

C *méthode déductive*

A RULEG

rushes: tirage journalier de toutes les scènes d'un film tournées au fur et à mesure d'une production afin de choisir les meilleures séquences pour la vision finale.

C *copie contact*

A rushes

rythme de progression: 1. vitesse à laquelle un individu ou un groupe est appelé à effectuer un apprentissage; **2.** vitesse à laquelle l'élève avance dans une séquence donnée d'items; la procédure habituelle est celle du rythme

individuel où l'élève effectue sa lecture et donne sa réponse à son propre rythme.
A 1. 2. pace

rythme individuel : procédure où l'apprenant contrôle lui-même le rythme de présentation des matériaux d'apprentissage.
C *enseignement/apprentissage à rythme individuel ; auto-évaluation*
A self-pacing

rythmes scolaires : aménagement des activités scolaires en fonction du temps biologique de l'élève, ou des biorythmes (c'est-à-dire en fonction des rythmes endocriniens, des rythmes de croissance, du rythme veille-sommeil, du rythme alimentaire, etc.).
A school work rhythms* ; time-of-day effects on pupil's performance*

S

saisie de données : enregistrement d'informations en vue de leur traitement informatique.
A data capture

salle (de cinéma) : local ou bâtiment servant à la projection de films.
A cinema

salle banalisée : local conçu et/ou adapté pour servir à divers types d'enseignement.
C *salle polyvalente ; salle spécialisée*
A general purpose space

salle de montage : local aménagé pour monter des films.
C *montage ; édition*
A cutting room

salle d'enseignement spécialisée : voir **salle spécialisée**

salle polyvalente : local conçu ou adapté spécifiquement, pour deux ou plusieurs utilisations pédagogiques combinées nécessitant, d'ordinaire, des locaux séparés.
C *salle banalisée ; salle spécialisée*
A multi-purpose room

salle spécialisée : local aménagé en vue de l'enseignement d'une discipline particulière : salle d'éducation physique, de travaux pratiques.
A special instruction space

satellite de radiodiffusion directe : satellite utilisé pour diffuser directement au public par l'intermédiaire d'un équipement de réception approprié, sans passer par une station réceptrice et un émetteur terrestre intermédiaires.
A direct broadcast satellite

satellite de distribution : satellite utilisé pour transmettre des signaux de radio et de télévision à un réseau d'organismes de diffusion ou à des émetteurs ; s'oppose à satellite de radiodiffusion directe.
A distribution satellite

satellite de communication : satellite servant à la transmission d'informations à partir de supports de toute nature : téléphone, télégraphe, telex, télécopie, radio, télévision, et dispositif de transfert de données entre ordinateurs. Le satellite peut avoir une orbite elliptique (orbite basse) ou synchrone (géostationnaire au-dessus de l'équateur).
A communications satellite

satellite national : satellite servant à émettre ou à relayer des signaux à l'intérieur du pays qui en contrôle la marche.
A domestic satellite

saturation de la couleur : quantité de couleur présente dans un sens donné à partir du blanc.
A colour saturation

238

saut: 1. passage conditionnel ou non d'un point d'un programme d'ordinateur à un autre. On dit aussi branchement; 2. rupture du déroulement d'une scène de film; 3. passage d'une question, d'un item dans un test.

A 1. jump; branch; 2. jump; 3. skip

sauter: transférer la suite de l'exécution d'un programme d'ordinateur à une instruction autre ue celle qui suit immédiatement; aller d'un point du programme à un autre sans passer par les étapes intermédiaires.

A to jump

sautillement: voir **scintillement**

sautillement d'image: voir **gigue**

savoir-faire: 1. capacité de pratiquer une activité, soit spontanément, soit par apprentissage; 2. performance observable, par opposition à un comportement non observable; comportements et conduites visibles qu'un sujet met en œuvre; 3. niveau exceptionnel de performance.

C *capacité*

A 1. 2. 3. skill; ability

scanneur: appareil ou dispositif capable de réaliser automatiquement le balayage continu de l'ensemble des canaux d'un récepteur.

C *analyseur*

A scanner

scénario: 1. document développé décrivant de façon détaillée le contenu et la traduction visuelle et sonore d'un film ou d'une émission; 2. hypothèse sur l'évolution d'une situation, utilisée en prospective.

C *découpage; descriptif; conducteur image*

A 1. script; treatment; 2. scenario

scénariste: professionnel composant des textes oui des dialogues pour des production audiovisuelles.

A script writer

scène: 1. plan unique ou ensemble de plans constituant une unité filmique complète dont l'action se déroule sans coupure dans un lieu ou un cadre donnés; 2. dans les arts du spectacle, emplacement où les artistes paraissent devant le public.

A 1. scene; 2. stage

schéma: représentation simplifiée d'un processus ou d'un dispositif à l'aide de symboles conventionnels ou de représentations graphiques.

C *graphique; tracé; organigramme; plan 3*

A diagramme

schéma de principe: voir **schéma fonctionnel**

schéma fonctionnel: représentation d'un système, appareil ou ordinateur dans laquelle les parties principales apparaissent sous forme de figures géométriques accompagnées d'indications appropriées montrant tout à la fois les fonctions essentielles et les relations entre les diverses parties.

C *organigramme*

A block diagram

scintillement: fluctuations de vitesse affectant l'enregistrement et la reproduction sonore et se traduisant par une variation de la hauteur du son. Le scintillement est une variation de vitesse plus rapide que le pleurage. On dit aussi sautillement.

A flutter

score: nombre exprimant le nombre d'épreuves ou d'éléments d'épreuve réussis à un test psychologique ou à un test de connaissances.

A score

score brut: résultat d'un test, d'une épreuve, avant correction et interprétation: par exemple nombre de bonnes réponses, nombre de bonnes réponses moins une fraction de mauvaises, temps requis pour accomplir la tâche, nombre d'erreurs ou toute autre mesure directe, non convertie et non interprétée. S'oppose à note étalonnée.

A raw score

scrambleur: voir **embrouilleur**

scripte: personne chargée de consigner les informations relatives aux prises de vues et de veiller à la continuité du tournage.

A script girl (USA); continuity girl (UK)

SECAM: système de télévision couleur utilisé par la France et la plupart des pays de l'Europe de l'Est; (SECAM: SEquentiel Couleur A Mémoire).

A SECAM

secteur (alimentation): alimentation électrique par un réseau de distribution.

A mains

section: structure pédagogique caractérisée à l'intérieur d'un même cycle d'enseignement, soit par des méthodes particulières, soit par la dominante des enseignements dispensés.

C *filière*

A track; stream

sémantique: étude de la signification des mots et des autres signes; ensemble des règles décrivant les relations entre les signes et les objets.

A semantics

sémantique générale: étude des effets de la signification des mots, des signes et des symboles, sur le comportement des individus et des groupes.

A general semantics

semi-conducteur: se dit d'un appareil dont les composants actifs (pour l'oscillation ou la détection) sont «à l'état solide» - c'est-à-dire, par opposition aux tubes électroniques à vide (lampes) - des transistors, diodes, circuits intégrés, etc., fabriqués à partir de solides tels le germanium ou le silicium.

A solid state

séminaire: 1. série limitée de cours ou de conférences faisant un large appel au dialogue avec les participants et consacré à l'étude exclusive d'un sujet dans le but de faire progresser les connaissances dans ce domaine particulier; **2.** système de formation intense dans un domaine limité. Les participants, qui ont déjà une formation, voire un métier, suivent un séminaire pour assimiler une technique ou une théorie récentes; **3.** mini-colloque, au cours duquel un nombre restreint de participants exposent en un temps relativement bref, d'une à deux semaines, les résultats de leurs travaux.

A 1. 2. 3. seminar

sémiologie: voir **sémiotique**

sémiotique: science des signes. Ses subdivisions principales sont la sémantique, la syntaxe et la pragmatique. Chacune d'elles, et la sémiotique elle-même, peut être pure, descriptive oui appliquée. La sémiotique pure élabore un langage pour parler des signes, la sémiotique descriptive étudie les signes eux-mêmes et la sémiotique appliquée utilise la connaissance des signes à diverses fins. Le terme sémiotique recouvre aujourd'hui toutes les acceptions de sémiologie.

A semiotics

sensibilité: 1. degré de réponse d'un instrument ou d'un organe de commande aux variations du signal d'entrée; **2.** capacité d'une épreuve ou d'un instrument de mesure à exprimer de faibles variations de l'objet de la mesure; **3.** photosensibilité de l'émulsion d'une pellicule. Elle est généralement exprimée sous forme d'une valeur numérique correspondant aux recommandations du fabricant concernant l'utilisation de la pellicule dans des conditions déterminées d'exposition et de développement.

A 1. sensitivity; 2. differential sensitivity; 3. emulsion speed

sépia: matière colorante brune utilisée dans les anciennes photographies.

A sepia

SEPMAG: voir **son magnétique séparé**

SEPOPT: voir **son optique séparé**

séquence: 1. unité d'action dans un film composée d'une série de scènes reliées les unes aux autres; **2.** en enseignement programmé, unité de programme composée de plusieurs cadres ou éléments.

A 1. 2. sequence

sérigraphie: procédé d'impression à l'aide d'un écran ou d'une trame de soie (ou d'un matériel similaire).

A silk-screen printing

serveur: 1. ordinateur qui dessert un certain nombre de machines, dispositifs ou utilisateurs dans un travail de transmission de données. On dit aussi «ordinateur hôte»; **2.** (abréviation de centre serveur) organisme gérant des banques de données et offrant un ou plusieurs services vidéotex.

A 1. host computer; server; 2. host; information spinner; on-line data service

seuil: 1. en psychologie de la perception, valeur minimum d'une stimulation capable de produire un effet perceptible. Seuil absolu: minimum de stimulation. Seuil différentiel: différence minimale entre deux stimulations, permettant de percevoir une variation; **2.** en approche systémique, valeur d'un composant à partir de laquelle une variation est possible au niveau des interactions ou des effets d'une action pédagogique.

A 1. 2. threshold

SGBD: voir **système de gestion de base de données**

sifflement: bruit de fond localisé dans les fréquences moyennes ou élevées et pouvant provenir d'un amplificateur, d'un disque, d'un câble ou d'une bande.

A hiss

signal: 1. signe transmis par une personne à une autre pour indiquer qu'une action convenue à un moment donné et dans un endroit fixé va s'accomplir; **2.** forme physique sous laquelle se transmet une information; **3.** stimulus provoquant l'apparition du réflexe conditionné.

A 1. 2. 3. signal

signal d'avertissement: signal optique conventionnel envoyé à un studio de diffusion ou à toute autre source de programme en vue de l'avertir de sa prochaine intervention dans le déroulement du programme.

C *indice; clignotement*

A cue

signal de commande: signal sonore enregistré sur la piste pilote d'une bande audio et invitant un opérateur à intervenir (par exemple: changer une diapositive).

A cue tone

signal vidéo composite: signal produit par une caméra de télévision ou une bande vidéo avant adjonction ou en l'absence de l'onde porteuse nécessaire à la diffusion par une station ou à la réception par un poste de télévision. Un moniteur de télévision sans syntoniseur peut utiliser un signal vidéo composite.

A composite video waveform

signe: 1. phénomène directement observable qui permet de conclure à l'existence d'un autre phénomène auquel il est associé; **2.** en sémiotique, association d'un concept et d'une image acoustique ou d'un signifié (ce qui est signifié) et d'un signifiant (ce qui signifie).

A 1. 2. sign

signe iconique: signe dans lequel le signifiant présente un certain degré de ressemblance perceptive (visuelle, auditive, etc.) avec son signifié. Si les mots «chat» et «miaou» sont deux signes pour l'animal chat, «miaou» a un plus grand degré d'iconicité que «chat».

C *analogie*

A iconic sign

signifiant: en sémiotique, aspect sonore, graphique ou visuel d'un signe.

C *signe 2.*

A significator

signifié: en sémiotique, ce qui est signifié par un signe, le concept.

A designatum; significant

simulateur: dispositif ou programme conçu pour reproduire les traits pertinents d'un environnement opérationnel et leurs variations en fonction des changements de conditions.

A simulator

simulation: 1. représentation de certains aspects du comportement d'un ensemble physique ou abstrait par le comportement d'un autre ensemble. Par exemple, représentation d'un phénomène physique au moyen d'opérations effectuées par un ordinateur, ou d'un système vivant par un modèle mathématique; **2.** méthode utilisée comme substitut dans des activités d'apprentissage pour rapprocher le plus possible les exercices et les moyens auxquels on a recours de la situation réelle où ce que l'on apprend doit trouver son application.

C *modèle*

A 1. 2. simulation

simulation sur ordinateur: technique permettant d'étudier le comportement futur d'un système à partir d'un modèle mathématique approprié programmé de manière à montrer l'évolution des différentes variables du phénomène que l'on cherche à analyser.

A computer simulation

SITE - satellite instructional television experiment: expérience effectuée en 1975-1976 en Inde avec utilisation du satellite ATS6 pour des essais de diffusion directe avec utilisation de récepteurs ordinaires dans les villages.

A SITE

(software): 1. anglicisme pour logiciel; **2.** terme générique utilisé abusivement pour désigner des documents (par exemple films, fixes fixes, enregistrements sonores) par opposition à l'équipement («hardware») nécessaire pour les présenter.

A 1. software; 2. materials

son creux: son grave de fort volume et de courte durée.

A boom

242

son magnétique séparé - SEPMAG: enregistrement du son d'un film sur une bande magnétique munie de perforations, et non pas latéralement sur la pellicule image.

C *piste de son magnétique*

A separate magnetic sound

son optique séparé - SEPOPT: enregistrement du son sur un support différent de celui du film lui-même.

C *piste optique*

A separate optical sound

sondage d'écoute: mesure, sur un échantillon, du nombre de personnes ou de familles qui regardent ou écoutent un programme donné de radio ou de télévision à un moment donné. Les principales techniques de mesure sont la tenue de journaux d'écoute ou de visionnement, les interviews à domicile ou par téléphone, et l'audiomètre.

A audience measurement

sono: voir **sonorisation**

sonorisation: 1. ensemble des opérations par lesquelles on ajoute les éléments sonores appropriés à une bande image; **2.** ensemble des appareils et installations utilisés pour diffuser des informations parlées ou de la musique dans un lieu public (sono).

C *synchronisation; musique de film*

A 1. dubbing; sound recording; scoring; 2. public address system

sortie: 1. première exploitation publique d'une production cinématographique; **2.** information ou ensemble d'informations résultant d'un traitement dans un ordinateur; **3.** dispositif, prise permettant la sortie d'un signal sur un appareil (sortie vidéo).

C *données de sortie*

A 1. release; 2. 3. output

souris: informatique, dispositif qui par son mouvement sur une surface permet de déplacer un curseur sur l'écran d'une visu.

A mouse

sous-exposition: exposition insuffisante (à la lumière) d'une pellicule ou d'un papier sensible due à un défaut de réglage de l'appareil de prise de vues ou de la tireuse.

A under-exposure

sous-programme: dans un système informatique, ensemble d'instructions décrivant une opération qui constitue un tout et qui est stocké de façon à pouvoir être appelé chaque fois que cette opération doit être exécutée.

A subroutine

sous-titres: mots, groupes de mots ou phrases apparaissant sur un document visuel pour expliquer, souligner ou clarifier un point, ou pour traduire dans une autre langue le dialogue enregistré.

A subtitles

spécialisé: voir **dédié**

spécimen: échantillon ou objet délibérément sélectionné pour examen, présentation ou étude et généralement choisi comme représentatif de sa catégorie.

A specimen

S-R: stimulus réponse

A S-R: stimulus response

stabilité: état caractérisé par une absence de vibration ou de mouvement.

A steadiness

stage: 1. période de formation ou de perfectionnement dans un service ou une entreprise, de durée généralement déterminée à l'avance, qui permet de compléter une formation théorique; **2.** réunion de formation, de perfectionnement ou d'information organisée à l'intention des maîtres ou des futurs maîtres de tous niveaux ou de toutes catégories.

A 1. practice period; 2. training course

standard: 1. niveau de performance qui a fait l'objet d'un étalonnage; **2.** caractérise un produit, un dispositif, une installation conforme aux normes et aux procédés courants.

A 1. 2. standard

statif de reproduction: support vertical ou horizontal équipé d'une monture ajustable permettant d'y fixer un appareil de prise de vues pour photographier de près des sujets plats.

A copystand

station: 1. centre de production et d'émissions de programmes de radiodiffusion; **2.** installation servant à émettre, capter, transmettre des signaux radiodiffusés; **3.** système connecté ou non à un ordinateur, conçu pour un domaine donné d'application comme une station graphique.

C *chaîne; canal*

A 1. 2. 3. station

station asservie: en télécommunication, station pouvant être commandée de manière automatique, généralement à distance.

A slave station

station au sol: station terrestre émettrice ou réceptrice servant de relais pour la réception ou la transmission de signaux en provenance de ou vers un satellite.

A ground station

station d'interrogation collective: voir **analyseur de réponses**

station satellite: relais de télévision séparé retransmettant les émissions diffusées en circuit ouvert par une station voisine pour en augmenter la couverture locale. A

A satellite station

stéréogramme: couple d'images opaques ou transparentes (généralement photographiques) produisant une sensation de relief comme dans la vision binoculaire normale, lorsque le visionnement s'effectue avec un équipement stéréoscopique.

A stereograph

stéréophonie: procédé de reproduction du son utilisant deux ou plusieurs sources ou pistes séparées et produisant une impressin de relief acoustique.

A stereophonic; stereo

stéréoscope: instrument optique muni de deux lentilles permettant à chaque œil de voir une image distincte, l'image combinée produisant une sensation de relief et de distance comme dans la vision binoculaire normale.

A stereoscope

stimulant: voir **récompense**

stockage: conservation de données dans la mémoire d'un ordinateur.

A storage; store (USA)

stratégie: combinaison et organisation dans le temps de l'ensemble des méthodes et moyens choisis pour atteindre des objectifs déterminés dans une situation donnée.

A strategy

stratégie alternative: dans une situation donnée, et en fonction d'un nouvel agencement des ressources et des contraintes, proposition d'une nouvelle combinaison des éléments qui modifie les résultats ou permet de les atteindre de manière plus rapide, plus économique ou plus adaptée.

C *approche systémique*

A alternative strategy

stratégie de l'éducation: stratégie qui s'applique au système éducatif tout entier.

A educational strategy

stratégie pédagogique: stratégie s'appliquant à des objectif d'apprentissage ou à la conduite de la classe.

A instructional strategy

stroboscope: dispositif d'éclairage émettant des éclairs lumineux intenses à intervalles calculés ou réguliers.

A strobe

structuration: technique ayant pour objet de découper un programme en blocs d'information ou en sous-programmes.

A structuring of content

structure de comportement: voir **pattern**

structure de données: voir **format 2.**

structure d'un cours: agencement d'un ensemble de modules d'enseignement réalisé en fonction d'objectifs d'apprentissage précis.

A course design

structuro-global: relatif à une théorie d'apprentissage des langues due à Peter Gube-rina et développée par la suite, qui met l'accent sur le fonctionnement structural du cerveau et l'appréhension globale d'unités de langue orale en situation. Ce terme est associé à un certain type de méthode audiovisuelle.

A structuro-global

studio: local spécialement conçu pour la réalisation des programmes de radio et de télévision, d'émissions et/ou d'enregistrements, de films et de photographies. Pour le son et la vidéo, le studios comportent généralement un local séparé où sont réunis tous les appareils autres que micros et caméras.

C *studio d'enregistrement*

A studio

studio d'enregistrement: local spécialement conçu, adapté ou équipé pour la prise de son. Un studio d'enregistrement comporte, généralement, une salle traitée acoustiquement, munie de microphones, où se trouvent les acteurs ou les interprètes et une salle insonorisée séparée pour les appareils et le personnel technique.

A sound studio

studio radio: voir **studio d'enregistrement**

studio son: voir **studio d'enregistrement**

subliminal: se dit d'un stimulus trop faible pour passer le seuil de la perception mais qui agit sur le comportement du sujet. On dit aussi infraliminaire.

A subliminal

suggestopédie: pédagogie mise au point par le Bulgare C. Lozanov sur la base de sa théorie de la suggestologie. Le but est de libérer (désuggestionner) l'étudiant de la tension créée par les normes et les stéréotypes sociaux afin d'accroître sa capacité à solliciter les réserves de mémoire et d'activité intellectuelle détenues au niveau paraconscient.

A suggestopedy

suivi: observation et étude du devenir d'un élève après un pronostic ou un traitement.

A follow-up

support: base matérielle sur laquelle est enregistré un message: film, disque, bande magnétique, etc.

A carrier

support d'information: tout dispositif amovible capable de stocker des informations réutilisables.

A data support

supports graphiques: voir **moyens graphiques**

sur bobine: film ou bande enroulé sur bobine, sans cassette ni cartouche.

A open reel

surexposition: fait d'exposer une pellicule plus longtemps que la normale, soit par erreur, soit délibérément, pour obtenir un effet particulier.

A overexposure

surimpression: 1. enregistrement photographique de deux ou plusieurs images sur la même pellicule. Les images peuvent être soit superposées, soit juxtaposées, selon toutes sortes de combinaisons, soit, parfois, entièrement séparées les unes des autres; **2.** technique consistant à superposer deux ou plusieurs images provenant de différentes caméras; **3.** superposition momentanée d'une image ou d'un son dans un programme.

A 1. double exposure; multiple exposure; 2. superimposition; 3. flash

surveillance: fonction qui consiste à suivre de façon continue le processus d'exécution matérielle d'une activité afin de veiller à ce que les diverses étapes – fourniture des apports, échelonnement des travaux, obtention des produits escomptés et autres mesures nécessaires – se déroulent conformément au plan et de pouvoir prendre les mesures correctives appropriées en cas de non-conformité ou d'insuffisance.

A monitoring

surveiller: voir **contrôler**

symétrique: amplificateur électronique constitué de deux lampes ou transistors qui travaillent à tour de rôle.

A push-pull

symétriseur: voir **transformateur symétrique-dissymétrique**

synchrone: 1. se dit de caméras vidéo commandées par un générateur d'impulsions de synchronisation commun; non-synchrone s'applique à des caméras non couplées ou des signaux vidéo distincts; **2.** caractérise un mode d'exploitation d'un système d'ordinateur dans lequel l'exécution de chaque instruction ou de chaque opération est astreinte à suivre le rythme déterminé par des signaux d'horloge; s'oppose à asynchrone.

A 1. 2. synchronous

synchronisation: 1. opération qui consiste à synchroniser l'analyse des lignes et des points de l'image vidéo; **2.** mettre en correspondance la bande image et la bande son d'un film.

C *postsynchronisation*

A 1. 2. synchronization

synchronisation labiale: enregistrement des paroles d'un personnage apparaissant à l'écran de telle sorte que le son corresponde au mouvement des lèvres.

A lip synchronization

synchroniseur: table de montage permettant de monter ensemble la pellicule image et la bande son d'un film.

A synchronizer

synergie: action, tâche ou opération effectuée en association et en collaboration par différents individus ou éléments d'un ensemble, l'effet total obtenu étant supérieur à la somme des effets pris isolément.

A synergy

synopsis: brève description du contenu projeté d'un film ou d'une émission.

A synopsis

syntagmatique: voir **pradigmatique**

synthétiseur vocal: dispositif électronique qui peut reproduire artificiellement la voix humaine.

A speech synthesizer

syntoniseur: voir **(tuner)**

systématique: 1. qui procède avec ordre, selon un programme rationnel; ne pas confondre avec systémique; **2.** voir **taxonomie.**

A 1. systematic; 2. taxonomy; classification

système: en informatique, nom générique pour désigner un ensemble d'équipements ou de programmes destinés à remplir plusieurs fonctions.

C *système auteur; système d'exploitation; système expert; système informatique; système tuteur intelligent*

A system

système auteur: outil logiciel conçu pour être une assistance à la production de logiciels d'application spécialisés, au moyen de commandes ou d'éditeurs spéciaux pour la création de textes, de graphiques et d'images animées et pour organiser le dialogue et l'analyse de la réponse de l'utilisateur. On dit aussi «système d'auteur».

C *éditeur de didacticiels; système expert*

A authoring system

système de gestion de base de données — SGBD: outil logiciel permettant de gérer une base de données, d'y introduire des informations, de les mettre à jour et de les retrouver.

C *gestionnaire de données*

A data base management system — DBMS

système d'enseignement ouvert: voir **enseignement ouvert**

système d'exploitation: logiciel destiné à commander l'exploitation des programmes; ensemble organisé de techniques, de règles et de procédures pour la mise en œuvre de l'ordinateur, indépendamment des programmes d'application.

A operating system

système didactique: ensemble intégré et structuré d'éléments d'un programme visant à faire atteindre des objectifs pédagogiques définis.

C *système d'instruction personnalisé; système multimédia*

A instructional system

système d'information en réseau: système qui transmet des informations alphanumériques ou graphiques qui sont stockées dans un ordinateur central et apparaissent sur l'écran d'un téléviseur domestique. Le système peut être unidirectionnel comme c'est le cas pour Ceefax, Oracle (Royaume-Uni) et la forme radiodiffusée de Telidon (Canada), ou interactif bidirectionnel, comme c'est le cas pour Prestel (Royaume-Uni), Antiope (France), Captain (Japon) ou la version interactive de Telidon.

C *videotex; téléinformatique; télématique; télétext*

A information network system

système d'instruction personnalisé: système particulier d'enseignement ou d'organisation du travail au niveau de l'enseignement supérieur où l'accent est mis sur le tutorat, l'adaptation de la programmation à chaque étudiant et le rythme individuel.

A personalized system of instruction; Keller plan

système d'intercommunication: voir **interphone**

système Dolby: procédé d'enregistrement et de reproduction du son réduisant le bruit sur les bandes magnétiques et les disques.

A Dolby system

système éducatif: au niveau national, l'ensemble des institutions et l'organisation structurelle qui permettent d'assurer l'instruction et l'éducation de la population.

A education system

système expert: progiciel exploitant les connaissances relatives à un domaine particulier et simulant les démarches du raisonnement d'un expert humain.

C *intelligence artificielle*

A expert system

système fermé/ouvert: un système fermé est un système coupé de son environnement. Son équilibre est donc en même temps sa mort, c'est-à-dire la cessation de tout échange et de toute interaction. Un système ouvert est un système qui est en relation permanente avec son environnement dont il reçoit les flux d'énergie, d'informations, de personnes. Cette ouverture lui permet de tendre vers un équilibre dynamique et une complexité de plus en plus grande.

A closed/open system

système informatique: combinaison de tous les moyens (équipement et logiciels) de saisie, de traitement et de transmission de l'information d'une application, utilisant un ou plusieurs calculateurs.

A data system

système interactif: système permettant des communications dans les deux sens, chaque partie pouvant agir activement sur l'autre.

A interactive system

système modulaire: 1. tout ensemble d'enseignement composé d'éléments indépendants, chacun d'eux pouvant être étudié comme une unité complète; **2.** équipement composé d'éléments constitutifs facilement substituables ou remplaçables.

C *modulaire*

A 1. 2. modular system

système multimédia: système didactique mettant en œuvre plusieurs médias de façon combinée et complémentaire.

A multimedia system

système tuteur intelligent: didacticiel construit à partir d'un système expert et capable d'interpréter, évaluer et corriger les réponses de l'élève et de présenter des stratégies d'apprentissage individualisées.

C *programme d'exercices; logiciel outil*

A intelligent tutoring system

système PPB: voir **rationalisation des choix budgétaires**

systémique: qui se rapporte à un système.

C *approche systémique; analyse systémique*

A systemic

T

table: recueil de données (numériques, expérimentales) groupées d'une façon systématique en vue d'une consultation aisée.

A table

tableau: 1. panneau disposé sur un plan vertical ou oblique, sur lequel on peut écrire de manière effaçable; **2.** présentation synoptique de données en vue de faciliter la consultation et la compréhension des rapports mutuels; **3.** mode de structuration des données qui permet de désigner un élément par sa position sur une grille à n dimensions (n = 1, 2, 3...).

A 1. marker board; board; black board; 2. table; chart; 3. array

tableau aimanté: plaque de métal ferreux sur lequel on peut fixer des objets à l'aide d'aimants.

A magnetic board

tableau de feutre: panneau fait de carton ou de contreplaqué recouvert de feutrine, feutre, papier floqué ou substance analogue et sur lequel peuvent adhérer des documents (images ou symboles) dont le verso est recouvert de la même substance ou de substances analogues.

A flannel board

tableau de papier: système composé d'un chevalet et de grandes feuilles de papier séparées, jointes par une extrémité, et pouvant être mises en évidence ou rabattues au-dessus du bord supérieur du cadre selon les besoins de la présentation.

A flip chart

tableau en velcro : panneau dont la surface est recouverte de minuscules boucles de nylon sur lequel des documents graphiques, revêtus au dos de minuscules crochets de nylon, peuvent s'accrocher par pression et demeurer fixés sans tomber.

A hook and loop board

tableau magnétique : voir **tableau aimanté**

tableau mural : panneau vertical utilisé comme auxiliaire d'enseignement pour des présentations visuelles de divers types.

A display board

tableau noir : surface unie d'ardoise, de verre ou autre matériau, utilisée pour écrire ou dessiner à l'aide d'un morceau de craie, d'un marqueur, d'un crayon ou de toute autre objet dont le tracé est facilement effaçable.

A blackboard

table de montage : dispositif permettant de visionner et de monter des films animés.

A editing table

table ronde : discussion ou débat réunissant plusieurs participants, souvent assis autour d'une table ronde, de sorte qu'aucune préséance n'est visiblement marquée.

A round table

tablette graphique : organe d'entrée d'un ordinateur qui permet à l'utilisateur d'entrer une information d'ordre graphique en dessinant ou en traçant un croquis ou une série de croquis sur une tablette.

A graphic tablet

tableur : outil logiciel destiné à la création et à la manipulation interactives de tableaux numériques visualisés. On dit aussi «feuille de calcul électronique».

C *logiciel outil*

A calc ; spreadsheet

tâche : activité constituant une unité de travail observable et/ou mesurable, effectuée par un individu ou une machine avec un résultat direct ou immédiat et qui, associé à d'autres, contribue à la réalisation d'un objectif ou d'un projet.

C *analyse des tâches*

A task

taches lumineuses : zones d'émulsion d'une pellicule qui ont été impressionnées autrement que par les propriétés optiques de l'objectif, par exemple en raison de reflets intérieurs entre les diverses surfaces des éléments de l'objectif ou à cause de tourelles de caméra, volets d'ouverture ou chargeurs à fermeture non hermétique.

A flare

tachistoscope : appareil servant à présenter, pendant un temps très bref, des stimuli visuels fixes utilisés pour l'étude de l'apprentissage, de l'attention et de la perception.

A tachistoscope

taux d'abandon : pourcentage d'élèves ou d'étudiants quittant l'école ou l'université avant la fin d'une année ou d'un cycle d'études.

A drop-out rate

taux d'erreur : pourcentage de réponses incorrectes à un item, un ensemble d'items ou l'ensemble d'un programme.

A error rate

taux de réussite : pourcentage des performances réussies à une épreuve.

A success rate

taxinomie, taxonomie : 1. science des lois de la classification des organismes vivants ; 2. taxinomie des objectifs pédagogiques. Classification d'un ensemble d'objectifs de l'éducation établie selon certains critères explicites.

A 1. taxonomy ; 2. taxonomy of educational objectives

TBC – time base corrector : voir **correcteur de base de temps**

team teaching: voir **enseignement en équipe**

technique Delphi: méthode de prévision de l'évolution des technologies dans laquelle les avis d'experts sont sollicités au moyen d'un questionnaire. Les réponses font l'objet d'une analyse et d'une synthèse qui est soumise à nouveau aux mêmes experts. L'opération peut être répétée plusieurs fois jusqu'à ce qu'il y ait une clarification suffisante des opinions.

A Delphi technique

technique des incidents critiques: technique permettant de déterminer quelles capacités sont nécessaires pour un travail particulier, afin de définir des niveaux de réussite fondés sur la confrontation avec des incidents réels. On utilise parfois des bandes et films d'incidents critiques dans la formation des enseignants pour étudier le comportement des maîtres ou des élèves dans des situations données.

A critical incident technique

technique d'étude: procédures utilisées pour faciliter les apprentissages intellectuels: technique de prise de notes de mémorisation et parfois même mode d'utilisation des ouvrages de référence ainsi que rédaction de fiches.

A study skill

technologie appropriée: ce terme, qui tend aujourd'hui à être d'un usage plus général que celui de technologie intermédiaire ou peu coûteuse, indique que la valeur d'une technologie ne réside pas seulement dans sa viabilité économique et ses qualités techniques, mais aussi dans son adaptation aux conditions socio-culturelles.

A appropriate technology

technologie de l'éducation: 1. à l'origine, moyens issus de la révolution des communications et qui peuvent servir à des fins éducatives comme par exemple les moyens audiovisuels, la télévision, les ordinateurs et les autres types d'équipement et de matériels pédagogiques; **2.** au sens nouveau et plus large, façon systématique de concevoir, d'appliquer et d'évaluer l'ensemble du processus d'enseignement/et d'apprentissage en tenant compte à la fois des moyens techniques, des moyens humains et des interactions entre les uns et les autres, de manière à aboutir à une éducation plus efficace. Dans ce second cas, la technologie de l'éducation utilise comme instrument théorique l'analyse systémique.

A educational technology

technologies de l'information: voir **nouvelles technologies de l'information**

technologie intermédiaire: voir **technologie appropriée**

technologie de l'enseignement: sous-ensemble de la technologie de l'éducation fondé sur l'idée que l'enseignement est un sous-ensemble de l'éducation. Elle a pour objet d'analyser les problèmes et de concevoir, expérimenter, évaluer et mettre en œuvre des solutions dans des situations où l'apprentissage est dirigé et contrôlé.

A instructional technology

teinte: attribut de la sensation visuelle de couleur qui suscite des dénominations de couleurs comme rouge, jaune, vert, bleu, pourpre, etc.

A hue

télé: 1. abrégé de télévision; **2.** « télé » plus substantif, a deux sens: a) à distance, au loin; exemple: téléenseignement, télécommunication, télécommande; b) relatif à la télévision; exemple: télécinéma.

A 1. TV; 2. tele; remote

téléchargement: chargement à distance par un procédé télématique d'un logiciel dans un ordinateur.

C *télélogiciel; téléinformatique; télétraitement*

A downloading

télécinéma: dispositif constitué d'une ou plusieurs caméras de télévision à poste fixe et de projecteurs appropriés. Il sert à transmettre des documents projetés (généralement des diapositives ou des films fixes ou animés) à un système de télévision.

A film chain

télécommande: 1. commande à distance d'un appareil par l'intermédiaire de fils, de signaux sonores, de rayons infra-rouges ou d'ondes électromagnétiques; **2.** dispositif (boîtier) permettant la commande de programmes de jeux.

C *accès à distance*

A 1. remote control; 2. paddle

télécommunication: toute transmission, émission ou réception de signes, de signaux, d'écrits, d'images, de sons ou de renseignements de toute nature par fil, radioélectricité, optique ou autres systèmes électromagnétiques.

A telecommunication

téléconférence: conférence dans laquelle les interlocuteurs sont répartis dans deux lieux ou plus, reliés entre eux par des moyens de télécommunication. On parle d'audioconférence lorsque les participants sont reliés par des systèmes téléphoniques qui permettent la transmission de la parole, et accessoirement des systèmes de télécopie ou de téléécriture qui permettent la transmission de documents graphiques. On parle de visioconférence ou de vidéoconférence lorsqu'il y a en plus transmission d'images animées des participants éloignés.

A teleconference; audioconference; videoconference

télécopie: procédé de reproduction à distance sous une forme identique à l'original de documents graphiques par des moyens de télécommunication.

C *fac-similé*

A facsimile transmission; fax

télédistribution: système de télévision dans lequel le signal est distribué par câbles; opposé de «radiodiffusion».

C *distribution par câble*

A cable television; cable casting

téléécriture: procédé de transmission d'informations graphiques au fur et à mesure de leur tracé manuscrit par des moyens de télécommunication avec affichage sur un écran.

A telewriting

250

téléenseignement: voir **enseignement à distance**

téléimprimeur: appareil émetteur et récepteur de télégraphie comportant un clavier alphanumérique pour l'émission et assurant à la réception l'impression des caractères.

A teleprinter; teletypewriter (USA)

téléinformatique: exploitation automatisée de systèmes informatiques par l'intermédiaire de réseaux de communication.

C *télématique*

A teleinformatics

téléleçon*: technique permettant de relier un enseignant ou un conférencier à des élèves en classe par l'intermédiaire de liaisons téléphoniques ordinaires donnant ainsi la possibilité à l'orateur de s'adresser, en même temps, à plusieurs classes situées dans des endroits différents; l'installation peut ausi offrir une possibilité de communication à double sens entre l'orateur et son public.

A telelecture

télélecteur: caméra de télévision, généralement fixée en position verticale, au-dessus d'une boîte lumineuse, pour la lecture de tout document (texte, carte, dessin), et l'étude d'objets divers

A overhead camera; TV reader

télélogiciel: terme générique pour désigner les programmes qui peuvent être chargés d'un ordinateur sur un autre par l'intermédaire d'un service vidéotex.

A telesoftware

télématique: contraction de *télé*communication et d'infor*matique*, terme créé pour désigner l'ensemble des services de nature ou d'origine informatique pouvant être fournis à travers un réseau de télécommunication.

C *téléinformatique*

A telematics

télémètre: accessoire d'un appareil de prise de vues indiquant la distance de l'appareil au sujet à photographier ou permettant de faire une mise au point correcte de l'objectif.

C *posemètre*

A range finder

téléobjectif: tout objectif photographique offrant, sous une forme compacte, une combinaison de deux systèmes dont l'un, antérieur, a une courte distance focale, alors que l'objectif dans son ensemble possède une grande distance focale. Aussi, au sens large, tout objectif de distance focale supérieure à la normale.

A telephoto lens

téléprojecteur: voir **projecteur d'images télévisées**

téléscripteur: tout appreil permettant d'écrire à distance par un procédé quelconque.

C *téléécriture; téléimprimeur*

A telewriter

télésouffleur: appareil permettant de lire un texte face à la caméra.

A teleprompter

Télétel: contraction de téléphone et de télévision. Nom du service français de vidéotex.

C *ANTIOPE, minitel*

A Teletel

télétex: terme normalisé pour designer un système de télétraitement pour les textes.

C *unité de traitement de texte; courier électronique*

A teletex

télétext(e): système unidirectionnel qui permet de consulter sur un récepteur de télévision domestique des informations alphanumériques et graphiques diffusées sur le réseau hertzien. On dit aussi vidéographie diffusée.

C *viewdata; vidéotex; Antiope*

A teletext

télétraitement: mode de traitement selon lequel les données sont émises ou reçues par des terminaux éloignés de l'ordinateur.

C *téléchargement*

A teleprocessing

téléuniversite: université donnant des enseignements à distance à des étudiants kadultes ou ne pouvant venir à l'université.

C *enseignement à distance*

A university at a distance

télévision à balayage lent: système de télévision où le signal vidéo se trouve comprimé à une largeur de bande adaptée à la transmission par lignes téléphoniques. La télévision à balayage lent ne peut généralement pas reproduire des images animées car il faut plusieurs secondes pour reconstituer une image.

A slow-scan television

télévision communautaire: voir **vidéoanimation**

télévision éducative: 1. utilisation de la télévision à des fins éducatives, formelles ou non formelles; **2.** tout ensemble de programmes de télévision, en circuit ouvert ou fermé, conçus pour couvrir une vaste gamme de sujets éducatifs et culturels.

C *radio éducative; télévision scolaire; enseignement télévisuel*

A 1. 2. educational television

télévision en circuit fermé: installation de télévision intégrée comprenant une unité de production ou de reproduction et un système de distribution par câbles ou par réseaux hertziens de programmes vidéo. En général, un circuit fermé dessert une zone restreinte: une salle de classe, une école, un campus universitaire.

A closed-circuit television

télévision scolaire: 1. ensemble de programmes de télévision essentiellement conçus pour être utilisés dans les écoles. Ils présentent généralement un caractère informatif oui didactique; **2.** ensemble des services chargés d'assurer la préparation, l'animation, la réalisation et l'exploitation pédagogique des émissions de télévision à usage d'enseignement.

C *radio scolaire; radio-télévision scolaire*

A 1. instructional television; 2. instructional television (service)

telex: 1. système de transmission à distance de messges dactylographiés au moyen de téléimprimeurs équipant les postes d'abonnés; **2.** message ainsi transmis.

A 1. 2. telex

TELIDON: voir **système d'information en réseau**

température de couleur: température absolue du corps noir qui émet un rayonnement ayant la même chromaticité que la source de lumière considérée (mesure exprimée en degrés Kelvin et généralement utilisée pour indiquer la couleur apparente de la lampe source).

A colour temperature

temps d'accès: intervalle entre l'instant où une unité de commande déclenche un appel de données et l'instant où ces données sont disponibles dans un système informatique.

A access time

temps d'antenne: temps imparti à chaque producteur ou animateur pour une émission radiodiffusée.

A broadcast(ing) time; on-air time

temps de latence: intervalle entre le moment de l'affichage d'un stimulus et le début de la réponse de l'élève.

A latency

temps d'immobilisation: période durant laquelle tout ou partie d'une installation n'est pas utilisable, pour cause de réparation ou d'entretien.

C *temps utilisable*

A down time

temps partagé: voir **partage de temps**

temps réel: 1. mode de traitement qui permet l'admission de données à un instant quelconque et l'obtention immédiate de résultats en un temps suffisamment court; **2.** caractérise un mode d'enregistrement ou duplication qui s'effectue au même rythme que le phénomène enregistré.

A 1. 2. real time

temps utilisable: temps pendant lequel un appareil est disponible et en état de marche.

C *temps d'immobilisation*

A up-time

terminal: 1. ensemble des connecteurs, des transformateurs et, si nécessaire, du convertisseur, montés à l'extrémité d'un récepteur de télévision par câble; **2.** organe d'entrée et de sortie qui permet de communiquer avec un ordinateur.

C *périphérique; imprimante; écran*

A terminal

terminal intelligent: voir **terminal programmable**

terminal passif: terminal qui permet seulement l'accès à un système informatique, sans possibilité de traitement de données.

A dumb terminal

terminal programmable: terminal qui est un ordinateur en lui-même en raison de ses possibilités propres, par exemple, la présence d'une mémoire.

A intelligent terminal

terre: le sol, considéré comme ayant un potentiel électrique égal à zéro; par analogie, toute masse jouant dans un circuit électrique le même rôle que le sol; par extension conducteur allant de l'appareil à la terre.

A earth (UK); ground (USA)

test à étalonnage critériel: voir **test critériel**

test à étalonnage normatif: voir **test normatif**

test centré sur la performance: voir **test de performance**

test critériel: type de test dans lequel un sujet est jugé sur la manière dont sa performance se situe par rapport à un niveau donné et non en relation avec la performance d'un groupe de référence.

C *test normatif (à étalonnage normatif)*

A criterion-referenced test

test d'acquisition: test destiné à mesurer le niveau acquis par un sujet dans un domaine donné.

A attainment test

test d'aptitude: test destiné à mesurer la capacité d'un sujet dans un domaine donné.

A aptitude test

test de capacité: test administré à des élèves en début d'apprentissage ou à tout autre moment ultérieur et destiné à mesurer leur niveau de performance.

A proficiency test

test de closure: test de mesure de la compétence de lecture et de compréhension qui fait appel à l'insertion ou à la suppression de mots appropriés dans un texte.

A cloze test

test de complètement: test demandant au sujet de compléter des phrases ou des images dont on a retiré certaines parties.

A completion test

test de connaissances: voir **test de rendement**

test de performance: test portant sur le résultat d'une activité, mais qui ne prétend pas mesurer la capacité qui la sous-tend.

A performance-based test

test de rendement: test conçu pour mesurer les savoirs, savoir-faire, compréhensions, etc. d'un sujet dans un domaine donné.

A achievement test

test de sortie: voir **test final**

test d'intelligence: méthode normalisée d'évaluation (collective ou individuelle) ayant pour but de mesurer, pour un individu donné, sa capacité à apprendre, à résoudre des problèmes comportant des éléments abstraits et à faire face à des situations nouvelles.

C *test d'aptitude; quotient intellectuel*

A intelligence test

test final: test administré à la fin d'un programme d'enseignement. On dit aussi test de sortie.

C *post-test*

A final test

test non verbal: test dont les items se composent de symboles, chiffres, nombres ou images, à l'exclusion de mots.

A non-verbal test

test normatif: test évaluant la performance d'un apprenant dans un domaine donné par rapport à une norme ou à un groupe de référence.

C *test critériel; test à étalonnage critériel*

A norm-referenced test

test objectif: test conçu pour éliminer, autant que possible, tout facteur de subjectivité de la part de ceux qui le passent et de ceux qui le dépouillent. Ce type d'épreuve comporte une série de questions concrètes demandant une réponse sous forme'd'un mot ou d'un signe graphique et ne nécessite ni expression verbale ni organisation d'éléments dans la réponse.

A objective-based test

test pronostique: test destiné à prédire une performance ou à déterminer l'aptitude à réaliser certains apprentissages dans un domaine ou un secteur spécifiques.

A prognosis test

tête d'effacement: dispositif intégré au système d'entraînement d'une bande magnétique dont la seule fonction est d'effacer les signaux précédemment enregistrés avant l'enregistrement de nouveaux signaux.

A erasing head

tête de lecture: dispositif reproduisant le son enregistré selon un des moyens habituellement utilisés.

A playback head

tête d'enregistrement: modulateur de lumière ou tête magnétique dont la fonction est de transformer des signaux sonores pour les inscrire sur une piste optique ou magnétique.

A recording head

tête magnétique: pièce électro-magnétique d'un équipement audio ou vidéo qui se trouve placée au contact de la couche d'oxyde de fer d'un film magnétique ou d'une bande magnétique et qui a pour fonction d'assurer les fonctions d'enregistrement, de lecture ou d'effacement (enregistrement sonore ou enregistrement vidéo).

A magnetic head

T group: voir **groupe de base**

thermocopie: procédé d'obtention de copies papier ou de transparents à partir d'un document à l'aide d'un copieur utilisant des supports sensibles à la chaleur.

A thermal process

thermocopieur: duplicateur permettant d'effectuer l'exposition et le développement d'images sur des clichés et papiers spéciaux en utilisant une source de rayons infrarouges.

A thermal copier

thésaurus: langage documentaire spécialisé caractérisé par l'utilisation de termes qui renvoient à des concepts. Ces termes, appelés descripteurs, sont agencés selon des relations de synonymie, de hiérarchie et d'association. En informatique documentaire, le thésaurus permet d'exploiter des bases de données car il sert à la fois à l'analyse des informations contenues dans les documents et à celle des questions posées par les utilisateurs des systèmes documentaires.

A thesaurus

tirage: 1. désignation par le sort; 2. le fait d'imprimer, de reproduire; 3. ensemble des opérations nécessaires à l'établissement d'une épreuve (généralement positive) sur du papier photographique à partir d'une pellicule (généralement négative) impressionnée et développée. Cela comprend les tirages par contact, les réductions et les agrandissements sur pellicule ou papier; 4. document graphique résultant du transfert sur un support permanent d'une image présentée sur un visuel; 5. ensemble d'exemplaires d'un livre ou d'un journal imprimés en une fois.

C *tirage optique*

A 1. sorting; 2. 3. printing; 4. hard copy; 5. run; press run; print run

tirage intermédiaire: tout film autre que l'original, utilisé seulement pour permettre de tirer des copies, comme un internégatif couleur ou un contretype négatif ou positif.

A intermediate

tirage optique: tirage d'une pellicule effectué sur une machine opérant par projection et non par contact direct.

A optical printing

tirage papier: document sur papier par opposition à un document présenté visuellement sur écran.

A hard copy

tiré à part: partie d'un livre, d'un article ou d'une revue ayant fait l'objet d'un tirage séparé pour une diffusion particulière.

A off-print

tireuse: appareil où défilent ensemble une pellicule impressionnée et une pellicule vierge. A l'intérieur du dispositif, la lumière, traversant la pellicule image vient impressionner la pellicule vierge pour constituer une succession d'images latentes.

A printer

tireuse optique: voir **truca**

titre: nom ou désignation d'un film.

A title caption

titre final: indication marquant de manière explicite la fin d'un document audiovisuel.

A end title

titre principal: nom donné à une production audiovisuelle et apparaissant au début de la projection du document.

A main title

tonalité: signal audio régulier et de fréquence unique.
A tone

top: bref signal sonore placé sur la piste pilote d'une bande audio ou vidéo pour servir de repère au montage.
A beep

topage: signal inscrit sur une bande audio ailleurs que sur la piste son et servant à commander le déroulement d'une présentation visuelle.
A separate track pulse

top de synchronisation: voir **impulsion de synchronisation**

tore: petit anneau de matériau magnétique employé pour mettre en mémoire des données.
A core

tourner: filmer un plan avec une caméra de cinéma ou effectuer les prises de vues d'un film.
A to shoot

tous les droits: terme du langage commun pour «tous les droits constituant le droit d'auteur».
A full rights

tracé: voir **graphique**

traceur: organe muni d'une plume qui fournit une représentation graphique à deux dimensions.
A plotter

traceur de courbes: dispositif de sortie d'un système informatique permettant de tracer des courbes sur papier par détermination successive des coordonnées des différents points.
A graph plotter; X-Y plotter

traduire: écrire dans un langage des informations écrites dans un autre langage.
A to translate

training: développement d'automatismes par répétition d'exercices.
C *exercice d'automatisation*
A training

traitement: ensemble d'opérations physiques ou chimiques effectuées sur une pellicule impressionnée pour développer et fixer sur papier les images qu'elle contient. Cela comprend des opérations spécifiques comme le développement, l'arrêt de l'action du révélateur, le fixage, le lavage, la clarification, le blanchiment et le virage.
A processing

traitement automatique de l'information: toute opération ou suite d'opérations systématiques sur des données, en appliquant des règles explicites ou implicites, comme des séries d'opérations discrètes telles que calculer, assembler, compiler, décoder, traduire, mettre en mémoire, extraire, transférer, générer, séparer, extraire, décaler, chercher, trier, fusionner, translittérer, lire, écrire, imprimer, effacer, perforer, etc. Dans une institution, le traitement des données peut être organisé d'une façon centralisée, lorsque toutes les opérations sont effectuées dans un même endroit, ou décentralisée.
A automatic data processing

traitement de texte: procédé électronique pour éditer et calibrer des textes rapidement et efficacement.
C *unité de traitement de texte; télétex*
A text processing

traitement par lots: mode de traitement de données ou réalisation de travaux suivant lequel les données à traiter et les programmes à effectuer ont été regroupés au préalable par lots. Dans ce mode, l'utilisateur ne peut pas agir sur les traitements en cours.
A batch processing

trame: ensemble des lignes d'une image télévisée décrites au cours d'un balayage vertical unique.
A raster

transcodeur: dispositif permettant d'assurer de façon automatique la transformation d'un signal de télévision d'un standard de couleur à un autre.

A transcoder

transducteur: dispositif permettant la transformation d'énergie électrique en énergie magnétique ou mécanique et vice-versa.

A transducer

transférer: faire passer un message d'un support à un autre.

A to transfer

transfert: 1. copie filmique d'un enregistrement de télévision ou vice-versa. Egalement, réenregistrement d'un signal de bande à bande ou de bande à piste son d'un film négatif; **2.** procédé technique consistant en l'utilisation de feuilles en matière plastique «porteuses» d'un certain nombre de signes qui sont transférables suivant le principe de la décalcomanie: il suffit au metteur en page de presser légèrement sur la feuille de plastique au-dessus du caractère concerné pour le reporter, en déposer le dessin sur la page en cours d'exécution; **3.** effet d'un apprentissage sur un apprentissage ultérieur; **4.** processus par lequel un sujet projette sur une autre personne des désirs inconscients.

A 1. 2. 3. 4. transfer

transfert à sec: méthode de réalisation de textes ou de documents graphiques à partir de feuilles originales sensibles à la pression.

C *lettrage*

A dry transfer

transformateur: appareil électrique permettant de changer la tension et le courant d'un circuit alternatif.

A transformer

transformateur symétrique-dissymétrique: dispositif reliant des récepteurs de télévision à certains câbles ou certaines annexes. On emploie aussi synthétiseur et balun.

A balun transformer

transistorisé: terme désignant divers types de composants électroniques ayant pour fonction d'assurer et de diriger la circulation d'électrons à l'intérieur de solides (par exemples transistors, diodes au germanium ou tores magnétiques).

C *semi-conducteur*

A solid state

transmettre: 1. dans un système informatique déplacer des données d'un emplacement à un autre emplacement: par exemple lire ou explorer des données à la source, les envoyer par l'intermédiaire d'un canal et les stocker à destination; **2.** envoyer un signal par voie hertzienne ou par câble.

C *émettre*

A 1. 2. to transmit

transmission: acheminement d'un signal d'un émetteur vers un récepteur.

C *communication; télécommunication*

A transmission; communication

transmission numérisée: acheminement de signaux de radio ou de télévision sous forme codée, généralement en utilisant des bits mathématiques ou des codes binaires permettant une régénération facile du signal sans apparition de bruit, déformation ou distorsion.

A digital transmission

transmodulation: pour un récepteur, modulation du signal utile appliqué à l'entrée d'un récepteur radioélectrique par le signal modulant d'une émission indésirable à fréquence proteuse différente, due à la non-linéarité des étages précédant le détecteur.

A cross modulation

transparent: terme générique pour tout type de documents visuels destinés à être regardés en utilisant une lumière transmise et non réfléchie, comme, par exemple, des diapositives ou des transparents pour rétroprojecteur.

C *opaque*

A transparency

256

transparents à rabats: transparents supplémentaires fixés sur le cadre d'un transparent principal projeté par rétroprojection. Leur contenu développe ou précise l'information présentée sur le transparent principal.

A overlay transparencies

transpondeur: relais émetteur convoyant la fréquence de signaux relayés sans démodulation et remodulation intermédiaires. On dit aussi répéteur.

A transponder

travail autonome: activités scolaires que des élèves effectuent en dehors du cadre contraignant imposé par le travail en classe, mais en consultant cependant périodiquement un ou plusieurs enseignants pour être dirigés et aidés dans leur travail et en ayant souvent comme objectif la réalisation de projets d'étude individuels. On dit aussi travail indépendant.

C *activités dirigées; enseignement individuel*

A independent study

travail dirigé: dans l'enseignement français, séance organisée par petits groupes (25 au maximum) pour les élèves du premier cycle du second degré, afin d'alléger les obligations scolaires de l'enfant à la maison, de faire acquérir une méthode de travail et faciliter l'observation de ses aptitudes.

C *travaux dirigés; activités dirigées*

A guided group study

travail en direction d'études: dans l'enseignement supérieur, mode de travail personnalisé, en face à face, s'effectuant avec un petit groupe d'étudiant, la discussion entre l'enseignant ou directeur d'études et les étudiants prenant souvent comme base l'analyse d'un travail écrit fait par un ou plusieurs étudiants.

A tutorial mode

travail en groupe: situation où les membres d'un groupe, travaillant en coopération plutôt qu'individuellement, échangent des idées et unisent leurs efforts pour attendre des objectifs communs

A group work

travail en laboratoire: activités d'apprentissage effectuées par des élèves dans un laboratoire conçu pour un travail individuel ou de groupe, sur une matière déterminée. L'objectif est l'application pratique de principes théoriques sous forme d'observation, d'expérimentation et de recherche.

A laboratory work

travail indépendant: voir **travail autonome**

travail individuel sur contrat*: disposition spécifique selon laquelle un élève a la possibilité de travailler à une tâche d'apprentissage définie, comme il l'entend et à son propre rythme, sans subir les contraintes rigides imposées par les activités du reste de la classe.

C *contrat pédagogique*

A student contract

travail par équipes*: méthode consistant à diviser une classe en groupes de cinq ou six élèves, chaque groupe ayant pour consigne d'écrire un rapport commun sur le même sujet ou des sujets différents. Ces groupes ou équipes fonctionnent comme des petits comités chargés de mener une enquête et de faire un rapport sur un problème particulier.

A syndicate group/method

travail sur projet: méthode demandant aux étudiants de présenter individuellement ou en groupes une thèse, un plan, un exposé oral ou un rapport écrit ou quelque autre travail, l'objectif véritable étant l'apprentissage et l'utilisation des techniques requises à cet effet.

A project method

travaux dirigés – TD: dans l'enseignement supérieur, travaux exécutés par des groupes d'étudiants sous la direction d'assistants, et en tout état de cause sans intervention directe du professeur durant leur déroulement. L'objectif est d'assimiler les principes introduits dans le cours magistral, notamment au moyen d'exercices d'application.

A tutorials; guided group work

travaux manuels: activités manuelles comme les travaux d'art appliqué, le travail sur bois, la couture, la menuiserie, la poterie.

A practicals

travaux pratiques: travail expérimental individuel par exemple en laboratoire pour réaliser des expériences de physique, de chimie, de biologie.

A practicals; practical work

travelling: déplacement de la caméra ou du microphone sur support mobile pour obtenir un effet d'éloignement ou de rapprochement ou pour suivre les déplacements d'un acteur.

A travelling; tracking; trucking (USA)

travelling avant/arrière: mouvement de caméra vers un sujet (travelling avant) ou à partir d'un sujet (travelling arrière).

A dolly in/out

travelling optique: voir **zoom**

trépied de caméra: support de caméra réglable, à trois pieds, souvent doté de barres de liaison et monté sur roulettes.

A tripod

trieuse: dispositif automatique employé pour présenter en une suite déterminée des cartes perforées ou des feuilles fixes codées et utilisées en informatique et en reprographie.

A sorter; collator

tronc commun: désigne généralement, au niveau secondaire et quelquefois au niveau supérieur, les parties essentielles du programme dispensées à tous les étudiants, quelles que soient les options, les filières ou les orientations ultérieures choisies.

A core curriculum

trousse pédagogique: voir **ensemble pédagogique**

truca: machine de laboratoire opérant le tirage par report optique et permettant des variatins de grandeur d'images d'une pellicule à l'autre.

A optical printer

trucage: voir **effets spéciaux**

tube: cylindre de verre rempli d'un gaz et contenant des électrodes servant pour l'éclairage ou la régulation électronique.

A tube

tube à rayons cathodiques: dispositif de sortie d'un appareil affichant des caractères ou des tracés par phosphorescence produits électriquement sur un écran de verre. L'écran d'un récepteur de télévision ordinaire est un exemple de tube à rayons cathodiques. On dit aussi écran cathodique.

A cathode-ray tube

tube image: tube à rayons cathodiques qui, associé à des dispositifs appropriés, assure la synthèse de l'image. Ecran d'un récepteur de télévision.

A picture tube; kinescope

(tuner): dispositif électronique recevant et sélectionnant des signaux de radio ou de télévision à partir d'une antenne et les transformant en signaux de fréquence radio ou télévision qui sont dirigés ensuite vers un étage d'amplification. Les tuners peuvent être incorporés à des récepteurs ou constituer des modules séparés.

A tuner

tuteur: 1. enseignant mis à la disposition d'un élève, ou d'un petit groupe d'élèves, pour les aider à organiser leurs activités d'apprentissage dans le cadre de l'emploi du temps; **2.** dans les systèmes d'enseignement ouvert, personne qui sert d'intermédiaire entre l'apprenant et les divers éléments du cours.

A 1. 2. tutor

tutoriel: voir **programme tuteur**

U

UHF: (ultra high frequency); désigne la bande 9, c'est-à-dire la gamme de fréquences comprise entre 300 et 3000 MHz, autrement dit les ondes décimétriques.
A ultra high frequency

UIT: Union Internationale des Télécommunications
A ITU

U-matic: voir **format vidéo**

UNISIST: programme intergouvernemental pour le développement de l'ensemble des normes, règles, méthodes des principes et techniques qui régissent le traitement et le transfert de l'information spécialisée, notamment par l'application des technologies modernes de l'informatique et des télécommunications.
A UNISIST

unité arithmétique: partie d'un ordinateur qui effectue des opérations arithmétiques et logiques.
A arithmetic unit

unité centrale: unité de matériel comprenant, dans un ordinateur, les dispositifs (logiques, arithmétiques) qui commandent l'interprétation et l'exécution des instructions.
A central processing unit; mainframe

unité de commande: partie de l'ordinateur qui commande les opérations de toutes les autres parties.
A control unit

unité de traitement de texte: terminal à clavier et à visuel permettant d'éditer électroniquement des textes.
A word processor

unité de valeur – UV: dans l'enseignement supérieur, désigne un enseignement semestriel ou annuel comportant des heures de cours et de travaux dirigés et sanctionné par un examen ou par un contrôle continu.
A credit

université des ondes: université utilisant la radio ou la télévision comme composantes pédagogiques principales d'un enseignement à distance.
C *enseignement à distance; téléuniversité*
A university of the air

université ouverte: terme originaire du Royaume-Uni. Il désigne une institution qui assure l'accès des adultes à l'enseignement supérieur, sans considération des titres académiques. L'enseignement s'effectue en combinant la correspondance, la radio et la télévision. Il est complété en partie par des séances de travaux dirigés.
A open university

université sans murs: université donnant une part importante de ses enseignements à l'extérieur des bâtiments universitaires et utilisant la plupart du temps des méthodes d'enseignement à distance.
C *université ouverte; enseignement à distance*
A university without walls

utilitaires: voir **programme de service.** Ne pas confondre avec «logiciels outils».

UV: voir **unité de valeur**

V

valeur nominale: spécifications des caractéristiques de puissance et de signal exigibles d'un appareil; puissance de sortie et qualité nominales d'un dispositif électronique.

A *rated power*

valeur nominale: spécifications des caractéristiques de puissance et de signal exigibles d'un appareil; puissance de sortie et qualité nominales d'un dispositif électronique.

A *rating*

validation: 1. démonstration de l'efficacité de matériaux, de systèmes didactiques ou de tests, au moyen de techniques d'évaluation sommative appropriées; **2.** reconnaissance institutionnelle par un examen ou un diplôme d'acquis scolaires.

C *expérimentation sur le terrain; preuve de succès d'apprentissage*

A 1. *validation*; 2. *certification*

validité: capacité d'une épreuve ou d'un instrument de mesure, à mesurer effectivement ce qu'il prétend mesurer; par exemple, capacité d'une épreuve d'aptitude intellectuelle à porter effectivement sur l'intelligence et non sur des acquisitions scolaires.

C *fiabilité; fidélité; sensibilité*

A *validity*

valise pédagogique: voir **ensemble pédagogique**

variance: 1. différence entre ce qui est attendu ou prédit et ce qui se produit en fait; **2.** degré de l'écart des mesures par rapport à la moyenne.

A 1. 2. *variance*

variateur: voir **gradateur**

vérification: examen ou contrôle qui vise à déterminer et à attester la mesure dans laquelle une condition, un processus ou un produit (réalisation) est conforme à des normes ou à des critères déterminés à l'avance.

A *audit*

verrouilleur de générateur de synchronisation: dispositif électronique permettant de maintenir synchronisées des images de télévision provenant de diverses sources.

A *genlock*

version originale – VO: copie d'un film sonore dans la langue d'origine par opposition à une version doublée.

A *original version; original language version*

VF – vidéofréquence: voir **fréquence vidéo**

VHF – very high frequency: désigne la bande 8, c'est-à-dire la gamme de fréquences comprise entre 30 et 300 MHz, c'est-à-dire les ondes métriques.

A *very high frequency*

vidéo: 1. abréviation de vidéofréquence. Technique audiovisuelle qui permet d'enregistrer sur un support magnétique l'image et le son au moyen d'un magnétoscope puis de reproduire cet enregistrement sur un écran de télévision; **2.** «vidéo» plus substantif: qui a trait à la production, la transmission ou la réception d'informations audiovisuelles utilisant la vidéofréquence.

A 1. 2. *video*

vidéoanimation: activité communautaire de production de télévision consistant à mettre un équipement de vidéo léger à la disposition des membres d'une collectivité; lorsque la vidéoanimation est associée à un réseau de télédistribution, on parle de télévision communautaire.

A *community video activities*

vidéobande: bande magnétique sur laquelle des signaux vidéo et audio sont ou peuvent être enregistrés.

C *format vidéo*

A videotape

vidéocassette: bande vidéo contenue dans un boîtier qui peut s'insérer aisément et instantanément sur un appareil enregistreur-lecteur ou lecteur conçu à cet effet, sans manipulation de la bande magnétique.

A videocassette

vidéoclip: courte séquence musicale en vidéo, généralement produite par un éditeur de disques à des fins promotionnelles.

A promo

vidéoconférence: voir **visioconférence**

vidéodisque: disque sur lequel sont enregistrés des signaux vidéo et audio pouvant être restitués par un récepteur de télévision. Un vidéodisque nécessite, pour être lu, un vidéolecteur compatible.

A videodisc

vidéo-fréquence: voir **fréquence vidéo**

vidéogramme: enregistrement vidéo sur bande ou cassette.

A videogram

vidéographie: procédé de télécommunication permettant de présenter à un usager des messages alphanumériques ou graphiques sur un écran de visualisation.

A videography

vidéographie diffusée: voir **télétext**

vidéographie interactive: voir **vidéotex**

vidéo interactive: système d'apprentissage individualisé résultant du couplage d'un lecteur de vidéodisque (ou de vidéocassette) avec un ordinateur de sorte que la sélection des séquences d'images est déterminée par les réponses de l'utilisateur. A ne pas confondre avec «vidéographie interactive» ou «vidéotex».

C *interactif*

A interactive video

vidéolecteur: appareil électronique pouvant lire les signaux vidéo et autres provenant d'un enregistrement vidéo réalisé sur bande vidéo ou vidéodisque. Il ne permet pas d'effectuer des enregistrements.

A video player

vidéo légère: équipement vidéo très léger et portatif, généralement utilisé pour le reportage et la vidéo non professionnelle.

C *camescope*

A light video equipment; light video

vidéophone: voir **visiophonie**

vidéo portable: voir **vidéo légère**

vidéotex: 1. terme générique accepté internationalement pour désigner tous les systèmes de transmission câblés ou radiodiffusés pour la transmission d'informations alphanumériques ou graphiques sur des récepteurs de télévision domestiques; **2.** système interactif permettant, à la demande de l'utilisateur (qui dispose d'un clavier), la visualisation sur un écran de télévision domestique de pages d'informations alphanumériques et graphiques, codées sous forme numérique et transmises par le réseau électronique. Ce réseau permet à l'utilisateur d'utiliser une voie de retour et de «dialoguer» avec l'ordinateur dans lequel sont stockées les informations. Synonyme: vidéographie interactive

C *télétext(e); système d'information en réseau*

A 1. 2. videotex

vidéotext: 1. terme impropre pour vidéotex; **2.** nom du système de télétext en République fédérale d'Allemagne et en Suisse.

A 1, 2. videotext

vidéothèque: collection de bandes vidéo et de vidéodisques et lieu où on les entrepose.

A videotape library

(**viewdata**) : terme générique utilisé en Grande-Bretagne pour désigner le télétext ; première appellation du système anglais PRESTEL, jusqu'à ce que l'Office des Brevets statue et refuse d'enregistrer cette dénomination, s'agissant d'un terme générique.

C *système d'information en réseau ; vidéotex*

A viewdata

virgule flottante : mode d'écriture des nombres dans lequel la virgule séparant la partie entière de la partie fractionnaire n'est pas fixée. Le nombre 338 peut s'écrire ainsi $3,38 \times 10^2$ ou $0,338 \times 10^3$.

A floating point notation

viseur : 1. partie d'une caméra ou d'un appareil photo permettant de cadrer le champ de prise de vues ; **2.** viseur électronique : petit moniteur de télévision incorporé à une caméra.

A 1. 2. viewfinder

visioconférence : téléconférence permettant un échange d'images de documents et la visualisation des orateurs.

C *audioconférence*

A videoconference

visionnement : 1. lecture d'un enregistrement vidéo ; **2.** projection sur écran d'un film ou d'autres documents visuels projetables.

A 1. viewing ; 2. screening

visionnement passif : visionnement de documents sans sollicitation active des spectateurs.

A passive viewing

visionnement préalable : visionnement ou étude d'un document, généralement non imprimé, avant achat. Ce visionnement peut avoir pour objet de décrire, d'annoter, d'analyser, de cataloguer le document ou d'en préparer une présentation.

A preview ; review

visionneuse : 1. appareil muni d'un système grossissant intégré ou d'un écran pour projection par transparence et destiné au visionnement de diapositives. Quelques modèles (généralement ceux pour projection par transparence) permettent le couplage avec des lecteurs d'enregistrement sonores d'accompagnement et peuvent être dotés d'une avance automatique des diapositives commandé par un signal sur la bande enregistrée ; **2.** dispositif de grossissement de films pour un visionnement individuel ou en petit groupe.

A 1. slide viewer ; 2. film viewer

visiophonie : association de la téléphonie et de la télévision permettant à deux correspondants de se voir l'un l'autre pendant leur conversation téléphonique.

A videophony ; picturephone

visu (n.f.) : terminal permettant la présentation visuelle et non permanente d'informations, généralement sur un moniteur vidéo. On dit aussi «visuel», «terminal à écran de visualisation».

A visual display unit – VDU

visualiser : 1. transmettre une information sous une forme visuelle ; **2.** faire apparaître sur un écran les résultats d'un traitement d'information sous forme alphanumérique ou graphique.

C *afficher*

A 1. 2. to display

visuel : 1. voir visu ; **2.** partie visuelle d'un film ou d'une émission de télévision.

A 1. VDU ; 2. visuals

vitesse de défilement de bande : vitesse à laquelle une bande magnétique défile devant un point fixe.

A tape speed

vitesse d'obturateur : intervalle de temps, mesuré en fractions de seconde, entre l'ouverture et la fermeture de l'obturateur d'un appareil de prise de vues.

A shutter speed

V.O.: voir **version originale**

voie: voir **canal**

voyant lumineux: voir **lampe témoin**

vue fixe: voir **diapositive**

vue par vue: voir **image par image**

VU mètre: appareil de contrôle du niveau du signal de modulation d'un programme sonore dont les caractéristiques sont normalisées.
A volume indicator

X

xérographie: procédé de copie électrostatique de positif à positif, utilisant une plaque ou un tambour photosensibles, recouvert d'une couche de sélénium et portant une charge électrostatique positive.
A xerography

Z

zéro: un état ou degré zéro se définit par l'absence de la caractéristique propre à un autre état pris comme terme de comparaison; par exemple, le degré zéro d'écriture filmique: simple enregistrement sans aucune élaboration cinématographique.
A zero point; absolute zero

zoom: **1.** variation très progressive de la distance focale d'un objectif. L'effet produit est semblable à celui d'un travelling avant ou arrière mais sans déplacement de caméra. A l'écran, dans le cas d'un zoom avant, le plan est graduellement grossi tandis que le champ couvert diminue, l'inverse se produisant pour un zoom arrière. On dit aussi travelling optique; **2.** voir **objectif à focale variable**.
A 1. zoom; 2. zoom lens

Bibliographie

Arnaud, J.F. *Dictionnaire de l'électronique.* Paris, Larousse, 1966.

Association française de normalisation. *Vocabulaire international de l'informatique: recueil de normes.* Paris, 1975.

Bureau d'études technico-économiques relatives à l'audio-visuel (France). *Guide pratique de la duplication et de l'impression: équipements et utilisation.* Paris, la Documentation française, 1980. 98 p.

Commission électrotechnique internationale. *Vocabulaire électronique international.* Genève. Fascicules: Télégraphie et téléphonie, 1970; Eclairage, 1970; Radiocommunications, 1970; Equipements et systèmes audiovisuels, magnétoscopiques et de télévision, 1977; Enregistrement et lecture du son et des images, 1977, 1977; Index général, 1979.

Conseil de l'Europe. *Vocabulaire du cinéma – multilingue.* Strasbourg, s.d.

Conseil international de la langue française. *Lexique photo-cinéma.* Fasc. 1: Enregistrement/restitution des images et des sons. Paris, 1972.

Conseil international de la langue française. *Vocabulaire de la radio-diffusion.* Paris, Hachette, 1973.

Dieuzeide, H. *Les techniques audio-visuelles dans l'enseignement.* Paris, Presses universitaires de France, 1965.

La Documentation française. *Guide pratique de la vidéo légère.* Paris, 1979. 156 p.

Dubois, J., et al. *Dictionnaire de linguistique.* Paris, Larousse, 1972. 516 p.

Fages, J.B.; Pagano, C. *Dictionnaire des média: technique, linguistique, sémiologie.* Paris, J.P. Delarge, 1971. 364 p.

Foulquié, P. *Dictionnaire de la langue pédagogique.* Paris, Presses universitaires de France, 1971. 492 p.

Galisson, R.; Coste, R. *Dictionnaire de didactique des langues.* Paris, Hachette, 1976. 612 p.

Ginguay, M.; Lauret, A. *Dictionnaire d'informatique.* 2ᵉ éd. Paris, Masson, 1982. 319 p.

Grenier, J.G. *Dictionnaire anglais-français d'électro-technique.* Joliette, Québec, Lanaudière, 1976. 260 p.

Hoytat, F.; Delepine-Messe, D. *Dictionnaire encyclopédique de pédagogie moderne.* Paris, Nathan; Bruxelles, Editions Labor, 1973. 340 p.

Internationales Zentralinstitut für das Jugend- und Bildungsfernsehen im Bayerischen Rundfunk. *Multilingual vocabulary of education radio and television terms.* München, Max Hueber Verlag, 1971. 189 p.

Lafon, R. *Vocabulaire de psychopédagogie et de psychiatrie de l'enfant.* 2ᵉ éd. revue et augmentée. Paris, Presses universitaires de France, 1969. 717 p.

Landsheere, G. De. *Dictionnaire de l'évaluation et de la recherche en éducation, avec lexique anglais-français.* Paris, Presses universitaires de France, 1979. 338 p.

Lefranc, R., éd. *Les techniques audio-visuelles au service de l'enseignement.* Paris, Armand Colin, 1963. 223 p.

Lelinisch, J.-P. *L'enseignement à distance.* Paris, Presses universitaires de France, 1981. 126 p. (Que sais-je?, 1983)

Leif, J. *Philosophie de l'éducation. Tome IV: Vocabulaire technique et critique de la pédagogie et des sciences de l'éducation.* Paris, Delagrave, 1974. 320 p.

Mialaret, G. *Lexique: Education.* Paris, Presses universitaires de France, 1981. 167 p.

Mialaret, G. *Vocabulaire de l'éducation.* Paris, Presses universitaires de France, 1979. 457 p.

Morvan, P. *Dictionnaire de l'informatique.* 6ᵉ éd. Paris, Larousse, 1985. 341 p.

Office national du film du Canada. *Glossaire/glossary.* Montréal, s.d.

Organisation internationale de normalisation. Traitement de l'information: matériel. Genève, 1982. (Recueil de normes ISO, 8.)

–. Traitement de l'information: logiciel. Genève, 1982. (Recueil de normes ISO, 9.)

–. Traitement de l'information: vocabulaire. Genève, 1982. (Recueil de normes ISO, 10.)

Pessis-Pasternak, Guitta. *Dictionnaire de l'audio-visuel, français-anglais, anglais-français.* Paris, Flammarion, 1976. 384 p.

Rigg, R.P. *L'audiovisuel au service de la formation: méthodes, matériels.* Paris, Entreprise moderne d'édition, 1971.

Titmus, C., et. al. *Terminology of adult education/Terminologie de l'éducation des adultes/Terminología de la educación de adultos.* Paris, Unesco, 1979. 154 p. (Ibedata)

Unesco. Section de l'enseignement technique et professionnel. *Terminology of technical and vocational education/Terminologie de l'enseignement technique et professionnel.* Paris, Unesco, 1978. 88 p. (Ibedata)

APPENDIX / ANNEXE

List of members of the working group constituted by ICEM
Liste des membres du groupe de travail constitué par le CIME

UNITED STATES / ÉTATS-UNIS
Anna L. Hyer
Howard Hitchens
Michael H. Molenda
Dr. Kenneth H. Silber
Raymond Wyman
Dr. Donald P. Ely
Clint Wallington

FRANCE
Robert Lefranc
Paul Chaix

FEDERAL REPUBLIC OF GERMANY / RÉPUBLIQUE FÉDÉRALE D'ALLEMAGNE
Hans Greetfeld

NORWAY / NORVÈGE
Erling Dale
Mr. Steigan

UNITED KINGDOM / ROYAUME-UNI
Richard Tucker
Mr. McCluskie

List of participants at the international meeting organized in Paris from 2 to 4 December 1981 by ICEM
Liste des participants à la réunion internationale organisée à Paris du 2 au 4 décembre 1981 par le CIME

BERGER, Guy,
Maître-Assistant,
Université de Paris VII,
72, rue du Temple,
75003 PARIS, France

BRUNSWIC, Etienne,
Head of the Section of Methods,
Materials and Techniques,
ED/SCM,
Unesco,
Place de Fontenoy,
75700 PARIS, France

CHAIX, Paul,
Assistant,
Ecole Normale Supérieure,
Grille du Parc d'Honneur,
92211 SAINT-CLOUD, France

FURTADO, Aida,
Documentalist,
UNESCO,
International Bureau of Education,
Palais Wilson,
GENEVA 1211, Switzerland

APPENDIX/ANNEXE

HYER, Anna L.,
Consultant,
7613 Wiley Dr.,
LORTON, VA. 22079, United States

KAYE, Anthony,
Senior Lecturer in Educational Technology,
Open University,
Milton Keynes, MK 6AA, United Kingdom

KIDD, Joan,
Reviser, English Translation Section,
Unesco

LEFRANC, Robert,
General Secretary,
International Council
of Educational Media (ICEM),
29, rue d'Ulm,
75230 PARIS CEDEX 05, France

SALOMON, Serge,
Reviser, French Translation Section,
Unesco

VALERIEN, Jean,
Conseiller au Ministère de l'Education,
5, Allée du Prunier Hardy,
92220 BAGNEUX, France

WHITING, Ann
Centre de Démonstration; ED/SCM,
Unesco

WYMAN, Raymond,
Professor,
University of Massachusetts,
11 Fairfield Street,
AMHERST, Mass. 01002, United States

ZIERER, Ernesto,
Professor of Linguistics,
National University of Trujillo,
Apartado 536,
TRUJILLO, Peru